ISBN 978-1-4510-0252-2
PIBN 10216682

Forgotten Books is a registered trademark of FB &c Ltd.
Copyright © 2015 FB &c Ltd.
FB &c Ltd, Dalton House, 60 Windsor Avenue, London, SW19 2RR.
Company number 08720141. Registered in England and Wales.

For support please visit www.forgottenbooks.com

1 MONTH OF
FREE
READING

at

www.ForgottenBooks.com

By purchasing this book you are eligible for one month membership to ForgottenBooks.com, giving you unlimited access to our entire collection of over 700,000 titles via our web site and mobile apps.

To claim your free month visit:

www.forgottenbooks.com/free216682

English
Français
Deutsche
Italiano
Español
Português

www.forgottenbooks.com

Mythology Photography **Fiction**
Fishing Christianity **Art** Cooking
Essays Buddhism Freemasonry
Medicine **Biology** Music **Ancient
Egypt** Evolution Carpentry Physics
Dance Geology **Mathematics** Fitness
Shakespeare **Folklore** Yoga Marketing
Confidence Immortality Biographies
Poetry **Psychology** Witchcraft
Electronics Chemistry History **Law**
Accounting **Philosophy** Anthropology
Alchemy Drama Quantum Mechanics
Atheism Sexual Health **Ancient History**
Entrepreneurship Languages Sport
Paleontology Needlework Islam
Metaphysics Investment Archaeology
Parenting Statistics Criminology
Motivational

THE
LIFE OF PASTEUR

BY RENÉ VALLERY-RADOT

TRANSLATED FROM THE FRENCH BY
MRS. R. L. DEVONSHIRE

WITH AN INTRODUCTION BY
SIR WILLIAM OSLER, BART., M.D., F.R.S.
REGIUS PROFESSOR OF MEDICINE, OXFORD UNIVERSITY

GARDEN CITY   NEW YORK
DOUBLEDAY, PAGE & COMPANY
1923

PRINTED IN GREAT BRITAIN BY
RICHARD CLAY & SONS, LIMITED
BUNGAY, SUFFOLK.

INTRODUCTION

L'homme en ce siècle a pris une connaissance toute nouvelle des ressource des
la nature et, par l'application de son intelligence il a commencé à les faire
fructifier. Il a refait, par la géologie et la paléontologie, l'histoire de la terre,
entraînée elle-même par la grande loi de l'évolution. Il connaît mieux, grâce à
Pasteur surtout, les conditions d'existence de son propre organisme et peut entre-
prendre d'y combattre les causes de destruction.—Monod, *L'Europe Con-
temporaine.*

WHETHER to admire more the man or his method, the life or
the work, I leave for the readers of this well-told story to
decide. Among the researches that have made the name of
Pasteur a household word in the civilised world, three are of
the first importance—a knowledge of the true nature of the
processes in fermentation—a knowledge of the chief maladies
which have scourged man and animals—a knowledge of the
measures by which either the body may be protected against
these diseases, or the poison neutralised when once within the
body.

I.

Our knowledge of disease has advanced in a curiously
uniform way. The objective features, the symptoms, naturally first attracted attention. The Greek physicians, Hippocrates, Galen, and Aretaeus, gave excellent accounts of many
diseases; for example, the forms of malaria. They knew, too,
very well, their modes of termination, and the art of prognosis
was studied carefully. But of the actual causes of disease they
knew little or nothing, and any glimmerings of truth were
obscured in a cloud of theory. The treatment was haphazard,
partly the outcome of experience, partly based upon false
theories of the cause of the disease. This may be said to have
been the sort of knowledge possessed by the profession until

men began to study the " seats and causes " of disease, and to search out the changes *inside* the body, corresponding to the outward symptoms and the external appearances. Morbid anatomy began to be studied, and in the hundred years from 1750 to 1850 such colossal strides were made that we knew well the post-mortem appearances of the more common diseases; the recognition of which was greatly helped by a study of the relation of the pathological appearances with the signs and symptoms. The 19th century may be said to have given us an extraordinarily full knowledge of the changes which disease produces in the solids and fluids of the body. Great advances, too, were made in the treatment of disease. We learned to trust Nature more and drugs less; we got rid (in part) of treatment by theory, and we ceased to have a drug for every symptom. But much treatment was, and still is, irrational, not based on a knowledge of the cause of the disease. In a blundering way many important advances were made, and even specifics were discovered—cinchona, for example, had cured malaria for a hundred and fifty years before Laveran found the cause. At the middle of the last century we did not know much more of the actual causes of the great scourges of the race, the plagues, the fevers and the pestilences, than did the Greeks. Here comes in Pasteur's great work. Before him Egyptian darkness; with his advent a light that brightens more and more as the years give us ever fuller knowledge. The facts that fevers were catching, that epidemics spread, that infection could remain attached to particles of clothing, etc., all gave support to the view that the actual cause was something alive, a *contagium vivum*. It was really a very old view, the germs of which may be found in the Fathers, but which was first clearly expressed—so far as I know—by Frascastorius, a Veronese physician in the 16th century, who spoke of the seeds of contagion passing from one person to another; and he first drew a parallel between the processes of contagion and the fermentation of wine. This was more than one hundred years before Kircher, Leeuwenhoek, and others, began to use the microscope and to see

animalculæ, etc., in water, and so gave a basis for the
" infinitely little " view of the nature of disease germs. And
it was a study of the processes of fermentation that led
Pasteur to the sure ground on which we now stand. Starting
as a pure chemist, and becoming interested in the science of
crystallography, it was not until his life at Lille, a town with
important brewing industries, that Pasteur became interested
in the biological side of chemical problems. Many years before
it had been noted by Cagniard-Latour that yeast was composed
of cells capable of reproducing themselves by a sort of budding,
and he made the keen suggestion that it was possibly through
some effect of their vegetation that the sugar was transformed.
But Liebig's view everywhere prevailed that the ferment was
an alterable, organic substance which exercised a catalytic
force, transforming the sugar. It was in August, 1857, that
Pasteur sent his famous paper on *Lactic Acid Fermentation*
to the Lille Scientific Society ; and in December of the same
year he presented to the Academy of Sciences a paper on
Alcoholic Fermentation, in which he concluded that the
deduplication of sugar into alcohol and carbonic acid is cor-
relevant to a phenomena of life. These studies had the signal
effect of diverting the man from the course of his previous more
strictly chemical studies. It is interesting to note how slowly
these views dislocated the dominant theories of Liebig. More
than ten years after their announcement I remember that we
had in our chemical lectures the catalytic theory very fully
presented.

Out of these researches arose a famous battle which kept
Pasteur hard at work for four or five years—the struggle over
spontaneous generation. It was an old warfare, but the
microscope had revealed a new world, and the experiments on
fermentation had lent great weight to the *omne vivum ex ovo*
doctrine. The famous Italians, Redi and Spallanzani, had led
the way in their experiments, and the latter had reached the
conclusion that there is no vegetable and no animal that has
not its own germ. But heterogenesis became the burning
question, and Pouchet in France, and Bastian in England,

led the opposition to Pasteur. The many famous experiments carried conviction to the minds of scientific men, and destroyed for ever the old belief in spontaneous generation. All along the analogy between disease and fermentation must have been in Pasteur's mind; and then came the suggestion: " What would be most desirable would be to push those studies far enough to prepare the road for a serious research into the origin of various diseases." If the changes in lactic, alcohol and butyric fermentations are due to minute living organisms, why should not the same tiny creatures make the changes which occur in the body in the putrid and suppurative diseases. With an accurate training as a chemist, having been diverted in his studies upon fermentation into the realm of biology, and nourishing a strong conviction of the identity between putrefactive changes of the body and fermentation, Pasteur was well prepared to undertake investigations, which had hitherto been confined to physicians alone.

The first outcome of the researches of Pasteur upon fermentation and spontaneous generation represents a transformation in the practice of surgery, which, it is not too much to say, has been one of the greatest boons ever conferred upon humanity. It had long been recognised that now and again a wound healed without the formation of pus, that is without suppuration, but both spontaneous and operative wounds were almost invariably associated with that change; and, moreover, they frequently became putrid, as it was then called—infected, as we should say; the general system became involved, and the patient died of blood poisoning. So common was this, particularly in old, ill-equipped hospitals, that many surgeons feared to operate, and the general mortality in all surgical cases was very high. Believing that from outside the germs came which caused the decomposition of wounds, just as from the atmosphere the sugar solution got the germs which caused the fermentation, a young surgeon at Glasgow, Joseph Lister, applied the principles of Pasteur's experiments to their treatment. It may be well here to quote from Lister's original paper in the *Lancet*, 1867 :—" Turning now to the question how the atmosphere produces decomposition of organic substances, we find that a flood of light has been thrown upon this most important subject by the philosophic researches of M. Pasteur, who has demonstrated by thoroughly convincing evidence that it is not to its oxygen or to any of its gaseous constituents that the air owes this property, but to minute particles suspended in it, which are the germs of various low forms of life, long since revealed by the microscope, and regarded as merely accidental concomitants of putrescence, but now shown by Pasteur to be its essential cause, resolving the complex organic compounds into substances of simpler chemical constitution, just as the yeast plant converts sugar into alcohol and carbonic acid." From these beginnings modern surgery took its rise, and the whole subject of wound infection, not only in relation to surgical diseases, but to child-bed fever, forms now one of the most brilliant chapters in the history of Preventive Medicine.

II.

Pasteur was early impressed with the analogies between fermentation and putrefaction and the infectious diseases, and in 1863 he assured the French Emperor that his ambition was " to arrive at the knowledge of the causes of putrid and contagious diseases." After a study upon the diseases of wines, which has had most important practical bearings, an opportunity came of the very first importance, which not only changed the whole course of his career, but had great influence in the development of medical science. A disease of the silkworm had, for some years, ruined one of the most important industries of France, and in 1865 the Government asked Pasteur to give up the laboratory work and teaching, and to devote his whole energies to the task of investigating it. The story of the brilliant success which followed years of application to the problem will be read with deep interest by every student of science. It was the first of his victories in the application of the experimental methods of a trained chemist to the problems of biology, and it placed his name high in the group of the most illustrious benefactors of practical industries.

The national tragedy of 1870–2 nearly killed Pasteur. He had a terrible pilgrimage to make in search of his son, a sergeant in Bourbaki's force. "The retreat from Moscow cannot have been worse than this," said the *savant*. In October, 1868, he had had a stroke of paralysis, from which he recovered in a most exceptional way, as it seemed to have diminished neither his enthusiasm nor his energy. In a series of studies on the diseases of beer, and on the mode of production of vinegar, he became more and more convinced that these studies on fermentation had given him the key to the nature of the infectious diseases. It is a remarkable fact that the distinguished English philosopher of the seventeenth century, the man who more than any one else of his century appreciated the importance of the experimental method, Robert Boyle, had said that he who could discover the nature of ferments and fermentation, would be more capable than anyone else of explaining the nature of certain diseases. The studies on spontaneous generation, and Lister's application of the germ theory to the treatment of wounds, had aroused the greatest interest in the medical world, and Villemin, in a series of most brilliant experiments, had demonstrated the infectivity of tuberculosis. An extraordinary opportunity now offered for the study of a widespread epidemic disease, known as anthrax, which in many parts of France killed from 25 to 30 per cent. of the sheep and cattle, and which in parts of Europe had been pandemic, attacking both man and beast. As far back as 1838 minute rods had been noted in the blood of animals which had died from the disease; and in 1863 Devaine thought that these little bodies, which he called bacteridia, were the cause of the disease. In 1876 a young German district physician, Robert Koch, began a career, which in interest and importance rivals that of the subject of this memoir. Koch confirmed in every point the old researches of Devaine; but he did much more, and for the first time isolated the organism in pure culture outside the body, grew successive generations, showed the

remarkable spore formation, and produced the disease artificially in animals by inoculating with the cultures. Pasteur
confirmed these results, and in the face of extraordinary opposition succeeded in convincing his opponents. Out of this study
came a still more important discovery, namely, that it was
possible so to attenuate or weaken the virus or poison that the
animal could be inoculated, and have a slight attack, recover,
and be protected against the disease. More than eighty years
had passed since, on May 14th, 1796, Jenner, with a small
bit of virus taken from a cow-pox on the hand of the milkmaid,
Sarah Newlme, had vaccinated a child, and thus proved that a
slight attack of one disease would protect the body from disease
of a similar character. It was an occasion famous in the
history of medicine, when, in the spring of 1881, at Melun, at
the farmyard of Pouilly le Fort, the final test case was determined, and the flock of vaccinated sheep remained well, while
every one of the unvaccinated, inoculated from the same
material, had died. It was indeed a great triumph.

The studies on chicken cholera, yellow fever, and on swine
plague helped to further the general acceptance of the germ
theory. I well remember at the great meeting of the International Congress in 1881, the splendid reception accorded to
the distinguished Frenchman, who divided with Virchow the
honours of the meeting. Finally came the work upon one of
the most dreaded of all diseases—hydrophobia, an infection of
a most remarkable character, the germ of which remains un-
discovered. The practical results of Pasteur's researches have
given us a prophylactic treatment of great efficacy. Before its
introduction the only means of preventing the development of
the disease was a thorough cauterisation of the disease wound
within half an hour after its infliction. Pasteur showed that
animals could be made immune to the poison, and devised a
method by which the infection conveyed by the bite could be
neutralised. Pasteur Institutes for the treatment of hydrophobia have been established in different countries, and where
the disease is widely prevalent have been of the greatest
benefit. Except at the London Congress, the only occasion

on which I saw the great master was in 1891 or 1892, when he demonstrated at the Institute to a group of us the technique of the procedure, and then superintended the inoculations of the day. A large number of persons are treated in the course of the year; a good many, of course, have not been bitten by mad dogs; but a very careful classification is made :—

(a) Includes persons bitten by dogs proved experimentally to have been mad.

(b) Persons bitten by dogs declared to be mad by competent veterinary surgeons.

(c) All other cases.

The mortality even in Class A is very slight, though many patients are not brought until late. Incidentally it may be remarked the lesson of this country in its treatment of hydrophobia is one of the most important ever presented in connection with an infectious disease. There are no Pasteur Institutes; there are no cases. Why? The simple muzzling order has prevented the transmission of the disease from dog to dog, and once exterminated in the dog, the possibility of the infection in man had gone. In 1888 the crowning work of Pasteur's life was the establishment of an Institute to serve as a centre of study on contagious disease, and a dispensary for the treatment of hydrophobia, which is to-day the most important single centre of research in the world. The closing years of his life were full of interest in the work of his colleagues and assistants, and he had the great satisfaction of participating, with his assistant Roux, in another great victory over the dread scourge, diphtheria. Before his death in 1895 he had seen his work prosper in a way never before granted to any great discoverer. To no one man has it ever been given to accomplish work of such great importance for the well-being of humanity. As Paul Bert expressed it in the report to the French Government, Pasteur's work constitutes three great discoveries, which may be thus formulated. 1. Each fermentation is produced by the development of a special microbe.

2. Each infectious disease is produced by the development within the organism of a special microbe.

3. The microbe of an infectious disease culture, under certain detrimental condition is attenuated in its pathogenic activity; from a virus it has become a vaccine.

In an address delivered in Edinburgh by Sir James Simpson in 1853, in which he extolled the recent advancement of physic, occur these words :—" I do not believe, that, at the present moment, any individual in the profession, who, in surgery or in midwifery, could point out some means of curing —or some prophylactic means of averting by antecedent treatment—the liability to these analogous or identical diseases— viz., surgical or puerperal fever—such a fortunate individual would, I say, make, in relation to surgery and midwifery, a greater and more important discovery than could possibly be attained by any other subject of investigation. Nor does such a result seem hopelessly unattainable." Little did he think that the fulfilment of these words was in the possession of a young Englishman who had just gone to Edinburgh as an assistant to his colleague, Professor Syme. Lister's recognition of the importance of Pasteur's studies led to the fulfilment within this generation of the pious hope expressed by Simpson. In Institutions and Hospitals surgical infection and puerperal fevers are things of the past, and for this achievement if for nothing else, the names of Louis Pasteur and Joseph Lister will go down to posterity among those of the greatest benefactors of humanity.

III.

In his growth the man kept pace with the scientist—heart and head held even sway in his life. To many whose estimate of French character is gained from " yellow " literature this story will reveal the true side of a great people, in whom filial piety, brotherly solicitude, generosity, and self-sacrifice are combined with a rare devotion to country. Was there ever a more charming picture than that of the family at Dôle! Napoleon's old sergeant, Joseph Pasteur, is almost as interesting a character as his illustrious son; and we follow the joys and sorrows of the home with unflagging attention. Rarely has a great man been able to pay such a tribute to his father as that paid by Pasteur :—" For thirty years I have been his constant care, I owe everything to him."

This is a biography for young men of science, and for others who wish to learn what science has done, and may do, for humanity. From it may be gleaned three lessons.

The value of method, of technique, in the hands of a great master has never been better illustrated. Just as Harvey, searching out Nature by way of experiment, opened the way for a study of the functions of the body in health, so did Pasteur, bringing to the problems of biology the same great *organon*, shed a light upon processes the nature of which had defied the analysis of the keenest minds. From Dumas's letter to Pasteur, quoted in Chapter VI., a paragraph may be given in illustration :—" The art of observation and that of experiment are very distinct. In the first case, the fact may either proceed from logical reasons or be mere good fortune; it is sufficient to have some penetration and the sense of truth in order to profit by it. But the art of experimentation leads from the first to the last link of the chain, without hesitation and without a blank, making successive use of Reason, which suggests an alternative, and of Experience, which decides on it, until, starting from a faint glimmer, the full blaze of light is reached." Pasteur had the good fortune to begin with chemistry, and with the science of crystallography, which demanded extraordinary accuracy, and developed that patient persistence so characteristic of all his researches.

In the life of a young man the most essential thing for happiness is the gift of friendship. And here is the second great lesson. As a Frenchman, Pasteur had the devotion that marks the students of that nation to their masters, living and dead. Not the least interesting parts of this work are the glimpses we get of the great teachers with whom he came in contact. What a model of a scientific man is shown in the character of Biot, so keenly alive to the interests of his young friend, whose brilliant career he followed with the devotion of a second father. One of the most touching incidents recorded in the book relates to Pasteur's election to the Academy of Sciences :—" The next morning when the gates of the Montparnasse cemetery were opened, a woman walked towards Biot's grave with her hands full of flowers. It was Mme. Pasteur who was bringing them to him . . . who had loved Pasteur with so deep an affection." Pasteur looked upon the cult of great men as a great principle in national education. As he said to the students of the University of Edinburgh :— " Worship great men " ; * and this reverence for the illustrious dead was a dominant element in his character, though the doctrines of Positivism seemed never to have had any attraction for him. A dark shadow in the scientific life is often thrown by a spirit of jealousy, and the habit of suspicious, carping criticism. The hall-mark of a small mind, this spirit should never be allowed to influence our judgment of a man's work, and to young men a splendid example is here offered of a man devoted to his friends, just and generous to his rivals, and patient under many trying contradictions and vexatious oppositions.

And the last great lesson is humility before the unsolved problems of the Universe. Any convictions that might be a comfort in the sufferings of human life had his respectful sympathy. His own creed was beautifully expressed in his eulogy upon *Littré* :—" He who proclaims the existence of the Infinite, and none can avoid it—accumulates in that affirmation more of the supernatural than is to be found in all the miracles of all the religions; for the notion of the Infinite presents that double character that it forces itself upon us and yet is incomprehensible. When this notion seizes upon our understanding, we can but kneel. . . . I see everywhere the inevitable expression of the Infinite in the world; through it, the supernatural is at the bottom of every heart. The idea of God is a form of the idea of the Infinite. As long as the mystery of the Infinite weighs on human thought, temples will be erected for the worship of the Infinite, whether God is called Brahma, Allah, Jehovah, or Jesus ; and on the pavement

* A great nation, said Disraeli, is a nation which produces great men.

b

of those temples, men will be seen kneeling, prostrated, annihilated in the thought of the Infinite." And modern Pantheism has never had a greater disciple, whose life and work set forth the devotion to an ideal—that service to humanity is service to God :—" Blessed is he who carries within himself a God, an ideal, and who obeys it : ideal of art, ideal of science, ideal of the gospel virtues, therein lie the springs of great thoughts and great actions ; they all reflect light from the Infinite."

The future belongs to Science. More and more she will control the destinies of the nations. Already she has them in her crucible and on her balances. In her new mission to humanity she preaches a new gospel. In the nineteenth century renaissance she has had great apostles, Darwin, for example, whose gifts of heart and head were in equal measure, but after re-reading for the third or fourth time the *Life of Louis Pasteur*, I am of the opinion, expressed recently by the anonymous writer of a beautiful tribute in the *Spectator*, " that he was the most perfect man who has ever entered the Kingdom of Science."

WILLIAM OSLER.

CONTENTS

CHAPTER XII

1884—1885

CHAPTER XIII

1885—1888

CHAPTER XIV
1889—1895

CHAPTER I

THE origin of even the humblest families can be traced back by persevering search through the ancient parochial registers. Thus the name of Pasteur is to be found written at the beginning of the seventeenth century in the old registers of the Priory of Mouthe, in the province of Franche Comté. The Pasteurs were tillers of the soil, and originally formed a sort of tribe in the small village of Reculfoz, dependent on the Priory, but they gradually dispersed over the country.

The registers of Miéges, near Nozeroy, contain an entry of the marriage of Denis Pasteur and Jeanne David, dated February 9, 1682. This Denis, after whom the line of Pasteur's ancestors follows in an unbroken record, lived in the village of Plénisette, where his eldest son Claude was born in 1683. Denis afterward sojourned for some time in the village of Douay, and ultimately forsaking the valley of Miéges came to Lemuy, where he worked as a miller for Claude François Count of Udressier, a noble descendant of a secretary of the Emperor Charles V.

Lemuy is surrounded by wide plains affording pasture for herds of oxen. In the distance the pine trees of the forest of Joux stand close together, like the ranks of an immense army, their dark masses deepening the azure of the horizon. It was in those widespreading open lands that Pasteur's ancestors lived. Near the church, overshadowed by old beech and lime trees, a tombstone is to be found overgrown with grass. Some members of the family lie under that slab naïvely inscribed : " Here lie, each by the side of the others . ."

In 1716, in the mill at Lemuy, ruins of which still exist, ,he marriage contract of Claude Pasteur was drawn up and iigned in the presence of Henry Girod, Royal notary of Salins. The father and mother declared themselves unable to write,

B

but we have the signatures of the affianced couple, Claude
Pasteur and Jeanne Belle, affixed to the record of the quaint
betrothal oath of the time. This Claude was in his turn a
miller at Lemuy, though at his death in 1746 he is only
mentioned as a labourer in the parish register. He had eight
children, the youngest, whose name was Claude Etienne, and
who was born in the village of Supt, a few kilometres from
Lemuy, being Louis Pasteur's great-grandfather.

What ambition, what love of adventures induced him to
leave the Jura plains to come down to Salins? A desire for
independence in the literal sense of the word. According to
the custom then still in force in Franche Comté (in contradiction to the name of that province, as Voltaire truly
remarks), there were yet some serfs, that is to say, people
legally incapable of disposing of their goods or of their persons.
They were part of the possessions of a nobleman or of the
lands of a convent or monastery. Denis Pasteur and his son
had been serfs of the Counts of Udressier. Claude Etienne
desired to be freed and succeeded in achieving this at the age
of thirty, as is proved by a deed, dated March 20, 1763, drawn
up in the presence of the Royal notary, Claude Jarry. Messire
Philippe-Marie-François, Count of Udressier, Lord of Ecleux,
Cramans, Lemuy and other places, consented "by special
grace" to free Claude Etienne Pasteur, a tanner, of Salins,
his serf. The deed stipulated that Claude Etienne and his
unborn posterity should henceforth be enfranchised from the
stain of mortmain. Four gold pieces of twenty-four livres
were paid then and there in the mansion of the Count of
Udressier by the said Pasteur.

The following year, he married Françoise Lambert. After
setting up together a small tannery in the Faubourg Champtave they enjoyed the fairy tale ideal of happiness : they had
ten children. The third, Jean Henri, through whom this
genealogy continues, was born in 1769. On June 25, 1779,
letters giving Claude Etienne Pasteur the freedom of the city
of Salins were delivered to him by the Town Council.

Jean Henri Pasteur, in his twentieth year, went to
Besançon to seek his fortune as a tanner, but was not successful. His wife, Gabrielle Jourdan, died at the age of twenty,
and he married again, but himself died at twenty-seven,
leaving one little son by his first marriage, Jean Joseph
Pasteur, born March 16, 1791. This child, who was to be

Louis Pasteur's father, was taken charge of by his grand-
mother at Salins; later on, his father's sisters, one married to
a wood merchant named Chamecin, and the other to Philibert
Bourgeois, Chamecin's partner, adopted the orphan. He was
carefully brought up, but without much learning; it was
considered sufficient in those days to be able to read the
Emperor's bulletins; the rest did not seem to matter very
much. Besides, Jean Joseph had to earn his living at the
tanner's trade, which had been his father's and his grandfather's before him.

Jean Joseph was drawn as a conscript in 1811, and went
through the Peninsular War in 1812 and 1813. He belonged
to the 3rd Regiment of the Line, whose mission was to pursue
in the northern Spanish provinces the guerillas of the famous
Espoz y Mina. A legend grew round this wonderful man; he
was said to make his own gunpowder in the bleak mountain
passes; his innumerable partisans were supplied with arms and
ammunition by the English cruisers. He dragged women and
old men after him, and little children acted as his scouts.
Once or twice however, in May, 1812, the terrible Mina was
very nearly caught; but in July he was again as powerful as
ever. The French had to organize mobile columns to again
occupy the coast and establish communications with France.
There was some serious fighting. Mina and his followers were
incessantly harassing the small French contingent of the 3rd
and 4th Regiments, which were almost alone. "How many
traits of bravery," writes Tissot, "will remain unknown which
on a larger field would have been rewarded and honoured!"

The records of the 3rd Regiment allow us to follow step by
step this valiant little troop, and among the rank and file,
doing his duty steadily through terrible hardships, that private
soldier (a corporal in July, 1812, and a sergeant in October,
1813) whose name was Pasteur. The battalion returned to
France at the end of January, 1814. It formed a part of that
Leval division which, numbering barely 8,000 men, had to
fight at Bar-sur-Aube against an army of 40,000 enemies. The
3rd Regiment was called "brave amongst the brave." "If
Napoleon had had none but such soldiers," writes Thiers in
his *History of the Consulate and the Empire*, "the result of
that great struggle would certainly have been different." The
Emperor, touched by so much courage, distributed crosses
among the men. Pasteur was made a sergeant-major on March

10, 1814, and received, two days later, the cross of the Legion of Honour.

At the battle of Arcis-sur-Aube (March 21) the Leval division had again to stand against 50,000 men—Russians, Austrians, Bavarians, and Wurtembergers. Pasteur's battalion, the 1st of the 3rd Regiment, came back to St. Dizier and went on by forced marches to Fontainebleau, where Napoleon had concentrated all his forces, arriving on April 4. The battalion was now reduced to eight officers and 276 men. The next day, at twelve o'clock, the Leval division and the remnant of the 7th corps were gathered in the yard of the Cheval Blanc Inn and were reviewed by Napoleon. The attitude of these soldiers, who had heroically fought in Spain and in France, and who were still offering their passionate devotion, gave him a few moments' illusion. Their enthusiasm and acclamations contrasted with the coldness, the reserve, the almost insubordinations of Generals like Ney, Lefebvre, Oudinot and MacDonald, who had just declared that to march on Paris would be folly.

Marmont's defection hastened events; the Emperor, seeing himself forsaken, abdicated. Jean Joseph Pasteur had not, like Captain Coignet, the sad privilege of witnessing the Emperor's farewell, his battalion having been sent into the department of Eure on April 9. On April 23 the white cockade replaced the tricolour.

On May 12, 1814, a royal order gave to the 3rd line Regiment the name of "Régiment Dauphin"; it was reorganized at Douai, where Sergeant-major Pasteur received his discharge from the service. He returned to Besançon with grief and anger in his heart : for him, as for many others risen from the people, Napoleon was a demi-god. Lists of victories, principles of equality, new ideas scattered throughout the nations, had followed each other in dazzling visions. It was a cruel trial for half-pay officers, old sergeants, grenadiers, peasant soldiers, to come down from this imperial epic to every-day monotony, police supervision, and the anxieties of poverty ; their wounded patriotism was embittered by feelings of personal humiliation. Jean Joseph resigned himself to his fate and went back to his former trade. The return from Elba was a ray of joy and hope in his obscure life, only to be followed by renewed darkness.

He was living in the Faubourg Champtave a solitary life in accordance with his tastes and character when this solitude was interrupted for an instant. The Mayor of Salins, a knight of Malta and an ardent royalist, ordered all the late soldiers of Napoleon, the " *brigands de la Loire* " as they were now called, to bring their sabres to the Mairie. Joseph Pasteur reluctantly obeyed ; but when he heard that these glorious weapons were destined to police service, and would be used by police agents, further submission seemed to him intolerable. He recognized his own sergeant-major's sabre, which had just been given to an agent,ˉand, springing upon the man, wrested the sword from him. Great excitement ensued—a mixture of indignation, irritation and repressed enthusiasm ; the numerous Bonapartists in the town began to gather together. An Austrian regiment was at that time still garrisoned in the town. The Mayor appealed to the colonel, asking him to repress this disobedience ; but the Austrian officer refused to interfere, declaring that he both understood and approved the military feelings which actuated the ex-sergeant-major. Pasteur was allowed to keep his sword, and returned home accompanied by sympathizers who were perhaps more noisily enthusiastic than he could have wished.

Having peacefully resumed his work he made the acquaintance of a neighbouring family of gardeners, whose garden faced his tannery on the other bank of the " Furieuse," a river rarely deserving its name. From the steps leading to the water Jean Joseph Pasteur often used to watch a young girl working in the garden at early dawn. She soon perceived that the "old soldier "—very young still ; he was but twenty-five years old— was interested in her every movement. Her name was Jeanne Etiennette Roqui.

Her parents, natives of Marnoz, a village about four kilometres from Salins, belonged to one of the most ancient plebeian families of the country. The Salins archives mention a Roqui working in vineyards as far back as 1555, and in 1659 there were Roqui lampmakers and plumbers. The members of this family were in general so much attached to each other that " to love like the Roqui" had become proverbial ; their wills and testaments mentioned legacies or gifts from brother to brother, uncle to nephew. In 1815 the father and mother of Jeanne Etiennette were living very quietly in the old Salins faubourg. Their daughter was modest, intelligent and kind ; Jean Joseph Pasteur asked for her hand in marriage. They seemed made for each other ; the difference in their natures only strengthened their mutual affection : he was reserved, almost secretive, with a slow and careful mind apparently absorbed in his own inner life; she was very active, full of imagination, and ready enthusiasm.

The young couple migrated to Dôle and settled down in the Rue des Tanneurs. Their first child only lived a few months; in 1818 a little daughter came. Four years later in a small room of their humble home, on Friday, December 27, 1822, at 2 a.m., Louis Pasteur was born.

Two daughters were born later—one at Dôle and the other at Marnoz, in the house of the Roqui. Jean Joseph Pasteur's mother-in-law, now a widow, considering that her great age no longer allowed her to administer her fortune, had divided all she possessed between her son Jean Claude Roqui, a landed proprietor at Marnoz, and Jeanne Etiennette her daughter.

Thus called away from Dôle by family interests, Jean Joseph Pasteur came to live at Marnoz. The place was not very favourable to his trade, though a neighbouring brook rendered the establishment of a tannery possible. The house, though many times altered, still bears the name of "Maison Pasteur." On one of the inner doors the veteran, who had a taste for painting, had depicted a soldier in an old uniform now become a peasant and tilling the soil. This figure stands against a background of grey sky and distant hills; leaning on his spade the man suspends his labours and dreams of past glories. It is easy to criticize the faults in the painting, but the sentimental allegory is full of feeling.

Louis Pasteur's earliest recollections dated from that time; he could remember running joyously along the Aiglepierre road. The Pasteur family did not remain long at Marnoz. A tannery was to let in the neighbourhood by the town of Arbois, near the bridge which crosses the Cuisance, and only a few kilometres from the source of the river. The house, behind its modest frontage, presented the advantage of a yard where pits had been dug for the preparation of the skins. Joseph Pasteur took this little house and settled there with his wife and children.

Louis Pasteur was sent at first to the "Ecole Primaire" attached to the college of Arbois. Mutual teaching was then the fashion; scholars were divided into groups : one child taught the rudiments of reading to others, who then spelt aloud in a sort of sing-song. The master, M. Renaud, went from group to group designating the monitors. Louis soon desired to possess this title, perhaps all the more so because he was the smallest scholar. But those who would decorate the early years of Louis Pasteur with wonderful legends would be disappointed : when a little later he attended the daily classes at the Arbois college he belonged merely to the category of good average pupils. He took several prizes without much difficulty ; he rather liked buying new lesson books, on the first page of which he proudly wrote his name. His father, who wished to instruct himself as well as to help his son, helped him with his home preparation. During holidays, the boy enjoyed his liberty. Some of his schoolfellows—Vercel, Charrière, Guillemin, Coulon—called for him to come out with them and he followed them with pleasure. He delighted in fishing parties on the Cuisance, and much admired the net throwing of his comrade Jules Vercel. But he avoided bird trapping ; the sight of a wounded lark was painful to him.

The doors of Louis Pasteur's home were not usually open except to his schoolboy friends, who, when they did not fetch him away, used to come and play in the tannery yard with remnants of bark, stray bits of iron, etc. Joseph Pasteur, though not considered a proud man, did not easily make friends. His language and manners were not those of a retired sergeant ; he never spoke of his campaigns and never entered a café. On Sundays, wearing a military-looking frock coat, spotlessly clean and adorned with the showy ribbon of the Legion of Honour (worn very large at that time), he invariably walked out towards the road from Arbois to Besançon. This road passes between vine-planted hills. On the left, on a wooded height above the wide plain towards Dôle, the ruins of the Vadans tower invest the whole landscape with a lingering glamour of heroic times. In these solitary meditations, he dwelt more anxiously on the future than on present difficulties, the latter being of little account in this hard-working family. What would become of this son of his, conscientious and studious, but, though already thirteen years old, with no apparent preference for anything but drawing? The epithet of *artist* given to Louis Pasteur by his Arboisian friends only half pleased the paternal vanity. And yet it is impossible not to be struck by the realism of his first original effort, a very bold pastel drawing. This pastel represents Louis' mother, one morning that she was going to market, with a white cap and a blue and green tartan shawl. Her son insisted on painting her just as she was. The portrait is full of sincerity and not unlike the work of a conscientious pre-Raphaelite. The powerful face is illumined by a pair of clear straightforward eyes.

Though they did not entertain mere acquaintances, the husband and wife were happy to receive those who seemed to them worthy of affection or esteem by reason of some superiority of the mind or of the heart. In this way they formed a friendship with an old army doctor then practising in the Arbois hospital, Dr. Dumont, a man who studied for the sake of learning and who did a great deal of good while avoiding popularity.

Another familiar friend was a philosopher named Bousson de Mairet. An indefatigable reader, he never went out without a book or pamphlet in his pocket. He spent his life in compiling from isolated facts annals in which the characteristics of the Francs-Comtois, and especially the Arboisians, were reproduced in detail, with labour worthy of a Benedictine monk. He often came to spend a quiet evening with the Pasteur family, who used to question him and to listen to his interesting records of that strange Arboisian race, difficult to understand, presenting as it does a mixture of heroic courage and that slightly ironical good humour which Parisians and Southerners mistake for naïveness. Arboisians never distrust themselves, but are sceptical where others are concerned. They are proud of their local history, and even of their rodomontades.

For instance, on August 4, 1830, they sent an address to the Parisians to express their indignation against the " Ordonnances " [1] and to assure them that all the available population of Arbois was ready to fly to the assistance of Paris. In April, 1834, a lawyer's clerk, passing one evening through Arbois by the coach, announced to a few *gardes nationaux* who were standing about that the Republic was proclaimed at Lyons. Arbois immediately rose in arms; the insurgents armed themselves with guns from the Hôtel de Ville. Louis Pasteur watched the

[1] *Ordonnances du 26 Juillet*, 1830. A royal Decree issued by Charles X under the advice of his minister, Prince de Polignac; it was based on a misreading of one of the articles of the Charter of 1814, and dissolved the new Chamber of Deputies before it had even assembled; it suppressed the freedom of the Press and created a new electoral system to the advantage of the royalist party. These *ordonnances* were the cause of the 1830 Revolution, which placed Louis Philippe of Orleans on the Throne. [Trans.]

arrival from Besançon of 200 grenadiers, four squadrons of light cavalry, and a small battery of artillery sent to reduce the rebels. The *sous-préfet* of Poligny having asked the rioters who were their leaders, they answered with one voice, " We are all leaders." A few days later the great, the good news was published in all the newspapers : " Arbois, Lyons, and Paris are pacified." The Arboisians called their neighbours " the Braggarts of Salins," probably with the ingenious intention of turning such a well-deserved accusation from themselves.

Louis Pasteur, whose mind already had a serious bent, preferred to these recent anecdotes such historical records as that of the siege of Arbois under Henry IV, when the Arboisians held out for three whole days against a besieging army of 25,000 men. His childish imagination, after being worked upon by these stories of local patriotism, eagerly seized upon ideals of a higher patriotism, and fed upon the glory of the French people as represented by the conquests of the Empire.

He watched his parents, day by day working under dire necessity and ennobling their weary task by considering their children's education almost as essential as their daily bread ; and, as in all things the father and mother took an interest in noble motives and principles, their material life was lightened and illumined by their moral life.

One more friend, the headmaster of Arbois college, M. Romanet, exerted a decisive influence on Louis Pasteur's career. This master, who was constantly trying to elevate the mind and heart of his pupils, inspired Louis with great admiration as well as with respect and gratitude. Romanet considered that whilst instruction doubled a man's value, education, in the highest sense of the word, increased it tenfold. He was the first to discover in Louis Pasteur the hidden spark that had not yet revealed itself by any brilliant success in the hardworking schoolboy. Louis' mind worked so carefully that he was considered slow ; he never affirmed anything of which he was not absolutely sure ; but with all his strength and caution he also had vivid imaginative faculties.

Romanet, during their strolls round the college playground, took pleasure in awakening with an educator's interest the leading qualities of this young nature—circumspection and enthusiasm. The boy, who had been sitting over his desk

with all-absorbing attention, now listened with sparkling eyes
to the kind teacher talking to him of his future and opening to
him the prospect of the great *Ecole Normale*.[1]

An officer of the Paris municipal guard, Captain Barbier,
who always came to Arbois when on leave, offered to look after
Louis Pasteur if he were sent to Paris. But Joseph Pasteur
—in spite of all—hesitated to send his son, not yet sixteen
years old, a hundred leagues away from home. Would it not
be wiser to let him go to Besançon college and come back to
Arbois college as professor? What could be more desirable
than such a position? Surely Paris and the Ecole Normale
were quite unnecessary! The question of money also had to
be considered.

"That need not trouble you," said Captain Barbier. "In
the Latin Quarter, Impasse des Feuillantines, there is a pre-
paratory school, of which the headmaster, M. Barbet, is a
Franc-Comtois. He will do for your son what he has done for
many boys from his own country—that is, take him at reduced
school fees."

Joseph Pasteur at last allowed himself to be persuaded, and
Louis' departure was fixed for the end of October, 1838. He
was not going alone : Jules Vercel, his dear school friend, was
also going to Paris to work for his "baccalauréat."[2] This
youth had a most happy temperament : unambitious, satisfied
with each day's work as it came, he took pride and pleasure
in the success of others, and especially in that of "Louis," as
he then and always fraternally called his friend. The two

[1] *Ecole Normale Supérieure*, under the supervision of the Ministry of
Public Instruction and Fine Arts, founded in 1808 by Napoleon I, with
the object of training young professors. Candidates must (1) be older
than eighteen and younger than twenty-one; (2) pass one written and
one vivâ voce examination; (3) be already in possession of their diploma
as *bachelier* of science or of letters, according to the branch of studies
which they wish to take up; and (4) sign an engagement for ten years'
work in public instruction. The professors of the Ecole Normale take
the title of *Maître des Conférences*. [Trans.]

[2] Baccalauréat (low Latin *bachalariatus*), first degree taken in a
French Faculty; the next is *licence*, and the next *doctorate*. It is
much more elementary than a bachelor's degree in an English university.
There are two baccalauréats : (1) the baccalauréat *ès lettres* required of
candidates for the Faculties of Medicine and of Law, to the Ecole
Normale Supérieure and to several public offices; (2) the baccalauréat *ès
sciences*, required for admission to the Schools of Medicine and of Pharmacy, to the Ecole Normale Supérieure (scientific section), and the
Polytechnic, Military and Foresters' Schools. [Trans.]

boys' friendship went some way to alleviate the natural anxieties felt by both families. The slowness and difficulty of travelling in those days gave to farewells a sort of solemn sadness; they were repeated twenty times whilst the horses were being harnessed and the luggage hoisted on to the coach in the large courtyard of the "Hôtel de la Poste." On that bleak October morning, amidst a shower of rain and sleet, the two lads had to sit under the tarpaulin behind the driver; there were no seats left inside or under the hood. In spite of Vercel's habit of seeing the right side of things and his joy in thinking that in forty-eight hours he, the country boy, would see the wonders of Paris—in spite of Pasteur's brave resolve to make the most of his unexpected opportunities of study, of the now possible entrance into the "Ecole Normale"—both looked with heavy hearts at the familiar scene they were leaving behind them—their homes, the square tower of Arbois church, the heights of the Ermitage in the grey distance.

Every native of Jura, though he affects to feel nothing of the kind, has, at the bottom of his heart, a strong feeling of attachment for the corner of the world where he has spent his childhood; as soon as he forsakes his native soil his thoughts return to it with a painful and persistent charm. The two boys did not take much interest in the towns where the coach stopped to change horses, Dôle, Dijon, Auxerre, Joigny, Sens, Fontainebleau, etc.

When Louis Pasteur reached Paris he did not feel like Balzac's student hero, confidently defying the great city. In spite of the strong will already visible in his pensive features, his grief was too deep to be reasoned away. No one at first suspected this; he was a reserved youth, with none of the desire to talk which leads weak natures to ease their sorrows by pouring them out; but, when all was quiet in the Impasse des Feuillantines and his sleeping comrades could not break in upon his regrets, he would lie awake for hours thinking of his home and repeating the mournful line—

> How endless unto watchful anguish
> Night doth seem.

The students of the Barbet school attended the classes of the Lycée St. Louis. In spite of his willingness and his passionate love of study, Louis was overcome with despair at being away from home. Never was homesickness more acute. "If

I could only get a whiff of the tannery yard," he would say to Jules Vercel, " I feel I should be cured." M. Barbet endeavoured in vain to amuse and turn the thoughts of this lad of fifteen so absorbed in his sorrow.   At last he thought it his duty to warn the parents of this state of mind, which threatened to become morbid.

One morning in November Louis Pasteur was told with an air of mystery that he was wanted. " They are waiting for you close by," said the messenger, indicating a small café at the corner of the street.   Louis entered and found a man sitting at a small table at the back of the shop, his face in his hands.   It was his father. " I have come to fetch you," he said simply. No explanations were necessary ; the father and son understood each other's longings.

What took place in Pasteur's mind when he found himself again at Arbois?   After the first few days of relief and joy, did he feel, when he went back to Arbois college, any regret, not to say remorse, at not having overcome his homesickness? Was he discouraged by the prospect of a restricted career in that small town?   Little is known of that period when his will had been mastered by his feelings ; but from the indecision of his daily life we may hazard a guess at the disquieted state of his mind at this time.   At the beginning of that year (1839) he returned for a time to his early tastes ; he went back to his coloured chalks, left aside for the last eighteen months, ever since one holiday time when he had drawn Captain Barbier, proudly wearing his uniform, and with the high colour of excellent health.

He soon got beyond the powers of his drawing master, M. Pointurier, a good man who does not seem to have seen any scientific possibilities in the art of drawing.

Louis' pastel drawings soon formed a portrait gallery of friends.   An old cooper of seventy, Father Gaidot, born at Dôle, but now living at Arbois, had his turn.   Gaidot appears in a festive costume, a blue coat and a yellow waistcoat, very picturesque with his wrinkled forehead and close-shaven cheeks. Then there are all the members of a family named Roch.   The father and the son are drawn carefully, portraits such as are often seen in country villages ; but the two daughters Lydia and Sophia are more delicately pencilled ; they live again in the youthful grace of their twenty summers.   Then we have a notary, the wide collar of a frock coat framing his rubicund face; a young woman in white; an old nun of eighty-two in a fluted cap, wearing a white hood and an ivory cross; a little boy of ten in a velvet suit, a melancholy-looking child, not destined to grow to manhood. Pasteur obligingly drew any one who wished to have a portrait. Among all these pastels, two are really remarkable. The first represents, in his official garb, a M. Blondeau, registrar of mortgages, whose gentle and refined features are perfectly delineated. The other is the portrait of a mayor of Arbois, M. Pareau; he wears his silver-embroidered uniform, with a white stock. The cross of the Legion of Honour and the tricolour scarf are discreetly indicated. The whole interest is centred in the smiling face, with hair brushed up à la Louis Philippe, and blue eyes harmonizing with a blue ground.

The compliments of this local dignitary and Romanet's renewed counsels at the end of the year—when Pasteur took more school prizes than he could carry—reawakened within him the ambition for the Ecole Normale.

There was no "philosophy"[1] class in the college of Arbois, and a return to Paris seemed formidable. Pasteur resolved to go to the college at Besançon, where he could go on with his studies, pass his baccalauréat and then prepare for the examinations of the Ecole Normale. Besançon is only forty kilometres from Arbois, and Joseph Pasteur was in the habit of going there several times a year to sell some of his prepared skins. This was by far the wisest solution of the problem.

On his arrival at the Royal College of Franche Comté Pasteur found himself under a philosophy master, M. Daunas,

---

[1] Philosophie class. In French secondary schools or *lycées* the forms or classes, in Pasteur's time, were arranged as follows, starting from the bottom—

1° huitième.
2° septième.
6° sixième (French grammar was begun).
5° cinquième (Latin was begun).
6° quatrième (Greek was begun).
7° troisième.
8° seconde.
9° Mathématiques élémentaires.   Rhétorique.
10° Mathématiques spéciales.   Philosophie.

The seconde students who intended to pass their *baccalauréat ès sciences* went into the mathématiques élémentaires class, whilst those who were destined for letters or the law entered the rhétorique class, from which they went on to the philosophie class. [Trans.]

who had been a student at the Ecole Normale and was a
graduate of the University; he was young, full of eloquence,
proud of his pupils, of awakening their faculties and directing
their minds. The science master, M. Darlay, did not inspire
the same enthusiasm; he was an elderly man and regretted
the good old times when pupils were less inquisitive.
Pasteur's questions often embarrassed him. Louis' reputation
as a painter satisfied him no longer, though the portrait he
drew of one of his comrades was exhibited. "All this does
not lead to the Ecole Normale," he wrote to his parents in
January, 1840. "I prefer a first place at college to 10,000
praises in the course of conversation. . . . We shall meet on
Sunday, dear father, for I believe there is a fair on Monday.
If we see M. Dannas, we will speak to him of the Ecole
Normale. Dear sisters, let me tell you again, work hard, love
each other. When one is accustomed to work it is impossible
to do without it; besides, everything in this world depends on
that. Armed with science, one can rise above all one's
fellows. . . . But I hope all this good advice to you is superfluous, and I am sure you spend many moments every day
learning your grammar. Love each other as I love you, while
awaiting the happy day when I shall be received at the Ecole
Normale." Thus was his whole life filled with tenderness as
well as with work. He took the degree of "bachelier ès
lettres" on August 29, 1840. The three examiners, doctors
"ès lettres," put down his answers as "good in Greek on
Plutarch and in Latin on Virgil, good also in rhetoric,
medicine, history and geography, good in philosophy, very
good in elementary science, good in French composition."

At the end of the summer holidays the headmaster of the
Royal College of Besançon, M. Répécaud, sent for him and
offered him the post of preparation master. Certain administrative changes and an increased number of pupils were the
reason of this offer, which proved the master's esteem for
Pasteur's moral qualities, his first degree not having been
obtained with any particular brilliancy.

The youthful master was to be remunerated from the month
of January, 1841. A student in the class of special mathematics, he was his comrades' mentor during preparation time.
They obeyed him without difficulty; simple and yet serious-
minded, his sense of individual dignity made authority easy
to him. Ever thoughtful of his distant home, he strengthened

the influence of the father and mother in the education of his sisters, who had not so great a love of industry as he had. On November 1, 1840—he was not eighteen yet—pleased to hear that they were making some progress, he wrote the following, which, though slightly pedantic, reveals the warmth of his feelings—" My dear parents, my sisters, when I received at the same time the two letters that you sent me I thought that something extraordinary had happened, but such was not the case. The second letter you wrote me gave me much pleasure; it tells me that—perhaps for the first time—my sisters have *willed*. To *will* is a great thing, dear sisters, for Action and Work usually follow Will, and almost always Work is accompanied by success. These three things, Will, Work, Success, fill human existence. Will opens the door to success both brilliant and happy; Work passes these doors, and at the end of the journey Success comes to crown one's efforts. And so, my dear sisters, if your resolution is firm, your task, be it what it may, is already begun; you have but to walk forward, it will achieve itself. If perchance you should falter during the journey, a hand would be there to support you. If that should be wanting, God, who alone could take that hand from you, would Himself accomplish its work.

May my words be felt and understood by you, dearest sisters. I impress them on your hearts. May they be your guide. Farewell. Your brother."

The letters he wrote, the books he loved, the friends he chose, bear witness to the character of Pasteur in those days of early youth. As he now felt, after the discouraging trial he had gone through in Paris, that the development of the will should hold the first place in education, he applied all his efforts to the bringing out of this leading force. He was already grave and exceptionally matured; he saw in the perfecting of self the great law of man, and nothing that could assist in that improvement seemed to him without importance. Books read in early life appeared to him to have an almost decisive influence. In his eyes a good book was a good action constantly renewed, a bad one an incessant and irreparable fault.

There lived at that time in Franche Comté an elderly writer, whom Sainte Beuve considered as the ideal of the upright man and of the man of letters. His name was Joseph Droz, and his moral doctrine was that vanity is the cause of many wrecked and aimless lives, that moderation is a form of wisdom and an element of happiness, and that most men sadden and trouble their lives by causeless worry and agitation. His own life was an example of his precepts of kindliness and patience, and was filled to the utmost with all the good that a pure literary conscience can bestow; he was all benevolence and cordiality. It seemed natural that he should publish one after another numberless editions of his *Essay on the Art of being Happy.*

"I have still," wrote Pasteur to his parents, "that little volume of M. Droz which he was kind enough to lend me. I have never read anything wiser, more moral or more virtuous. I have also another of his works; nothing was ever better written. At the end of the year I shall bring you back these books. One feels in reading them an irresistible charm which penetrates the soul and fills it with the most exalted and generous feelings. There is not a word of exaggeration in what I am writing. Indeed I take his books with me to the services on Sundays to read them, and I believe that in so acting, in spite of all that thoughtless bigotry might say, I am conforming to the very highest religious ideas."

Those ideas Droz might have summarized simply by Christ's words, "Love ye one another." But this was a time of circumlocution. Young people demanded of books, of discourses, of poetry, a sonorous echo of their own secret feelings. In the writings of the Besançon moralist, Pasteur saw a religion such as he himself dreamed of, a religion free from all controversy and all intolerance, a religion of peace, love and devotion.

A little later, Silvio Pellico's *Miei Prigioni* developed in him an emotion which answered to his instinctive sympathy for the sorrows of others. He wrote advising his sisters to read "that interesting work, where you breathe with every page a religious perfume which exalts and ennobles the soul." In read *Miei Prigioni* his sisters would light upon a passage on fraternal love and all the deep feelings which it represents.

"For my sisters," he wrote in another letter, "I bought, a few days ago, a very pretty book; I mean by very pretty something very interesting. It is a little volume which took the Montyon[1] prize a few years ago, and it is called, *Picciola.*

[1] Prix Montyon : a series of prizes founded at the beginning of the nineteenth century by Baron de Montyon, a distinguished philanthropist, and conferred on literary works for their moral worth, and on individuals

How could it have deserved the Montyon prize," he added, with an edifying respect for the decisions of the Academy, "if the reading of it were not of great value?"

"You know," he announced to his parents when his appointment was definitely settled, "that a supplementary master has board and lodging and 300 francs a year!" This sum appeared to him enormous. He added, on January 20: "At the end of this month money will already be owing to me; and yet I assure you I am not really worth it."

Pleased with this situation, though such a modest one, full of eagerness to work, he wrote in the same letter: "I find it an excellent thing to have a room of my own; I have more time to myself, and I am not interrupted by those endless little things that the boys have to do, and which take up a good deal of time. Indeed I am already noticing a change in my work; difficulties are getting smoothed away because I have more time to give to overcoming them; in fact I am beginning to hope that by working as I do and shall continue to do I may be received with a good rank at the Ecole. But do not think that I am overworking myself at all; I take every recreation necessary to my health."

Besides his ordinary work, he had been entrusted with the duty of giving some help in mathematics and physical science to the youths who were reading for their baccalauréat.

As if reproaching himself with being the only member of the family who enjoyed the opportunity of learning, he offered to pay for the schooling of his youngest sister Josephine in a girls' college at Lons-le-Saulnier. He wrote, "I could easily do it by giving private lessons. I have already refused to give some to several boys at 20 or 25 fr. a month. I refused because I have not too much time to give to my work." But he was quite disposed to waive this motive in deference to superior judgment. His parents promised to think over this fraternal wish, without however accepting his generous suggestion, offering even to supplement his small salary of 24 francs a month by a little allowance, in case he wished for a few private lessons to prepare himself more thoroughly for the Ecole Normale. They quite recognized his right to advise;

for acts of private virtue or self-sacrifice. The laureates are chosen every year by the Académie Française, and in this way many obscure heroes are deservedly rewarded, and many excellent books brought to public notice. [Trans.]

C

and—as he thought that his sister should prepare herself beforehand for the class she was to enter—he wrote to his mother with filial authority, "Josephine should work a good deal until the end of the year, and I would recommend to Mother that she should not continually be sent out on errands; she must have time to work."

Michelet, in his recollections, tells of his hours of intimacy with a college friend named Poinsat, and thus expresses himself: "It was an immense, an insatiable longing for confidences, for mutual revelations." Pasteur felt something of the sort for Charles Chappuis, a *philosophie* student at Besançon college. He was the son of a notary at St. Vit, one of those old-fashioned provincial notaries, who, by the dignity of their lives, their spirit of wisdom, the perpetual preoccupation of their duty, inspired their children with a sense of responsibility. His son had even surpassed his father's hopes. Of this generous, gentle-faced youth there exists a lithograph signed "Louis Pasteur." A book entitled *Les Graveurs du XIXme Siècle* mentions this portrait, giving Pasteur an unexpected form of celebrity. Before the *Graveurs*, the *Guide de l'Amateur des Œuvres d'Art* had already spoken of a pastel drawing discovered in the United States near Boston. It represents another schoolfellow of Pasteur's, who, far from his native land, carefully preserved the portrait of Chappuis as well as his own. Everything that friendship can give in strength and disinterestedness, everything that, according to Montaigne—who knew more about it even that Michelet "makes souls merge into each other so that the seam which originally joined them disappears," was experienced by Pasteur and Chappuis. Filial piety, brotherly solicitude, friendly confidences—Pasteur knew the sweetness of all these early human joys; the whole of his life was permeated with them. The books he loved added to this flow of generous emotions. Chappuis watched and admired this original nature, which, with a rigid mind made for scientific research and always seeking the proof of everything, yet read Lamartine's *Meditations* with enthusiasm. Differing in this from many science students, who are indifferent to literature—just as some literature students affect to disdain science—Pasteur kept for literature a place apart. He looked upon it as a guide for general ideas. Sometimes he would praise to excess some writer or orator merely because he had found in one page or in one sentence the expression of an exalted sentiment. It was with Chappuis that he exchanged his thoughts, and together they mapped out a life in common. When Chappuis went to Paris, the better to prepare himself for the Ecole Normale, Pasteur felt an ardent desire to go with him. Chappuis wrote to him with that open spontaneity which is such a charm in youth, "I shall feel as if I had all my Franche Comté with me when you are here." Pasteur's father feared a crisis like that of 1838, and, after hesitating, refused his consent to an immediate departure. "Next year," he said.

In October, 1841, though still combining the functions of master and student, Pasteur resumed his attendance of the classes for special mathematics. But he was constantly thinking of Paris, "Paris, where study is deeper." One of Chappuis' comrades, Bertin, whom Pasteur had met during the holidays, had just entered the Ecole Normale at the head of the list after attending in Paris a class of special mathematics.

"If I do not pass this year," Pasteur wrote to his father on November 7, "I think I should do well to go to Paris for a year. But there is time to think of that and of the means of doing so without spending too much, if the occasion should arise. I see now what great advantage there is in giving two years to mathematics; everything becomes clearer and easier. Of all our class students who tried this year for the Ecole Polytechnique and the Ecole Normale, not a single one has passed, not even the best of them, a student who had already done one year's mathematics at Lyons. The master we have now is very good. I feel sure I shall do a great deal this year."

He was twice second in his class; once he was first in physics. "That gives me hope for later on," he said. He wrote about another mathematical competition, "If I get a good place it will be well deserved, for this work has given me a pretty bad headache; I always do get one, though, whenever we have a competition." Then, fearful of alarming his parents, he hastily adds, "But those headaches never last long, and it is only an hour and a half since we left off."

Anxious to stifle by hard work his growing regrets at not having followed Chappuis to Paris, Pasteur imagined that he might prepare himself for the Ecole Polytechnique as well as for the Ecole Normale. One of his masters, M. Bouché, had led him to hope that he might be successful. "I shall try this year for both schools," Pasteur wrote to his friend (January 22, 1842). " I do not know whether I am right in deciding to do so. One thing tells me that I am wrong : it is the idea that we might thus be parted ; and when I think of that, I firmly believe that I cannot possibly be admitted this year into the Ecole Polytechnique. I feel quite superstitious about it. I have but one pleasure, your letters and those from my family. Oh ! do write often, very long letters ! "

Chappuis, concerned at this sudden resolve, answered in terms that did credit to his heart and youthful wisdom. " Consult your tastes, think of the present, of the future. You must think of yourself ; it is your own fate that you have to direct. There is more glitter on the one side ; on the other the gentle quiet life of a professor, a trifle monotonous perhaps, but full of charm for him who knows how to enjoy it. You too appreciated it formerly, and I learned to do so when we thought we should both go the same way. Anyhow, go where you think you will be happy, and think of me sometimes. I hope your father will not blame me. I believe he looks upon me as your evil genius. These last holidays I wanted you to come to me, then I advised you to go to Paris ; each time your father created some obstacle ! But do what he wishes, and never forget that it is perhaps because he loves you too much that he never does what you ask him."

Pasteur soon thought no more of his Polytechnic fancy, and gave himself up altogether to his preparation for the Ecole Normale. But the study of mathematics seemed to him dry and exhausting. He wrote in April, " One ends by having nothing but figures, formulas and geometrical forms before one's eyes. . . . On Thursday I went out and I read a charming story, which, much to my astonishment, made me weep. I had not done such a thing for years. Such is life."

On August 13, 1842, he went up for his examination (*baccalauréat ès sciences*) before the Dijon Faculty. He passed less brilliantly even than he had done for the *baccalauréat ès lettres*. In chemistry he was only put down as " *médiocre.*" On August 26 he was declared admissible to the examinations for the Ecole Normale. But he was only fifteenth out of twenty-two candidates. He considered this too low a place, and resolved to try again the following year. In October, 1842, he started for Paris with Chappuis. On the eve of his departure Louis drew a last pastel, a portrait of his father. It is a powerful face, with observation and meditation apparent in the eyes, strength and caution in the mouth and chin.

Pasteur arrived at the Barbet Boarding School, no longer a forlorn lad, but a tall student capable of teaching and engaged for that purpose. He only paid one-third of the pupil's fees, and in return had to give to the younger pupils some instruction in mathematics every morning from six to seven. His room was not in the school, but in the same Impasse des Feuillantines; two pupils shared it with him.

" Do not be anxious about my health and work," he wrote to his friends a few days after his arrival. " I need hardly get up till 5.45; you see it is not so very early." He went on outlining the programme of his time. " I shall spend my Thursdays in a neighbouring library with Chappuis, who has four hours to himself on that day. On Sundays we shall walk and work a little together; we hope to do some Philosophy on Sundays, perhaps too on Thursdays; I shall also read some literary works. Surely you must see that I am not homesick this time."

Besides attending the classes of the Lycée St. Louis, he also went to the Sorbonne [1] to hear the Professor, who, after taking Gay-Lussac's place in 1832, had for the last ten years delighted his audience by an eloquence and talent which opened boundless horizons before every mind.

In a letter dated December 9, 1842, Pasteur wrote, " I attend at the Sorbonne the lectures of M. Dumas, a celebrated chemist. You cannot imagine what a crowd of people come to these lectures. The room is immense, and always quite full. We have to be there half an hour before the time to get a good place, as you would in a theatre; there is also a great deal of applause; there are always six or seven hundred people."

[1] Sorbonne. Name given to the Paris Faculty of Theology and the buildings in which it was established. It was originally intended by its founder, Robert de Sorbon (who was chaplain to St. Louis, King of France, 1270) as a special establishment to facilitate theological studies for poor students. This college became one of the most celebrated in the world, and produced so many clever theologians that it gave its name to all the members of the Faculty of Theology. It was closed during the Revolution in 1789, and its buildings, which had been restored by Richelieu in the seventeenth century, were given to the Université in 1808. Since 1821 they have been the seat of the Universitarian Academy of Paris, and used for the lectures of the Faculties of Theology, of Letters, and of Sciences. [Trans.]

Under this rostrum, Pasteur became, in his own words, a
" disciple " full of the enthusiasm inspired by Dumas.

Happy in this industrious life, he wrote in response to an
expression of his parents' provincial uneasiness as to the
temptations of the Latin Quarter. " When one wishes to keep
straight, one can do so in this place as well as in any other; it
is those who have no strength of will that succumb."

He made himself so useful at Barbet's that he was soon
kept free of all expense. But the expenses of his Parisian life
are set out in a small list made about that time. His father
wished him to dine at the Palais Royal on Thursdays and
Sundays with Chappuis, and the price of each of those dinners
came to a little less than two francs. He had, still with the
inseparable Chappuis, gone four times to the theatre and once
to the opera. He had also hired a stove for his stone-floored
room; for eight francs he had bought some firewood, and also a
two-franc cloth for his table, which he said had holes in it,
and was not convenient to write on.

At the end of the school year, 1843, he took at the Lycée
St. Louis two " Accessits,"[1] and one first prize in physics,
and at the " *Concours Général* "[2] a sixth " Accessit " in
physics. He was admitted fourth on the list to the Ecole
Normale. He then wrote from Arbois to M. Barbet, telling
him that on his half-holidays he would give some lessons at
the school of the Impasse des Feuillantines as a small token
of his gratitude for past kindness. " My dear Pasteur,"
answered M. Barbet, " I accept with pleasure the offer you
have made me to give to my school some of the leisure that
you will have during your stay at the Ecole Normale. It will
indeed be a means of frequent and intimate intercourse
between us, in which we shall both find much advantage."

Pasteur was in such a hurry to enter the Ecole Normale
that he arrived in Paris some days before the other students.
He solicited permission to come in as another might have
begged permission to come out. He was readily allowed to
sleep in the empty dormitory. His first visit was to M. Barbet.
The Thursday half-holiday, usually from one to seven, was

---

[1] Accessit. A distinction accorded in French schools to those who
have come nearest to obtaining the prize in any given subject. [Trans.]

[2] Concours Général. An open competition held every year at the Sorbonne between the *élite* of the students of all the colleges in France,
from the highest classes down to the *quatrième*. [Trans.]

now from one to eight. "There is nothing more simple," he said, "than to come regularly at six o'clock on Thursdays and give the schoolboys a physical science class."

"I am very pleased," wrote his father, "that you are giving lessons at M. Barbet's. He has been so kind to us that I was anxious that you should show him some gratitude; be therefore always most obliging towards him. You should do so, not only for your own sake, but for others; it will encourage him to show the same kindness to other studious young men, whose future might depend upon it."

Generosity, self-sacrifice, kindliness even to unknown strangers, cost not the least effort to the father and son, but seemed to them the most natural thing possible. Just as their little house at Arbois was transformed by a ray of the ideal, the broken down walls of the old Ecole Normale—then a sort of annexe of the Louis Le Grand college, and looking, said Jules Simon, like an old hospital or barracks—reflected within them the ideas and sentiments which inspire useful lives. Joseph Pasteur wrote (Nov. 18, 1843): "The details you give me on the way your work is directed please me very much; everything seems organized so as to produce distinguished scholars. Honour be to those who founded this School." Only one thing troubled him, he mentioned it in every letter. "You know how we worry about your health; you do work so immoderately. Are you not injuring your eyesight by so much night work? Your ambition ought to be satisfied now that you have reached your present position!" He also wrote to Chappuis: "Do tell Louis not to work so much; it is not good to strain one's brain. That is not the way to succeed but to compromise one's health." And with some little irony as to the cogitations of Chappuis the philosopher: "Believe me, you are but poor philosophers if you do not know that one can be happy even as a poor professor in Arbois College."

Another letter, December, 1843, to his son this time: "Tell Chappuis that I have bottled some 1834 bought on purpose to drink the health of the Ecole Normale during the next holidays. There is more wit in those 100 litres than in all the books on philosophy in the world; but, as to mathematical formulæ, there are none, I believe. Mind you tell him that we shall drink the first bottle with him. Remain two good friends."

Pasteur's letters during this first period at the Normale have been lost, but his biography continues without a break, thanks to the letters of his father. "Tell us always about your studies, about your doings at Barbet's. Do you still attend M. Pouillet's lectures, or do you find that one science hampers the other? I should think not; on the contrary, one should be a help to the other." This observation should be interesting to a student of heredity; the idea casually mentioned by the father was to receive a vivid demonstration in the life-work of the son.

CHAPTER II

PASTEUR often spent his leisure moments in the library of the Ecole Normale. Those who knew him at that time remember him as grave, quiet, almost shy. But under these reflective characteristics lay the latent fire of enthusiasm. The lives of illustrious men, of great scientists, of great patriots inspired him with a generous ardour. To this ardour he added a great eagerness of mind; whether studying a book, even a commonplace one—for he was so conscientious that he did not even know what it was to " skim " through a book—or coming away from one of J. B. Dumas' lectures, or writing his student's notes in his small fine handwriting, he was always thirsting to learn more, to devote himself to great researches. There seemed to him no better way of spending a holiday than to be shut up all Sunday afternoon at the Sorbonne laboratory or coaxing a private lesson from the celebrated Barruel, Dumas' curator.

Chappuis—anxious to obey the injunctions of Pasteur's father, who in every letter repeated " Do not let him work too much ! " desirous also of enjoying a few hours' outing with his friend—used to wait philosophically, sitting on a laboratory stool, until the experiments were over. Conquered by this patient attitude and reproachful silence Pasteur would take off his apron, saying half angrily, half gratefully, " Well, let us go for a walk." And, when they were out in the street, the same serious subjects of conversation would inevitably crop up—classes, lectures, readings, etc.

One day, in the course of those long talks in the gardens of the Luxembourg, Pasteur carried Chappuis with him very far away from philosophy. He began to talk of tartaric acid and of paratartaric acid. The former had been known since 1770, thanks to the Swedish chemist Scheele, who discovered it in

the thick crusty formations within wine barrels called "tartar"; but the latter was disconcerting to chemists. In 1820
an Alsatian manufacturer, Kestner, had obtained by chance,
whilst preparing tartaric acid in his factory at Thann, a very
singular acid which he was unable to reproduce in spite of
various attempts. He had kept some of it in stock. Gay-
Lussac, having visited the Thann factory in 1826, studied this
mysterious acid; he proposed to call it *racemic* acid. Berzélius
studied it in his turn, and preferred to call it *paratartaric*.
Either name may be adopted; it is exactly the same thing:
men of letters or in society are equally frightened by the word
paratartaric or racemic. Chappuis certainly was when Pasteur
repeated to him word for word a paragraph by a Berlin chemist
and crystallographer named Mitscherlich. Pasteur had pondered over this paragraph until he knew it by heart; often
indeed, absorbed in reading the reports for 1844 of the
Académie des Sciences, in the dark room which was then the
library of the Ecole Normale, he had wondered if it were possible to get over a difficulty which seemed insurmountable to
scientists such as Mitscherlich and Biot. This paragraph
related to two saline combinations—tartrate and paratartrate
of soda or ammonia—and may be epitomized as follows: in
these two substances of similar crystalline form, the nature and
number of the atoms, their arrangement and distances are the
same. Yet dissolved tartrate rotates the plane of polarized
light and paratartrate remains inactive.

Pasteur had the gift of making scientific problems interesting in a few words, even to minds least inclined to that particular line of thought. He rendered his listener's attention very
easy; no question surprised him and he never smiled at ignorance. Though Chappuis, absorbed in the series of lectures on
philosophy given at that time by Jules Simon, was deep in a
train of thought very far away from Mitscherlich's perplexities,
he gradually became interested in this optical inactivity of paratartrate, which so visibly affected his friend. Pasteur liked to
look back into the history of things, giving in this way a
veritable life to his explanations. Thus, à propos of the optical
phenomenon which puzzled Mitscherlich, Pasteur was speaking to his friend of crystallized carbonate of lime, called Iceland
spar, which presents a double refraction—that is to say: if you
look at an object through this crystal, you perceive two repro-
ductions of that object. In describing this, Pasteur was not

giving to Chappuis a vague notion of some piece of crystal in a glass case, but was absolutely evoking a vision of the beautiful crystal, perfectly pure and transparent, brought from Iceland in 1669 to a Danish physicist. Pasteur almost seemed to experience the surprise and emotion of this scientist, when, observing a ray of light through this crystal, he saw it suddenly duplicated. Pasteur also spoke enthusiastically of an officer of Engineers under the First Empire, Etienne Louis Malus. Malus was studying double refraction, and holding in his hands a piece of spar crystal, when, from his room in the Rue de l'Enfer, it occurred to him to observe through the crystal the windows of the Luxembourg Palace, then lighted up by the setting sun. It was sufficient to make the crystal rotate slowly round the visual ray (as on an axis) to perceive the periodic variations in the intensity of the light reflected by the windows. No one had yet suspected that light, after being reflected under certain conditions, would acquire properties quite different from those it had before its reflection. Malus gave the name of polarized light to light thus modified (by reflection in this particular case). Scientists admitted in those days, in the theory of emission, the existence of luminous molecules, and they imagined that these molecules " suffered the same effects simultaneously when they had been reflected on glass at a certain angle. . They were all turned in the same direction." Pouillet, speaking of this discovery of Malus in the class on physics that Pasteur attended, explained that the consequent persuasion was " that those molecules had rotatory axes and poles, around which their movements could be accomplished under certain influences."

Pasteur spoke feverishly of his regrets that Malus should have died at thirty-seven in the midst of his researches; of Biot, and of Arago, who became illustrious in the path opened by Malus. He explained to Chappuis that, by means of a polarizing apparatus, it could be seen that certain quartz crystals deflected to the right the plane of polarized light, whilst others caused it to turn to the left. Chappuis also learned that some natural organic material, such as solutions of sugar or of tartaric acid, when placed in such an apparatus, turned to the right the plane of polarization, whilst others, like essence of turpentine or quinine, deflected it to the left; whence the expression " rotatory polarization."

These would seem dry researches, belonging altogether to

the domain of science. And yet, thanks to the saccharimeter, which is a polarizing apparatus, a manufacturer can ascertain the quantity of pure sugar contained in the brown sugar of commerce, and a physiologist can follow the progress of diabetes.

Chappuis, who knew what powers of investigation his friend could bring to bear on the problem enunciated by Mitscherlich, thought with regret that the prospect of such examinations as that for the *licence* and for the *agrégation* did not allow Pasteur to concentrate all his forces on such a special scientific point. But Pasteur was resolved to come back definitely to this sub-jcot as soon as he should have become " *docteur ès sciences.*"

When writing to his father he did not dwell upon tartrate and paratartrate; but his ambition was palpable. He was ever eager to do double work, to go up for his examination at the very earliest. " Before being a captain," answered the old sergeant-major, " you must become a lieutenant."

These letters give one the impression of living amongst those lives, perpetually reacting upon each other. The thoughts of the whole family were centred upon the great School, where that son, that brother, was working, in whom the hopes of each were placed. If one of his bulky letters with the large post mark was too long in coming, his father wrote to reproach him gently : " Your sisters were counting the days. Eighteen days, they said! Louis has never kept us waiting so long! Can he be ill? It is a great joy to me," adds the father, " to note your attachment to each other. May it always remain so."

The mother had no time to write much; she was burdened with all the cares of the household and with keeping the books of the business. But she watched for the postman with a tender anxiety increased by her vivid imagination. Her thoughts were ever with the son whom she loved, not with a selfish love, but for himself, sharing his happiness in that he was working for a useful career.

So, between that corner in the Jura and the Ecole Normale, there was a continual exchange of thoughts; the smallest inci-dents of daily life were related. The father, knowing that he should inform the son of the fluctuations of the family budget, spoke of his more or less successful sales of leathers at the Besançon fair. The son was ever hunting in the progress of industry anything that could tend to lighten the father's heavy handicraft. But though the father declared himself ready to examine Vauquelin's new tanning process, which obviated the necessity of keeping the skins so long in the pits, he asked himself with scrupulous anxiety whether leathers prepared in that way would last as long as the others. Could he safely guarantee them to the shoemakers, who were unanimous in praising the goods of the little tannery-yard, but alas equally unanimous in forgetting to reward the disinterested tanner by prompt payment? He supplied his family with the necessaries of life : what more did he want? When he had news of his *Normalien* he was thoroughly happy. He associated himself with his son's doings, sharing his enthusiasm over Dumas' lectures, and taking an interest in Pouillet's classes : Pouillet was a Franc-Comtois, and had been a student at the Ecole Normale ; he was now Professor of Physics at the Sorbonne and a member of the *Institut*.[1] When Balard, a lecturer at the Ecole, was nominated to the Académie des Sciences, Louis told his father of it with the delight of an admiring pupil.

Like J. B. Dumas, Balard had been an apothecary's pupil. When he spoke of their humble beginnings, Dumas was wont to say rather pompously—"Balard and I were initiated into our scientific life under the same conditions." When, at the age of forty-two, he was made a member of the Institute, Balard could not contain his joy ; he was quite a Southerner in his language and gestures, and the adjective *exubérant* might have been invented for him. But this same Southerner, ever on the move as he was, belonged to a special race : he always kept ·his word. "I was glad to note your pleasure at this nomination," wrote Joseph Pasteur to his son ; "it proves

[1] *Institut de France.* Name given collectively to the five following societies—

1. *Académie Française*, founded by Richelieu in 1635 in order to polish and maintain the purity of the French language. It is composed of forty Life members, and publishes from time to time a dictionary which is looked upon as a standard test of correct French.

2. *Académie des Inscriptions et Belles Lettres*, founded by Colbert in 1663.

3. *Académie des Sciences*, also founded by Colbert in 1666. It has published most valuable reports ever since 1699.

4. *Académie des Beaux-Arts*, which includes the Academies of Painting, of Sculpture, of Music, and of Architecture.

5. *Académie des Sciences Morales et Politiques.*

It was in 1795 that these ancient academies, which had been suppressed two years before by the Revolution, were reorganized and combined together to form the *Institut de France*. [Trans.]

that you are grateful to your masters." About that same time
the headmaster of Arbois College, M. Romanet, used to read
out to the older boys the letters, always full of gratitude, which
he received from Louis Pasteur. These letters reflected life
in Paris, such as Pasteur understood it—a life of hard work
and exalted ambition. M. Romanet, in one of his replies,
asked him to become librarian *in partibus* for the college and
to choose and procure books on science and literature. The
headmaster also begged of the young man some lectures for
the *rhétorique* class during the holidays. "It would seem to
the boys like an echo of the Sorbonne lectures! And you
would speak to us of our great scientific men," added M.
Romanet, "amongst whom we shall one day number him who
once was one of our best pupils and will ever remain one of
our best friends."

A corresponding member of Arbois College, and retained as
vacation lecturer, Pasteur now undertook a yet more special
task. He had often heard his father deplore his own lack of
instruction, and knew well the elder man's desire for knowledge. By a touching exchange of parts, the child to whom
his father had taught his alphabet now became his father's
teacher; but with what respect and what delicacy did this filial
master express himself! "It is in order that you may be able
to help Josephine that I am sending you this work to do." He
took most seriously his task of tutor by correspondence; the
papers he sent were not always easy. His father wrote (Jan.
2, 1845)—"I have spent two days over a problem which I
afterwards found quite easy; it is no trifle to learn a thing and
teach it directly afterwards." And a month later : "Josephine
does not care to rack her brains, she says; however I promise
you that you will be pleased with her progress by the next
holidays."

The father would often sit up late at night over rules of
grammar and mathematical problems, preparing answers to
send to his boy in Paris.

Some Arboisians, quite forgotten now, imagined that they
would add lustre to the local history. General Baron Delort,
a peer of France,[1] aide de camp to Louis Philippe, Grand Cross

[1] *Peers of France.* A supreme Council formed originally of the First
Vassals of the Crown; became in 1420 one of the Courts of Parliament.
In 1789 the Peerage was suppressed, but reinstated in 1814 by the
Restoration, when it again formed part of the Legislative Corps; there
were then hereditary peers and life-peers. In 1831 the hereditary

of the Legion of Honour and the first personage in Arbois where he beguiled his old age by translating Horace—used to go across the Cuisance bridge without so much as glancing at the tannery where the Pasteur family lived. Whilst the general in his thoughts bequeathed to the town of Arbois his books, his papers, his decorations, even his uniform, he was far from foreseeing that the little dwelling by the bridge would one day become the cynosure of all eyes.

Months went by and happy items of news succeeded one another. The *Normalien* was chiefly interested in the transformations of matter, and was practising in order to become capable of assisting in experiments; difficulties only stimulated him. At the chemistry class that he attended, the process of obtaining phosphorus was merely explained, on account of the length of time necessary to obtain this elementary substance; Pasteur, with his patience and desire for proven knowledge, was not satisfied. He therefore bought some bones, burnt them, reduced them to a very fine ash, treated this ash with sulphuric acid, and carefully brought the process to its close. What a triumph it seemed to him when he had in his possession sixty grammes of phosphorus, extracted from bones, which he could put into a phial labelled " phosphorus." This was his first scientific joy.

Whilst his comrades ironically (but with some discernment) called him a " laboratory pillar," some of them, more intent upon their examinations, were getting ahead of him.—M. Darboux, the present " doyen " of the Faculty [1] of Science, finds in the Sorbonne registers that Pasteur was placed 7th at the *licence* examination; two other students having obtained equal marks with him, the jury (Balard, Dumas and Delafosse), mentioned his name after theirs.

Those who care for archives would find in the *Journal Général de l'Instruction Publique* of September 17, 1846, a report of the *agrégation* [2] competition (physical science). Out

peerage was abolished and life-peers were nominated by the King under certain restrictions. This House of Peers was suppressed in 1848, and in 1852 the Senate was instituted in its stead. [Trans.]

[1] *Facultés*, Government establishments for superior studies; there are in France Faculties of Theology, of Law, of Medicine, of Sciences and of Letters, distributed among the larger provincial towns as well as in Paris. The administrator of a faculty is styled *doyen* (dean) and is chosen among the professors. [Trans.]

[2] *Agrégation.* An annual competition for recruiting professors for

of fourteen candidates only four passed and Pasteur was the third. His lessons on physics and chemistry caused the jury to say, "He will make an excellent professor."

Many *Normaliens* of that time fancied themselves called to a destiny infinitely superior to his. Some of them, in later times, used to complacently allude to this momentary superiority when speaking to their pupils. Of all Pasteur's acquaintances Chappuis was the only one who divined the future. "You will see what Pasteur will be," he used to say, with an assurance generally attributed to friendly partiality. Chappuis—Pasteur's confidant—was well aware of his friend's powers of concentration.

Balard also realised this; he had the happy idea of taking the young *agrégé* into his laboratory, and intervened vehemently when the Minister of Public Instruction desired—a few months later—that Pasteur should teach physics in the Tournon Lycée. It would be rank folly, Balard declared, to send 500 kilometres away from Paris a youth who only asked for the modest title of curator, and had no ambition but to work from morning till night, preparing for his doctor's degree. There would be time to send him away later on. It was impossible to resist this torrent of words founded on solid sense. Balard prevailed.

Pasteur was profoundly grateful to him for preserving him from exile to the little town in Ardèche; and, as he added to his Franc-Comtois patience and reflective mind a childlike heart and deep enthusiasm, he was delighted to remain with a master like Balard, who had become celebrated, at the age of twenty-four, as the discoverer of bromin.

At the end of 1846, a newcomer entered Balard's laboratory, a strange delicate-looking man, whose ardent eyes were at the same time proud and yet anxious. This man, a scientist and a poet, was a professor of the Bordeaux Faculty, named Auguste Laurent. Perhaps he had had some friction with his Bordeaux chiefs, possibly he merely wished for a change; at all events, he now desired to live in Paris. Laurent was already known in the scientific world, and had recently been made a correspondent of the Académie des Sciences. He had foreseen and confirmed the theory of substitutions, formulated by Dumas as early as 1834 before the Académie. Dumas had

faculties and secondary schools or *lycées*. A candidate for the *lycées agrégation* must have passed his *licence* examination. [Trans.]

expressed himself thus : " Chlorine possesses the singular power of seizing upon the hydrogen in certain substances, and of taking its place atom by atom."

This theory of substitutions was—according to a simple and vivid comparison of Pasteur's—a way of looking upon chemical bodies as upon " molecular edifices, in which one element could be replaced by another without disturbing the structure of the edifice ; as if one were to replace, one by one, every stone of a monument by a new stone." Original researches, new and bold ideas, appealed to Pasteur. But his cautious mind prevented his boldness from leading him into errors, surprises or hasty conclusions. " That is possible," he would say, " but we must look more deeply into the subject."

When asked by Laurent to assist him with some experiments upon certain theories, Pasteur was delighted at this suggested collaboration, and wrote to his friend Chappuis : " Even if the work should lead to no results worth publishing, it will be most useful to me to do practical work for several months with such an experienced chemist."

It was partly due to Laurent, that Pasteur entered more deeply into the train of thought which was to lead him to grapple with Mitscherlich's problem. " One day " (this is a manuscript note of Pasteur's) " one day it happened that M. Laurent—studying, if I mistake not, some tungstate of soda, perfectly crystallized and prepared from the directions of another chemist, whose results he was verifying—showed me through the microscope that this salt, apparently very pure, was evidently a mixture of three distinct kinds of crystals, easily recognizable with a little experience of crystalline forms. The lessons of our modest and excellent professor of mineralogy, M. Delafosse, had long since made me love crystallography ; so, in order to acquire the habit of using the goniometer, I began to carefully study the formations of a very fine series of combinations, all very easily crystallized, tartaric acid and the tartrates." He appreciated any favourable influence on his work ; we find in the same note : " Another motive urged me to prefer the study of those particular forms. M. de la Provostaye had just published an almost complete work concerning them ; this allowed me to compare as I went along my own observations with those, always so precise, of that clever scientist."

Pasteur and Laurent's work in common was interrupted.

D

Laurent was appointed as Dumas' assistant at the Sorbonne. Pasteur did not dwell upon his own disappointment, but rejoiced to see honour bestowed upon a man whom he thought worthy of the first rank. Some judges have thought that Laurent, in his introductory lesson, was too eager to expound his own ideas; but is not every believer an apostle? When a mind is full of ideas, it naturally overflows. It is probable that Pasteur in Laurent's place would have kept his part as an assistant more in the background. He did not give vent to the slightest criticism, but wrote to Chappuis. "Laurent's lectures are as bold as his writings, and his lessons are making a great sensation amongst chemists." Whether one of criticism or of approbation, this sensation was a living element of success. In order to answer some insinuations concerning Laurent's ambition and constant thirst for change, Pasteur proclaimed in his thesis on chemistry how much he had been "enlightened by the kindly advice of a man so distinguished, both by his talent and by his character." "

This essay was entitled "*Researches into the saturation capacity of arsenious acid. A study of the arsenites of potash, soda and ammonia.*" This, to Pasteur's mind, was but school-boy work. He had not yet, he said, enough practice and experience in laboratory work. "In physics," he wrote to Chappuis, "I shall only present a programme of some re-searches that I mean to undertake next year, and that I merely indicate in my essay."

This essay on physics was a "*Study of phenomena relative to the rotatory polarization of liquids.*" In it he rendered full homage to Biot, pointing out the importance of a branch of science too much neglected by chemists; he added that it was most useful, in order to throw light upon certain difficult chemical problems, to obtain the assistance of crystallography and physics. "Such assistance is especially needed in the present state of science."

These two essays, dedicated to his father and mother, were read on August 23, 1847. He only obtained one white ball and two red ones for each. "We cannot judge of your essays," wrote his father, in the name of the whole family, "but our satisfaction is no less great. As to a doctor's degree, I was far from hoping as much; all *my* ambition was satisfied with the *agrégation.*" Such was not the case with his son.

" Onwards " was his motto, not from a desire for a diploma, but from an insatiable thirst for knowledge.

After spending a few days with his family and friends, he wanted to go to Germany with Chappuis to study German from morning till night. The prospect of such industrious holidays enchanted him. But he had forgotten a student's debt. " I cannot carry out my project," he sadly wrote, on September 8, 1847; " I am more than ruined by the cost of printing my thesis."

On his return to Paris he shut himself up in the laboratory. "I am extremely happy. I shall soon publish a paper on crystallography." His father writes (December 25, 1847) : " We received your letter yesterday ; it is absolutely satisfactory, but it could not be otherwise coming from you ; you have long, indeed ever, been all satisfaction to me." And in response to his son's intentions of accomplishing various tasks, fully understanding that nothing will stop him : " You are doing right to make for your goal ; it was only out of excessive affection that I have often written in another sense. I only feared that you might succumb to your work ; so many noble youths have sacrificed their health to the love of science. Knowing you as I do, this was my only anxiety."

After being reproved for excessive work, Louis was reprimanded for too much affection (January 1, 1848). " The presents you sent have just arrived ; I shall leave it to your sisters to write their thanks. For my part, I should prefer a thousand times that this money should still be in your purse, and thence to a good restaurant, spent in some good meals that you might have enjoyed with your friends. There are not many parents, my dearest boy, who have to write such things to their son ; my satisfaction in you is indeed deeper than I can express." At the end of this same letter, the mother adds in her turn : " My darling boy, I wish you a happy new year. Take great care of your health. Think what a worry it is to me that I cannot be with you to look after you. Sometimes I try to console myself for your absence by thinking how fortunate I am in having a child able to raise himself to such a position as yours is—such a happy position, as it seems to be from your last letter but one." And in a strange sentence, where it would seem that a presentiment of her approaching death made worldly things appear at their true value :

" Whatever happens to you, do not grieve; nothing in life is more than a chimera. Farewell, my son."

On March 20, 1848, Pasteur read to the Académie des Sciences a portion of his treatise on "*Researches on Dimorphism.*" There are some substances which crystallize in two different ways. Sulphur, for instance, gives quite dissimilar crystals according to whether it is melted in a crucible or dissolved in sulphide of carbon. Those substances are called dimorphous. Pasteur, kindly aided by the learned M. Delafosse (with his usual gratefulness he mentions this in the very first pages) had made out a list—as complete as possible—of all dimorphous substances. When M. Romanet, of Arbois College, received this paper he was quite overwhelmed. " It is much too stiff for you," he said with an infectious modesty to Vercel, Charrière, and Coulon, Pasteur's former comrades. Perhaps the head master desired to palliate his own incompetence in the eyes of coming generations, for on the title page of the copy of Pasteur's booklet still to be found in the Arbois library, he wrote this remark, which he signed with his initial R. :—" *Dimorphisme* ; this word is not even to be found in the *Dictionnaire de l'Académie* " ! ! The approbation of several members of the Académie des Sciences compensated for the somewhat summary judgment of M. Romanet, whose good wishes continued to follow the rapid course of his old pupil.

After this very special study, dated at the beginning of 1848, one might imagine the graduate-curator closing his ears to all outside rumours and little concerned with political agitation, but that would be doing him an injustice. Those who witnessed the Revolution of 1848 remember how during the early days France was exalted with the purest patriotism. Pasteur had visions of a generous and fraternal Republic; the words *drapeau* and *patrie* moved him to the bottom of his soul. Lamartine [1] as a politician inspired him with an enthusiastic confidence; he delighted in the sight of a poet leader of men. Many others shared the same illusions. France, as Louis Veuillot has it, made the mistake of choosing her band-master

---

[1] This celebrated poet took a large share in the Revolution of 1848, when his popularity became enormous. His political talents, however, apart from his wonderful eloquence, were less than mediocre, and he retired into private life within three years.

His " Meditations," " Jocelyn," " Recueillements," etc., etc., are beautiful examples of lyrical poetry, and may be considered as forming part of the literature of the world. [Trans.]

as colonel of the regiment. Enrolled with his fellow students, Pasteur wrote thus to his parents : " I am writing from the Orleans Railway, where as a *garde national*[1] I am stationed. I am glad that I was in Paris during the February days[2] and that I am here still; I should be sorry to leave Paris just now. It is a great and a sublime doctrine which is now being unfolded before our eyes . . . and if it were necessary I should heartily fight for the holy cause of the Republic." " What a transformation of our whole being ! " has written one who was then a candidate to the Ecole Normale, already noted by his masters for his good sense, Francisque Sarcey. " How those magical words of liberty and fraternity, this renewal of the Republic, born in the sunshine of our twentieth year, filled our hearts with unknown and absolutely delicious sensations ! With what a gallant joy we embraced the sweet and superb image of a people of free men and brethren ! The whole nation was moved as we were ; like us, it had drunk of the intoxicating cup. The honey of eloquence flowed unceasingly from the lips of a great poet, and France believed, in childlike faith, that his word was efficacious to destroy abuses, cure evils and soothe sorrows."

One day when Pasteur was crossing the Place du Panthéon, he saw a gathering crowd around a wooden erection, decorated with the words : *Autel de la Patrie*. A neighbour told him that pecuniary offerings might be laid upon this altar. Pasteur goes back to the Ecole Normale, empties a drawer of all his savings, and returns to deposit it in thankful hands.

[1] Garde Nationale. A city militia, intended to preserve order and to maintain municipal liberties; it was improvised in 1789, and its first Colonel was General Lafayette, of American Independence fame. Its cockade united the King's white to the Paris colours, blue and red, and thus was inaugurated the celebrated Tricolour.

The National Guard was preserved by the Restoration, but Charles X disbanded it as being dangerously Liberal in its tendencies. It re-formed itself of its own accord in 1830, and helped to overthrow the elder branch of Bourbon. It proved a source of disorder in 1848 and was reorganized under the second Empire, but, having played an active and disastrous part in the Commune (1871), it was disarmed and finally suppressed. [Trans.]

[2] February days. The Republicans had organized a banquet in Paris for February 22, 1848. The Government prohibited it, with the result that an insurrection took place. Barricades were erected and some fighting ensued; on the 24th, the insurgents were masters of the situation. Louis Philippe abdicated (vainly) in favour of his grandson, the Comte de Paris, and fled to England. [Trans.]

"You say," wrote his father on April 28, 1848, "that you
have offered to France all your savings, amounting to 150
francs. You have probably kept a receipt of the office where
this payment was made, with mention of the date and place?"
And considering that this action should be made known, he
advises him to publish it in the journal *Le National* or *La
Réforme* in the following terms, "Gift to the *Patrie* : 150
francs, by the son of an old soldier of the Empire, Louis
Pasteur of the Ecole Normale." He wrote in the same letter,
"You should raise a subscription in your school in favour of
the poor Polish exiles who have done so much for us ; it would
be a good deed."

After those days of national exaltation, Pasteur returned to
his crystals. He studied tartrates under the influence of
certain ideas that he himself liked to expound. Objects considered merely from the point of view of form, may be divided
into two great categories. First, those objects which, placed
before a mirror, give an image which can be superposed to
them : these have a symmetrical plan ; secondly, those which
have an image which cannot be superposed to them : they are
dissymmetrical. A chair, for instance, is symmetrical, or a
straight flight of steps. But a spiral staircase is not symmetrical, its own image cannot be laid over it. If it turns to
the right, its image turns to the left. In the same way the
right hand cannot be superposed to the left hand, a righthand
glove does not fit a left hand, and a right hand seen in a mirror
gives the image of a left hand.

Pasteur noticed that the crystals of tartaric acid and the
tartrates had little faces, which had escaped even the profound
observation of Mitscherlich and La Provostaye. These faces,
which only existed on one half of the edges or similar angles,
constituted what is called a hemihedral form. When the
crystal was placed before a glass the image that appeared could
not be superposed to the crystal ; the comparison of the two
hands was applicable to it. Pasteur thought that this aspect
of the crystal might be an index of what existed within the
molecules, dissymmetry of form corresponding with molecular
dissymmetry. Mitscherlich had not perceived that his tartrate
presented these little faces, this dissymmetry, whilst his paratartrate was without them, was in fact not hemihedral. Therefore, reasoned Pasteur, the deviation to the right of the plane
of polarization produced by tartrate and the optical neutrality

of paratartrates would be explained by a structural law. The first part of these conclusions was confirmed; all the crystals of tartrate proved to be hemihedral. But when Pasteur came to examine the crystals of paratartrate, hoping to find none of them hemihedral, he experienced a keen disappointment. The paratartrate also was hemihedral, but the faces of some of the crystals were inclined to the right, and those of others to the left. It then öccurred to Pasteur to take up these crystals one by one and sort them carefully, putting on one side those which turned to the left, and on the other those which turned to the right. He thought that by observing their respective solutions in the polarizing apparatus, the two contrary hemihedral forms would give two contrary deviations; and then, by mixing together an equal number of each kind, as no doubt Mitscherlich had done, the resulting solution would have no action upon light, the two equal and directly opposite deviations exactly neutralizing each other.

With anxious and beating heart he proceeded to this experiment with the polarizing apparatus and exclaimed, "I have it!" His excitement was such that he could not look at the apparatus again; he rushed out of the laboratory, not unlike Archimedes. He met a curator in the passage, embraced him as he would have embraced Chappuis, and dragged him out with him into the Luxembourg garden to explain his discovery. Many confidences have been whispered under the shade of the tall trees of those avenues, but never was there greater or more exuberant joy on a young man's lips. He foresaw all the consequences of his discovery. The hitherto incomprehensible constitution of paratartaric or racemic acid was explained; he differentiated it into righthand tartaric acid, similar in every way to the natural tartaric acid of grapes, and lefthand tartaric acid. These two distinct acids possess equal and opposite rotatory powers which neutralize each other when these two substances, reduced to an aqueous solution, combine spontaneously in equal quantities.

"How often," he wrote to Chappuis (May 5), whom he longed to have with him, "how often have I regretted that we did not both take up the same study, that of physical science. We who so often talked of the future, we did not understand. What splendid work we could have undertaken and would be undertaking now; and what could we not have done united by the same ideas, the same love of science, the same ambition!

I would we were twenty and with the three years of the Ecole before us!" Always fancying that he could have done more, he often had such retrospective regrets. He was impatient to begin new researches, when a sad blow fell upon him—his mother died almost suddenly of apoplexy. "She succumbed in a few hours," he wrote to Chappuis on May 28, "and when I reached home she had already left us. I have asked for a holiday." He could no longer work; he remained steeped in tears and buried in his sorrow. For weeks his intellectual life was suspended.

In Paris, in the scientific world perhaps even more than in any other, everything gets known, repeated, discussed. Pasteur's researches were becoming a subject of conversation. Balard, with his strident voice, spoke of them in the library at the Institute, which is a sort of drawing-room for talkative old Academicians. J. B. Dumas listened gravely; Biot, old Biot, then seventy-four years old, questioned the story with some scepticism. "Are you quite sure?" he would ask, his head a little on one side, his words slow and slightly ironical. He could hardly believe, on first hearing Balard, that a new doctor, fresh from the Ecole Normale, should have overcome a difficulty which had proved too much for Mitscherlich. He did not care for long conversations with Balard, and as the latter continued to extol Pasteur, Biot said, "I should like to investigate that young man's results."

Besides Pasteur's deference for all those whom he looked upon as his teachers, he also felt a sort of general gratitude for their services to Science. Partly from an infinite respect and partly from an ardent desire to convince the old scientist, he wrote on his return to Paris to Biot, whom he did not know personally, asking him for an interview. Biot answered : " I shall be pleased to verify your results if you will communicate them confidentially to me. Please believe in the feelings of interest inspired in me by all young men who work with accuracy and perseverance."

An appointment was made at the Collège de France,[1] where Biot lived. Every detail of that interview remained for ever

[1] Collège de France. An establishment of superior studies founded in Paris by Francis I in 1530, and where public lectures are given on languages, literature, history, mathematics, physical science, etc. It was formerly independent, but is now under the jurisdiction of the Ministry of Public Instruction. [Trans.]

fixed in Pasteur's memory. Biot began by fetching some paratartaric acid. "I have most carefully studied it," he said to Pasteur; "it is absolutely neutral in the presence of polarized light." Some distrust was visible in his gestures and audible in his voice. "I shall bring you everything that is necessary," continued the old man, fetching doses of soda and ammonia. He wanted the salt prepared before his eyes.

After pouring the liquid into a crystallizer, Biot took it into a corner of his room to be quite sure that no one would touch it. "I shall let you know when you are to come back," he said to Pasteur when taking leave of him. Forty-eight hours later some crystals, very small at first, began to form; when there was a sufficient number of them, Pasteur was recalled. Still in Biot's presence, Pasteur withdrew, one by one, the finest crystals and wiped off the mother-liquor adhering to them. He then pointed out to Biot the opposition of their hemihedral character, and divided them into two groups—left and right.

"So you affirm," said Biot, "that your righthand crystals will deviate to the right the plane of polarization, and your lefthand ones will deviate it to the left?"

"Yes," said Pasteur.

"Well, let me do the rest."

Biot himself prepared the solutions, and then sent again for Pasteur. Biot first placed in the apparatus the solution which should deviate to the left. Having satisfied himself that this deviation actually took place, he took Pasteur's arm and said to him these words, often deservedly quoted: "My dear boy, I have loved Science so much during my life, that this touches my very heart."

"It was indeed evident," said Pasteur himself in recalling this interview, "that the strongest light had then been thrown on the cause of the phenomenon of rotatory polarization and hemihedral crystals; a new class of isomeric substances was discovered; the unexpected and until then unexampled constitution of the racemic or paratartaric acid was revealed; in one word a great and unforeseen road was opened to science."

Biot now constituted himself the sponsor in scientific matters of his new young friend, and undertook to report upon Pasteur's paper entitled: "*Researches on the relations which may exist between crystalline form, chemical composition, and the direction of rotatory power*"—destined for the Académie des Sciences.

Biot did full justice to Pasteur; he even rendered him
homage, and—not only in his own name but also in that of his
three colleagues, Regnault, Balard, and Dumas—he suggested
that the Académie should declare its highest approbation of
Pasteur's treatise.

Pasteur did not conceive greater happiness than his laboratory
life, and yet the laboratories of that time were very unlike what
they are nowadays, as we should see if the laboratories of the
Collège de France, of the Sorbonne, of the Ecole Normale had
been preserved. They were all that Paris could offer Europe,
and Europe certainly had no cause to covet them. Nowadays
the most humble college, in the smallest provincial town, would
not accept such dens as the State offered (when it offered them
any) to the greatest French scientists. Claude Bernard,
Magendie's curator, worked at the Collège de France in a regular cellar. Wurtz only had a lumber-room in the attics of the
Dupuytren Museum. Henri Sainte Claire Deville, before he became head of the Besançon Faculty, had not even as much; he
was relegated to one of the most miserable corners of the Rue
Lafarge. J. B. Dumas did not care to occupy the unhealthy
room reserved for him at the Sorbonne; his father-in-law,
Alexandre Brongniart, having given him a small house in the
Rue Cuvier, opposite the Jardin des Plantes, he had had it
transformed into a laboratory and was keeping it up at his own
expense. He was therefore comfortably situated, but he was
exceptionally fortunate. Every scientist who had no private
means to draw upon had to choose between the miserable
cellars and equally miserable garrets which were all that the
State could offer. And yet it was more tempting than a Professor's chair in a College or even in a Faculty, for there one
could not give oneself up entirely to one's work.

Nothing would have seemed more natural than to leave
Pasteur to his experiments. But his appointment to some
definite post could no longer be deferred, in spite of Balard's
tumultuous activity. The end of the summer vacation was
near, there was a vacancy: Pasteur was made a Professsor of
Physics at the Dijon Lycée. The Minister of Public Instruction consented to allow him to postpone his departure until the
beginning of November, in order to let him finish some work
begun under the eye of Biot, who thought and dreamt of
nothing but these new investigations. During thirty years
Biot had studied the phenomena of rotatory polarization. He

had called the attention of chemists to these phenomena, but his call had been unheeded. Continuing his solitary labour, he had—in experimenting on cases both simple and complex—studied this molecular rotatory power, without suspecting that this power bore a definite relation to the hemihedral form of some crystals. And now that the old man was a witness of a triumphant sequel to his own researches, now that he had the joy of seeing a young man with a thoughtful mind and an enthusiastic heart working with him, now that the hope of this daily collaboration shed a last ray on the close of his life, Pasteur's departure for Dijon came as a real blow. "If at least," he said, "they were sending you to a Faculty!" He turned his wrath on to the Government officials. "They don't seem to realize that such labours stand above everything else! If they only knew it, two or three such treatises might bring a man straight to the Institut!"

Nevertheless Pasteur had to go. M. Pouillet gave him a letter for a former Polytechnician,[1] now a civil engineer at Dijon, a M. Parandier, in which he wrote—

"M. Pasteur is a most distinguished young chemist. He has just completed some very remarkable work, and I hope it will not be long before he is sent to a first-class Faculty. I need add nothing else about him; I know no more honest, industrious, or capable young man. Help him as much as you can at Dijon; you will not regret it."

Those first weeks away from his masters and from his beloved pursuits seemed very hard to Pasteur. But he was anxious to prove himself a good teacher. This duty appeared to him to be a noble ideal, and to involve a wide responsibility. He felt none of the self satisfaction which is sometimes a source of strength to some minds conscious of their superiority to others. He did not even do himself the justice of feeling that he was

[1] Polytechnician. A student of the Ecole Polytechnique, a military and engineering school under the jurisdiction of the Minister of War, founded in 1794. Candidates for admission must be older than sixteen and younger than twenty, but the limit of age is raised to twenty-five in the case of private soldiers and non-commissioned officers. They must also have passed their *baccalauréat ès lettres* or *ès sciences*—preferably the latter. After two years' residence (compulsory) students pass a leaving examination, and are entered according to their list number as engineers of the Navy, Mines, or Civil Works, or as officers in the military Engineers or in the Artillery; the two last then have to go through one of the military training schools (Ecoles d'Application). [Trans.]

absolutely sure of his subject. He wrote to Chappuis (November 20, 1848) : " I find that preparing my lessons takes up a great deal of time. It is only when I have prepared a lesson very carefully that I succeed in making it very clear and capable of compelling attention. If I neglect it at all I lecture badly and become unintelligible."

He had both first and second year pupils; these two classes took up all his time and all his strength. He liked the second class; it was not a very large one. " They all work," Pasteur wrote, "some very intelligently." As to the first year class, what could he do with eighty pupils? The good ones were kept back by the bad. " Don't you think," he wrote, " that it is a mistake not to limit classes to fifty boys at the most? It is with great difficulty that I can secure the attention of all towards the end of the lesson. I have only found one means, which is to multiply experiments at the last moment."

Whilst he was eagerly and conscientiously giving himself up to his new functions—not without some bitterness, for he really was entitled to an appointment in a Faculty, and he could not pursue his favourite studies—his masters were agitating on his behalf. Balard was clamouring to have him as an assistant at the Ecole Normale. Biot was appealing to Baron Thenard. This scientist was then Chairman of the Grand Council of the Université.[1] He had been a pupil of Vauquelin, a friend of Laplace, and a collaborator of Gay-Lussac; he had lectured during thirty years at the Sorbonne, at the Collège de France, and at the Ecole Polytechnique; he could truthfully boast that he had had 40,000 pupils. He was, like J. B. Dumas, a born professor. But, whilst Dumas was always self possessed and dignified in his demeanour, his very smile serious, Thenard, a native of Burgundy, threw his whole personality into his work, a broad smile on his beaming face.

He was now (1848) seventy years old, and the memory of his

---

[1] *Université.* The celebrated body known as Université de Paris, and instituted by Philippe Auguste in 1200, possessed great privileges from its earliest times. It had the monopoly of teaching and a jurisdiction of its own. It took a share in public affairs on several occasions, and had long struggles to maintain against several religious orders. The Université was suppressed by the Convention, but re-organized by Napoleon I in 1808. It is now subdivided into sixteen *Académies Universitaires*, each of which is administered by a Rector. The title of Grand Master of the Université always accompanies that of Minister of Public Instruction. [Trans.]

teaching, the services rendered to industry by his discoveries, the *éclat* of his name and titles contrasted with his humble origin, all combined to render him more than a Chancellor of the University; he was in fact a sort of Field Marshal of science, and all powerful. Three years previously he had much scandalized certain red-tape officials by choosing three very young men—Puiseux, Delesse, and H. Sainte Claire Deville—as professors for the new Faculty of Science at Besançon. He had accentuated this authoritative measure by making Sante Claire Deville Dean of the Faculty. In the unknown professor of twenty-six, he had divined the future celebrated scientist.

At the end of the year 1848 Pasteur solicited the place of assistant to M. Delesse, who was taking a long leave of absence. This would have brought him near Arbois, besides placing him in a Faculty. He asked for nothing more. Thenard, who had Biot's report in his hands, undertook to transmit to the Minister this modest and natural request. He was opposed by an unexpected argument—the presentation of assistantships belonged to each Faculty. This custom was unknown to Pasteur. Thenard was unable to overcome this routine formality. Pasteur thought that the unanimous opinion of Thenard, Biot, and Pouillet ought to have prevailed. "I can practically do nothing here," he wrote on the sixth of December, thinking of his interrupted studies. "If I cannot go to Besançon, I shall go back to Paris as a curator."

His father, to whom he paid a visit for the new year, persuaded him to look upon things more calmly, telling him that wisdom repudiated too much hurry. Louis deferred to his father's opinion to the extent of writing, on January 2, 1849, to the Minister of Public Instruction, begging him to overlook his request. However, the members of the Institute who had taken up his cause did not intend to be thwarted by minor difficulties. Pasteur's letter was hardly posted when he received an assistantship, not at the Besançon Faculty but at Strasburg, to take the place of M. Persoz, Professor of Chemistry, who was desirous of going to Paris.

Pasteur, on his arrival at Strasburg (January 15) was welcomed by the Professor of Physics, his old school friend, the Franc-Comtois Bertin. "First of all, you are coming to live with me," said Bertin gleefully. "You could not do better; it is a stone's throw from the Faculté." By living with Bertin, Pasteur acquired a companion endowed with a rare combination of qualities—a quick wit and an affectionate heart. Bertin was too shrewd to be duped, and a malicious twinkle often lit up his kindly expression ; with one apparently careless word, he would hit the weak point of the most self satisfied. He loved those who were simple and true, hence his affection for Pasteur. His smiling philosophy contrasted with Pasteur's robust faith and ardent impetuosity. Pasteur admired, but did not often imitate, the peaceful manner with which Bertin, affirming that a disappointment often proved to be a blessing in disguise, accepted things as they came. In order to prove that this was no paradox, Bertin used to tell what had happened to him in 1839, when he was mathematical preparation master at the College of Luxeuil. He was entitled to 200 francs a month, but payment was refused him. This injustice did not cause him to recriminate, but he quietly tendered his resignation. He went in for the Ecole Normale examination, entered the school at the head of the list, and subsequently became Professor of Physics at the Strasburg Faculty. "If it had not been for my former disappointment, I should still be at Luxeuil." He was now perfectly satisfied, thinking that nothing could be better than to be a Professor in a Faculty ; but this absence of any sort of ambition did not prevent him from giving his teaching the most scrupulous attention. He prepared his lessons with extreme care, endeavouring to render them absolutely clear. He took great personal interest in his pupils, and often helped them with his advice in the interval between class hours. This excellent man's whole life was spent in working for others, and to be useful was ever to him the greatest satisfaction.

Perhaps Pasteur was stimulated by Bertin's example to give excessive importance to minor matters in his first lessons. He writes : "I gave too much thought to the style of my two first lectures, and they were anything but good ; but I think the subsequent ones were more satisfactory, and I feel I am improving." His lectures were well attended, for the numerous industries of Alsace gave to chemistry quite a place by itself.

Everything pleased him in Strasburg save its distance from Arbois. He who could concentrate his thoughts for weeks, for months even, on one subject, who could become as it were a prisoner of his studies, had withal an imperious longing for family life. His rooms in Bertin's house suited him all the better that they were large enough for him to entertain one of his relations. His father wrote in one of his letters : " You say that you will not marry for a long time, that you will ask one of your sisters to live with you. I could wish it for you and for them, for neither of them wishes for a greater happiness. Both desire nothing better than to look after your comfort; you are absolutely everything to them. One may meet with sisters as good as they are, but certainly with none better.''

Louis Pasteur's circle of dear ones was presently enlarged by his intimacy with another family. The new Rector of the Academy of Strasburg, M. Laurent, had arrived in October. He was no relation to the chemist of the same name, and the place he was about to take in Pasteur's life was much greater than that held by Auguste Laurent at the time when they were working together in Balard's laboratory.

After having begun, in 1812, as preparation master in the then Imperial College of Louis le Grand, M. Laurent had become, in 1826, head master of the College of Riom. He found at Riom more tutors than pupils; there were only three boys in the school ! Thanks to M. Laurent, those three soon became one hundred and thirty-four. From Riom he was sent to Guéret, then to Saintes, to save a college in imminent danger of disappearing; there were struggles between the former head master and the Mayor, the town refused the subsidies, all was confusion. Peace immediately followed his arrival. " Those who have known him,'' wrote M. Pierron in the *Revue de l'Instruction Publique*, " will not be surprised at such miracles coming from a man so intelligent and so active, so clever, amiable, and warm-hearted.'' Wherever he was afterwards sent, at Orleans, Angoulême, Douai, Toulouse, Cahors, he worked the same charm, born of kindness. At Strasburg, he had made of the Académie a home where all the Faculty found a simple and cordial welcome. Madame Laurent was a modest woman who tried to efface herself, but whose exquisite qualities of heart and mind could not remain hidden. The eldest of her daughters was married to M. Zevort, whose name became doubly dear to the Université. The two younger ones, brought up in habits of industry and unselfishness which seemed natural to them, brightened the home by their youthful gaiety.

When Pasteur on his arrival called on this family, he had the feeling that happiness lay there. He had seen at Arbois how, through the daily difficulties of manual labour, his parents looked at life from an exalted point of view, appreciating it from that standard of moral perfection which gives dignity and grandeur to the humblest existence. In this family—of a higher social position than his own—he again found the same high ideal, and, with great superiority of education, the same simple-mindedness. When Pasteur entered for the first time the Laurent family circle, he immediately felt the delightful impression of being in a thoroughly congenial atmosphere; a communion of thoughts and feelings seemed established after the first words, the first looks exchanged between him and his hosts.

In the evening, at the restaurant where most of the younger professors dined, he heard others speak of the kindliness and strict justice of the Rector; and everyone expressed respect for his wonderfully united family.

At one of M. Laurent's quiet evening "at homes," Bertin was saying of Pasteur, "You do not often meet with such a hard worker; no attraction ever can take him away from his work." The attraction now came, however, and it was such a powerful one that, on February 10, only a fortnight after his arrival, Pasteur addressed to M. Laurent the following official letter :—

" SIR,—

" An offer of the greatest importance to me and to your family is about to be made to you on my behalf; and I feel it my duty to put you in possession of the following facts, which may have some weight in determining your acceptance or refusal.

" My father is a tanner in the small town of Arbois in the Jura, my sisters keep house for him, and assist him with his books, taking the place of my mother whom we had the misfortune to lose in May last.

" My family is in easy circumstances, but with no fortune; I do not value what we possess at more than 50,000 francs, and, as for me, I have long ago decided to hand over to my sisters the whole of what should be my share. I have therefore absolutely no fortune. My only means are good health, some courage, and my position in the Université.

"I left the Ecole Normale two years ago, an *agrégé* in physical science. I have held a Doctor's degree eighteen months, and I have presented to the Académie a few works which have been very well received, especially the last one, upon which a report was made which I now have the honour to enclose.

"This, Sir, is all my present position. As to the future, unless my tastes should completely change, I shall give myself up entirely to chemical research. I hope to return to Paris when I have acquired some reputation through my scientific labours. M. Biot has often told me to think seriously about the Institute; perhaps I may do so in ten or fifteen years' time, and after assiduous work; but this is but a dream, and not the motive which makes me love Science for Science's sake.

"My father will himself come to Strasburg to make this proposal of marriage.

"Accept, Sir, the assurance of my profound respect, etc.

"P.S.—I was twenty-six on December 27."

A definite answer was adjourned for a few weeks. Pasteur, in a letter to Madame Laurent, wrote, "I am afraid that Mlle. Marie may be influenced by early impressions, unfavourable to me. There is nothing in me to attract a young girl's fancy. But my recollections tell me that those who have known me very well have loved me very much."

Of these letters, religiously preserved, fragments like the following have also been obtained. "All that I beg of you, Mademoiselle (he had now been authorised to address himself directly to her) is that you will not judge me too hastily, and therefore misjudge me. Time will show you that below my cold, shy and unpleasing exterior, there is a heart full of affection for you!" In another letter, evidently remorseful at forsaking the laboratory, he says, "I, who did so love my crystals!"

He loved them still, as is proved by an answer from Biot to a proposal of Pasteur's. In order to spare the old man's failing sight, Pasteur had the ingenious idea of cutting out of pieces of cork, with exquisite skill, some models of crystalline types greatly enlarged. He had tinted the edges and faces, and nothing was easier than to recognize their hemihedral character. "I accept with great pleasure," wrote Biot on April 7, "the offer you make me of sending me a small quantity of your two acids, with models of their crystalline types." He meant the righthand tartaric acid and the lefthand tartaric acid, which Pasteur—not to pronounce too hastily on their identity with ordinary tartaric acid—then called *dextroracemic* and *lævoracemic*.

Pasteur wished to go further; he was now beginning to study the crystallizations of formate of strontian. Comparing them with those of the paratartrates of soda and ammonia, surprised and uneasy at the differences he observed, he once exclaimed, " Ah ! formate of strontian, if only I had got you ! " to the immense amusement of Bertin, who long afterwards used to repeat this invocation with mock enthusiasm.

Pasteur was about to send these crystals to Biot, but the latter wrote, "Keep them until you have thoroughly investigated them. . . . You can depend on my wish to serve you in every circumstance when my assistance can be of any use to you, and also on the great interest with which you have inspired me."

Regnault and Senarmont had been invited by Biot to examine the valuable samples received from Strasburg, the dextroracemic and lævoracemic acids. Biot wrote to Pasteur, " We might make up our minds to sacrifice a small portion of the two acids in order to reconstitute the racemic, but we doubt whether we should be capable of discerning it with certainty by those crystals when they are formed. You must show it us yourself, when you come to Paris for the holidays. Whilst arranging my chemical treasures, I came upon a small quantity of racemic acid which I thought I had lost. It would be sufficient for the microscopical experiments that I might eventually have to make. So if the small phial of it that you saw here would be useful to you, let me know, and I will willingly send it. In this, as in everything else, you will always find me most anxious to second you in your labours."

This period was all happiness. Pasteur's father and his sister Josephine came to Strasburg. The proposal of marriage was accepted, the father returned to Arbois, Josephine staying behind. She remained to keep house and to share the everyday life of her brother, whom she loved with a mixture of pride, tenderness and solicitude. In her devoted sisterly generosity, she resigned herself to the thought that her happy dream must be of short duration. The wedding was fixed for May 29.

"I believe," wrote Pasteur to Chappuis, "that I shall be very happy. Every quality I could wish for in a wife I find in her. You will say, 'He is in love!' Yes, but I do not think I exaggerate at all, and my sister Josephine quite agrees with me."

CHAPTER III

FROM the very beginning Mme. Pasteur not only admitted, but approved, that the laboratory should come before everything else. She would willingly have adopted the typographic custom of the Académie des Sciences Reports, where the word Science is always spelt with a capital S. It was indeed impossible to live with her husband without sharing his joys, anxieties and renewed hopes, as they appeared day by day reflected in his admirable eyes—eyes of a rare grey-green colour like the sparkle of a Ceylon gem. Before certain scientific possibilities, the flame of enthusiasm shone in those deep eyes, and the whole stern face was illumined. Between domestic happiness and prospective researches, Pasteur's life was complete. But this couple, who had now shared everything for more than a year, was to suffer indirectly through the new law on the liberty of teaching.

Devised by some as an effort at compromise between the Church and the University, considered by others as a scope for competition against State education, the law of 1850 brought into the Superior Council of Public Instruction four archbishops or bishops, elected by their colleagues. In each Department[1] an Academy Council was instituted, and, in this parcelling out of University jurisdiction, the right of presence was recognized as belonging to the bishop or his delegate. But all these advantages did not satisfy those who called themselves Catholics before everything else. The rupture between Louis Veuillot on one side and, on the other, Falloux and Montalembert, the principal authors of this law, dates from that time.

[1] *Départements.* The present divisions of French territory, numbering eighty-seven in all. Each department is administered by a *préfet*, and subdivided into *arrondissements*, each of which has a *sous-préfet*. [Trans.]

" What we understood by the liberty of teaching," wrote
Louis Veuillot, " was not a share given to the Church, but the
destruction of monopoly. . . . No alliance with the University !
Away with its books, inspectors, examinations, certificates,
diplomas ! All that means the hand of the State laid on the
liberty of the citizen ; it is the breath of incredulity on the
younger generation." Confronted by the violent rejection of
any attempt at reconciliation and threatened interference with
the University on the part of the Church, the Government was
trying to secure to itself the whole teaching fraternity.

The primary schoolmasters groaned under the heavy yoke
of the prefects. "These deep politicians only know how to
dismiss   . The rectors will become the valets of the prefects . . ." wrote Pasteur with anger and distress in a letter
dated July, 1850. After the primary schools, the attacks now
reached the colleges. The University was accused of attending exclusively to Latin verse and Greek translations, and of
neglecting the souls of the students. Romieu, who ironically
dubbed the University "Alma Parens," and attacked it most
bitterly, seemed hardly fitted for the part of justiciary. He
was a former pupil of the Ecole Polytechnique, who wrote
vaudevilles until he was made a prefect by Louis Philippe.
He was celebrated for various tricks which amused Paris and
disconcerted the Government, much to the joy of the Prince de
Joinville,[1] who loved such mystifications. After the fall of
Louis Philippe, Romieu became a totally different personality.
He had been supposed to take nothing seriously ; he now put a
tragic construction on everything. He became a prophet of
woe, declaring that " gangrene was devouring the souls of
eight year old children." According to him, faith, respect, all
was being destroyed ; he anathematized Instruction without
Education, and stigmatized village schoolmasters as "obscure
apostles " charged with " preaching the doctrines of revolt."
This violence was partly oratory, but oratory does not minimize
violence, it excites it. Every pamphleteer ends by being a
bond-slave to his own phraseology.

When Romieu appeared in Strasburg as an Envoy Extraordinary entrusted by the Government with a general inquiry,
he found that M. Laurent did not answer to that ideal of a

[1] *Prince de Joinville.* Third son of Louis Philippe, and an Admiral
in the French navy. It was he who was sent to fetch Napoleon's remains
from St. Helena. [Trans.]

functionary which was entertained by a certain party. M. Laurent had the very highest respect for justice; he distrusted the upstarts whose virtues were very much on the surface; he never decided on the fate of an inferior without the most painstaking inquiry; he did not look on an accidental mistake as an unpardonable fault; he refused to take any immediate and violent measures : all this caused him to be looked upon with suspicion. " The influence of the Rector " (thus ran Romieu's official report) " is hardly, if at all, noticeable. He should be replaced by a safe man."

The Minister of Public Instruction, M. de Parieu, had to bow before the formal wish of the Minister of the Interior, founded upon peremptory arguments of this kind. M. Laurent was offered the post of Rector at Châteauroux, a decided step downward. He refused, left Strasburg, and, with no complaint or recriminations, retired into private life at the age of fifty-five.

It was when this happy family circle was just about to be enlarged that its quiet was thus broken into by this untoward result of political agitation. M. Laurent's youngest daughter soon after became engaged to M. Loir, a professor at the Strasburg Pharmaceutical School, who had been a student at the Ecole Normale, and who ultimately became Dean of the Faculty of Sciences at Lyons. He was then preparing, assisted by Pasteur, his " thesis " for the degree of Doctor of Science In this he announced some new results based on the simultaneous existence of hemihedral crystalline forms and the rotatory power. He wrote, "I am happy to have brought new facts to bear upon the law that M. Pasteur has enunciated."

" Why are you not a professor of physics or chemistry ! " wrote Pasteur to Chappuis ; " we should work together, and in ten years' time we would revolutionize chemistry. There are wonders hidden in crystallization, and, through it, the inmost construction of substances will one day be revealed. If you come to Strasburg, you *shall* become a chemist ; I shall talk to you of nothing but crystals."

The vacation was always impatiently awaited by Pasteur. He was able to work more, and to edit the result of his researches in an extract for the Académie des Sciences. On October 2 his friend received the following letter : "On Monday I presented this year's work to the 'Institut.' I read a long extract from it, and then gave a vivâ voce demonstration relative to some crystallographic details. This demonstration, which I had been specially desired to give, was quite against the prevailing customs of the Académie. I gave it with my usual delight in that sort of thing, and it was followed with great attention. Fortunately for me, the most influential members of the Académie were present. M. Dumas sat almost facing me. I looked at him several times, and he expressed by an approving nod of his head that he understood and was much interested. He asked me to his house the next day, and congratulated me. He said, amongst other things, that I was a proof that when a Frenchman took up crystallography he knew what he was about, and also that if I persevered, as he felt sure I should, I should become the founder of a school.

" M. Biot, whose kindness to me is beyond all expression, came to me after my lecture and said, ' It is as good as it can possibly be.' On October 14 he will give his report on my work ; he declares I have discovered a very California. Do not suppose I have done anything wonderful this year. This is but a satisfactory consequence of preceding work."

In his report (postponed until October 28) Biot was more enthusiastic. He praised the numerous and unforeseen results brought out by Pasteur within the last two years. "He throws light upon everything he touches," he said.

To be praised by Biot was a rare favour ; his diatribes were better known. In a secret committee of the Académie des Sciences (January, 1851) the Académie had to pronounce on the merits of two candidates for a professorship at the Collège de France : Balard, a professor of the Faculty of Science, chief lecturer of the Ecole Normale, and Laurent the chemist, who in order to live had been compelled to accept a situation as assayer at the Mint. Biot, with his halting step, arrived at the Committee room and spoke thus : " The title of Member of the Institute is the highest reward and the greatest honour that a French scientist can receive, but it does not constitute a privilege of inactivity that need only be claimed in order to obtain everything. . . . For several years, M. Balard has been in possession of two large laboratories where he might have executed any work dictated to him by his zeal, whilst nearly all M. Laurent's results have been effected by his unaided personal efforts at the cost of heavy sacrifices. If you give the college

vacancy to M. Balard, you will add nothing to the opportunities
for study which he already has; but it will take away from M.
Laurent the means of work that he lacks and that we have
now the opportunity of providing for him. The chemical
section, and indeed the whole Academy will easily judge on
which side are scientific justice and the interests of future
progress."

Biot had this little speech printed and sent a copy of it to
Pasteur. The incident led to a warm dispute, and Biot lost
his cause. Pasteur wrote to Chappuis, "M. Biot has done
everything that was possible to do in order that M. Laurent
should win, and the final result is a great grief to him. But
really," the younger man added, more indulgent than the old
man, and divided between his wishes for Laurent and the fear
of the sorrow Balard would have felt, "M. Balard would not
have deserved so much misfortune. Think of the disgrace it
would have been to him if there had been a second vote favourable to Laurent, especially coming from the Institute of which
he is a member." At the end of that campaign, Biot in a fit
of misanthropy which excepted Pasteur alone, and knowing
that Pasteur had spoken with effusion of their mutual feelings,
wrote to him as follows : "I am touched by your acknowledgment of my deep and sincere affection for you, and I thank you
for it. But whilst keeping your attachment for me as I
preserve mine for you, let me for the future rejoice in it in the
secret recesses of my heart and of yours. The world is jealous
of friendships however disinterested, and my affection for you
is such that I wish people to feel that they honour themselves
by appreciating you, rather than that they should know that
you love me and that I love you. Farewell. Persevere in
your good feelings as in your splendid career, and be happy.
Your friend."

The character of Biot, a puzzle to Sainte Beuve, seems easier
to understand after reading those letters, written in a small
conscientious hand. The great critic wrote : "Who will give
us the secret key to Biot's complex nature, to the curiosities,
aptitudes, envies, prejudices, sympathies, antipathies, folds
and creases of every kind in his character?" Even with no
other documents, the history of his relations with Pasteur
would throw light upon this nature, not so "complex" after
all. From the day when Pasteur worked out his first experiment before Biot, at first suspicious, then astonished and

finally touched to the heart, until the period of absolute mutual confidence and friendship, we see rising before us the image of this true scientist, with his rare independence, his good-will towards laborious men and his mercilessness to every man who, loving not Science for its own sake, looked upon a discovery as a road to fortune, pecuniary or political.

He loved both science and letters, and, now that age had bent his tall form, instead of becoming absorbed in his own recollections and the contemplation of his own labours, he kept his mind open, happy to learn more every day and to anticipate the future of Pasteur.

During the vacation of 1851 Pasteur came to Paris to bring Biot the results of new researches on aspartic and malic acids, and he desired his father to join him in order to efface the sad impression left by his former journey in 1838. Biot and his wife welcomed the father and son as they would have welcomed very few friends. Touched by so much kindness, Joseph Pasteur on his return in June wrote Biot a letter full of gratitude, venturing at the same time to send the only thing it was in his power to offer, a basket of fruit from his garden. Biot answered as follows : " Sir, my wife and I very much appreciate the kind expressions in the letter you have done me the honour of writing me. Our welcome to you was indeed as hearty as it was sincere, for I assure you that we could not see without the deepest interest such a good and honourable father sitting at our modest table with so good and distinguished a son. I have never had occasion to show that excellent young man any feelings but those of esteem founded on his merit, and an affection inspired by his personality. It is the greatest pleasure that I can experience in my old age, to see young men of talent working industriously and trying to progress in a scientific career by means of steady and persevering labour, and not by wretched intriguing. That is what has made your son dear to me, and his affection for me adds yet to his other claims and increases that which I feel for him. We are therefore even with one another. As to your kindness in wishing that I should taste fruit from your garden, I am very grateful for it, and I accept it as cordially as you send it."

Pasteur had also brought Biot some other products—a case full of new crystals. Starting from the external configuration of crystals, he penetrated the individual constitution of their molecular groups, and from this point of departure, he then had recourse to the resources of chemistry and optics. Biot never ceased to admire the sagacity of the young experimentalist who had turned what had until then been a mere crystallographic character into an element of chemical research.

Equally interested by the general consequences of these studies, so delicate and so precise, M. de Senarmont wished in his turn to examine the crystals. No one approved more fully than he the expressions of the old scientist, who ended in this way his 1851 report : "If M. Pasteur persists in the road he has opened, it may be predicted of him that what he has found is nothing to what he will find." And, delighted to see the important position that Pasteur was taking at Strasburg and the unexpected extension of crystallography, Biot wrote to him : "I have read with much interest the thesis of your brother-in-law, M. Loir. It is well conceived and well written, and he establishes with clearness many very curious facts. M. de Senarmont has also read it with very great pleasure, and I beg you will transmit our united congratulations to your brother-in-law." Biot added, mixing as he was wont family details with scientific ideas : "We highly appreciated your father, the rectitude of his judgment, his firm, calm, simple reason and the enlightened love he bears you."

"My plan of study is traced for this coming year," wrote Pasteur to Chappuis at the end of December. "I am hoping to develop it shortly in the most successful manner. . . . I think I have already told you that I am on the verge of mysteries, and that the veil which covers them is getting thinner and thinner. The nights seem to me too long, yet I do not complain, for I prepare my lectures easily, and often have five whole days a week that I can give up to the laboratory. I am often scolded by Mme. Pasteur, but I console her by telling her that I shall lead her to fame."

He already foresaw the greatness of his work. However he dare not speak of it, and kept his secret, save with the confidante who was now a collaborator, ever ready to act as secretary, watching over the precious health of which he himself took no account, an admirable helpmeet, to whom might be applied the Roman definition, *socia rei humanæ atque divinæ*. Never did life shower more affection upon a man. Everything at that time smiled upon him. Two fair children in the home, great security in his work, no enemies, and the comfort of receiving the approval and counsel of masters who inspired him with a feeling of veneration.

"At my age," wrote Biot to Pasteur, "one lives only in the interest one takes in those one loves. You are one of the small number who can provide such food for my mind." And alluding in that same letter (December 22, 1851) to four reports successively approved of by Balard, Dumas, Regnault, Chevreul, Senarmont and Thenard : "I was very happy to see, in those successive announcements of ideas of so new and so far-reaching a nature, that you have said—and that we have made you say—nothing that should now be contradicted or objected to in one single point. I still have in my hands the pages of your last paper concerning the optical study of malic acid. I have not yet returned them to you, as I wish to extract from them some results that I shall place to your credit in a paper I am now writing."

It was no longer Biot and Senarmont only who were watching the growing importance of Pasteur's work. At the beginning of the year 1852 the physicist Regnault thought of making Pasteur a corresponding member of the Institute. Pasteur was still under thirty. There was a vacancy in the General Physics section, why not offer it to him? said Regnault, with his usual kindliness. Biot shook his head : "It is to the Chemistry section that he ought to belong." And, with the courage of sincere affection, he wrote to Pasteur, "Your work marks your place in chemistry rather than physics, for in chemistry you are in the front rank of inventors, whilst in physics you have applied processes already known rather than invented new ones. Do not listen to people, who, without knowing the ground, would cause you to desire, and even to hastily obtain, a distinction which would be above your real and recognized claims   Besides, you can see for yourself how much your work of the last four years has raised you in every one's estimation. And that place, which you have made for yourself in the general esteem, has the advantage of not being subject to the fluctuations of the ballot. Farewell, dear friend, write to me when you have time, and be assured that my interest in hard workers is about the only thing which yet makes me wish to live. Your friend."

Pasteur gratefully accepted these wise counsels. In an excess of modesty, he wrote to Dumas that he should not apply

as candidate even if a place for a correspondent were vacant in
the Chemistry section. "Do you then believe," answered
Dumas with a vivacity very unlike his usual solemn calmness,
"do you believe that we are insensible to the glory which your
work reflects on French chemistry, and on the Ecole from
whence you come? The very day I entered the Ministry, I
asked for the Cross [1] for you. I should have had in giving it to
you myself a satisfaction which you cannot conceive. I don't
know whence the delay and difficulty arise. But what I do
know is that you make my blood boil when you speak in your
letter of the necessity of leaving a free place in chemistry to
the men you mention, one or two excepted   . What opinion
have you then of our judgment? When there *is* a vacant
place, you shall be presented, supported and elected. It is a
question of justice and of the great interests of science : we
shall make them prevail. . . . When the day comes, there will
be means found to do what is required for the interests of
science, of which you are one of the firmest pillars, and one of
the most glorious hopes. Heartily yours."

"My dear father," wrote Pasteur, sending his father a copy
of this letter, "I hope you will be proud of M. Dumas' letter.
It surprised me very much. I did not believe that my work
deserved such a splendid testimony, though I recognize its
great importance."

Thus were associated in Pasteur the full consciousness of his
great mental power with an extreme ingenuousness. Instead
of the pride and egotism provoked, almost excusably, in so
many superior men by excessive strength, his character presented the noblest delicacy.

Another arrangement occurred to Regnault : that he himself
should accept the direction of the Sèvres Manufactory, and
give up to Pasteur his professorship at the Ecole Polytechnique.
Others suggested that Pasteur should become chief lecturer at
the Ecole Normale. Rumours of these possibilities reached
Strasburg, but Pasteur's thoughts were otherwise absorbed.
He was concerned with the manner in which he could modify
the crystalline forms of certain substances which, though
optically active, did not at the first view present the hemihedral
character, and with the possibility of provoking the significant
faces by varying the nature of the dissolving agents. Biot was

[1] Of the Legion of Honour.

anxious that he should not be disturbed in these ingenious researches, and advised him to remain at Strasburg in terms as vigorous as any of his previous advice. '' As to the accidents which come from or depend on men's caprice, be strong-minded enough to disdain them yet awhile. Do not trouble about anything, but pursue indefatigably your great career. You will be rewarded in the end, the more certainly and un-questionably that you will have deserved it more fully. The time is not far when those who can serve you efficiently will feel as much pride in doing so as shame and embarrassment in not having done so already.''

When Pasteur came to Paris in August, for what he might have called his annual pilgrimage, Biot had reserved for him a most agreeable surprise. Mitscherlich was in Paris, where he had come, accompanied by another German crystallo-grapher, G. Rose, to thank the Académie for appointing him a foreign Associate. They both expressed a desire to see Pasteur, who was staying in a hotel in the Rue de Tournon. Biot, starting for his daily walk round the Luxembourg Garden, left this note : '' Please come to my house to-morrow at 8 a.m., if possible with your products. M. Mitscherlich and M. Rose are coming at 9 to see them.'' The interview was lengthy and cordial. In a letter to his father—who now knew a great deal about crystals and their forms, thanks to Pasteur's lucid explanations—we find these words. '' I spent two and a half hours with them on Sunday at the Collège de France, showing them my crystals. They were much pleased, and highly praised my work. I dined with them on Tuesday at M. Thenard's ; you will like to see the names of the guests : Messrs. Mitscherlich, Rose, Dumas, Chevreul, Regnault, Pelouze, Péligot, C. Prévost, and Bussy. You see I was the only outsider, they are all members of the Académie. . . But the chief advantage of my meeting these gentlemen is that I have heard from them the important fact that there is a manufacturer in Germany who again produces some racemic acid. I intend to go and see him and his products, so as to study thoroughly that singular substance.''

At the time when scientific novels were in fashion, a whole chapter might have been written on Pasteur in search of that acid. In order to understand in a measure his emotion on learning that a manufacturer in Saxony possessed this mysterious acid, we must remember that the racemic acid—

produced for the first time by Kestner at Thann in 1820, through a mere accident in the manufacture of tartaric acid— had suddenly ceased to appear, in spite of all efforts to obtain it again.   What then was the origin of it?

Mitscherlich believed that the tartars employed by this Saxony manufacturer came from Trieste. "I shall go to Trieste," said Pasteur ; "I shall go to the end of the world. I *must* discover the source of racemic acid, I must follow up the tartars to their origin."   Was the acid existent in crude tartars, such as Kestner received in 1820 from Naples, Sicily, or Oporto?   This was all the more probable from the fact that from the day when Kestner began to use semi-refined tartars he had no longer found any racemic acid.   Should one conclude that it remained stored up in the mother-liquor?

With a feverish impetuosity that nothing could soothe, Pasteur begged Biot and Dumas to obtain for him a mission from the Ministry or the Académie.   Exasperated by red tape delays, he was on the point of writing directly to the President of the Republic. "It is a question," he said, "that France should make it a point of honour to solve through one of her children."   Biot endeavoured to moderate this excessive impatience. "It is not necessary to set the Government in motion for this," he said, a little quizzically. "The Academy, when informed of your motives might very well contribute a few thousand francs towards researches on the racemic acid." But when Mitscherlich gave Pasteur a letter of recommendation to the Saxony manufacturer, whose name was Fikentscher and who lived near Leipzig, Pasteur could contain himself no longer, and went off, waiting for nothing and listening to no one. His travelling impressions were of a peculiar nature.   We will extract passages from a sort of diary addressed to Madame Pasteur so that she might share the emotions of this pursuit. He starts his campaign on the 12th September. "I do not stop at Leipzig, but go on to Zwischau, and then to M. Fikentscher.   I leave him at nightfall and go back to him the next morning very early.   I have spent all to-day, Sunday, with him.   M. Fikentscher is a very clever man, and he has shown me his whole manufactory in every detail, keeping no secrets from me. . . . His factory is most prosperous. It comprises a group of houses which, from a distance. and situated on a height as they are, look almost like a little village.

It is surrounded by 20 hectares [1] of well cultivated ground.
All this is the result of a few years' work. As to *the* question,
here is a little information that you will keep strictly to yourself for the present. M. Fikentscher obtained racemic acid
for the first time about twenty-two years ago. He prepared at
that time rather a large quantity. Since then only a very small
amount has been formed in the process of manufacture and he
has not troubled to preserve it. When he used to obtain most,
his tartars came from Trieste. This confirms, though not in
every point, what I heard from M. Mitscherlich. Anyhow,
here is my plan : Having no laboratory at Zwischau, I have just
returned to Leipzig with two kinds of tartars that M.
Fikentscher now uses, some of which come from Austria, and
some from Italy. M. Fikentscher has assured me that I
should be very well received here by divers professors, who
know my name very well, he says. To-morrow Monday morning, I will go to the Université and set up in some laboratory
or other. I think that in five or six days I shall have finished
my examination of these tartars. Then I shall start for
Vienna, where I shall stay two or three days and rapidly study
Hungarian tartars. . . . Finally I shall go to Trieste, where I
shall find tartars of divers countries, notably those of the
Levant, and those of the neighbourhood of Trieste itself. On
arriving here at M. Fikentscher's I have unfortunately discovered a very regrettable circumstance. It is that the tartars
he uses have already been through one process in the country
from which they are exported, and this process is such that it
evidently eliminates and loses the greater part of the racemic
acid. At least I think so. I must therefore go to the place
itself. If I had enough money I should go on to Italy ; but
that is impossible, it will be for next year. I shall give ten
years to it if necessary ; but it will not be, and I am sure that
in my very next letter I shall be able to tell you that I have
some good results. For instance, I am almost sure to find a
prompt means of testing tartars from the point of view of
racemic acid. That is a point of primary importance for my
work. I want to go quickly through examining all these
different tartars ; that will be my first study.   M.
Fikentscher will take nothing for his products. It is true that
I have given him hints and some of my own enthusiasm. He

[1] Hectare : French measure of surface, about 2½ acres. [Trans.]

wants to prepare for commercial purposes some *left* tartaric acid, and I have given him all the necessary crystallographic indications. I have no doubt he will succeed."

Leipzig, Wednesday, September 15, 1852 " My dear Marie, I do not want to wait until I have the results of my researches before writing to you again. And yet I have nothing to tell you, for I have not left the laboratory for three days, and I know nothing of Leipzig but the street which goes from the Hôtel de Bavière to the Université. I come home at dusk, dine, and go to bed. I have only received, in M. Erdmann's study, the visit of Professor Hankel, professor of physics of the Leipzig Université, who has translated all my treatises in a German paper edited by M. Erdmann. He has also studied hemihedral crystals, and I enjoyed talking with him. 1 shall also soon meet the professor of mineralogy, M. Naumann.

" To-morrow only shall I have a first result concerning racemic acid. I shall stay about ten days longer in Leipzig. It is more than I told you, and the reason lies in rather a happy circumstance. M. Fikentscher has kindly written to me and to a firm in Leipzig, and I heard yesterday from the head of that firm that, very likely, they can get me to-morrow some tartars absolutely crude and of the same origin as M. Fikentscher's. The same gentleman has given me some information about a factory at Venice, and will give me a letter of recommendation to a firm in that city, also for Trieste. In this way the journey I proposed to make in that town will not simply be a pleasure trip. . . . I shall write to M. Biot as soon as I have important results. To-day has been a good day, and in about three or four more you will no doubt receive a satisfactory letter."

Leipzig, September 18, 1852. " My dear Marie, the very question which has brought me here is surrounded with very great difficulties. . . . I have only studied one tartar thoroughly since I have been here ; it comes from Naples and has been refined once. It contains racemic acid, but in such infinitesimal proportions that it can only be detected by the most delicate process. It is only by manufacture on a very large scale that a certain quantity could be prepared. But I must tell you that the first operation undergone by this tartar must have deprived it almost entirely of racemic acid. Fortunately M. Fikentscher is a most enlightened man, he perfectly understands the importance of this acid and he is

prepared to follow most minutely the indications that I shall
give him in order to obtain this singular substance in quantities
such that it can again be easily turned into commercial use.
I can already conceive the history of this product. M. Kestner
must have had at his disposal in 1820 some Neapolitan tartars,
as indeed he said he had, and he must have operated on crude
tartar. That is the whole secret. . . . But is it certain that
almost the whole of the acid is lost in the first manufacture
undergone by tartar? I believe it is. But it must be proved.
There are at Trieste and at Venice two tartar refineries of
which I have the addresses. I also have letters of introduction.
I shall examine there (if I find a laboratory) the residual products, and I shall make minute inquiries respecting the places
the tartars used in those two cities come from. Finally, I shall
procure a few kilogrammes, which I shall carefully study when
I get back to France. . . ."

Freiberg, September 23, 1852. "I arrived on the evening
of the 21st at Dresden, and I had to wait until eleven the next
morning to have my passport *visé*, so I could not start for
Freiberg before seven p.m. I took advantage of that day to
visit the capital of Saxony, and I can assure you that I saw
some admirable things. There is a most beautiful museum
containing pictures by the first masters of every school. I
spent over four hours in the galleries, noting on my catalogue
the pictures I most enjoyed. Those I liked I marked with a
cross; but I soon put two, three crosses, according to the
degree of my enthusiasm. I even went as far as four.

"I also visited what they call the green vault room, an
absolutely unique collection of works of art, gems, jewels . . .
then some churches, avenues, admirable bridges across the
Elbe. .

"I then started for Freiberg at 7. . . . My love of crystals
took me first to the learned Professor of mineralogy, Breithaupt,
who received me as one would not be received in France.
After a short colloquy, he passed into the next room, came back
in a black tail-coat with three little decorations in his button
hole, and told me he would first present me to the Baron von
Beust, Superintendent of Factories, so as to obtain a permit
to visit the latter. . . . Then he took me for a walk, talking
crystals the whole time. . . ."

P.S.—"Mind you tell M. Biot how I was received; it will
please him."

F

Vienna, September 27, 1852. "Yesterday, Monday morning, I set out to call upon several people. Unfortunately, I
hear that Professor Schrotten is at Wiesbaden, at a scientific
congress, as well as M. Seybel, a manufacturer of tartaric acid.
M. Miller, a merchant for whom I had a letter of recommendation, was kind enough to ask M. Seybel's business manager
for permission for me to visit the factory in his absence. He
refused, saying he was not authorized. But I did not give in;
I asked for the addresses of Viennese professors, and I fortunately came upon that of a very well known scientific man,
M. Redtenbacher, who has been kind to me beyond all
description. At 6 a.m. he came to my hotel, and we took the
train at 7 for the Seybel manufactory, which is at a little distance from Vienna. We were received by the chemist of the
factory, who made not the slightest difficulty in introducing
us into the sanctuary, and after many questions we ended by
being convinced that the famous racemic acid was seen there
last winter. . . . I reserve for later many details of great
interest, for here they have operated for years on crude tartar.
I came away very happy.

"There is another factory of tartaric acid in Vienna. We
go there; I repeat through M. Redtenbacher my string of
questions. They have seen nothing. I ask to see their
products, and I come upon a barrel full of tartaric acid crystals,
on the surface of which I think I perceive *the* substance. A
first test made with dirty old glasses then and there confirms
my doubts; they become a certainty a few moments later at
M. Redtenbacher's laboratory. We dine together; then we
go back to the factory, where we learn, miraculous to relate,
that they are just now embarrassed in their manufacturing
process, and, almost certainly, the product which hinders them
—though it is in a very small quantity, and they take it for
sulphate of potash—is no other than racemic acid. I wish I
could give you more details of this eventful day. I was to
have left Vienna to-day, but, as you will understand, I shall
stay until I have unravelled this question. I have already in
the laboratory three kinds of products from the factory. To-
morrow night, or the day after, I shall know what to think. . . .

"You remember what I used to say to you and to M. Dumas,
that almost certainly the first operation which tartar goes
through in certain factories causes it to lose all or nearly all its
racemic acid. Well, in the two Viennese factories, it is only

two years since they began to operate on crude tartar, and it is only two years since they first saw the supposed sulphate of potash, the supposed sulphate of magnesia. For, at M. Seybel's, they had taken for sulphate of magnesia the little crystals of racemic acid.

" Shortly, this is as far as I have come—I spare you many details :—

1. " The Naples tartar contains racemic acid.

2. " The Austrian tartar (neighbourhood of Vienna) contains racemic acid.

3. " The tartars of Hungary, Croatia, Carniola contain racemic acid.

4. " The tartar of Naples contains notably more than the latter, for it presents racemic acid even after one refining process, whilst that from Austria and Hungary only presents it when in the crude state

" I believe it now to be extremely probable that I shall find some racemic acid in French tartars, but in very small quantities ; and if it is not detected it is because all the circumstances of the manufacture of tartaric acid are unknown or unappreciated, or because some little precaution is neglected that would preserve it or make it visible.

" You see, dear Marie, how useful was my journey."

" *Vienna, September* 30, 1852.   I am not going to Trieste ; I shall start for Prague this evening."

" *Prague, October* 1, 1852.   Here is a startling piece of news.   I arrive in Prague; I settle down in the Hôtel d'Angleterre, have lunch, and call on M. Rochleder, Professor of chemistry, so that he may introduce me to the manufacturer. I go to the chemist of the factory, Dr. Rassmann, for whom I had a letter from M. Redtenbacher, his former master.   That letter contained all the questions that I usually make to the manufacturers of tartaric acid.

" Dr. Rassmann hardly took time to read the letter ; he saw what it dealt with, and said to me : ' I have long obtained racemic acid.   The Paris Pharmaceutical Society offered a prize for whoever manufactured it.   It is a product of manufacture; I obtain it with the assistance of tartaric acid.'   I took the chemist's hand affectionately, and made him repeat what he had said.   Then I added : ' You have made one of the greatest discoveries that it is possible to make in chemistry. Perhaps you do not realise as I do the full importance of it.

But allow me to tell you that, with my ideas, I look upon that discovery as impossible. I do not ask for your secret; I shall await the publication of it with the greatest impatience. So that is really true? You take a kilogramme of pure tartaric acid, and with that you make racemic acid?'

"'Yes,' he said; 'but it is still' . . . and as he had some difficulty in expressing himself, I said : 'It is still surrounded with great difficulties?'

''Yes, monsieur.'

"Great heavens! what a discovery! if he had really done what he says! But no; it is impossible. There is an abyss to cross, and chemistry is yet too young."

Second letter, same date. "M. Rassmann is mistaken He has never obtained racemic acid with pure tartaric acid. He does what M. Fikentscher and the Viennese manufacturers do, with slight differences, which confirm the general opinion I expressed in my letter to M. Dumas a few days ago."

That letter, and also another addressed to Biot, indicated that racemic acid was formed in varying quantities in the mother-liquor, which remained after the purification of crude tartars.

"I can at last," Pasteur wrote from Leipzig to his wife, "turn my steps again towards France. I want it; I am very weary."

In an account of this journey in a newspaper called *La Vérité* there was this sentence, which amused everybody, Pasteur included : "Never was treasure sought, never adored beauty pursued over hill and vale with greater ardour."

But the hero of scientific adventures was not satisfied. He had foreseen by the examination of crystalline forms, the correlation between hemihedral dissymmetry and rotatory power; this was, to his mind, a happy foresight. He had afterwards succeeded in separating the racemic acid, inactive on polarized light, into two acids, left and right, endowed with equal but contrary rotatory powers; this was a discovery deservedly qualified as memorable by good judges in those matters. Now he had indicated the mother-liquor as a source of racemic acid, and this was a precious observation that Kestner, who was specially interested in the question, confirmed in a letter to the Académie des Sciences (December, 1852), sending at the same time three large phials of racemic acid, one of which, made of thin glass, broke in Biot's hands. But a great advance, apparently unrealizable, remained yet to be accomplished. Could not racemic acid be produced by the aid of tartaric acid?

Pasteur himself, as he told the optimist Rassmann, did not believe such a transformation possible. But, by dint of ingenious patience, of trials, of efforts of all sorts, he fancied he was nearing the goal. He wrote to his father : "I am thinking of one thing only, of the hope of a brilliant discovery which seems not very far. But the result I foresee is so extraordinary that I dare not believe it." He told Biot and Senarmont of this hope. Both seemed to doubt. "I advise you," wrote Senarmont, "not to speak until you can say : 'I obtain racemic acid artificially with some tartaric acid, of which I have myself verified the purity ; the artificial acid, like the natural, divides itself into equal equivalents of left and right tartaric acids, and those acids have the forms, the optical properties, all the chemical properties of those obtained from the natural acid.' Do not believe that I want to worry you ; the scruples I have for you I should have for myself ; it is well to be doubly sure when dealing with such a fact." But with Biot, Senarmont was less reserved ; he believed the thing done. He said so to Biot, who, prudent and cautious, still desirous of warning Pasteur, wrote to him on May 27, 1853, speaking of Senarmont : "The affection with which your work, your perseverance and your moral character have inspired him makes him desire impossible prodigies for you. My friendship for you is less hastily hopeful and harder to convince. However, enjoy his friendship fully, and be as unreserved with him as you are with me. You can do so in full security ; I do not know a stronger character than his. I have said and repeated to him how happy I am to see the affection he bears you. For there will be at least one man who will love you and understand you when I am gone. Farewell ; enough sermons for to-day ; a man must be as I am, in his eightieth year, to write such long homilies. Fortunately you are accustomed to mine, and do not mind them."

At last, on the first of June, here is the letter announcing the great fact : "My dear father, I have just sent out the following telegram : *Monsieur Biot, Collège de France, Paris. I transform tartaric acid into racemic acid; please inform MM. Dumas and Senarmont.* Here is at last that racemic acid (which I went to seek at Vienna) artificially obtained through tartaric acid. I long believed that that transformation was impossible. This discovery will have incalculable consequences."

" I congratulate you," answered Biot on the second of June. " Your discovery is now complete. M. de Senarmont will be as delighted as I am. Please congratulate also Mme. Pasteur from me ; she must be as pleased as you." It was by maintaining tartrate of cinchonin at a high temperature for several hours that Pasteur had succeeded in transforming tartaric acid into racemic acid. Without entering here into technical details (which are to be found in a report of the Paris Pharmaceutical Society, concerning the prize accorded to Pasteur for the artificial production of racemic acid) it may be added that he had also produced the neutral tartaric acid—that is : with no action on polarized light—which appeared at the expense of racemic acid already formed. There were henceforth four different tartaric acids :—(1) the right or dextro-tartaric acid ; (2) the left or lævo-tartaric acid ; (3) the combination of the right and the left or racemic acid ; and (4) the meso-tartaric acid, optically inactive.

The reports of the Académie des Sciences also contain accounts of occasional discoveries, of researches of all kinds accessory to the history of racemic acid. Thus aspartic acid had caused Pasteur to make a sudden journey from Strasburg to Vendôme. A chemist named Dessaignes—who was municipal receiver of that town, and who found time through sheer love of science for researches on the constitution of divers substances—had announced a fact which Pasteur wished to verify , it turned out to be inaccurate.

One whole sitting of the Académie, the third of January, 1853, was given up to Pasteur's name and growing achievements.

After all this Pasteur came back to Arbois with the red ribbon of the Legion of Honour. He had not won it in the same way as his father had, but he deserved it as fully. Joseph Pasteur, delighting in his illustrious son, wrote effusively to Biot ; indeed the old scientist had had his share in this act of justice. Biot answered in the following letter, which is a further revelation of his high and independent ideal of a scientific career.

" Monsieur, your good heart makes out my share to be greater than it is. The splendid discoveries made by your worthy and excellent son, his devotion to science, his indefatig-able perseverance, the conscientious care with which he fulfils the duties of his situation, all this had made his position such that there was no need to solicit for him what he had so long deserved. But one might boldly point out that it would be a real loss to the Order if he were not promptly included within its ranks. That is what I did, and I am very glad to see that the too long delay is now at an end. I wished for this all the more as I knew of your affectionate desire that this act of justice should be done. Allow me to add, however, that in our pro-fession our real distinction depends on us alone, fortunately, and not on the favour or indifference of a minister. In the position that your son has acquired, his reputation will grow with his work, no other help being needed ; and the esteem he already enjoys, and which will grow day by day, will be accorded to him, without gainsaying or appeal, by the Grand Jury of scientists of all nations—an absolutely just tribunal, the only one we recognize.

"Allow me to add to my congratulations the expression of the esteem and cordial affection with which you have in-spired me."

On his return to Strasburg Pasteur went to live in a house in the Rue des Couples, which suited him as being near the Académie and his laboratory ; it also had a garden where his children could play. He was full of projects, and what he called the "spirit of invention" daily suggested some new undertaking. The neighbourhood of Germany, at that time a veritable hive of busy bees, was a fertile stimulant to the French Faculty at Strasburg.

But material means were lacking. When Pasteur received the prize of 1,500 francs given him by the Pharmaceutical So-ciety, he gave up half of it to buying instruments which the Strasburg laboratory was too poor to afford. The resources then placed by the State at his disposal by way of contribution to the expenses of a chemistry class only consisted of 1,200 francs under the heading "class expenses." Pasteur had to pay the wages of his laboratory attendant out of it. Now that he was better provided, thanks to his prize, he renewed his studies on crystals.

Taking up an octahedral crystal, he broke off a piece of it, then replaced it in its mother-liquor. Whilst the crystal was growing larger in every direction by a deposit of crystalline par-

ticles, a very active formation was taking place on the mutilated part; after a few hours the crystal had again assumed its
original shape. The healing up of wounds, said Pasteur, might
be compared to that physical phenomenon. Claude Bernard,
much struck later on by these experiments of Pasteur's and
recalling them with much praise, said in his turn—

" These reconstituting phenomena of crystalline redintegration
afford a complete comparison with those presented by living
beings in the case of a wound more or less deep. In the crystal
as in the animal, the damaged part heals, gradually taking back
its original shape, and in both cases the reformation of tissue
is far more active in that particular part than under ordinary
evolutive conditions."

Thus those two great minds saw affinities hidden under facts
apparently far apart. Other similarities yet more unexpected
carried Pasteur away towards the highest region of speculation.
He spoke with enthusiasm of molecular dissymmetry; he saw
it everywhere in the universe. These studies in dissymmetry
gave birth twenty years later to a new science arising immediately out of his work, viz. stereo-chemistry, or the chemistry of
space. He also saw in molecular dissymmetry the influence of
a great cosmic cause—

" The universe," he said one day, " is a dissymmetrical
whole. I am inclined to think that life, as manifested to us,
must be a function of the dissymmetry of the universe and of
the consequences it produces. The universe is dissymmetrical;
for, if the whole of the bodies which compose the solar system
were placed before a glass moving with their individual movements, the image in the glass could not be superposed to the
reality. Even the movement of solar life is dissymmetrical.
A luminous ray never strikes in a straight line the leaf where
vegetable life creates organic matter. Terrestrial magnetism,
the opposition which exists between the north and south poles
in a magnet, that offered us by the two electricities positive
and negative, are but resultants from dissymmetrical actions
and movements."

" Life," he said again, " is dominated by dissymmetrical
actions. I can even foresee that all living species are primor-
dially, in their structure, in their external forms, functions of
cosmic dissymmetry."

And there appeared to him to be a barrier between mineral
or artificial products and products formed under the influence

of life. But he did not look upon it as an impassable one, and he was careful to say, "It is a distinction of fact and not of absolute principle." As nature elaborates immediate principles of life by means of dissymmetrical forces, he wished that the chemist should imitate nature, and that, breaking with methods founded upon the exclusive use of symmetrical forces, he should bring dissymmetrical forces to bear upon the production of chemical phenomena. He himself, after using powerful magnets to attempt to introduce a manifestation of dissymmetry into the form of crystals, had had a strong clockwork movement constructed, the object of which was to keep a plant in continual rotatory motion first in one direction then in another. He also proposed to try to keep a plant alive, from its germination under the influence of solar rays reversed by means of a mirror directed by a heliostat.

But Biot wrote to him : "I should like to be able to turn you from the attempts you wish to make on the influence of magnetism on vegetation. M. de Senarmont agrees with me. To begin with, you will spend a great deal on the purchase of instruments with the use of which you are not familiar, and of which the success is very doubtful. They will take you away from the fruitful course of experimental researches which you have followed hitherto, where there is yet so much for you to do, and will lead you from the certain to the uncertain."

"Louis is rather too preoccupied with his experiments," wrote Mme. Pasteur to her father-in-law; "you know that those he is undertaking this year will give us, if they succeed, a Newton or a Galileo."

But success did not come. "My studies are going rather badly," wrote Pasteur in his turn (December 30) "I am almost afraid of failing in all my endeavours this year, and of having no important achievement to record by the end of next year. I am still hoping, though I suppose it was rather mad to undertake what I have undertaken."

Whilst he was thus struggling, an experiment, which for others would have been a mere chemical curiosity, interested him passionately. Recalling one day how his first researches had led him to the study of ferments : "If I place," he said, "one of the salts of racemic acid, paratartrate or racemate of ammonia, for instance, in the ordinary conditions of fermentation, the dextro-tartaric acid alone ferments, the other remains in the liquor. I may say, in passing, that this is the best means of preparing lævo-tartaric acid. Why does the dextro-tartaric acid alone become putrefied? Because the ferments of that fermentation feed more easily on the right than on the left molecules."

" I have done yet more," he said much later, in a last lecture to the Chemical Society of Paris ; " I have kept alive some little seeds of *penicillium glaucum*—that mucor which is to be found everywhere—on the surface of ashes and paratartaric acid and I have seen the lævo-tartaric acid appear . . . "

What seemed to him startling in those two experiments was to find molecular dissymmetry appear as a modifying agent on chemical affinities in a phenomenon of the physiological order.

By an interesting coincidence it was at the very moment when his studies were bringing him towards fermentations that he was called to a country where the local industry was to be the strongest stimulant to his new researches.

IN September, 1854, he was made Professor and Dean of the new Faculté des Sciences at Lille. "I need not, Sir," wrote the Minister of Public Instruction, M. Fortoul, in a letter where private feelings were mixed with official solemnity, "recall to your mind the importance which is attached to the success of this new Faculty of Science, situated in a town which is the richest centre of industrial activity in the north of France. By giving you the direction of it, I show the entire confidence which I have placed in you. I am convinced that you will fulfil the hopes which I have founded upon your zeal."

Built at the expense of the town, the Faculté was situated in the Rue des Fleurs. In the opening speech which he pronounced on December 7, 1854, the young Dean expressed his enthusiasm for the Imperial decree of August 22, which brought two happy innovations into the Faculties of Science : (1) The pupils might, for a small annual sum, enter the laboratory and practise the principal experiments carried out before them at the classes ; and (2) a new diploma was created. After two years of practical and theoretical study the young men who wished to enter an industrial career could obtain this special diploma and be chosen as foremen or overseers. Pasteur was overjoyed at being able to do useful work in that country of distilleries, and to attract large audiences to the new Faculty. " Where in your families will you find," he said, to excite indolent minds—" where will you find a young man whose curiosity and interest will not immediately be awakened when you put into his hands a potato, when with that potato he may produce sugar, with that sugar alcohol, with that alcohol æther and vinegar? Where is he that will not be happy to tell his family in the evening that he has just been working out an electric telegraph? And, gentlemen, be convinced of this, such studies are seldom if ever forgotten. It is somewhat as if geography were to be taught by travelling; such geography is remembered because one has seen the places. In the same way your sons will not forget what the air we breathe contains when they have once analysed it, when in their hands and under their eyes the admirable properties of its elements have been resolved."

After stating his wish to be directly useful to these sons of manufacturers and to put his laboratory at their disposal, he eloquently upheld the rights of theory in teaching—

"Without theory, practice is but routine born of habit. Theory alone can bring forth and develop the spirit of invention. It is to you specially that it will belong not to share the opinion of those narrow minds who disdain everything in science which has not an immediate application. You know Franklin's charming saying? He was witnessing the first demonstration of a purely scientific discovery, and people round him said : 'But what is the use of it?' Franklin answered them : 'What is the use of a new-born child?' Yes, gentlemen, what is the use of a new-born child? And yet, perhaps, at that tender age, germs already existed in you of the talents which distinguish you! In your baby boys, fragile beings as they are, there are incipient magistrates, scientists, heroes as valiant as those who are now covering themselves with glory under the walls of Sebastopol. And thus, gentlemen, a theoretical discovery has but the merit of its existence : it awakens hope, and that is all. But let it be cultivated, let it grow, and you will see what it will become.

"Do you know when it first saw the light, this electric telegraph, one of the most marvellous applications of modern science? It was in that memorable year, 1822 : Oersted, a Danish physicist, held in his hands a piece of copper wire, joined by its extremities to the two poles of a Volta pile. On his table was a magnetized needle on its pivot, and he suddenly saw (by chance you will say, but chance only favours the mind which is prepared) the needle move and take up a position quite different from the one assigned to it by terrestrial magnetism. A wire carrying an electric current deviates a magnetized needle from its position. That, gentlemen, was the birth of the modern telegraph. Franklin's interlocutor might well have said when the needle moved : 'But what is the use of that?' And yet that discovery was barely twenty years old when it produced by its application the almost supernatural effects of the electric telegraph!"

The small theatre where Pasteur gave his chemistry lessons soon became celebrated in the students' world.

The faults had disappeared with which Pasteur used to reproach himself when he first taught at Dijon and later at Strasburg. He was sure of himself, he was clear in his explanations; the chain of thought, the fitness of words, all was perfect. He made few experiments, but those were decisive. He endeavoured to bring out every observation or comparison they might suggest. The pupil who went away delighted from the class did not suspect the care each of those apparently easy lessons had cost. When Pasteur had carefully prepared all his notes, he used to make a summary of them; he had these summaries bound together afterwards. We may thus sketch the outline of his work; but who will paint the gesture of demonstration, the movement, the grave penetrating voice, the life in short?

After a few months the Minister wrote to M. Guillemin, the rector, that he was much pleased with the success of this Faculty of Sciences at Lille, " which already owes it to the merit of the teaching—solid and brilliant at the same time— of that clever Professor, that it is able to rival the most flourishing Faculties." The Minister felt he must add some official advice : " But M. Pasteur must guard against being carried away by his love for science, and he must not forget that the teaching of the Faculties, whilst keeping up with scientific theory, should, in order to produce useful and far-reaching results, appropriate to itself the special applications suitable to the real wants of the surrounding country."

A year after the inauguration of the new Faculty, Pasteur wrote to Chappuis : " Our classes are very well attended; I have 250 to 300 people at my most popular lectures, and we have twenty-one pupils entered for laboratory experiments. I believe that this year, like last year, Lille holds the first rank for that innovation, for I am told that at Lyons there were but eight entries." It was indeed a success to distance Lyons. " The zeal of all is a pleasure to watch (January, 1856). It reaches that point that four of the professors take the trouble to have their manuscript lessons printed; there are already 120 subscribers for the course of applied mechanics.

" Our building is fortunately completed; it is large and handsome, but will soon become insufficient owing to the progress of practical teaching.

" We are very comfortably settled on the first floor, and I have (on the ground floor immediately below) what I have always wished for, a laboratory where I can go at any time. This week, for instance, the gas remains on, and operations follow their course whilst I am in bed. In this way I try to make up a little of the time which I have to give to the direction of all the rather numerous departments in our Faculties. Add to this that I am a member of two very active societies, and that I have been entrusted, at the suggestion of the Conseil-Général,[1] with the testing of manures for the département of the Nord, a considerable work in this rich agricultural land, but one which I have accepted eagerly, so as to popularize and enlarge the influence of our young Faculty.

" Do not fear lest all this should keep me from the studies I love. I shall not give them up, and I trust that what is already accomplished will grow without my help, with the growth that time gives to everything that has within it the germ of life. Let us all work; that only is enjoyable. I am quoting M. Biot, who certainly is an authority on that subject. You saw the share he took the other day in a great discussion at the Académie des Sciences; his presence of mind, high reasoning powers, and youthfulness were magnificent, and he is eighty-four ! "

In a mere study on Pasteur as a scientific man, the way in which he understood his duties as Dean would only be a secondary detail. It is not so here, the very object of this book being to paint what he was in all the circumstances, all the trials of life. Besides his professional obligations, his kindness in leaving his laboratory, however hard the sacrifice, bears witness to an ever present devotion. For instance, he took his pupils round factories and foundries at Aniche, Denain, Valenciennes, St. Omer. In July, 1856, he organized for the same pupils a tour in Belgium. He took them to visit factories, iron foundries, steel and metal works, questioning the foremen with his insatiable curiosity, pleased to induce in his tall students a desire to learn. All returned from these trips with more pleasure in their work; some with the fiery enthusiasm that Pasteur wished to see.

---

[1] *Conseil-Général de département.* A representative assembly for the general management of each département, somewhat similar to the County Councils in England. [Trans.]

The sentence in his Lille speech, "in the fields of observation, chance only favours the mind which is prepared," was particularly applicable to him. In the summer of 1856 a Lille manufacturer, M. Bigo, had, like many others that same year, met with great disappointments in the manufacture of beetroot alcohol. He came to the young Dean for advice. The prospect of doing a kindness, of communicating the results of his observations to the numerous hearers who crowded the small theatre of the Faculty, and of closely studying the phenomena of fermentation which preoccupied him to such a degree, caused Pasteur to consent to make some experiments. He spent some time almost daily at the factory. On his return to his laboratory—where he only had a student's microscope and a most primitive coke-fed stove—he examined the globules in the fermentation juice, he compared filtered with non-filtered beetroot juice, and conceived stimulating hypotheses often to be abandoned in face of a fact in contradiction with them. Above some note made a few days previously, where a suggested hypothesis had not been verified by fact, he would write : " error," "erroneous," for he was implacable in his criticism of himself.

M. Bigo's son, who studied in Pasteur's laboratory, has summed up in a letter how these accidents of manufacture became a starting point to Pasteur's investigations on fermentation, particularly alcoholic fermentation. "Pasteur had noticed through the microscope that the globules were round when fermentation was healthy, that they lengthened when alteration began, and were quite long when fermentation became lactic. This very simple method allowed us to watch the process and to avoid the failures in fermentation which we used so often to meet with. I had the good fortune to be many times the confidant of the enthusiasms and disappointments of a great man of science." Young Bigo indeed remembered the series of experiments, the numerous observations noted, and how Pasteur, whilst studying the causes of those failures in the distillery, had wondered whether he was not confronted with a general fact, common to all fermentations. Pasteur was on the road to a discovery the consequences of which were to revolutionize chemistry. During months and months he worked to assure himself that he was not a prey to error.

In order to appreciate the importance of the ideas which

from that small laboratory were about to inundate the world, and in order to take account of the effort necessitated to obtain the triumph of a theory which was to become a doctrine, it is necessary to go back to the teachings of that time upon the subject of fermentations. All was darkness, pierced in 1836 by a momentary ray of light. The physicist Cagniard-Latour, studying the ferment of beer called yeast, had observed that that ferment was composed of cells " susceptible of reproduction by a sort of budding, and probably acting on sugar through some effect of their vegetation." Almost at the same time the German doctor Schwann was making analogous observations. However, as the fact seemed isolated, nothing similar being met with elsewhere, Cagniard-Latour's remark was but a curious parenthesis in the history of fermentations.

When such men as J. B. Dumas said that perhaps there might be a sequel to Cagniard-Latour's statement, they emitted the idea so timidly that, in a book *On Contagion* published at Montpellier in 1853, Anglada, the well known author, expressed himself thus—

" M. Dumas, who is an authority, looks upon the act of fermentation as *strange and obscure*; he declares that it gives rise to phenomena the knowledge of which is only tentative at present. Such a competent affirmation is of a nature to discourage those who claim to unravel the mysteries of contagion by the comparative study of fermentation. What is the advantage of explaining one through the other since both are equally mysterious ! " This word, *obscure*, was to be found everywhere. Claude Bernard used the same epithet at the Collège de France in March, 1850, to qualify those phenomena.

Four months before the request of the Lille manufacturer, Pasteur himself, preparing on a loose sheet of paper a lesson on fermentation, had written these words : " What does fermentation consist of ?—Mysterious character of the phenomenon.—A word on lactic acid." Did he speak in that lesson of his ideas of future experiments? Did he insist upon the mystery he intended to unveil? With his powers of concentration it is probable that he restrained himself and decided to wait another year.

The theories of Berzelius and of Liebig then reigned supreme. To the mind of Berzelius, the Swedish chemist, fermentation was due to contact. It was said that there was a catalytic force. In his opinion, what Cagniard-Latour believed he had seen, was but "an immediate vegetable principle, which became precipitated during the fermentation of beer, and which, in precipitating, presented forms analogous to the simpler forms of vegetable life, but formation does not constitute life."

In the view of the German chemist Liebig, chemical decomposition was produced by influence : the ferment was an extremely alterable organic substance which decomposed, and in decomposing set in motion, by the rupture of its own elements, the molecules of the fermentative matter ; it was the dead portion of the yeast, that which had lived and was being altered, which acted upon the sugar. These theories were adopted, taught, and to be found in all treatises on chemistry.

A vacancy at the Académie des Sciences took Pasteur away from his students for a time and obliged him to go to Paris. Biot, Dumas, Balard and Senarmont had insisted upon his presenting himself in the section of mineralogy. He felt himself unfit for the candidature. He was as incapable of election manœuvres as he was full of his subject when he had to convince an interlocutor or to interest an audience in his works on crystallography. (These works had just procured the bestowal on him of the great Rumford medal, conferred by the London Royal Society.) During this detested canvassing campaign he had one happy day : he was present on February 5, 1857, at the reception of Biot by the Académie Française.

Biot, who had entered the Académie des Sciences fifty-four years earlier, and was now the oldest member of the Institute, took advantage of his great age to distribute, in the course of his speech, a good deal of wise counsel, much applauded by Pasteur from the ranks of the audience. Biot, with his calm irony, aimed this epigram at men of science who disdained letters : "Their science was not the more apparent through their want of literary culture." He ended by remarks which formed a continuation of his last letter to Pasteur's father. Making an appeal to those whose high ambition is to consecrate themselves to pure science, he proudly said : "Perhaps your name, your existence will be unknown to the crowd. But you will be known, esteemed, sought after by a small number of eminent men scattered over the face of the earth, your rivals, your peers in the intellectual Senate of minds ; they alone have the right to appreciate you and to assign to you your rank, a well-merited rank, which no princely will, no popular caprice can give or take away, and which will remain yours as long as you remain faithful to Science, which bestows it upon you."

Guizot, to whom it fell to welcome Biot to the Académie, rendered homage to his independence, to his worship of disinterested research, to his ready counsels. "The events which have overturned everything around you," he said, "have never turned the course of your free and firm judgment, or of your peaceful labours." On that occasion the decline of Biot's life seemed like a beautiful summer evening in the north, before nightfall, when a soft light still envelops all things. No disciple ever felt more emotion than Pasteur when participating in that last joy of his aged master. In Regnault's laboratory, a photograph had been taken of Biot seated with bent head and a weary attitude, but with the old sparkle in his eyes. Biot offered it to Pasteur, saying : "If you place this proof near a portrait of your father, you will unite the pictures of two men who have loved you very much in the same way."

Pasteur, between two canvassing visits, gave himself the pleasure of going to hear a young professor that every one was then speaking of. "I have just been to a lecture by Rigault, at the Collège de France," he wrote on March 6, 1857 "The room is too small, it is a struggle to get in. I have come away delighted; it is a splendid success for the Université, there is nothing to add, nothing to retrench. Fancy a professor in one of the Paris lycées making such a début at the Collège de France !"

Pasteur preferred Rigault to St. Marc Girardin. "And Rigault is only beginning !" But, under Rigault's elegance and apparent ease, lurked perpetual constraint. One day that St. Marc Girardin was congratulating him, "Ah," said Rigault, "you do not see the steel corsets that I wear when I am speaking !" That comparison suited his delicate, ingenious, slightly artificial mind, never unrestrained even in simple conversation, at the same time conscientious and self-conscious. He who had once written that "Life is a work of art to be fashioned by a skilful hand if the faculties of the mind are to be fully enjoyed," made the mistake of forcing his nature. He died a few months after that lecture.

Pasteur's enthusiastic lines about Rigault show the joy he felt at the success of others. He did not understand envy, ill-will, or jealousy, and was more than astonished, indeed amazed, when he came across such feelings. One day that he had read an important paper at the Académie des Sciences, " Would you believe it," he wrote to his father, " I met a Paris Professor of chemistry the very next day, whom I know to have been present, who had indeed come purposely to hear my reading, and he never said a word ! I then remembered a saying of M. Biot's : ' When a colleague reads a paper and no one speaks to him about it afterwards, it is because it has been thought well of ' "

The election was at hand. Pasteur wrote (March 11) : " My dear father, I am certain to fail." He thought he might count upon twenty votes ; thirty were necessary. He resigned himself philosophically. His candidature would at any rate bring his works into greater prominence. In spite of a splendid report by Senarmont, enumerating the successive steps by which Pasteur had risen since his first discoveries concerning the connection between internal structure and external crystalline forms, Pasteur only obtained sixteen votes.

On his return to Lille he set to work with renewed energy ; he took up again his study of fermentations, and in particular that of sour milk, called lactic fermentation ; he made notes of his experiments day by day ; he drew in a notebook the little globules, the tiny bodies that he found in a grey substance sometimes aranged in a zone. Those globules, much smaller than those of yeast, had escaped the observation of chemists and naturalists because it was easy to confound them with other products of lactic fermentation. After isolating and then scattering in a liquid a trace of that grey substance, Pasteur saw some well-characterized lactic fermentation appear. That matter, that grey substance was indeed the ferment.

Whilst all the writings of the chemists who followed in the train of Liebig and Berzelius united in rejecting the idea of an influence of life in the cause of fermentations, Pasteur recognized therein a phenomenon correlative to life. That special lactic yeast, Pasteur could see budding, multiplying, and offering the same phenomena of reproduction as beer yeast.

It was not to the Académie des Sciences, as is generally believed, that Pasteur sent the paper on lactic fermentation, the fifteen pages of which contained such curious and unexpected facts. With much delicacy of feeling, Pasteur made to the Lille Scientific Society this communication (August, 1857) which the Académie des Sciences only saw three months later.

How was it that he desired to leave this Faculty at Lille to which he had rendered such valuable service? The Ecole Normale was going through difficult times. "In my opinion," wrote Pasteur with a sadness that betrayed his attachment to the great school, "of all the objects of care to the authorities, the Ecole Normale should be the first; it is now but the shadow of its former self." He who so often said, "Do not dwell upon things already acquired!" thought that the Lille Faculty was henceforth sure of its future and needed him no longer. Was it not better to come to the assistance of the threatened weak point? At the Ministry of Public Instruction his wish was understood and approved of. Nisard had just been made Director of the Ecole Normale with high and supreme powers; his sub-director of literary studies was M. Jacquinet. The administration was reserved for Pasteur, who was also entrusted with the direction of the scientific studies. To that task were added "the surveillance of the economic and hygienic management, the care of general discipline, intercourse with the families of the pupils and the literary or scientific establishments frequented by them."

The rector of the Lille Faculty announced in these terms the departure of the Dean : " Our Faculty loses a professor and a scientist of the very first order. You have yourselves, gentlemen, been able to appreciate more than once all the vigour and clearness of that mind at once so powerful and so capable."

At the Ecole Normale, Pasteur's labours were not at first seconded by material convenience. The only laboratory in the Rue d'Ulm building was occupied by Henri Sainte Claire Deville who, in 1851, had taken the place of Balard, the latter leaving the Ecole Normale for the Collège de France. Dark rooms, a very few instruments, and a credit of 1,800 francs a year, that was all Sainte Claire Deville had been able to obtain. It would have seemed like a dream to Pasteur. He had to organize his scientific installation in two attics under the roof of the Ecole Normale; he had no assistance of any kind, not even that of an ordinary laboratory attendant. But his courage was not of the kind which evaporates at the first obstacle, and no difficulty could have kept him from work : he climbed the stairs leading to his pseudo-laboratory with all the cheerfulness of a soldier's son. Biot—who had been grieved to see the chemist Laurent working in a sort of cellar, where that scientist's health suffered (he died at forty-three)—was angry that Pasteur should

be relegated to an uninhabitable garret. Neither did he understand the " economic and hygienic surveillance " attributed to
Pasteur. He hoped Pasteur would reduce to their just proportions those secondary duties. "They have made him an administrator," he said with mock pomposity; "let them
believe that he will administrate." Biot was mistaken. The
de minimis non curat did not exist for Pasteur.

On one of his agenda leaves, besides subjects for lectures, we
find notes such as these : " Catering ; ascertain what weight of
meat per pupil is given out at the Ecole Polytechnique. Courtyard to be strewn with sand. Ventilation of classroom. Dining
hall door to be repaired." Each detail was of importance in his
eyes, when the health of the students was in question.

He inaugurated his garret by some work almost as celebrated
as that on lactic fermentation. In December, 1857, he presented to the Académie des Sciences a paper on alcoholic
fermentation. " I have submitted," he said, "alcoholic fermentation to the method of experimentation indicated in the
notes which I recently had the honour of presenting to the
Académie. The results of those labours should be put on the
same lines, for they explain and complete each other." And
in conclusion · " The deduplication of sugar into alcohol and
carbonic acid is correlative to a phenomenon of life, an organization of globules . . . "

The reports of the Académie des Sciences for 1858 show how
Pasteur recognized complex phenomena in alcoholic fermentation. Whilst chemists were content to say : " So much sugar
gives so much alcohol and so much carbonic acid," Pasteur
went further. He wrote to Chappuis in June : " I find that
alcoholic fermentation is constantly accompanied by the production of glycerine ; it is a very curious fact. For instance, in one
litre of wine there are several grammes of that product which
had not been suspected." Shortly before that he had also recognized the normal presence in alcoholic fermentation of succinic
acid. " I should be pursuing the consequences of these facts,"
he added, " if a temperature of 36° C. did not keep me from my
laboratory. I regret to see the longest days in the year lost to
me. Yet I have grown accustomed to my attic, and I should be
sorry to leave it. Next holidays I hope to enlarge it. You too
are struggling against material hindrances in your work ; let it
stimulate us, my dear fellow, and not discourage us. Our discoveries will have the greater merit."

The year 1859. was given up to examining further facts concerning fermentation. Whence came those ferments, those microscopic bodies, those transforming agents, so weak in appearance, so powerful in reality? Great problems were working in his mind; but he was careful not to propound them hastily, for he was the most timid, the most hesitating of men until he held proofs in his hands. "In experimental science," he wrote, "it is always a mistake not to doubt when facts do not compel you to affirm."

In September he lost his eldest daughter. She died of typhoid fever at Arbois, where she was staying with her grandfather. On December 30 Pasteur wrote to his father: "I cannot keep my thoughts from my poor little girl, so good, so happy in her little life, whom this fatal year now ending has taken away from us. She was growing to be such a companion to her mother and to me, to us all   But forgive me, dearest father, for recalling these sad memories. She is happy; let us think of those who remain and try as much as lies in our power to keep from them the bitterness of this life."

CHAPTER V

ON January 30, 1860, the Académie des Sciences conferred on Pasteur the Prize for Experimental Physiology. Claude Bernard, who drew up the report, recalled how much Pasteur's experiments in alcoholic fermentation, lactic fermentation, the fermentation of tartaric acid, had been appreciated by the Académie. He dwelt upon the great physiological interest of the results obtained. "It is," he concluded, "by reason of that physiological tendency in Pasteur's researches, that the Commission has unanimously selected him for the 1859 Prize for Experimental Physiology."

That same January, Pasteur wrote to Chappuis : "I am pursuing as best I can these studies on fermentation which are of great interest, connected as they are with the impenetrable mystery of Life and Death. I am hoping to mark a decisive step very soon by solving, without the least confusion, the celebrated question of spontaneous generation. Already I could speak, but I want to push my experiments yet further. There is so much obscurity, together with so much passion, on both sides, that I shall require the accuracy of an arithmetical problem to convince my opponents by my conclusions. I intend to attain even that."

This progress was depicted to his father in the following letter, dated February 7, 1860—

" I think I told you that I should read a second and last lecture on my old researches on Friday, at the Chemical Society, before several members of the Institute—amongst others, Messrs. Dumas and Claude Bernard. That lecture has had the same success as the first. M. Biot heard about it the next day through some distinguished persons who were in the audience, and sent for me in order to kindly express his great satisfaction.

" After I had finished, M. Dumas, who occupied the chair,

rose and addressed me in these words.   After praising the zeal I had brought to this novel kind of teaching at the Society's request, and the *so great penetration I had given proof of, in the course of the work I had just expounded*, he added, ' *The Académie, sir, rewarded you a few days ago for other profound researches; your audience of this evening will applaud you as one of the most distinguished professors we possess.*'

" All I have underlined was said in those very words by M. Dumas, and was followed by great applause.

" All the students of the scientific section of the Ecole Normale were present ; they felt deeply moved and several of them have expressed their emotion to me.

" As for myself, I saw the realization of what I had foreseen. You know how I have always told you confidentially that time would see the growth of my researches on the molecular dissymmetry of natural organic products.   Founded as they were on varied notions borrowed from divers branches of science—crystallography, physics, and chemistry—those studies could not be followed by most scientists so as to be fully understood.   On this occasion I presented them in the aggregate with some clearness and power and every one was struck by their importance.

" It is not by their form that these two lectures have delighted my hearers, it is by their contents ; it is the future reserved to those great results, so unexpected, and opening such entirely new vistas to physiology.   I have dared to say so, for at these heights all sense of personality disappears, and there only remains that sense of dignity which is ever inspired by true love of science.

" God grant that by my persevering labours I may bring a little stone to the frail and ill-assured edifice of our knowledge of those deep mysteries of Life and Death where all our intellects have so lamentably failed.

" P.S.—Yesterday I presented to the Academy my researches on spontaneous generation ; they seemed to produce a great sensation.   More later."

When Biot heard that Pasteur wished to tackle this study of spontaneous generation, he interposed, as he had done seven years before, to arrest him on the verge of his audacious experiments on the part played by dissymmetrical forces in the development of life.   Vainly Pasteur, grieved at Biot's disapprobation, explained that this question, in the course of such researches, had become an imperious necessity; Biot would not be convinced. But Pasteur, in spite of his quasi-filial attachment to Biot, could not stop where he was; he had to go through to the end.

"You will never find your way out," cried Biot.

"I shall try," said Pasteur modestly.

Angry and anxious, Biot wished Pasteur to promise that he would relinquish these apparently hopeless researches. J. B. Dumas, to whom Pasteur related the more than dis-couraging remonstrances of Biot, entrenched himself behind this cautious phrase—

"I would advise no one to dwell too long on such a subject."

Senarmont alone, full of confidence in the ingenious curiosity of the man who could read nature by dint of patience, said that Pasteur should be allowed his own way.

It is regrettable that Biot—whose passion for reading was so indefatigable that he complained of not finding enough books in the library at the Institute—should not have thought of writing the history of this question of spontaneous genera-tion. He could have gone back to Aristotle, quoted Lucretius, Virgil, Ovid, Pliny. Philosophers, poets, naturalists, all be-lieved in spontaneous generation. Time went on, and it was still believed in. In the sixteenth century, Van Helmont—who should not be judged by that one instance—gave a cele-brated recipe to create mice : any one could work that prodigy by putting some dirty linen in a receptacle, together with a few grains of wheat or a piece of cheese. Some time later an Italian, Buonanni, announced a fact no less fantastic : certain timberwood, he said, after rotting in the sea, produced worms which engendered butterflies, and those butterflies became birds.

Another Italian, less credulous, a poet and a physician, Francesco Redi, belonging to a learned society calling itself The Academy of Experience, resolved to carefully study one of those supposed phenomena of spontaneous generation. In order to demonstrate that the worms found in rotten meat did not appear spontaneously, he placed a piece of gauze over the meat. Flies, attracted by the odour, deposited their eggs on the gauze. From those eggs were hatched the worms, which had until then been supposed to begin life spontaneously in the flesh itself. This simple experiment marked some pro-gress. Later on another Italian, a medical professor of

Padua, Vallisneri, recognized that the grub in a fruit is also hatched from an egg deposited by an insect before the development of the fruit.

The theory of spontaneous generation, still losing ground, appeared to be vanquished when the invention of the microscope at the end of the seventeenth century brought fresh arguments to its assistance. Whence came those thousands of creatures, only distinguishable on the slide of the microscope, those infinitely small beings which appeared in rain water as in any infusion of organic matter when exposed to the air? How could they be explained otherwise than through spontaneous generation, those bodies capable of producing 1,000,000 descendants in less than forty-eight hours.

The world of salons and of minor courts was pleased to have an opinion on this question. The Cardinal of Polignac, a diplomat and a man of letters, wrote in his leisure moments a long Latin poem entitled the *Anti-Lucretius*. After scouting Lucretius and other philosophers of the same school, the cardinal traced back to one Supreme Foresight the mechanism and organization of the entire world. By ingenious developments and circumlocutions, worthy of the Abbé Delille, the cardinal, while vaunting the wonders of the microscope, which he called "eye of our eye," saw in it only another prodigy offered us by Almighty Wisdom. Of all those accumulated and verified arguments, this simple notion stood out : " The earth, which contains numberless germs, has not produced them. Everything in this world has its germ or seed."

Diderot, who disseminated so many ideas (since borrowed by many people and used as if originated by them), wrote in some tumultuous pages on nature : "Does living matter combine with living matter? how? and with what result? And what about dead matter? "

About the middle of the eighteenth century the problem was again raised on scientific ground. Two priests, one an Englishman, Needham, and the other an Italian, Spallanzani, entered the lists. Needham, a great partisan of spontaneous generation, studied with Buffon some microscopic animalculæ. Buffon afterwards built up a whole system which became fashionable at that time. The force which Needham found in matter, a force which he called productive or vegetative, and which he regarded as charged with the formation of the organic world, Buffon explained by saying that there are certain primitive and incorruptible parts common to animals and to vegetables. These organic molecules cast themselves into the moulds or shapes which constituted different beings. When one of those moulds was destroyed by death, the organic molecules became free ; ever active, they worked the putrefied matter, appropriating to themselves some raw particles and forming, said Buffon, "by their reunion, a multitude of little organized bodies, of which some, like earthworms, and fungi, seem to be fair-sized animals or vegetables, but of which others, in almost infinite numbers, can only be seen through the microscope."

All those bodies, according to him, only existed through spontaneous generation. Spontaneous generation takes place continually and universally after death and sometimes during life. Such was in his view the origin of intestinal worms. And, carrying his investigations further, he added, " The eels in flour paste, those of vinegar, all those so-called microscopic animals, are but different shapes taken spontaneously, according to circumstances, by that ever active matter which only tends to organization."

The Abbé Spallanzani, armed with a microscope, studied these infinitesimal beings. He tried to distinguish them and their mode of life. Needham had affirmed that by enclo..ing putrescible matter in vases and by placing those vases on warm ashes, he produced animalculæ. Spallanzani suspected : firstly that Needham had not exposed the vases to a sufficient degree of heat to kill the seeds which were inside ; and secondly, that seeds could easily have entered those vases and given birth to animalculæ, for Needham had only closed his vases with cork stoppers, which are very porous.

" I repeated that experiment with more accuracy," wrote Spallanzani. " I used hermetically sealed vases. I kept them for an hour in boiling water, and after having opened them and examined their contents within a reasonable time I found not the slightest trace of animalculæ, though I had examined with the microscope the infusions from nineteen different vases."

Thus dropped to the ground, in Spallanzani's eyes, Needham's singular theory, this famous vegetative force, this occult virtue. Yet Needham did not own himself beaten. He retorted that Spallanzani had much weakened, perhaps destroyed, the vegetative force of the infused substances by leaving his vases in boiling water during an hour. He advised him to try with less heat.

The public took an interest in this quarrel. In an opuscule entitled *Singularities of Nature* (1769), Voltaire, a born journalist, laughed at Needham, whom he turned into an Irish Jesuit to amuse his readers. Joking on this race of so-called eels which began life in the gravy of boiled mutton, he said " At once several philosophers exclaimed at the wonder and said, ' There is no germ; all is made, all is regenerated by a vital force of nature.' ' Attraction,' said one; ' Organized matter,' said another, ' they are organic molecules which have found their casts.' Clever physicists were taken in by a Jesuit."

In those pages, lightly penned, nothing remained of what Voltaire called " the ridiculous mistake, the unfortunate experiments of Needham, so triumphantly refuted by M. Spallanzani and rejected by whoever has studied nature at all." " It is now demonstrated to sight and to reason that there is no vegetable, no animal but has its own germ.'" In his *Philosophic Dictionary*, at the word God, " It is very strange," said Voltaire, " that men should deny a creator and yet attribute to themselves the power of creating eels ! " The Abbé Needham, meeting with these religious arguments, rather unexpected from Voltaire, endeavoured to prove that the hypothesis of spontaneous generation was in perfect accordance with religious beliefs. But both on Needham's side and on Spallanzani's there was a complete lack of conclusive proofs.

Philosophic argumentation always returned to the fore. As recently as 1846 Ernest Bersot (a moralist who became later a director of the Ecole Normale) wrote in his book on Spiritualism : " The doctrine of spontaneous generation pleases simplicity-loving minds; it leads them far beyond their own expectations. But it is yet only a private opinion, and, were it recognized, its virtue would have to be limited and narrowed down to the production of a few inferior animals."

That doctrine was about to be noisily re-introduced.

On December 20, 1858, a correspondent of the Institute, M. Pouchet, director of the Natural History Museum of Rouen, sent to the Académie des Sciences a *Note on Vegetable and Animal Proto-organisms spontaneously Generated in Artificial Air and in Oxygen Gas*. The note began thus : " At this time when, seconded by the progress of science, several naturalists are endeavouring to reduce the domain of spontaneous generation or even to deny its existence altogether, I have undertaken a series of researches with the object of elucidating this vexed question." Pouchet, declaring that he had taken excessive precautions to preserve his experiments from any cause of error, proclaimed that he was prepared to demonstrate that "animals and plants could be generated in a medium absolutely free from atmospheric air, and in which, therefore, no germ of organic bodies could have been brought by air."

On one copy of that communication, the opening of a four years' scientific campaign, Pasteur had underlined the passages which he intended to submit to rigorous experimentation. The scientific world was discussing the matter; Pasteur set himself to work.

A new installation, albeit a summary one, allowed him to attempt some delicate experiments. At one of the extremities of the façade of the Ecole Normale, on the same line as the doorkeeper's lodge, a pavilion had been built for the school architect and his clerk. Pasteur succeeded in obtaining possession of this small building, and transformed it into a laboratory. He built a drying stove under the staircase; though he could only reach the stove by crawling on his knees, yet this was better than his old attic. He also had a pleasant surprise —he was given a curator. He had deserved one sooner, for he had founded the institution of *agrégés préparateurs*. Remembering his own desire, on leaving the Ecole Normale, to have a year or two for independent study, he had wished to facilitate for others the obtaining of those few years of research and perhaps inspiration. Thanks to him, five places as laboratory curators were exclusively reserved to Ecole Normale students who had taken their degree (*agrégés*). The first curator who entered the new laboratory was Jules Ranlin, a young man with a clear and sagacious mind, a calm and tenacious character, loving difficulties for the sake of overcoming them.

Pasteur began by the microscopic study of atmospheric air. "If germs exist in atmosphere," he said, "could they not be arrested on their way?" It then occurred to him to draw —through an aspirator—a current of outside air through a tube containing a little plug of cotton wool. The current as it passed deposited on this sort of filter some of the solid corpuscles contained in the air; the cotton wool often became black with those various kinds of dust. Pasteur assured himself that amongst various detritus those dusts presented spores and germs. "There are therefore in the air some organized corpuscles. Are they germs capable of vegetable productions, or of infusions? That is the question to solve." He undertook a series of experiments to demonstrate that the most putrescible liquid remained pure indefinitely if placed out of the reach of atmospheric dusts. But it was sufficient to place in a pure liquid a particle of the cotton-wool filter to obtain an immediate alteration.

A year before starting any discussion Pasteur wrote to Pouchet that the results which he had attained were "not founded on facts of a faultless exactitude. I think you are wrong, not in believing in spontaneous generation (for it is difficult in such a case not to have a preconceived idea), but in affirming the existence of spontaneous generation. In experimental science it is always a mistake not to doubt when facts do not compel affirmation. . . . In my opinion, the question is whole and untouched by decisive proofs. What is there in air which provokes organization? Are they germs? is it a solid? is it a gas? is it a fluid? is it a principle such as ozone? All this is unknown and invites experiment."

After a year's study, Pasteur reached this conclusion: "Gases, fluids, electricity, magnetism, ozone, things known or things occult, there is nothing in the air that is conditional to life, except the germs that it carries."

Pouchet defended himself vigorously. To suppose that germs came from air seemed to him impossible. How many millions of loose eggs or spores would then be contained in a cubic millimetre of atmospheric air?

"What will be the outcome of this giant's struggle?" grandiloquently wrote an editor of the *Moniteur Scientifique* (April, 1860). Pouchet answered this anonymous writer by advising him to accept the doctrine of spontaneous generation adopted of old by so many "men of genius." Pouchet's principal disciple was a lover of science and of letters, M. Nicolas Joly, an *agrégé* of natural science, doctor of medicine, and professor of physiology at Toulouse. He himself had a pupil, Charles Musset, who was preparing a thesis for his doctor's degree under the title: *New Experimental Researches on Heterogenia, or Spontaneous Generation.* By the words heterogenia or spontaneous generation Joly and Musset agreed in affirming that "they did not mean a creation out of nothing, but the production of a new organized being, lacking parents, and of which the primordial elements are drawn from ambient organic matter."

Thus supported, Pouchet multiplied objections to the views of Pasteur, who had to meet every argument. Pasteur intended to narrow more and more the sphere of discussion. It was an ingenious operation to take the dusts from a cotton-wool filter, to disseminate them in a liquid, and thus to determine the alteration of that liquid; but the cotton wool itself was an organic substance and might be suspected. He therefore substituted for the cotton wool a plug of asbestos fibre, a mineral substance. He invented little glass flasks with a long curved neck; he filled them with an alterable liquid, which he deprived of germs by ebullition; the flask was in communication with the outer air through its curved tube, but the atmospheric germs were deposited in the curve of the neck without reaching the liquid; in order that alteration should take place, the vessel had to be inclined until the point where the liquid reached the dusts in the neck.

But Pouchet said, "How could germs contained in the air be numerous enough to develop in every organic infusion? Such a crowd of them would produce a thick mist as dense as iron." Of all the difficulties this last seemed to Pasteur the hardest to solve. Could it not be that the dissemination of germs was more or less thick according to places? "Then," cried the heterogenists, "there would be sterile zones and fecund zones, a most convenient hypothesis, indeed!" Pasteur let them laugh whilst he was preparing a series of flasks reserved for divers experiments. If spontaneous generation existed, it should invariably occur in vessels filled with the same alterable liquid. "Yet it is ever possible," affirmed Pasteur, "to take up in certain places a notable though limited volume of ordinary air, having been submitted to no physical or chemical change, and still absolutely incapable of producing any alteration in an eminently putrescible liquor." He was ready to prove that nothing was easier than to increase or to reduce the number either of the vessels where productions should appear or of the vessels where those productions should be lacking. After introducing into a series of flasks of a capacity of 250 cubic centimetres a very easily corrupted liquid, such as yeast water, he submitted each flask to ebullition. The neck of those vessels was ended off in a vertical point. Whilst the liquid was still boiling, he closed, with an enameller's lamp, the pointed opening through which the steam had rushed out, taking with it all the air contained in the vessel. Those flasks were indeed calculated to satisfy both partisans or adversaries of spontaneous generation. If the extremity of the neck of one of these vessels was suddenly broken, all the ambient air rushed into the flask, bringing in all the suspended dusts; the bulb was closed again at once with the assistance of a jet of flame. Pasteur could then carry it away and place it in a temperature of 25–30° C., quite suitable for the development of germs and mucors.

In those series of tests some flasks showed some alteration, others remained pure, according to the place where the air had been admitted. During the beginning of the year 1860 Pasteur broke his bulb points and enclosed ordinary air in many different places, including the cellars of the Observatory of Paris. There, in that zone of an invariable temperature, the absolutely calm air could not be compared to the air he gathered in the yard of the same building. The results were also very different : out of ten vessels opened in the cellar, closed again and placed in the stove, only one showed any alteration ; whilst eleven others, opened in the yard, all yielded organized bodies.

In a letter to his father (June, 1860), Pasteur wrote : " I have been prevented from writing by my experiments, which continue to be very curious. But it is such a wide subject that I have almost too many ideas of experiments. I am still being contradicted by two naturalists, M. Pouchet of Rouen and M. Joly of Toulouse. But I do not waste my time in answering them ; they may say what they like, truth is on my side. They do not know how to experiment; it is not an easy art; it demands, besides certain natural qualities, a long practice which naturalists have not generally acquired nowadays."

When the long vacation approached, Pasteur, who intended to go on a voyage of experiments, laid in a store of glass flasks. He wrote to Chappuis, on August 10, 1860 : " I fear from your letter that you will not go to the Alps this year. . . . Besides the pleasure of having you for a guide, I had hoped to utilize your love of science by offering you the modest part of curator. It is by some study of air on heights afar from habitations and vegetation that I want to conclude my work on so-called spontaneous generation. The real interest of that work for me lies in the connection of this subject with that of ferments which I shall take up again November."

Pasteur started for Arbois, taking with him seventy-three flasks; he opened twenty of them not very far from his father's tannery, on the road to Dôle, along an old road, now a path which leads to the mount of the Bergère. The vine labourers who passed him wondered what this holiday tourist could be doing with all those little phials; no one suspected that he was penetrating one of nature's greatest secrets. "What would you have?" merrily said his old friend, Jules Vercel; "it amuses him!" Of those twenty vessels, opened some distance away from any dwelling, eight yielded organized bodies.

Pasteur went on to Salins and climbed Mount Poupet, 850 metres above the sea-level. Out of twenty vessels opened, only five were altered. Pasteur would have liked to charter a balloon in order to prove that the higher you go the fewer germs you find, and that certain zones absolutely pure contain none at all. It was easier to go into the Alps.

He arrived at Chamonix on September 20, and engaged a guide to make the ascent of the Montanvert. The very next morning this novel sort of expedition started. A mule carried the case of thirty-three vessels, followed very closely by Pasteur, who watched over the precious burden and walked alongside of precipices supporting the case with one hand so that it should not be shaken.

When the first experiments were started an incident occurred. Pasteur has himself related this fact in his report to the Académie. "In order to close again the point of the flasks after taking in the air, I had taken with me an eolipyle spirit-lamp. The dazzling whiteness of the ice in the sunlight was such that it was impossible to distinguish the jet of burning alcohol, and as moreover that was slightly moved by the wind, it never remained on the broken glass long enough to hermetically seal my vessel. All the means I might have employed to make the flame visible and consequently directable would inevitably have given rise to causes of error by spreading strange dusts into the air. I was therefore obliged to bring back to the little inn of Montanvert, unsealed, the flasks which I had opened on the glacier."

The inn was a sort of hut, letting in wind and rain. The thirteen open vessels were exposed to all the dusts in the room

H

where Pasteur slept; nearly all of them presented alterations.

In the meanwhile the guide was sent to Chamonix where a
tinker undertook to modify the lamp in view of the coming
experiment.

The next morning, twenty flasks, which have remained celebrated in the world of scientific investigators, were brought to
the Mer de Glace. Pasteur gathered the air with infinite precautions; he used to enjoy relating these details to those people
who call everything easy. After tracing with a steel point a
line on the glass, careful lest dusts should become a cause of
error, he began by heating the neck and fine point of the bulb
in the flame of the little spirit-lamp. Then raising the vessel
above his head, he broke the point with steel nippers, the long
ends of which had also been heated in order to burn the dusts
which might be on their surface and which would have been
driven into the vessel by the quick inrush of the air. Of those
twenty flasks, closed again immediately, only one was altered.
"If all the results are compared that I have obtained until
now," he wrote, on March 5, 1880, when relating this journey
to the Académie, "it seems to me that it can be affirmed that
the dusts suspended in atmospheric air are the exclusive origin,
the necessary condition of life in infusions."

And in an unnoticed little sentence, pointing already then to
the goal he had in view, " What would be most desirable would
be to push those studies far enough to prepare the road for a
serious research into the origin of various diseases." The
action of those little beings, agents not only of fermentation but
also of disorganization and putrefaction, already dawned upon
him.

While Pasteur was going from the Observatoire cellars to the
Mer de Glace, Pouchet was gathering air on the plains of
Sicily, making experiments on Etna, and on the sea. He saw
everywhere, he wrote, "air equally favourable to organic
genesis, whether surcharged with detritus in the midst of our
populous cities, or taken on the summit of a mountain, or on
the sea, where it offers extreme purity. With a cubic deci-
metre of air, taken where you like, I affirm that you can ever
produce legions of microzoa."

And the heterogenists proclaimed in unison that "every
where, strictly everywhere, air is constantly favourable to life."
Those who followed the debate nearly all leaned towards

Pouchet. "I am afraid," wrote a scientific journalist in *La Presse* (1860), "that the experiments you quote, M. Pasteur, will turn against you. . . . The world into which you wish to take us is really too fantastic. . . ."

And yet some adversaries should have been struck by the efforts of a mind which, while marching forward to establish new facts, was ever seeking arguments against itself, and turned back to strengthen points which seemed yet weak. In November, Pasteur returned to his studies on fermentations in general and lactic fermentation in particular. Endeavouring to bring into evidence the animated nature of the lactic ferment, and to indicate the most suitable surroundings for the self-development of that ferment, he had come across some complications which hampered the purity and the progress of that culture. Then he had perceived another fermentation, following upon lactic fermentation and known as butyric fermentation. As he did not immediately perceive the origin of this butyric acid—which causes the bad smell in rancid butter—he ended by being struck by the inevitable coincidence between the (then called) infusory animalculæ and the production of this acid.

"The most constantly repeated tests," he wrote in February, 1861, "have convinced me that the transformation of sugar, mannite and lactic acid into butyric acid is due exclusively to those Infusories, and they must be considered as the real butyric ferment." Those vibriones that Pasteur described as under the shape of small cylindric rods with rounded ends, sliding about, sometimes in a chain of three or four articles, he sowed in an appropriate medium, as he sowed beer yeast. But, by a strange phenomenon, "those infusory animalculæ," he said, "live and multiply indefinitely, without requiring the least quantity of air. And not only do they live without air, but air actually kills them. It is sufficient to send a current of atmospheric air during an hour or two through the liquor where those vibriones were multiplying to cause them all to perish and thus to arrest butyric fermentation, whilst a current of pure carbonic acid gas passing through that same liquor hindered them in no way. Thence this double proposition," concluded Pasteur; "the butyric ferment is an infusory; that infusory lives without free oxygen." He afterwards called anaërobes those beings which do not require air, in opposition to the name of aërobes given to other microscopic beings who require air to live.

Biot, without knowing all the consequences of these studies, had not been long in perceiving that he had been far too sceptical, and that physiological discoveries of the very first rank would be the outcome of researches on so-called spontaneous generation. He would have wished, before he died, not only that Pasteur should be the unanimously selected candidate for the 1861 Zecker prize in the Chemistry Section, but also that his friend, forty-eight years younger than himself, should be a member of the Institute. At the beginning of 1861, there was one vacancy in the Botanical Section. Biot took advantage of the researches pursued by Pasteur within the last three years, to say and to print that he should be nominated as a candidate. "I can hear the commonplace objection : he is a chemist, a physicist, not a professional botanist. . . . But that very versatility, ever active and ever successful, should be a title in his favour   Let us judge of men by their works and not by the destination more or less wide or narrow that they have marked out for themselves. Pasteur made his début before the Académie in 1848, with the remarkable treatise which contained by implication the resolution of the paratartaric acid into its two components, right and left. He was then twenty-six ; the sensation produced is not forgotten. Since then, during the twelve years which followed, he has submitted to your appreciation twenty-one papers, the last ten relating to vegetable physiology. All are full of new facts, often very unexpected, several very far reaching, not one of which has been found inaccurate by competent judges. If to-day, by your suffrage, you introduce M. Pasteur into the Botanical Section, as you might safely have done for Théodore de Saussure or Ingenhousz, you will have acquired for the Académie and for that particular section an experimentalist of the same order as those two great men."

Balard, who in this academic campaign made common cause with Biot, was also making efforts to persuade several members of the Botanical Section. He was walking one day in the Luxembourg with Moquin-Tandon, pouring out, in his rasping voice, arguments in favour of Pasteur. " Well," said Moquin-Tandon, " let us go to Pasteur's, and if you find a botanical work in his library I shall put him on the list." It was a witty form given to the scruples of the botanists. Pasteur only had twenty-four votes ; Duchartre was elected.

The study of a microscopic fungus, capable by itself of

transforming wine into vinegar, the bringing to light of the action of that mycoderma, endowed with the power of taking oxygen from air and fixing it upon alcohol, thus transforming the latter into acetic acid ; the most ingenious experiments to demonstrate the absolute and exclusive power of the little plant, all gave reason to Biot's affirmation that such skill in the observation of inferior vegetables equalled any botanist's claim. Pasteur, showing that the interpretations of the causes which act in the formation of vinegar were false, and that alone the microscopic fungus did everything, was constantly dwelling on this power of the infinitesimally small. "Mycoderma," he said, "can bring the action of combustion of the oxygen in air to bear on a number of organic materia. If microscopic beings were to disappear from our globe, the surface of the earth would be encumbered with dead organic matter and corpses of all kinds, animal and vegetable. It is chiefly they who give to oxygen its powers of combustion. Without them, life would become impossible because death would be incomplete."

Pasteur's ideas on fermentation and putrefaction were being adopted by disciples unknown to him   "I am sending you," he wrote to his father, " a treatise on fermentation, which was the subject of a recent competition at the Montpellier Faculty. This work is dedicated to me by its author, whom I do not know at all, a circumstance which shows that my results are spreading and exciting some attention.

" I have only read the last pages, which have pleased me ; if the rest is the same, it is a very good *résumé*, entirely conceived in the new direction of my labours, evidently well understood by this young doctor.

" M. Biot is very well, only suffering a little from insomnia. He has, fortunately for his health, finished that great account of my former results which will be the greatest title I can have to the esteem of scientists."

Biot died without having realized his last wish, which was to have Pasteur for a colleague. It was only at the end of the year 1862 that Pasteur was nominated by the Mineralogical Section for the seat of Senarmont. This new candidature did not go without a hitch. In his study on tartrates, Pasteur, as will be remembered, had discovered that their crystalline forms were hemihedral. When he examined the characteristic faces, he held the crystal in a particular way and said : " It is hemihedral on the right side." A German mineralogist, named

Rammelsberg, holding the crystal in the opposite direction, said : "It is hemihedral on the left side." It was a mere matter of conventional orientation ; nothing was changed in the scientific results announced by Pasteur. But some adversaries made a weapon of that inverted crystal; not a dangerous weapon, thought Pasteur at first, fancying that a few words would clear the misunderstanding. But the campaign persisted, with insinuations, murmurs, whisperings. When Pasteur saw this simple difference in the way the crystal was held stigmatised as a cause of error, he desired to cut short this quarrel made in Germany. He then had with him no longer Raulin, but M. Duclaux, who was beginning his scientific life. M. Duclaux remembers one day when Pasteur, seeing that incontrovertible arguments were required, sent for a cabinet maker with his tools. He superintended the making of a complete wooden set of the crystalline forms of tartrates, a gigantic set, such as Gulliver might have seen in Brobdingnag if he had studied geometrical forms in that island. A coating of coloured paper finished the work ; green paper marked the hemihedral face. A member of the Philomathic Society, Pasteur asked the Society to give up the meeting of November 8, 1862, to the discussion of that subject. Several of his colleagues vainly endeavoured to dissuade him from that intention ; Pasteur hearkened to no one. He took with him his provision of wooden crystals, and gave a vivid and impassioned lecture. " If you know the question," he asked his adversaries, " where is your conscience? If you know it not, why meddle with it ? " And with one of his accustomed sudden turns, " What is all this? " he added. " One of those incidents to which we all, more or less, are exposed by the conditions of our career; no bitterness remains behind. Of what account is it in the presence of those mysteries, so varied, so numerous, that we all, in divers directions, are working to clear? It is true I have had recourse to an unusual means of defending myself against attacks not openly published, but I think that means was safe and loyal, and deferential towards you. And," he added, thinking of Biot and Senarmont, " will you have my full confession? You know that I had during fifteen years the inestimable advantage of the intercourse of two men who are no more, but whose scientific probity shone as one of the beacons of the Académie des Sciences. Before deciding on the course I have now followed, I questioned my memory and endeavoured to revive their advice, and it seemed to me that they would not have disowned me."

M. Duclaux said about this meeting : "Pasteur has since then won many oratorical victories. I do not know of a greater one than that deserved by that acute and penetrating improvisation. He was still much heated as we were walking back to the Rue d'Ulm, and I remember making him laugh by asking him why, in the state of mind he was in, he had not concluded by hurling his wooden crystals at his adversaries' heads."

On December 8, 1862, Pasteur was elected a member of the Académie des Sciences; out of sixty voters he received thirty-six suffrages.

The next morning, when the gates of the Montparnasse cemetery were opened, a woman walked towards Biot's grave with her hands full of flowers. It was Mme. Pasteur who was bringing them to him who lay there since February 5, 1862, and who had loved Pasteur with so deep an affection.

A letter picked up at a sale of autographs, one of the last Biot wrote, gives a finishing touch to his moral portrait. It is addressed to an unknown person discouraged with this life. " Sir,—The confidence you honour me with touches me. But I am not a physician of souls. However, in my opinion, you could not do better than seek remedies to your moral suffering in work, religion, and charity. A useful work taken up with energy and persevered in will revive by occupation the forces of your mind. Religious feelings will console you by inspiring you with patience. Charity manifested to others will soften your sorrows and teach you that you are not alone to suffer in this life. Look around you, and you will see afflicted ones more to be pitied than yourself. Try to ease their sufferings; the good you will do to them will fall back upon yourself and will show you that a life which can thus be employed is not a burden which cannot, which must not be borne."

On his entering the Académie des Sciences, Balard and Dumas advised Pasteur to let alone his wooden crystals and to continue his studies on ferments. He undertook to demonstrate that " the hypothesis of a phenomenon of mere contact is not more admissible than the opinion which placed the ferment character exclusively in dead albuminoid matter. Whilst continuing his researches on beings which could live without air, he tried, as he went along, à propos of spontaneous generation, to find some weak point in his work. Until now the liquids he had used, however alterable they were, had been brought up to boiling point. Was there not some new and decisive experiment to make? Could he not study organic matter as constituted by life and expose to the contact of air deprived of its germs some fresh liquids, highly putrescible, such as blood and urine? Claude Bernard, joining in these experiments of Pasteur's, himself took some blood from a dog. This blood was sealed up in a glass phial, with every condition of purity, and the phial remained in a stove constantly heated up to 30° C. from March 3 until April 20, 1862, when Pasteur laid it on the Académie table. The blood had suffered no sort of putrefaction; neither had some urine treated in the same way. "The conclusions to which I have been led by my first series of experiments," said Pasteur before the Académie, "are therefore applicable in all cases to organic substances."

While studying putrefaction, which is itself but a fermentation applied to animal materia, while showing the marvellous power of the infinitesimally small, he foresaw the immensity of the domain he had conquered, as will be proved by the following incident. Some time after the Académie election, in March, 1863, the Emperor, who took an interest in all that took place in the small laboratory of the Rue d'Ulm, desired to speak with Pasteur. J. B. Dumas claimed the privilege of presenting his former pupil, and the interview took place at the Tuileries. Napoleon questioned Pasteur with a gentle, slightly dreamy insistence. Pasteur wrote the next day : " I assured the Emperor that all my ambition was to arrive at the knowledge of the causes of putrid and contagious diseases."

In the meanwhile, the chapter on ferments was not yet closed; Pasteur was attracted by studies on wine. At the beginning of the 1863 holidays, just before starting for Arbois, he drew up this programme with one of his pupils : " From the 20th to the 30th (August) preparation in Paris of all the vessels, apparatus, products, that we must take. September 1, departure for the Jura; installation; purchase of the products of a vineyard. Immediate beginning of tests of all kinds. We shall have to hurry; grapes do not keep long."

Whilst he was preparing this vintage tour, which he intended to make with three " Normaliens," Duclaux, Gernez and Lechartier, the three heterogenists, Pouchet, Joly and Musset, proposed to use that same time in fighting Pasteur on his own ground. They started from Bagnères-de-Luchon followed by several guides and taking with them all kinds of provisions and some little glass flasks with a slender pointed neck. They crossed the pass of Venasque without incident, and decided to go further, to the Rencluse. Some isard-stalkers having come towards the strange-looking party, they were signalled away; even the guides were invited to stand aside. It was necessary to prevent any dusts from reaching the bulbs, which were thus opened at 8 p.m. at a height of 2,083 metres. But eighty-three metres higher than the Montanvert did not seem to them enough, they wished to go higher. "We shall sleep on the mountain," said the three scientists. Fatigue and bitter cold, they withstood everything with the courage inspired by a problem to solve. The next morning they climbed across that rocky chaos, and at last reached the foot of one of the greatest glaciers of the Maladetta, 3,000 metres above the sea-level. "A very deep narrow crevasse," says Pouchet, "seemed to us the most suitable place for our experiments." Four phials (filled with a decoction of hay) were opened and sealed again with precautions that Pouchet considered as exaggerated.

Pouchet, in his merely scientific report, does not relate the return journey, yet more perilous than the ascent. At one of the most dangerous places, Joly slipped, and would have rolled into a precipice, but for the strength and presence of mind of one of the guides. All three at last came back to Luchon, forgetful of dangers run, and glorying at having reached 1,000 metres higher than Pasteur. They triumphed when they saw alteration in their flasks! "Therefore," said Pouchet, "the air of the Maladetta, and of high mountains in general, is not incapable of producing altera-tion in an eminently putrescible liquor; therefore heterogenia or the production of a new being devoid of parents, but formed at the expense of ambient organic matter, is for us a reality."

The Academy of Sciences was taking more and more interest in this debate. In November, 1863, Joly and Musset expressed a wish that the Academy should appoint a Com-mission, before whom the principal experiments of Pasteur and of his adversaries should be repeated. On this occasion Flourens expressed his opinion thus : " I am blamed in certain quarters for giving no opinion on the question of spontaneous generation. As long as my opinion was not formed, I had nothing to say. It is now formed, and I give it : M. Pasteur's experiments are decisive. If spontaneous generation is real, what is required to obtain animalculæ? Air and putrescible liquor. M. Pasteur puts air and putrescible liquor together and nothing happens. Therefore spontaneous generation is not. To doubt further is to misunderstand the question."

Already in the preceding year, the Académie itself had evidenced its opinion by giving Pasteur the prize of a competition proposed in these terms : '' To attempt to throw some new light upon the question of so-called spontaneous generation by well-conducted experiments." Pasteur's treatise on *Organized Corpuscles existing in Atmosphere* had been unanimously preferred. Pasteur might have entrenched himself behind the suffrages of the Academy, but begged it, in order to close those incessant debates, to appoint the Commission demanded by Joly and Musset.

The members of the Commission were Flourens, Dumas, Brongniart, Milne-Edwards, and Balard. Pasteur wished that the discussion should take place as soon as possible, and it was fixed for the first fortnight in March. But Pouchet, Joly and Musset asked for a delay on account of the cold. '' We consider that it might compromise, perhaps prevent, our results, to operate in a temperature which often goes below zero even in the south of France. How do we know that it will not freeze in Paris between the first and fifteenth of March?'' They even asked the Commission to adjourn experiments until the summer. '' I am much surprised," wrote Pasteur, '' at the delay sought by Messrs. Pouchet, Joly and Musset; it would have been easy with a stove to raise the temperature to the degree required by those gentlemen. For my part I hasten to assure the Academy that I am at its disposal, and that in summer, or in any other season, I am ready to repeat my experiments."

Some evening scientific lectures had just been inaugurated at the Sorbonne; such a subject as spontaneous generation was naturally on the programme. When Pasteur entered the large lecture room of the Sorbonne on April 7, 1864, he must have been reminded of the days of his youth, when crowds came, as to a theatrical performance, to hear J. B. Dumas speak. Dumas' pupil, now a master, in his turn found a still greater crowd invading every corner. Amongst the professors and students, such celebrities as Duruy,

Alexandre Dumas senior, George Sand, Princess Mathilde, were being pointed out. Around them, the inevitable "smart" people who must see everything and be seen everywhere, without whom no function favoured by fashion would be complete; in short what is known as the "Tout Paris." But this "Tout Paris" was about to receive a novel impression, probably a lasting one. The man who stood before this fashionable audience was not one of those speakers who attempt by an insinuating exordium to gain the good graces of their hearers; it was a grave-looking man, his face full of quiet energy and reflective force. He began in a deep, firm voice, evidently earnestly convinced of the greatness of his mission as a teacher: "Great problems are now being handled, keeping every thinking man in suspense; the unity or multiplicity of human races; the creation of man 1,000 years or 1,000 centuries ago, the fixity of species, or the slow and progressive transformation of one species into another; the eternity of matter; the idea of a God unnecessary. Such are some of the questions that humanity discusses nowadays."

He had now, he continued, entered upon a subject accessible to experimentation, and which he had made the object of the strictest and most conscientious studies. Can matter organize itself? Can living beings come into the world without having been preceded by beings similar to them? After showing that the doctrine of spontaneous generation had gradually. lost ground, he explained how the invention of the microscope had caused it to reappear at the end of the seventeenth century, "in the face of those beings, so numerous, so varied, so strange in their shapes, the origin of which was connected with the presence of all dead vegetable and animal matter in a state of disorganization." He went on to say how Pouchet had taken up this study, and to point out the errors that this new partisan of an old doctrine had committed, errors difficult to recognize at first. With perfect clearness and simplicity, Pasteur explained how the dusts which are suspended in air contain germs of inferior organized beings and how a liquid preserved, by certain precautions, from the contact of these germs can be kept indefinitely, giving his audience a glimpse of his laboratory methods.

"Here," he said, "is an infusion of organic matter, as limpid as distilled water, and extremely alterable. It has been prepared to-day. To-morrow it will contain animalculæ, little infusories, or flakes of mouldiness.

"I place a portion of that infusion into a flask with a long neck, like this one. Suppose I boil the liquid and leave it to cool. After a few days, mouldiness or animalculæ will develop in the liquid. By boiling, I destroyed any germs contained in the liquid or against the glass; but that infusion being again in contact with air, it becomes altered, as all infusions do. Now suppose I repeat this experiment, but that, before boiling the liquid, I draw (by means of an enameller's lamp) the neck of the flask into a point, leaving, however, its extremity open. This being done, I boil the liquid in the flask, and leave it to cool. Now the liquid of this second flask will remain pure not only two days, a month, a year, but three or four years—for the experiment I am telling you about is already four years old, and the liquid remains as limpid as distilled water. What difference is there, then, between those two vases? They contain the same liquid, they both contain air, both are open! Why does one decay and the other remain pure? The only difference between them is this: in the first case, the dusts suspended in air and their germs can fall into the neck of the flask and arrive into contact with the liquid, where they find appropriate food and develop; thence microscopic beings. In the second flask, on the contrary, it is impossible, or at least extremely difficult, unless air is violently shaken, that dusts suspended in air should enter the vase; they fall on its curved neck. When air goes in and out of the vase through diffusions or variations of temperature, the latter never being sudden, the air comes in slowly enough to drop the dusts and germs that it carries at the opening of the neck or in the first curves.

"This experiment is full of instruction; for this must be noted, that everything in air save its dusts can easily enter the vase and come into contact with the liquid. Imagine what you choose in the air—electricity, magnetism, ozone, unknown forces even, all can reach the infusion. Only one thing cannot enter easily, and that is dust, suspended in air. And the proof of this is that if I shake the vase violently two or three times, in a few days it contains animalculæ or mouldiness. Why? because air has come in violently enough to carry dust with it.

"And, therefore, gentlemen, I could point to that liquid and say to you, I have taken my drop of water from the immensity of creation, and I have taken it full of the elements appropriated to the development of inferior beings. And I wait, I watch, I question it, begging it to recommence for me the beautiful spectacle of the first creation. But it is dumb, dumb since these experiments were begun several years ago; it is dumb because I have kept it from the only thing man cannot produce, from the germs which float in the air, from Life, for Life is a germ and a germ is Life. Never will the doctrine of spontaneous generation recover from the mortal blow of this simple experiment.''

The public enthusiastically applauded these words, which ended the lecture :

'' No, there is now no circumstance known in which it can be affirmed that microscopic beings came into the world without germs, without parents similar to themselves. Those who affirm it have been duped by illusions, by ill-conducted experiments, spoilt by errors that they either did not perceive or did not know how to avoid.''

In the meanwhile, besides public lectures and new studies, Pasteur succeeded in ''administering'' the Ecole Normale in the most complete sense of the word. His influence was such that students acquired not a taste but a passion for study; he directed each one in his own line, he awakened their instincts. It was already through his wise inspiration that five ''Normaliens agrégés'' should have the chance of the five curators' places; but his solicitude did not stop there. If some disappointment befell some former pupil, still in that period of youth which doubts nothing or nobody, he came vigorously to his assistance; he was the counsellor of the future. A few letters will show how he understood his responsibility.

A Normalien, Paul Dalimier, received 1st at the *agrégation* of Physics in 1858, afterwards Natural History curator at the Ecole, and who, having taken his doctor's degree, asked to be sent to a Faculty, was ordered to go to the Lycée of Chaumont.

In the face of this almost disgrace he wrote a despairing letter to Pasteur. He could do nothing more, he said, his career was ruined. ''My dear sir,'' answered Pasteur, ''I much regret that I could not see you before your departure for Chaumont. But here is the advice which I feel will be useful to you. Do not manifest your just displeasure; but attract attention from the very first by your zeal and talent. In a word, aggravate, by your fine discharge of your new duties, the injustice which has been committed. The discouragement expressed in your last letter is not worthy of a man of science. Keep but three objects before your eyes : your class, your pupils and the work you have begun. . . Do your duty to the best of your ability. without troubling about the rest."

Pasteur undertook the rest himself. He went to the Ministry to complain of the injustice and unfairness, from a general point of view, of that nomination.

" Sir," answered the Chaumont exile, " I have received your kind letter. My deep respect for every word of yours will guarantee my intention to follow your advice. I have given myself up entirely to my class. I have found here a Physics cabinet in a deplorable state, and I have undertaken to re-organise it."

He had not time to finish : justice was done, and Paul Dalimier was made *maître des conférences* at the Ecole Normale. He died at twenty-eight.

The wish that masters and pupils should remain in touch with each other after the three years at the Ecole Normale had already in 1859 inspired Pasteur to write a report on the desirableness of an annual report entitled, *Scientific Annals of the Ecole Normale.*

The initiative of pregnant ideas often is traced back to France. But, through want of tenacity, she allows those same ideas to fall into decay and they are taken up by other nations, transplanted, developed, until they come back unrecognized to their mother country. Germany had seen the possibilities of such a publication as Pasteur's projected *Annals.* Renan wrote about that time to the editors of the *Revue Germanique,* a Review intended to draw France and Germany together : " In France, nothing is made public until achieved and ripened. In Germany, a work is given out provisionally, not as a teaching, but as an incitement to think, as a ferment for the mind."

Pasteur felt all the power of that intellectual ferment. In the volume entitled *Centenary of the Ecole Normale,* M. Gernez has recalled Pasteur's enthusiasm when he spoke of those *Annals.* Was it not for former pupils, away in the provinces, a means of collaborating with their old masters and of keeping in touch with Paris?

It was in June, 1864, that Pasteur presented the first number of this publication to the Académie des Sciences. M. Gernez, who was highly thought of by Pasteur, has not related in the *Centenary* that the book opened with some of his own researches on the rotatory power of certain liquids and their steam.

At that same time, the heterogenists had at last placed themselves at the disposal of the Académie and were invited to meet Pasteur before the Natural History Commission at M. Chevreul's laboratory. "I affirm," said Pasteur, "that in any place it is possible to take up from the ambient atmosphere a determined volume of air containing neither egg nor spore and producing no generation in putrescible solutions." The Commission declared that, the whole contest bearing upon one simple fact, one experiment only should take place. The heterogenists wanted to recommence a whole series of experiments, thus reopening the discussion. The Commission refused, and the heterogenists, unwilling to concede the point, retired from the field, repudiating the arbiters that they had themselves chosen.

And yet Joly had written to the Académie, "If one only of our flasks remains pure, we will loyally own our defeat." A scientist who later became Permanent Secretary of the Académie des Sciences, Jamin, wrote about this conflict: "The heterogenists, however they may have coloured their retreat, have condemned themselves. If they had been sure of the fact—which they had solemnly engaged to prove or to own themselves vanquished,—they would have insisted on showing it, it would have been the triumph of their doctrine."

The heterogenists appealed to the public. A few days after their defeat, Joly gave a lecture at the Faculty of Medicine. He called the trial, as decided on by the Commission, a " circus competition "; he was applauded by those who saw other than scientific questions in the matter. The problem was now coming down from mountains and laboratories into the arena of society discussions. If all comes from a germ, people said, whence came the first germ? We must bow before that mystery, said Pasteur; it is the question of the origin of all things, and absolutely outside the domain of scientific research. But an invincible curiosity exists amongst most men which cannot admit that science should have the wisdom to content itself with the vast space between the beginning of the world and the unknown future. Many people transform a question of fact into a question of faith. Though Pasteur had brought into his researches a solely scientific preoccupation, many people approved or blamed him as the defender of a religious cause.

Vainly had he said, "There is here no question of religion, philosophy, atheism, materialism, or spiritualism. I might even add that they do not matter to me as a scientist. It is a question of fact; when I took it up I was as ready to be convinced by experiments that spontaneous generation exists as I am now persuaded that those who believe it are blind-folded."

It might have been thought that Pasteur's arguments were in support of a philosophical theory! It seemed impossible to those whose ideas came from an ardent faith, from the influence of their surroundings, from personal pride or from interested calculations to understand that a man should seek truth for its own sake and with no other object than to proclaim it. Hostilities were opened, journalists kept up the fire. A priest, the Abbé Moigno spoke of converting unbelievers through the proved non-existence of spontaneous generation. The celebrated novelist, Edmond About, took up Pouchet's cause with sparkling irony. "M. Pasteur preached at the Sorbonne amidst a concert of applause which must have gladdened the angels."

Thus, among the papers and reviews of that time we can follow the divers ideas brought out by these discussions. Guizot, then almost eighty, touched on this problem with the slightly haughty assurance of one conscious of having given much thought to his beliefs and destiny. "Man has not been formed through spontaneous generation, that is by a creative and organizing force inherent in matter; scientific observation daily overturns that theory, by which, moreover, it is impossible to explain the first appearance upon the earth of man in his complete state." And he praised "M. Pasteur, who has brought into this question the light of his scrupulous criticism."

Nisard was a wondering witness of what took place in the small laboratory of the Ecole Normale. Ever preoccupied by the relations between science and religion, he heard with some surprise Pasteur saying modestly, "Researches on primary causes are not in the domain of Science, which only recognizes facts and phenomena which it can demonstrate."

Pasteur did not disinterest himself from the great problems which he called the eternal subjects of men's solitary meditations. But he did not admit the interference of religion with science any more than that of science with religion.

His eagerness during a conflict was only equalled by his absolute forgetfulness after the conflict was over. He answered some one who, years later, reminded him of that past so full of attacks and praises. "A man of science should think of what will be said of him in the following century, not of the insults or the compliments of one day."

Pasteur, anxious to regain lost time, hurried to return to his studies on wine. "Might not the diseases of wines," he said at the Académie des Sciences in January, 1864, "be caused by organized ferments, microscopic vegetations, of which the germs would develop when certain circumstances of temperature, of atmospheric variations, of exposure to air, would favour their evolution or their introduction into wines? . . . I have indeed reached this result that the alterations of wines are co-existent with the presence and multiplication of microscopic vegetations." Acid wines, bitter wines, "ropy" wines, sour wines, he had studied them all with a microscope, his surest guide in recognizing the existence and form of the evil.

As he had more particularly endeavoured to remedy the cause of the acidity which often ruins the Jura red or white wines in the wood, the town of Arbois, proud of its celebrated rosy and tawny wines, placed an impromptu laboratory at his disposal during the holidays of 1864; the expenses were all to be covered by the town. "This spontaneous offer from a town dear to me for so many reasons," answered Pasteur to the Mayor and Town Council, "does too much honour to my modest labours, and the way in which it is made covers me with confusion." He refused it however, fearing that the services he might render should not be proportionate to the generosity of the Council. He preferred to camp out with his curators in an old coffee room at the entrance of the town, and they contented themselves with apparatus of the most primitive description, generally made by some local tinker or shoeing smith.

The problem consisted, in Pasteur's view, in opposing the development of organized ferments or parasitic vegetations, causes of the diseases of wines. After some fruitless endeavours to destroy all vitality in the germs of these parasites, he found that it was sufficient to keep the wine for a few moments at a temperature of 50° C. to 60° C. "I have also ascertained that wine was never altered by that preliminary operation, and as nothing prevents it afterwards from undergoing the gradual action of the oxygen in the air—the only cause, as I think, of its improvement with age—it is evident that this process offers every advantage."

It seems as if that simple and practical means, applicable to every quality of wine, now only had to be tried. But not so. Every progress is opposed by prejudice, petty jealousies, indolence even. A devoted obstinacy is required in order to overcome this opposition. Pasteur's desire was that his country should benefit by his discovery. An Englishman had written to him : " People are astonished in France that the sale of French wines should not have become more extended here since the Commercial Treaties. The reason is simple enough. At first we eagerly welcomed those wines, but we soon had the sad experience that there was too much loss occasioned by the diseases to which they are subject."

Pasteur was in the midst of those discussions, experimental sittings, etc., when J. B. Dumas suddenly asked of him the greatest of sacrifices, that of leaving the laboratory.

CHAPTER VI

An epidemic was ruining in terrible proportions the industry of the cultivation of silkworms. J. B. Dumas had been desired, as Senator, to draw up a report on the wishes of over 3,500 proprietors in sericicultural departments, all begging the public authorities to study the question of the causes of the protracted epidemic. Dumas was all the more preoccupied as to the fate of sericiculture that he himself came from one of the stricken departments. He was born on July 14, 1800, in one of the back streets of the town of Alais, to which he enjoyed returning as a celebrated scientist and a dignitary of the Empire. He gave much attention to all the problems which interested the national prosperity and considered that the best judges in these matters were the men of science. He well knew the conscientious tenacity—besides other characteristics—which his pupil and friend brought into any undertaking, and anxiously urged him to undertake this study. "Your proposition," wrote Pasteur in a few hurried lines, "throws me into a great perplexity; it is indeed most flattering and the object is a high one, but it troubles and embarrasses me l Remember, if you please, that I have never even touched a silkworm. If I had some of your knowledge on the subject I should not hesitate; it may even come within the range of my present studies. However, the recollection of your many kindnesses to me would leave me bitter regrets if I were to decline your pressing invitation. Do as you like with me." On May 17, 1865, Dumas wrote : " I attach the greatest value to seeing your attention fixed on the question which interests my poor country; the distress is beyond anything you can imagine."

Before his departure for Alais, Pasteur had read an essay on the history of the silkworm, published by one of his col-

leagues, Quatrefages, born like Dumas in the Gard. Quatrefages attributed to an Empress of China the first knowledge
of the art of utilizing silk, more than 4,000 years ago. The
Chinese, in possession of the precious insect, had jealously
preserved the monopoly of its culture, even to the point of
making it a capital offence to take beyond the frontiers of the
Empire the eggs of the silkworm. A young princess, 2,000
years later, had the courage to infringe this law for love of
her betrothed, whom she was going to join in the centre of
Asia, and also through the almost equally strong desire to
continue her fairy-like occupation after her marriage.

Pasteur appreciated the pretty legend, but was more interested in the history of the acclimatizing of the mulberry
tree. From Provence Louis XI took it to Touraine : Catherine
de Medici planted it in Orléanais. Henry IV had some mulberry trees planted in the park at Fontainebleau and in the
Tuileries where they succeeded admirably. He also encouraged a *Treatise on the Gathering of Silk* by Olivier de
Serres. This earliest agricultural writer in France was much
appreciated by the king, in spite of the opposition of Sully,
who did not believe in this new fortune for France. Docu-
mentary evidence is lacking as to the development of the silk
industry.

From 1700 to 1788, wrote Quatrefages, France produced
annually about 6,000,000 kilogrammes of cocoons. This was
decreased by one-half under the Republic; wool replaced silk
perhaps from necessity, perhaps from affectation.

Napoleon I restored that luxury. The sericicultural industry
prospered from the Imperial Epoch until the reign of Louis
Philippe, to such an extent as to reach in one year a total of
20,000,000 kilogrammes of cocoons, representing 100,000,000
francs. The name of Tree of Gold given to the mulberry, had
never been better deserved.

Suddenly all these riches fell away. A mysterious disease
was destroying the nurseries. " Eggs, worms, chrysalides,
moths, the disease may manifest itself in all the organs,"
wrote Dumas in his report to the Senate. " Whence does it
come? how is it contracted? No one knows. But its invasion is recognized by little brown or black spots." It was
therefore called " corpuscle disease "; it was also designated
as " *gattine* " from the Italian *gattino*, kitten ; the sick worms
held up their heads and put out their hooked feet like cats about

to scratch. But of all those names, that of "pébrine" adopted by Quatrefages was the most general. It came from the patois word *pébré* (pepper). The spots on the diseased worms were, in fact, rather like pepper grains.

The first symptoms had been noticed by some in 1845, by others in 1847. But in 1849 it was a disaster. The South of France was invaded. In 1853, seed had to be procured from Lombardy. After one successful year the same disappointments recurred. Italy was attacked, also Spain and Austria. Seed was procured from Greece, Turkey, the Caucasus, but the evil was still on the increase; China itself was attacked, and, in 1864, it was only in Japan that healthy seed could be found.

Every hypothesis was suggested, atmospheric conditions, degeneration of the race of silkworms, disease of the mulberry tree, etc.—books and treatises abounded, but in vain.

When Pasteur started for Alais (June 16, 1865), entrusted with this scientific mission by the Minister of Agriculture, his mind saw but that one point of interrogation, "What caused these fatal spots?" On his arrival he sympathetically questioned the Alaisians. He received confused and contradictory answers, indications of chimerical remedies; some cultivators poured sulphur or charcoal powder on the worms, some mustard meal or castor sugar; ashes and soot were used, quinine powders, etc. Some cultivators preferred liquids, and syringed the mulberry leaves with wine, rum or absinthe. Fumigations of chlorine, of coal tar, were approved by some and violently objected to by others. Pasteur, more desirous of seeking the origin of the evil than of making a census of these remedies, unceasingly questioned the nursery owners, who invariably answered that it was something like the plague or cholera. Some worms languished on the frames in their earliest days, others in the second stage only, some passed through the third and fourth moultings, climbed the twig and spun their cocoon. The chrysalis became a moth, but that diseased moth had deformed antennæ and withered legs, the wings seemed singed. Eggs (technically called seed) from those moths were inevitably unsuccessful the following year. Thus, in the same nursery, in the course of the two months that a larva takes to become a moth, the pébrine disease was alternately sudden or insidions : it burst out or disappeared, it hid itself within the chrysalis and reappeared in the moth or the eggs of a moth which had seemed sound. The discouraged Alaisians thought that nothing could overcome pébrine.

Pasteur did not admit such resignation. But he began by one aspect only of the problem. He resolved to submit those corpuscles of the silkworm which had been observed since 1849 to microscopical study. He settled down in a small *magnanerie* near Alais; two series of worms were being cultivated. The first set was full grown; it came from some Japanese seed guaranteed as sound, and had produced very fine cocoons. The cultivator intended to keep the seed of the moths to compensate himself for the failure of the second set, also of Japanese origin, but not officially guaranteed. The worms of this second series were sickly and did not feed properly. And yet these worms, seen through the microscope, only exceptionally presented corpuscles; whilst Pasteur was surprised to find some in almost every moth or chrysalis from the prosperous nursery. Was it then elsewhere than in the worms that the secret of the pébrine was to be found?

Pasteur was interrupted in the midst of his experiments by a sudden blow. Nine days after his arrival, a telegram called him to Arbois: his father was very ill. He started, full of anguish, remembering the sudden death of his mother before he had had time to reach her, and that of Jeanne, his eldest daughter, who had also died far away from him in the little house at Arbois. His sad presentiment oppressed him during the whole of the long journey, and was fully justified; he arrived to find, already in his coffin, the father he so dearly loved and whose name he had made an illustrious one.

In the evening, in the empty room above the tannery, Pasteur wrote: "Dear Marie, dear children, the dear grandfather is no more; we have taken him this morning to his last resting place, close to little Jeanne's. In the midst of my grief I have felt thankful that our little girl had been buried there. . . . Until the last moment I hoped I should see him again, embrace him for - the last time . . . but when I arrived at the station I saw some of our cousins all in black, coming from Salins; it was only then that I understood that I could but accompany him to the grave.

"He died on the day of your first communion, dear Cécile; those two memories will remain in your heart, my poor child. I had a presentiment of it when that very morning, at the hour when he was struck down, I was asking you to pray for

the grandfather at Arbois. Your prayers will have been acceptable unto God, and perhaps the dear grandfather himself knew
of them and rejoiced with dear little Jeanne over Cécile's
piety.

"I have been thinking all day of the marks of affection I
have had from my father. For thirty years I have been his
constant care, I owe everything to him. When I was young
he kept me from bad company and instilled into me the habit
of working and the example of the most loyal and best-filled
life. He was far above his position both in mind and in character. . . . You did not know him, dearest Marie, at the
time when he and my mother were working so hard for the
children they loved, for me especially, whose books and schooling cost so much. . . . And the touching part of his affection for me is that it never was mixed with ambition. You
remember that he would have been pleased to see me the headmaster of Arbois College? He foresaw that advancement
would mean hard work, perhaps detrimental to my health.
And yet I am sure that some of the success in my scientific
career must have filled him with joy and pride; his son! his
name! the child he had guided and cherished! My dear
father, how thankful I am that I could give him some satisfaction!

"Farewell, dearest Marie, dear children. We shall often
talk of the dear grandfather. How glad I am that he saw you
all again a short time ago, and that he lived to know little
Camille. I long to see you all, but must go back to Alais, for
my studies would be retarded by a year if I could not spend
a few days there now.

"I have some ideas on this disease, which is indeed a scourge
for all those southern departments. The one *arrondissement*
of Alais has lost an income of 120,000,000 francs during the
last fifteen years. M. Dumas is a million times right; it must
be seen to, and I am going to continue my experiments. I am
writing to M. Nisard to have the admission examinations in my
absence, which can easily be done."

Nisard wrote to him (June 19): "My dear friend, I heard
of your loss, and I sympathize most cordially with you. . . .
Take all the time necessary to you. You are away in the
service of science, probably of humanity. Everything will be
done according to your precise indications. I foresee no
difficulty . . . , everything is going on well at the Ecole.

In spite of your reserve—which is a part of your talent—I see that you are on the track, as M. Biot would have said, and that you will have your prey. Your name will stand next to that of Olivier de Serres in the annals of sericiculture."

On his return to Alais Pasteur went back to his observations with his scientific ardour and his customary generous eagerness to lighten the burden of others. He wrote in the introduction to his *Studies on Silkworm Disease* the following heartfelt lines—

" A traveller coming back to the Cévennes mountains after an absence of fifteen years would be saddened to see the change wrought in that countryside within such a short time. Formerly he might have seen robust men breaking up the rock to build terraces against the side and up to the summit of each mountain; then planting mulberry trees on these terraces. These men, in spite of their hard work, were then bright and happy, for ease and contentment reigned in their homes.

" Now the mulberry plantations are abandoned, the ' golden tree ' no longer enriches the country, faces once beaming with health and good humour are now sad and drawn. Distress and hunger have succeeded to comfort and happiness."

Pasteur thought with sorrow of the sufferings of the Cévenol populations. The scientific problem was narrowing itself down. Faced by the contradictory facts that one successful set of cocoons had produced corpuscled moths, while an apparently unsuccessful set of worms showed neither corpuscles nor spots, he had awaited the last period of these worms with an impatient curiosity. He saw, amongst those which had started spinning, some which as yet showed no spots and no corpuscles. But corpuscles were abundant in the chrysalides, those especially which were in full maturity, on the eve of becoming moths; and none of the moths were free from them. Perhaps the fact that the disease appeared in the chrysalis and moth only explained the failures of succeeding series. " It was a mistake," wrote Pasteur (June 26, 1865), " to look for the symptom, the corpuscle, exclusively in the eggs or the worms; either might carry in themselves the germ of the disease, without presenting distinct and microscopically visible corpuscles. The evil developed itself chiefly in the chrysalides and the moths, it was there that it should chiefly be sought. There should be an infallible means of procuring healthy seed by having recourse to moths free from corpuscles.

This idea was like a searchlight flashed into the darkness. Pasteur thus formulated his hypothesis : " Every moth containing corpuscles must give birth to diseased seed. If a moth only has a few corpuscles, its eggs will provide worms without any, or which will only develop them towards the end of their life. If the moth is much infected, the disease will show itself in the earliest stages of the worm, either by corpuscles or by other unhealthy symptoms."

Pasteur studied hundreds of moths under the microscope. Nearly all, two or three couples excepted, were corpuscled, but that restricted quantity was increased by a precious gift. Two people, who had heard Pasteur ventilate his theories, brought him five moths born of a local race of silkworms and nurtured in the small neighbouring town of Anduze in the Turkish fashion, i.e. without any of the usual precautions consisting in keeping the worms in nurseries heated at an equal temperature. Everything having been tried, this system had also had its turn, without any appreciable success. By a fortunate circumstance, four out of those five moths were healthy.

Pasteur looked forward to the study in comparisons that the following spring would bring when worms were hatched both from the healthy and the diseased seed. In the meanwhile, only a few of the Alaisians, including M. Pagès, the Mayor, and M. de Lachadenède, really felt any confidence in these results. Most of the other silkworm cultivators were disposed to criticize everything, without having the patience to wait for results. They expressed much regret that the Government should choose a " mere chemist " for those investigations instead of some zoologist or silkworm cultivator. Pasteur only said, " Have patience."

He returned to Paris, where fresh sorrow awaited him Camille, his youngest child, only two years old, was seriously ill. He watched over her night after night, spending his days at his task in the laboratory, and returning in the evening to the bedside of his dying child. During that same period he was asked for an article on Lavoisier by J. B. Dumas, who had been requested by the Government to publish his works.

" No one," wrote Dumas to Pasteur—" has read Lavoisier with more attention than you have ; no one can judge of him better. . . . The chance which caused me to be born before you has placed me in communication with surroundings and with men in whom I have found the ideas and feelings which have guided me in this work. But, had it been yours, I should have allowed no one else to be the first in drawing the world's attention to it. It is from this motive, also from a certain conformity of tastes and of principles which has long made you dear to me, that I now ask you to give up a few hours to Lavoisier."

"My dear and illustrious master," answered Pasteur (July 18, 1865), "in the face of your letter and its expressions of affectionate confidence, I cannot refuse to submit to you a paper which you must promise to throw away if it should not be exactly what you want. I must also ask you to grant me much time, partly on account of my inexperience, and partly on account of the fatigue both mental and bodily imposed on me by the illness of our dear child."

Dumas replied : "Dear friend and colleague, I thank you for your kind acquiescence in Lavoisier's interests, which might well be your own, for no one at this time represents better than you do his spirit and method,—a method in which reasoning had more share than anything else.

"The art of observation and that of experimentation are very distinct. In the first case, the fact may either proceed from logical reasons or be mere good fortune; it is sufficient to have some penetration and the sense of truth in order to profit by it. But the art of experimentation leads from the first to the last link of the chain, without hesitation and without a blank, making successive use of Reason, which suggests an alternative, and of Experience, which decides on it, until, starting from a faint glimmer, the full blaze of light is reached. Lavoisier made this art into a method, and you possess it to a degree which always gives me a pleasure for which I am grateful to you.

"Take your time. Lavoisier has waited seventy years! It is a century since his first results were produced! What are weeks and months?

"I feel for you with all my heart! I know how heartrending are those moments by the deathbed of a suffering child. I hope and trust this great sorrow will be spared you, as indeed you deserve that it should be."

The promise made by Dumas to give to France an edition of Lavoisier's works dated very far back. It was in May, 1836, in one of his eloquent lectures at the Collège de France, that Dumas had declared his intention of raising a scientific monument to the memory of this, perhaps the greatest of all French scientists. He had hoped that a Bill would be passed by the Government of Louis Philippe decreeing that this edition of Lavoisier's works would be produced at the expense of the State. But the usual obstacles and formalities came in the way. Governments succeeded each other, and it was only in 1861 that Dumas obtained the decree he wished for and that the book appeared.

Certainly Pasteur knew and admired as much as any one the discoveries of Lavoisier. But, in the presence of the series of labours accomplished, in spite of many other burdens, during that life cut off in its prime by the Revolutionary Tribunal (1792), labours collated for the first time by Dumas, Pasteur was filled with a new and vivid emotion. His logic in reasoning and his patience in observing nature had in no wise diminished the impetuous generosity of his feelings; a beautiful book, a great discovery, a brilliant exploit or a humble act of kindness would move him to tears. Concerning such a man as Lavoisier, Pasteur's curiosity became a sort of worship. He would have had the history of such a life spread everywhere. "Though one discovery always surpasses another, and though the chemical and physical knowledge accumulated since his time has gone beyond all Lavoisier's dreams," wrote Pasteur, " his work, like that of Newton and a few other rare spirits, will remain ever young. Certain details will age, as do the fashions of another time, but the foundation, the method, constitute one of those great aspects of the human mind, the majesty of which is only increased by years. . . . "

Pasteur's article appeared in the *Moniteur* and was much praised by the celebrated critic Sainte Beuve, whose literary lectures were often attended by Pasteur, between 1857 and 1861. The chronological order that we are following in this history of Pasteur's life allows us to follow the ideas and feelings with which he lived his life of hard daily work combined with daily devotion to others. Joys and sorrows can be chronicled, thanks to the confidences of those who loved him. His fame is indeed part of the future, but the tenderness which he inspired revives the memories of the past.

In September, 1865, little Camille died. Pasteur took the tiny coffin to Arbois and went back to his work. A letter written in November alludes to the depth of his grief.

It was à propos of a candidature to the Académie des

Sciences, Sainte Beuve was asked to help that of a young friend of his, Charles Robin. Robin occupied a professor's chair specially created for him at the *Faculté de Médecine*; he had made a deep microscopical study of the tissues of living bodies, of cellular life, of all which constitutes histology. He was convinced that outside his own studies, numerous questions would fall more and more into the domain of experimentation, and he believed that the faith in spiritual things could not " stand the struggle against the spirit of the times, wholly turned to positive things." He did not, like Pasteur, understand the clear distinction between the scientist on the one hand and the man of sentiment on the other, each absolutely independent. Neither did he imitate the reserve of Claude Bernard who did not allow himself to be pressed' by any urgent questioner into enrolment with either the believers or the unbelievers, but answered : " When I am in my laboratory, I begin by shutting the door on materialism and on spiritualism ; I observe facts alone ; I seek but the scientific conditions under which life manifests itself." Robin was a disciple of Auguste Comte, and proclaimed himself a Positivist, a word which for superficial people was the equivalent of materialist. The same efforts which had succeeded in keeping Littré out of the Académie Française in 1863 were now attempted in order to keep Robin out of the Académie des Sciences in 1865.

Sainte Beuve, whilst studying medicine, had been a Positivist ; his quick and impressionable nature had then turned to a mysticism which had inspired him to pen some fine verses. He had now returned to his former philosophy, but kept an open mind, however, criticism being for him not the art of dictating, but of understanding, and he was absolutely averse to irrelevant considerations when a candidature was in question.

The best means with Pasteur, who was no diplomat, was to go straight to the point. Sainte Beuve therefore wrote to him : " Dear Sir, will you allow me to be indiscreet enough to solicit your influence in favour of M. Robin, whose work I know you appreciate?

" M. Robin does not perhaps belong to the same philosophical school as you do ; but it seems to me—from an outsider's point of view—that he belongs to the same scientific school. If he should differ essentially—whether in metaphysics or otherwise—would it not be worthy of a great scientist to take none but positive work into account? Nothing more, nothing less.

"Forgive me ; I have much resented the injustice towards you of certain newspapers, and I have sometimes asked myself if there were not some simple means of showing up all that nonsense, and of disproving those absurd and ill-intentioned statements. If M. Robin deserves to be of the Académie why should he not attain to it through you?

"My sense of gratitude towards you for those four years during which you have done me the honour of including such a man as you are in my audience, also a feeling of friendship, are carrying me too far. I intended to mention this to you the other day at the Princess's ; she had wished me to do so, but I feel bolder with a pen.   "

The Princess in question was Princess Mathilde. Her salon, a rendezvous of men of letters, men of science and artists, was a sort of second Academy which consoled Théophile Gautier for not belonging to the other. Sainte Beuve prided himself on being, so to speak, honorary secretary to this accomplished and charming hostess.

Pasteur answered by return of post. "Sir and illustrious colleague, I feel strongly inclined towards M. Robin, who would represent a new scientific element at the Academy—the microscope applied to the study of the human organism. I do not trouble about his philosophical school save for the harm it may do to his work. . . . I confess frankly, however, that I am not competent on the question of our philosophical schools. Of M. Comte I have only read a few absurd passages ; of M. Littré I only know the beautiful pages you were inspired to write by his rare knowledge and some of his domestic virtues. My philosophy is of the heart and not of the mind, and I give myself up, for instance, to those feelings about eternity which come naturally at the bedside of a cherished child drawing its last breath. At those supreme moments, there is something in the depths of our souls which tells us that the world may be more than a mere combination of phenomena proper to a mechanical equilibrium brought out of the chaos of the elements simply through the gradual action of the forces of matter. I admire them all, our philosophers ! We have experiments to straighten and modify our ideas, and we constantly find that nature is other than we had imagined. They, who are always guessing, how can they know ! . . ."

Sainte Beuve was probably not astonished at Pasteur's somewhat hasty epithet applied to Auguste Comte, whom he had
himself defined as " an obscure, abstruse, often diseased brain."
After Robin's election he wrote to his "dear and learned colleague "—

" I have not allowed myself to thank you for the letter, so
beautiful, if I may say so, so deep and so exalted in thought,
which you did me the honour of writing in answer to mine.
Nothing now forbids me to tell you how deeply I am struck
with your way of thinking and with your action in this
scientific matter."

That "something in the depths of our souls " of which
Pasteur spoke in his letter to Sainte Beuve, was often perceived in his conversation; absorbed as he was in his
daily task, he yet carried in himself a constant aspiration
towards the Ideal, a deep conviction of the reality of the
Infinite and a trustful acquiescence in the Mystery of the
universe.

During the last term of the year 1865, he turned from his
work for a time in order to study cholera. Coming from Egypt,
the scourge had lighted on Marseilles, then on Paris, where it
made in October more than two hundred victims per day; it
was feared that the days of 1832 would be repeated, when the
deaths reached twenty-three per 1,000. Claude Bernard,
Pasteur, and Sainte Claire Deville went into the attics of the
Lariboisière hospital, above a cholera ward.

" We had opened," said Pasteur, "one of the ventilators
communicating with the ward; we had adapted to the opening
a glass tube surrounded by a refrigerating mixture, and we
drew the air of the ward into our tube, so as to condense
into it as many as we could of the products of the air in the
ward."

Claude Bernard and Pasteur afterwards tried blood taken
from patients, and many other things; they were associated in
those experiments, which gave no result. Henri Sainte Claire
Deville once said to Pasteur, " Studies of that sort require
much courage." " What about duty? " said Pasteur simply,
in a tone, said Deville afterwards, worth many sermons. The
cholera did not last long; by the end of the autumn all danger
had disappeared.

Napoleon the Third loved science, and found in it a sense
of assured stability which politics did not offer him. He de-

sired Pasteur to come and spend a week at the Palace of Compiègne.

The very first evening a grand reception took place. The diplomatic world was represented by M. de Budberg, ambassador of Russia, and the Prussian ambassador, M. de Goltz. Among the guests were : Dr. Longet, celebrated for his researches and for his *Treatise on Physiology*, a most original physician, whose one desire was to avoid patients and so have more time for pure science ; Jules Sandean, the tender and delicate novelist, with his somewhat heavy aspect of a captain in the Garde Nationale ; Paul Baudry, the painter, then in the flower of his youth and radiant success ; Paul Dubois, the conscientious artist of the *Chanteur Florentin* exhibited that very year ; the architect, Viollet le Duc, an habitué of the palace. The Emperor drew Pasteur aside towards the fireplace, and the scientist soon found himself instructing his Sovereign, talking about ferments and molecular dissymmetry.

Pasteur was congratulated by the courtiers on the favour shown by this immediate confidential talk, and the Empress sent him word that she wished him to talk with her also. Pasteur remembered this conversation, an animated one, a little disconnected, chiefly about animalculæ, infusories and ferments. When the guests returned to the immense corridor into which the rooms opened, each with the name of the guests on the door, Pasteur wrote to Paris for his microscope and for some samples of diseased wines.

The next morning a stag hunt was organized ; riders in handsome costumes, open carriages drawn by six horses and containing guests, entered the forest ; a stag was soon brought to bay by the hounds. In the evening, after dinner, there was a torchlight procession in the great courtyard. Amid a burst of trumpets, the footmen in state livery, standing in a circle, held aloft the flaming torches. In the centre, a huntsman held part of the carcase of the stag and waved it to and fro before the greedy eyes of the hounds, who, eager to hurl themselves upon it, and now restrained by a word, then let loose, and again called back all trembling at their discomfiture, were at length permitted to rush upon and devour their prey.

The next day offered another item on the programme, a visit to the castle of Pierrefonds, marvellously restored by

Viollet le Duc at the expense of the Imperial purse. Pasteur, who, like the philosopher, might have said, "I am never bored but when I am being entertained," made his arrangements so that the day should not be entirely wasted. He made an appointment for his return with the head butler, hoping to find a few diseased wines in the Imperial cellar. That department, however, was so well administered that he was only able to find seven or eight suspicious-looking bottles. The tall flunkeys, who scarcely realized the scientific interest offered by a basketful of wine bottles, watched Pasteur more or less ironically as he returned to his room, where he had the pleasure of finding his microscope and case of instruments sent from the Rue d'Ulm. He remained upstairs, absorbed as he would have been in his laboratory, in the contemplation of a drop of bitter wine revealing the tiny mycoderma which caused the bitterness.

In the meanwhile some of the other guests were gathered in the smoking room, smilingly awaiting the Empress's five o'clock tea, whilst others were busy with the preparations for the performance of Racine's *Plaideurs*, which Provost, Regnier, Got, Delaunay, Coquelin, and Mademoiselle Jouassain were going to act that very evening in the theatre of the palace.

On the Sunday, at 4 p.m., he was received privately by their Majesties, for their instruction and edification. He wrote in a letter to a friend: "I went to the Emperor with my microscope, my wine samples, and all my paraphernalia. When I was announced, the Emperor came up to meet me and asked me to come in. M. Conti, who was writing at a table, rose to leave the room, but was invited to stay. Then he fetched the Empress, and I began to show their Majesties various objects under the microscope and to explain them; it lasted a whole hour."

The Empress had been much interested, and wished that her five o'clock friends—who were waiting in the room where tea was served—should also acquire some notions of these studies. She merrily took up the microscope, laughing at her new occupation of laboratory attendant, and arrived thus laden in the drawing-room, much to the surprise of her privileged guests. Pasteur came in behind her, and gave a short and simple account of a few general ideas and precise discoveries.

In the same way, the preceding week, Le Verrier[1] had spoken of his planet, and Dr. Longet had given a lecture on the circulation of the blood. That butterfly world of the Court, taking a momentary interest in scientific things, did not foresee that the smallest discovery made in the poor laboratory of the Rue d'Ulm would leave a more lasting impression than the fêtes of the Tuileries of Fontainebleau and of Compiègne.

In the course of their private interview, Napoleon and Eugénie manifested some surprise that Pasteur should not endeavour to turn his discoveries and their applications to a source of legitimate profit. "In France," he replied, "scientists would consider that they lowered themselves by doing so."

He was convinced that a man of pure science would complicate his life, the order of his thoughts, and risk paralysing his inventive faculties, if he were to make money by his discoveries. For instance, if he had followed up the industrial results of his studies on vinegar, his time would have been too much and too regularly occupied, and he would not have been free for new researches.

"My mind is free," he said. "I am as full of ardour for the new question of silkworm disease as I was in 1863, when I took up the wine question."

What he most wished was to be able to watch the growth of the silkworms from the very first day, and to pursue without interruption this serious study in which the future of France was interested. That, and the desire to have one day a laboratory adequate to the magnitude of his works were his only ambitions. On his return to Paris he obtained leave to go back to Alais.

"My dear Raulin," wrote Pasteur to his former pupil in January, 1866. "I am again entrusted by the Minister of Agriculture with a mission for the study of silkworm disease, which will last at least five months, from February 1 to the end of June. Would you care to join me?"

[1] Le Verrier, a celebrated astronomer, at that time Director of the Paris Observatory. His calculations led him to surmise the existence of the planet Neptune, which was discovered accordingly. Adam, an English astronomer, attained the same result, by the same means, at the same time, each of the two scientists being in absolute ignorance of the work of the other. Le Verrier was the first to publish his discovery. [Trans.]

Raulin excused himself; he was then preparing, with his accustomed slow conscientiousness, his doctor's thesis, a work afterwards considered by competent judges to be a master piece.

"I must console myself," wrote Pasteur, expressing his regrets, "by thinking that you will complete your excellent thesis."

One of Raulin's fellow students at the Ecole Normale, M. Gernez, was now a professor at the Collège Louis le Grand. His mind was eminently congenial to Pasteur's. Duruy, then Minister of Public Instruction, was ever anxious to smooth down all difficulties in the path of science : he gave a long leave of absence to M. Gernez, in order that he might take Raulin's place. Another young *Normalien*, Maillot, prepared to join the scientific party, much to his delight. The three men left Paris at the beginning of February. They began by spending a few days in an hotel at Alais, trying to find a suitable house where they would set up their temporary laboratory. After a week or two in a house within the town, too far, to be convenient, from the restaurant where they had their meals, Maillot discovered a lonely house at the foot of the Mount of the Hermitage, a mountain once covered with flourishing mulberry trees, but now abandoned, and growing but a few olive trees.

This house, at Pont Gisquet, not quite a mile from Alais, was large enough to hold Pasteur, his family and his pupils ; a laboratory was soon arranged in an empty orangery.

"Then began a period of intense work," writes M. Gernez. "Pasteur undertook a great number of trials, which he himself followed in their minutest details; he only required our help over similar operations by which he tested his own. The result was that above the fatigues of the day, easily borne by us strong young men, he had to bear the additional burden of special researches, importunate visitors, and an equally importunate correspondence, chiefly dealing out criticisms "

Madame Pasteur, who had been detained in Paris for her children's education, set out for Alais with her two daughters. Her mother being then on a visit to the rector of the Chambéry Academy, M. Zevort, she arranged to spend a day or two in that town. But hardly had she arrived when her daughter Cécile, then twelve years old, became ill with typhoid fever.

Madame Pasteur had the courage not to ask her husband to leave his work and come to her; but her letters alarmed him, and the anxious father gave up his studies for a few days and arrived at Chambéry. The danger at that time seemed averted, and he only remained three days at Chambéry. Cécile, apparently convalescent, had recovered her smile, that sweet, indefinable smile which gave so much charm to her serious, almost melancholy face. She smiled thus for the last time at her little sister Marie-Louise, about the middle of May, lying on a sofa by a sunny window.

On May 21, her doctor, Dr. Flesschutt, wrote to Pasteur : "If the interest I take in the child were not sufficient to stimulate my efforts, the mother's courage would keep up my hopes and double my ardent desire for a happy issue." Cécile died on May 23 after a sudden relapse. Pasteur only arrived at Chambéry in time to take to Arbois the remains of the little girl, which were buried near those of his mother, of his two other daughters, Jeanne and Camille, and of his father, Joseph Pasteur. The little cemetery indeed represented a cup of sorrows for Pasteur.

"Your father has returned from his sad journey to Arbois," wrote Madame Pasteur from Chambéry to her son who was at school in Paris. "I did think of going back to you, but I could not leave your poor father to go back to Alais alone after this great sorrow." Accompanied by her who was his greatest comfort, and who gave him some of her own courage, Pasteur came back to the Pont Gisquet and returned to his work. M. Duclaux in his turn joined the hard-working little party.

At the beginning of June, Duruy, with the solicitude of a Minister who found time to be also a friend, wrote affectionately to Pasteur—

"You are leaving me quite in the dark, yet you know the interest I take in your work. Where are you? and what are you doing? Finding out something I feel certain. . . ."

Pasteur answered, "Monsieur le Ministre, I hasten to thank you for your kind reminder. My studies have been associated with sorrow; perhaps your charming little daughter, who used to play sometimes at M. Le Verrier's, will remember Cécile Pasteur among other little girls of her age that she used to meet at the Observatoire. My dear child was coming with her mother to spend the Easter holidays with me at Alais,

when, during a few days' stay at Chambéry, she was seized
with an attack of typhoid fever, to which she succumbed
after two months of painful suffering. I was only able to be
with her for a few days, being kept here by my work, and
full of deceiving hopes for a happy issue from that terrible
disease.

"I am now wholly wrapped up in my studies, which alone
take my thoughts from my deep sorrow.

"Thanks to the facilities which you have put in my way,
I have been able to collect a quantity of experimental observations, and I think I understand on many points this disease
which has been ruining the South for fifteen or twenty years.
I shall be able on my return to propose to the Commission of
Sericiculture a practical means of fighting the evil and suppressing it in the course of a few years.

"I am arriving at this result that there is no silkworm
disease. There is but an exaggeration of a state of things
which has always existed, and it is not difficult, in my view, to
return to the former situation, even to improve on it. The
evil was sought for in the worm and even in the seed ; that was
something, but my observations prove that it develops chiefly
in the chrysalis, especially in the mature chrysalis, at the
moment of the moth's formation, on the eve of the function
of reproduction. The microscope then detects its presence
with certitude, even when the seed and the worm seem very
healthy. The practical result is this : you have a nursery full ; it
has been successful or it has not ; you wish to know whether to
smother the cocoons or whether to keep them for reproduction.
Nothing is simpler. You hasten the development of about 100
moths through an elevation of temperature, and you examine
these moths through the microscope, which will tell you what
to do.

"The sickly character is then so easy to detect that a woman
or a child can do it. If the cultivator should be a peasant,
without the material conditions required for this study, he can
do this : instead of throwing away the moths after they have
laid their eggs, he can bottle a good many of them in brandy
and send them to a testing office or to some experienced person
who will determine the value of the seed for the following
year."

The Japanese Government sent some cases of seed supposed
to be healthy to Napoleon III, who distributed them in the

silkworm growing departments. Pasteur, in the meanwhile, was stating the results he had arrived at, and they were being much criticized. In order to avoid the pébrine, which was indeed the disease caused by the corpuscles so clearly visible through the microscope, he averred that no seed should be used that came from infected moths. In order to demonstrate the infectious character of the pébrine he would give to some worms meals of leaves previously contaminated by means of a brush dipped in water containing corpuscles. The worms absorbed the food, and the disease immediately appeared and could be found in the chrysalides and moths from those worms.

"I hope I am in the right road—close to the goal, perhaps, but I have not yet reached it," wrote Pasteur to his faithful Chappuis; "and as long as the final proof is not acquired complications and errors are to be feared. Next year, the growth of the numerous eggs I have prepared will obviate my scruples, and I shall be sure of the value of the preventive means I have indicated. It is tiresome to have to wait a year before testing observations already made; but I have every hope of success."

While awaiting the renewal of the silkworm season, he was busy editing his book on wine, full of joy at contributing to the national riches through practical application of his observations. It was, in fact, sufficient to heat the wines by the simple process already at that time known in Austria as *pasteurisation*, to free them from all germs of disease and make them suitable for keeping and for exportation. He did not accord much attention to the talk of old gourmets who affirmed that wines thus "mummified" could not mellow with age, being convinced on the contrary that the most delicate wines could only be improved by heating. "The ageing of wines," he said, "is due, not to fermentation, but to a slow oxidation which is favoured by heat."

He alluded in his book to the interest taken by Napoleon III in those researches which might be worth millions to France. He also related how the Imperial solicitude had been awakened, and acknowledged gratitude for this to General Favé, one of the Emperor's aides de camp.

The General, on reading the proofs, declared that his name must disappear. Pasteur regretfully gave in to his scruples, but wrote the following words on the copy presented to General Favé: "General, this book contains a serious omission—that of your name: it would be an unpardonable one had it not been

made at your own request, according to your custom of keeping your good works secret. Without you, these studies on
wine would not exist; you have helped and encouraged them.
Leave me at least the satisfaction of writing that name on the
first page of this copy, of which I beg you to accept the
homage, while renewing the expression of my devoted gratitude.''

Another incident gives us an instance of Pasteur's kindness
of heart. In the year 1866 Claude Bernard suffered from a
gastric disease so serious that his doctors, Rayer and Davaine,
had to admit their impotence. Bernard was obliged to leave
his laboratory and retire to his little house at St. Julien (near
Villefranche), his birthplace. But the charm of his recollections of childhood was embittered by present sadness. His
mind full of projects, his life threatened in its prime, he had
the courage, a difficult thing to unselfish people, of resolutely
taking care of himself. But preoccupied solely with his own
diet, his own body now a subject for experiments, he became
a prey to a deep melancholia. Pasteur, knowing to what extent
moral influences react on the physique, had the idea of writing
a review of his friend's works, and published it in the *Moniteur
Universel* of November 7, 1866, under the following title:
*Claude Bernard: the Importance of his Works, Teaching and
Method.* He began thus: ''Circumstances have recently
caused me to re-peruse the principal treatises which have
founded the reputation of our great physiologist, Claude
Bernard.

''I have derived from them so great a satisfaction, and my
admiration for his talent has been confirmed and increased to
such an extent that I cannot resist the somewhat rash desire
of communicating my impressions. . . .''

Amongst Claude Bernard's discoveries, Pasteur chose that
which seemed to him most instructive, and which Claude
Bernard himself appreciated most: ''When M. Bernard became in 1854 a candidate for the Académie des Sciences, his
discovery of the glycogenic functions of the liver was neither
the first nor the last among those which had already placed
him so high in the estimation of men of science; yet it was
by that one that he headed his list of the claims which could
recommend him to the suffrages of the illustrious body. That
preference on the part of the master decides me in mine.''

Claude Bernard had begun by meditating deeply on the

disease known as diabetes and which is characterized, as every-body knows, by a superabundance of sugar in the whole of the organism, the urine often being laden with it. But how is it, wondered Claude Bernard, that the quantity of sugar expelled by a diabetic patient can so far surpass that with which he is provided by the starchy or sugary substances which form part of his food? How is it that the presence of sugary matter in the blood and its expulsion through urine are never completely arrested, even when all sugary or starchy alimentation is suppressed? Are there in the human organism sugar-producing phenomena unknown to chemists and physiologists? All the notions of science were contrary to that mode of thinking; it was affirmed that the vegetable kingdom only could produce sugar, and it seemed an insane hypothesis to suppose that the animal organism could fabricate any. Claude Bernard dwelt upon it however, his principle in experimentation being this : "When you meet with a fact opposed to a prevailing theory, you should adhere to the fact and abandon the theory, even when the latter is supported by great authorities and generally adopted."

This is what he imagined, summed up in a few words by Pasteur—

" Meat is an aliment which cannot develop sugar by the digestive process known to us. Now M. Bernard having fed some carnivorous animals during a certain time exclusively with meat, he assured himself, with his precise knowledge of the most perfect means of investigation offered him by chemistry, that the blood which enters the liver by the portal vein and pours into it the nutritive substances prepared and rendered soluble by digestion is absolutely devoid of sugar; whilst the blood which issues from the liver by the hepatic veins is always abundantly provided with it. M. Claude Bernard has also thrown full light on the close connection which exists between the secretion of sugar in the liver and the influence of the nervous system. He has demonstrated, with a rare sagacity, that by acting on some determined portion of that system it was possible to suppress or exaggerate at will the production of sugar. He has done more still; he has discovered within the liver the existence of an absolutely new substance which is the natural source whence this organ draws the sugar that it produces."

Pasteur, starting from this discovery of Claude Bernard's,

spoke of the growing close connection between medicine and physiology. Then, with his constant anxiety to incite students to enthusiasm, he recommended them to read the lectures delivered by Bernard at the Collège de France. Speaking of the *Introduction to the Study of Experimental Medicine*, Pasteur wrote : "A long commentary would be necessary to present this splendid work to the reader ; it is a monument raised to honour the method which has constituted Physical and Chemical Science since Galileo and Newton, and which M. Bernard is trying to introduce into physiology and pathology. Nothing so complete, so profound, so luminous has ever been written on the true principles of the difficult art of experimentation. . . . This book will exert an immense influence on medical science, its teaching, its progress, its language even." Pasteur took pleasure in adding to his own tribute praise from other sources. He quoted, for instance, J. B. Dumas' answer to Duruy, who asked him, "What do you think of this great physiologist? " " He is not a great physiologist ; he is Physiology itself." "I have spoken of the man of science," continued Pasteur. " I might have spoken of the man in everyday life, the colleague who has inspired so many with a solid friendship, for I should seek in vain for a weak point in M. Bernard ; it is not to be found. His personal distinction, the noble beauty of his physiognomy, his gentle kindliness attract at first sight ; he has no pedantry, none of a scientist's usual faults, but an antique simplicity, a perfectly natural and unaffected manner, while his conversation is deep and full of ideas. . . ." Pasteur, after informing the public that the graver symptoms of Bernard's disease had now disappeared, ended thus : "May the publicity now given to these thoughts and feelings cheer the illustrious patient in his enforced idleness, and assure him of the joy with which his return will be welcomed by his friends and colleagues."

The very day after this article reached him (November 19, 1860) Bernard wrote to Pasteur : "My dear friend,—I received yesterday the *Moniteur* containing the superb article you have written about me. Your great praise indeed makes me proud, though I feel I am yet very far from the goal I would reach. If I return to health, as I now hope I may do, I think I shall find it possible to pursue my work in a more methodical order and with more complete means of demonstration, better indicating the general idea towards which my various efforts converge. In the meanwhile it is a very precious encouragement to me to be approved and praised by a man such as you. Your works have given you a great name, and have placed you in the first rank among experimentalists of our time. The admiration which you profess for me is indeed reciprocated ; and we must have been born to understand each other, for true science inspires us both with the same passion and the same sentiments.

"Forgive me for not having answered your first letter ; but I was really not equal to writing the notice you wanted. I have deeply felt for you in your family sorrow ; I have been through the same trial, and I can well understand the sufferings of a tender and delicate soul such as yours."

Henri Sainte Claire Deville, who was as warm-hearted as he was witty, had, on his side, the ingenious idea of editing an address of collective wishes for Claude Bernard, who answered : "My dear friend,—You are evidently as clever in inventing friendly surprises as in making great scientific discoveries. It was indeed a most charming idea, and one for which I am very grateful to you—that of sending me a collective letter from my friends. I shall carefully preserve that letter : first, because the feelings it expresses are very dear to me ; and also because it is a collection of illustrious autographs which should go down to posterity. I beg you will transmit my thanks to our friends and colleagues, E. Renan, A. Maury, F. Ravaisson and Bellaguet. Tell them how much I am touched by their kind wishes and congratulations on my recovery. It is, alas, not yet a cure, but I hope I am on a fair way to it.

"I have received the article Pasteur has written about me in the *Moniteur* ; that article paralysed the vasomotor nerves of my sympathetic system, and caused me to blush to the roots of my hair. I was so amazed that I don't know what I wrote to Pasteur ; but I did not dare say to him that he had wrongly exaggerated my merits. I know he believes all that he writes, and I am happy and proud of his opinion, because it is that of a scientist and experimentalist of the very first rank. Nevertheless, I cannot help thinking that he has seen me through the prism of his kindly heart, and that I do not deserve such excessive praise. I am more than thankful for all the marks of esteem and friendship which are showered upon me. They make me cling closer to life, and feel that I should be very foolish not to take care of myself and continue to live amongst those who love me, and who deserve my love for all the happiness they give me. I intend to return to Paris some time this month, and, in spite of your kind advice, I should like to take up my Collège de France classes again this winter. I hope to be allowed not to begin before January. But we shall talk of all this in Paris. I remain your devoted and affectionate friend."

To end this academic episode, we will quote from Joseph Bertrand's letter of thanks to Pasteur, who had sent him the article : ". . . The public will learn, among other things, that the eminent members of the Academy admire and love each other sometimes with no jealousy. This was rare in the last century, and, if all followed your example, we should have over our predecessors one superiority worth many another."

Thus Pasteur showed himself a man of sentiment as well as a man of science; the circle of his affections was enlarging, as was the scope of his researches, but without any detriment to the happy family life of his own intimate circle. That little group of his family and close friends identified itself absolutely with his work, his ideas and his hopes, each member of it willingly subordinating his or her private interests to the success of his investigations. He was at that time violently attacked by his old adversaries as well as his new contradictors. Pouchet announced everywhere that the question of spontaneous generation was being taken up again in England, in Germany, in Italy and in America. Joly, Pouchet's inseparable friend, was about to make some personal studies and to write some general considerations on the new silkworm campaign. Pasteur, who had confidently said, "The year 1867 must be the last to bear the complaints of silkworm cultivators!" went back to Alais in January, 1867. But, before leaving Paris, Pasteur wrote out for himself a list of various improvements and reforms which he desired to effect in the administration of the Ecole Normale, showing that his interest in the great school had by no means abated, in spite of his necessary absence. He brought with him his wife and daughter, and Messrs. Gernez and Maillot; M. Duclaux was to come later. The worms hatched from the eggs of healthy moths and those from diseased ones were growing more interesting every day; they were in every instance exactly what Pasteur had prophesied they would be. But besides studying his own silkworms, he liked to see what was going on in neighbouring *magnaneries*. A neighbour in the Pont Gisquet, a cultivator of the name of Cardinal, had raised with great success a brood originating from the famous Japanese seed. He was disappointed, however, in the eggs produced by the moths, and Pasteur's microscope revealed the fact that those moths were all corpuscled, in spite of their healthy origin. Pasteur did not suspect that origin, for the worms had shown health and vigour through all their stages of growth, and seemed to have issued from healthy parents. But Cardinal had raised another brood, the produce of unsound seed, immediately above these healthy worms. The excreta from this second brood could fall on to the frames of those below them, and the healthy worms had become contaminated. Pasteur demonstrated that the pébrine contagion might take place in one or two different ways : either from direct contact between the worms on the same frame, or by the soiling of the food from the very infectious excreta. The remedy for the pébrine seemed now found. "The corpuscle disease," said Pasteur, "is as easily avoided as it is easily contracted." But when he thought he had reached his goal a sudden difficulty rose in his way. Out of sixteen broods of worms which he had raised, and which presented an excellent appearance, the sixteenth perished almost entirely immediately after the first moulting. "In a brood of a hundred worms," wrote Pasteur, "I picked up fifteen or twenty dead ones every day, black and rotting with extraordinary rapidity. . . . They were soft and flaccid like an empty bladder. I looked in vain for corpuscles ; there was not a trace of them."

Pasteur was temporarily troubled and discouraged. But he consulted the writings of former students of silkworm diseases, and, when he discovered vibriones in those dead worms, he did not doubt that he had under his eyes a well characterized example of the flachery disease—a disease independent and distinct from the pébrine. He wrote to Duruy, and acquainted him with the results he had obtained and the obstacles he encountered. Duruy wrote back on April 9, 1867—

"Thank you for your letter and the good news it contains.

"Not very far from you, at Avignon, a statue has been erected to the Persian who imported into France the cultivation of madder ; what then will not be done for the rescuer of two of our greatest industries ! Do not forget to inform me when you have mastered the one or two lame facts which still stand in the way. As a citizen, as head of the Université, and, if I may say so, as your friend, I wish I could follow your experiments day by day.

" You know that I should like to found a special college at Alais. Please watch for any useful information on that subject. We will talk about it on your return.

" I am obliged to M. Gernez for his assiduous and intelligent collaboration with you."

This letter from the great Minister is all the more interesting that it is dated from the eve of the day when the law on the reorganization of primary teaching was promulgated.

The introduction into the curriculum of historical and geographical notions; the inauguration of 10,000 schools and 30,000 adult classes; the transformation of certain flagging classical colleges into technical training schools; a constant struggle to include the teaching of girls in Université organization; reforms and improvements in general teaching; the building of laboratories, etc., etc.—into the accomplishment of all these projects Duruy carried his bold and methodical activity. No one was more suited than he to the planning out of a complete system of national education. He and Pasteur were indeed fitted to understand each other, for each had in the same degree those three forms of patriotism : love for the land, memories for the past, and hero worship.

In May, 1867, Pasteur received at Alais the news that a grand prize medal of the 1867 exhibition was conferred upon him for his works on wines. He hastened to write to Dumas—

" My dear master, . . . Nothing has surprised me more— or so agreeably,—than the news of this Exhibition prize medal, which I was far from expecting. It is a new proof of your kindness, for I feel sure that I have to thank you for originating such a favour. I shall do all I can to make myself worthy of it by my perseverance in putting all difficulties aside from the subject I am now engaged in, and in which the light is growing brighter every day. If that flachery disease had not come to complicate matters, everything would be well by now. I cannot tell you how absolutely sure I now feel of my conclusions concerning the corpuscle disease. I could say a great deal about the articles of Messrs. Béchamp, Estor and Balbiani, but I will follow your advice and answer nothing . . "

Dumas had been advising Pasteur not to waste his time by

answering his adversaries and contradictors. Pasteur's system was making way; ten microscopes were set up, here and there, in the town of Alais; most seed merchants were taking up the examination of the dead moths, and the Pont-Gisquet colony had samples brought in daily for inspection. "I have already prevented many failures for next year," he wrote to Dumas (June, 1867), "but I always beg as a favour that a little of the condemned seed may be raised, so as to confirm the exactness of my judgment."

His system was indeed quite simple; at the moment when the moths leave their cocoons and mate with each other, the cultivator separates them and places each female on a little square of linen where it lays its eggs. The moth is afterwards pinned up in a corner of the same square of linen, where it gradually dries up; later on, in autumn or even in winter, the withered moth is moistened in a little water, pounded in a mortar, and the paste examined with a microscope. If the least trace of corpuscles appears the linen is burnt, together with the seed which would have perpetuated the disease.

Pasteur came back to Paris to receive his medal; perhaps his presence was not absolutely necesary, but he did not question the summons he received. He always attached an absolute meaning to words and to things, not being one of those who accept titles and homage with an inward and ironical smile.

The pageant of that distribution of prizes was well worth seeing, and July 1, 1867, is now remembered by many who were children at that time. Paris afforded a beautiful spectacle; the central avenue of the Tuileries garden, the Place de la Concorde, the Avenue des Champs Elysées, were lined along their full length by regiments of infantry, dragoons, Imperial Guards, etc., etc., standing motionless in the bright sunshine, waiting for the Emperor to pass. The Imperial carriage, drawn by eight horses, escorted by the Cent-Gardes in their pale blue uniform, and by the Lancers of the Household, advanced in triumphant array. Napoleon III sat next to the Empress, the Prince Imperial and Prince Napoleon facing them. From the Palais de l'Elysée, amidst equally magnificent ceremonial, the Sultan Abdul-Aziz and his son arrived; then followed a procession of foreign princes: the Crown Prince of Prussia, the Prince of Wales, Prince Humbert of Italy, the Duke and Duchess of Aosta, the Grand Duchess Marie of Russia, all of whom have since borne a part in

European politics. They entered the Palais de l'Industrie and sat around the throne. From the ground to the first floor an immense stand was raised, affording seats for 17,000 persons. The walls were decorated with eagles bearing olive branches, symbolical of strength and peace. The Emperor in his speech dwelt upon these hopes of peace, whilst the Empress in white satin, wearing a diadem, and surrounded by white-robed princesses, brightly smiled at these happy omens.

On their names being called out, the candidates who had won Grand Prizes, and those about to be promoted in the Legion of Honour, went up one by one to the throne. Marshal Vaillant handed each case to the Emperor, who himself gave it to the recipient. This old Field-Marshal, with his rough bronzed face, who had been a captain in the retreat from Moscow and was now a Minister of Napoleon III, seemed a natural and glorious link between the First and the Second Empires. He was born at Dijon in humble circumstances, of which he was somewhat proud, a very cultured soldier, interested in scientific things, a member of the Institute. The names of certain members of the Legion of Honour promoted to a higher rank, such as Gérôme and Meissonier, that of Ferdinand de Lesseps, rewarded for the achievement of the Suez Canal, excited great applause. Pasteur was called without provoking an equal curiosity : his scientific discoveries, in spite of their industrial applications, being as yet known but to a few. "I was struck," writes an eye-witness, "with his simplicity and gravity ; the seriousness of his life was visible in his stern, almost sad eyes."

At the end of the ceremony, when the Imperial procession left the Palais de l'Industrie, an immense chorus, accompanied by an orchestra, sang *Domine salvum fac imperatorem.*

On his return to his study in the Rue d'Ulm, Pasteur again took up the management of the scientific studies of the Ecole Normale. But an incident put an end to his directorship, while bringing perturbation into the whole of the school. Sainte Beuve was the indirect cause of this small revolution. The Senate, of which he was a member, had had to examine a protest from 102 inhabitants of St. Etienne against the introduction into their popular libraries of the works of Voltaire, J. J. Rousseau, Balzac, E. Renan, and others. The committee had approved this petition in terms which identified the report with the petition itself. Sainte Beuve, too exclusively literary in his tastes, and too radical in his opinions to be popular in the Senate, rose violently against this absolute and arbitrary judgment, forgetting everything but the jeopardy of free opinions before the excessive and inquisitorial zeal of the Senate. His speech was very unfavourably received, and one of his colleagues, M. Lacaze, aged sixty-eight, challenged him to a duel. Sainte Beuve, himself then sixty-three years old, refused to enter into what he called "the summary jurisprudence which consists in strangling a question and suppressing a man within forty-eight hours."

The students of the Ecole Normale deputed one of their number to congratulate Sainte Beuve on his speech, and wrote the following letter —

"We have already thanked you for defending freedom of thought when misjudged and attacked; now that you have again pleaded for it, we beg you to receive our renewed thanks.

"We should be happy if the expression of our grateful sympathy could console you for this injustice. Courage is indeed required to speak in the Senate in favour of the independence and the rights of thought; but the task is all the more glorious for being more difficult. Addresses are now being sent from everywhere; you will forgive the students of the Ecole Normale for having followed the general lead and having sent their address to M. Sainte Beuve."

This letter was published in a newspaper. Etienne Arago published it without remembering the Université by-laws which forbade every sort of political manifestation to the students. It had given pleasure to Sainte Beuve, the pleasure that elderly men take in the applause of youth; but he soon became uneasy at the results of this noisy publicity.

Nisard, the Director of the school, could not very well tolerate this breach of discipline. In spite of the entreaties of Sainte Beuve, the student who had signed the letter was provisionally sent back to his family. His comrades revolted at this and imperiously demanded his immediate restoration. Pasteur attempted to pacify them by speaking to them, but failed utterly; his influence was very great over his own pupils, the students on the scientific side, but the others, the "littéraires," were the most violent on this question, and he was not diplomatic and conciliating enough to bring them round. They rose in a body, marched to the door, and the whole school was soon parading the streets. " Before such disorder," concluded the *Moniteur*, relating the incident (July 10), "the authorities were obliged to order an immediate closure. The school will be reconstituted and the classes will reopen on October 15."

Both the literary and the political world were temporarily agitated; the Minister was interviewed. M. Thiers wrote to Pasteur on July 10: "My dear M. Pasteur,—I have been talking with some members of the Left, and I am certain or almost certain, that the Ecole Normale affair will be smoothed over in the interest of the students. M. Jules Simon intends to work in that direction; keep this information for yourself, and do the best you can on your side."

At the idea that the Ecole was about to be reconstituted, that is, that the three great chiefs, Nisard, Pasteur and Jacquinet, would be changed, deep regret was manifested by Pasteur's scientific students. One of them, named Didon, expressed it in these terms: "If your departure from the school is not definitely settled, if it is yet possible to prevent it, all the students of the Ecole will be only too happy to do everything in their power. . . . As for me, it is impossible to express my gratitude towards you. No one has ever shown me so much interest, and never in my life shall I forget what you have done for me."

Pasteur's interest in young men, his desire to excite in them scientific curiosity and enthusiasm, were now so well known that Didon and several others who had successfully passed the entrance examinations both for the Ecole Polytechnique and the Ecole Normale, had chosen to enter the latter in order to be under him; by the *Normaliens* of the scientific section, he was not only understood and admired, but beloved, almost worshipped.

Sainte Beuve, who continued to be much troubled at the consequences of his speech, wrote to the Minister of Public Instruction in favour of the rusticated student. Duruy thought so much of Sainte Beuve that the student, instead of being exiled to some insignificant country school, was made professor of *seconde* in the college of Sens. But it was specified that in the future no letter should be written, no public responsibility taken in the name of the Ecole without the authorization of the Director.

Nisard left; Dumas had just been made President of the

Monetary Commission, thus leaving vacant a place as Inspector-General of Higher Education. Duruy, anxious to do Pasteur justice, thought this post most suitable to him as it would allow him to continue his researches. The decree was about to be signed, when Balard, professor of chemistry at the Faculty of Sciences, applied for the post. Pasteur wrote respectfully to the Minister of Public Instruction (July 31) : "Your Excelleney must know that twenty years ago, when I left the Ecole Normale, I was made a curator, thanks to M. Balard, who was then a professor at the Ecole Normale. A grateful pupil cannot enter into competition with a revered master, especially for a post where considerations of age and experience should have great weight."

When Pasteur spoke of his masters, dead or living, Biot or Senarmont, Dumas or Balard, it might indeed have been thought that to them alone he owed it that he was what he was. He was heard on this occasion, and Balard obtained the appointment.

Nisard was succeeded by M. F. Bouillier, whose place as Inspector-General of Secondary Education devolved on M. Jacquinet. The directorship of scientific studies was given to Pasteur's old and excellent friend, the faithful Bertin. After teaching in Alsace for eighteen years, he had become *maître des conférences* at the Ecole Normale in 1866, and also assistant of Regnault at the Collège de France. It had only been by dint of much persuasion that Pasteur had enticed him to Paris. "What is the good?" said the unambitious Bertin ; "beer is not so good in Paris as in Strasburg. . . . Pasteur does not understand life ; he is a genius, that is all !" But, under this apparent indolence, Bertin was possessed of the taste for and the art of teaching ; Pasteur knew this, and, when Bertin was appointed, Pasteur's fears for the scientific future of his beloved Ecole were abated. Duruy, much regretting the break of Pasteur's connection with the great school, offered him the post of *maître des conférences*, besides the chair of chemistry which Balard's appointment had left vacant at the Sorbonne. But Pasteur declined the tempting offer ; he knew the care and trouble that his public lectures cost him, and felt that the two posts would be beyond his strength ; if his time were taken up by that double task it would be almost impossible for him to pursue his private researches, which under no circumstances would he abandon.

He carried his scruples so far as to give up his chemistry professorship at the School of Fine Arts, where he had been lecturing since 1863. He had endeavoured in his lessons to draw the attention of his artist pupils, who came from so many distant places, to the actual principles of Science. "Let us always make application our object," he said, "but resting on the stern and solid basis of scientific principles. Without those principles, application is nothing more than a series of recipes and constitutes what is called routine. Progress with routine is possible, but desperately slow."

Another reason prevented him from accepting the post offered him at the Ecole Normale; this was that the tiny pavilion which he had made his laboratory was much too small and too inconvenient to accommodate the pupils he would have to teach. The only suitable laboratory at the Ecole was that of his friend, Henri Sainte Claire Deville, and Pasteur was reluctant to invade it. He had a great affection for his brilliant colleague, who was indeed a particularly charming man, still youthful in spite of his forty-nine summers, active, energetic, witty. "I have no wit," Pasteur would say quite simply. Deville was a great contrast to his two great friends, Pasteur and Claude Bernard, with their grave meditative manner. He enjoyed boarding at the Ecole and having his meals at the students' table, where his gaiety brightened and amused everybody, effacing the distance between masters and pupils and yet never losing by this familiar attitude a particle of the respect he inspired.

Sometimes, however, when preoccupied with the heavy expenses of his laboratory, he would invite himself to lunch with Duruy, from whom—as from the Emperor or any one else—he usually succeeded in coaxing what he wanted. The general state of things connected with higher education was at that time most deplorable. The Sorbonne was as Richelieu had left it—the Museum was sadly inadequate. At the Collège de France, it was indeed impossible to call by the name of laboratory the narrow, damp and unhealthy cellars, which Claude Bernard called "scientists' graves," and where he had contracted the long illness from which he was only just recovering.

Duruy understood and deplored this penury, but his voice was scarcely heard in cabinet councils, the other Ministers being absorbed in politics. Pasteur, whose self-effacing modesty disappeared when the interests of science were in question, presented to Napoleon, through the medium of his enlightened aide de camp, General Favé, the following letter, a most interesting one, for, in it, possibilities of future discoveries are hinted at, which later became accomplished facts.

"Sire,—My researches on fermentations and on microscopic organisms have opened to physiological chemistry new roads, the benefit of which is beginning to be felt both by agricultural industries and by medical studies. But the field still to be explored is immense. My great desire would be to explore it with a new ardour, unrestrained by the insufficiency of material means.

"I should wish to have a spacious laboratory, with one or two outhouses attached to it, which I could make use of when making experiments possibly injurious to health, such as might be the scientific study of putrid and infectious diseases.

"How can researches be attempted on gangrene, virus or inoculations, without a building suitable for the housing of animals, either dead or alive? Butchers' meat in Europe reaches an exorbitant price, in Buenos Ayres it is given away. How, in a small and incomplete laboratory, can experiments be made, and various processes tested, which would facilitate its transport and preservation? The so-called 'splenic fever' costs the Beauce [1] about 4,000,000 francs annually; it would be indispensable to go and spend some weeks in the neighbourhood of Chartres during several consecutive summers, and make minute observations.

"These researches and a thousand others which correspond in my mind to the great act of transformation after death of organic matter, and the compulsory return to the ground and atmosphere of all which has once been living, are only compatible with the installation of a great laboratory. The time has now come when experimental science should be freed from its bonds "

The Emperor wrote to Duruy the very next day, desiring that Pasteur's wish should be acceded to. Duruy gladly acquiesced and plans began to be drawn out. Pasteur, who scarcely dared believe in these bright hopes, was consulted about the situation, size, etc., of the future building, and

[1] Ancient name of the high flat ground surrounding Chartres and including parts of the Departments of Eure et Loir, Loir et Cher, Loiret and Seine et Oise. These plains are very fertile, the soil being extremely rich, and produce cereals chiefly. [Trans.]

looked forward to obtaining the help of Ranlin, his former pupil, when he had room enough to experiment on a larger scale. The proposed site was part of the garden of the Ecole Normale, where the pavilion already existing could be greatly added to.

In the meanwhile Pasteur was interviewed by the Mayor and the President of the Chamber of Commerce of Orleans, who begged him to come to Orleans and give a public lecture on the results of his studies on vinegar. He consented with pleasure, ever willing to attempt awakening the interest of the public in his beloved Science—" Science, which brings man nearer to God."

It was on the Monday, November 11, at 7.30 p.m., that Pasteur entered the lecture room at Orleans. A great many vinegar manufacturers, some doctors, apothecaries, professors, students, even ladies, had come to hear him. An account in a contemporary local paper gives us a description of the youngest member of the Académie des Sciences as he appeared before the Orleans public. He is described as of a medium height, his face pale, his eyes very bright through his glasses, scrupulously neat in his dress, with a tiny Legion of Honour rosette in his button hole.

He began his lecture with the following simple words : " The Mayor and the President of the Chamber of Commerce having heard that I had studied the fermentation which produces vinegar, have asked me to lay before the vinegar makers of this town the results of my work. I have hastened to comply with their request, fully sharing in the desire which instigated it, that of being useful to an industry which is one of the sources of the fortune of your city and of your department."

He tried to make them understand scientifically the well known fact of the transformation of wine into vinegar. He showed that all the work came from a little plant, a microscopic fungus, the *mycoderma aceti*. After exhibiting an enlarged picture of that mycoderma, Pasteur explained that the least trace of that little vinegar-making plant, sown on the surface of any alcoholic and slightly acid liquid, was sufficient to produce a prodigious extension of it ; in summer or artificial heat, said Pasteur, a surface of liquid of the same area as the Orleans Lecture room could be covered in forty-eight hours. The mycodermic veil is sometimes smooth and hardly visible, sometimes wrinkled and a little greasy to the touch. The fatty matter which accompanies the development of the plant keeps it on the surface, air being necessary to the plant; it would otherwise perish and the acetification would be arrested. Thus floating, the mycoderma absorbs oxygen from the air and fixes it on the alcohol, which becomes transformed into acetic acid.

Pasteur explained all the details in his clear powerful voice. Why,.in an open bottle, does wine left to itself become vinegar? Because, thanks to the air, and to the mycoderma aceti (which need never be sown, being ever mixed with the invisible dusts in the air), the chemical transformation of wine into vinegar can take place. Why does not a full, closed bottle become acetified? Because the mycoderma cannot multiply in the absence of air. Wine and air heated in the same vessel will not become sour, the high temperature having killed the germs of mycoderma aceti both in the wine itself and in the dusts suspended in the air. But, if a vessel containing wine previously heated is exposed to the free contact of ordinary air, the wine may become sour, for, though the germs in the wine have been killed, other germs may fall into it from the air and develop.

Finally, if pure alcoholized water does not become acetified, though germs can drop into it from the air, it is because it does not offer to those germs the food necessary to the plant —food which is present in wine but not in alcoholized water. But if a suitable aliment for the little plant is added to the water, acetification takes place.

When the acetification is complete, the mycoderma, if not submerged, continues to act, and, when not arrested in time, its oxidating power becomes dangerous; having no more alcohol to act upon, it ends by transforming acetic acid itself into water and carbonic acid gas, and the work of death and destruction is thus achieved.

Speaking of that last phase of the mycoderma aceti, he went on to general laws—laws of the universe by which all that has lived must disappear. "It is an absolute necessity that the matter of which living beings are formed should return after their death to the ground and to the atmosphere in the shape of mineral or gaseous substances, such as steam, carbonic acid gas, ammoniac gas or nitrogen—simple principles easily displaced by movements of the atmosphere and in which life is again enabled to seek the elements of its indefinite perpetuity. It is chiefly through acts of fermentation and slow combustion that this law of dissolution and return to a gaseous state is accomplished.''

Coming back to his special subject, he pointed out to vinegar manufacturers the cause of certain failures and the danger of certain errors.

It was imagined for instance that some microscopic beings, anguillulæ, of which Pasteur projected an enlarged wriggling image on the screen, and which were to be found in the tubs of some Orleans vinegar works, were of some practical utility. Pasteur explained their injurious character : as they require air to live, and as the mycoderma, in order to accomplish its work, is equally dependent on oxygen, a struggle takes place between the anguillulæ and the mycoderma. If acetification is successful, if the mycoderma spreads and invades everything, the vanquished anguillulæ are obliged to take refuge against the sides of the barrel, from which their little living army watches the least accidental break of the veil. Pasteur, armed with a magnifying glass, had many times witnessed the struggle for life which takes place between the little fungi and the tiny animals, each fighting for the surface of the liquid. Sometimes, gathering themselves into masses, the anguillulæ succecd in sinking a fragment of the mycodermic veil and victoriously destroying the action of the drowned plants.

Pasteur related all this in a vivid manner, evidently happy that his long and delicate laboratory researches should now pass into the domain of industry. He had been pleased to find that some Orleans wine merchants heated wine according to his advice in order to preserve it; and he now informed them that the temperature of 55° C. which killed germs and vegetations in wine could be applied with equal success to vinegar after it was produced. The active germs of the mycoderma aceti were thus arrested at the right moment, the anguillulæ were killed and the vinegar remained pure and unaltered. "Nothing," concluded Pasteur, "is more agreeable to a man who has made science his career than to increase the number of discoveries, but his cup of joy is full when the result of his observations is put to immediate practical use."

This year 1867 marks a specially interesting period in Pasteur's life. At Alais he had shown himself an incomparable observer, solely preoccupied with the silkworm disease, thinking, speaking of nothing else. He would rise long before any one else so as to begin earlier the study of the experiments he had started, and would give his thought and attention to some detail for hours at a time. After this minute observation he would suddenly display a marvellous ingenuity in varying tests, foreseeing and avoiding causes of error, and at last, after so many efforts, a clear and decisive experiment would come, as it had done in the cases of spontaneous generation and of ferments.

The contrasts in his mind had their parallel in his character : this usually thoughtful, almost dreamy man, absorbed in one idea, suddenly revealed himself a man of action if provoked by some erroneous newspaper report or some illogical statement, and especially when he heard of some unscrupulous silkworm seed merchant sowing ruin in poor *magnaneries* for the sake of a paltry gain. When, on his return to Paris, he found himself mixed up with the small revolution in the Ecole Normale, he was seen to efface himself modestly before his masters when honours and titles came in question. Now he had interrupted his researches in order to do a kindness to the people of Orleans, who, practical as they were, and perhaps a little disdainful of laboratory theories, had been surprised to find him as careful of the smallest detail as they themselves were.

He was then in the full maturity of his forty-five years. His great intuition, his imagination, which equalled any poet's, often carried him to a summit whence an immense horizon lay before him ; he would then suddenly doubt this imagination, resolutely, with a violent effort, force his mind to start again along the path of experimental method, and, surely and slowly, gathering proofs as he went, he would once more reach his exalted and general ideas. This constant struggle within himself was almost dramatic ; the words " Perseverance in Effort," which he often used in the form of advice to others, or as a programme for his own work, seemed to bring something far away, something infinite before his dreamy eyes.

At the end of the year, an obstacle almost arrested the great experiments he contemplated. He heard that the promises made to him were vanishing away, the necessary credit having been refused for the building of the new laboratory. And this, Pasteur sadly reflected, when millions and millions of francs were being spent on the Opera house ! Wounded in his feelings, both as a scientist and a patriot, he prepared for the *Moniteur*, then the official paper, an article destined to shake the culpable indifference of public authorities.

" . . . The boldest conceptions," he wrote, "the most legitimate speculations can be embodied but from the day when they are consecrated by observation and experiment. Laboratories and discoveries are correlative terms; if you suppress laboratories, Physical Science will become stricken with barrenness and death; it will become mere powerless information instead of a science of progress and futurity; give it back its laboratories, and life, fecundity and power will reappear. Away from their laboratories, physicists and chemists are but disarmed soldiers on a battlefield.

"The deduction from these principles is evident : if the conquests useful to humanity touch your heart—if you remain confounded before the marvels of electric telegraphy, of anæsthesia, of the daguerreotype and many other admirable discoveries—if you are jealous of the share your country may boast in these wonders—then, I implore you, take some interest in those sacred dwellings meaningly described as *laboratories*. Ask that they may be multiplied and completed. They are the temples of the future, of riches and of comfort. There humanity grows greater, better, stronger; there she can learn to read the works of Nature, works of progress and universal harmony, while humanity's own works are too often those of barbarism, of fanaticism and of destruction.

" Some nations have felt the wholesome breath of truth. Rich and large laboratories have been growing in Germany for the last thirty years, and many more are still being built; at Berlin and at Bonn two palaces, worth four million francs each, are being erected for chemical studies. St. Petersburg has spent three and a half million francs on a Physiological Institute; England, America, Austria, Bavaria have made most generous sacrifices. Italy too has made a start.

" And France?

"France has not yet begun. . . ." He mentioned the sepulchre-like cellar where the great physiologist, Claude Bernard, was obliged to live; " and where? " wrote Pasteur. " In the very establishment which bears the name of the mother country, the Collège de France ! " The laboratory of the Sorbonne was no better—a damp, dark room, one metre below the level of the street. He went on, demonstrating that the provincial Faculties were as destitute as those of Paris. " Who will believe me when I affirm that the budget of Public Instruction provides not a penny towards the progress of physical

science in laboratories, that it is through a tolerated administrative fiction that some scientists, considered as professors,
are permitted to draw from the public treasury towards the
expenses of their own work, some of the allowance made to
them for teaching purposes."

The manuscript was sent to the *Moniteur* at the beginning
of January, 1868.   It had lately been publishing mild articles
on Mussulman architecture, then on herring fishing in Norway.
The official whose business it was to read over the articles sent
to the paper literally jumped in his chair when he read this
fiery denunciation; he declared those pages must be modified,
cut down; the Administration could not be attacked in that
way, especially by one of its own functionaries!   M. Dalloz,
the editor of the paper, knew that Pasteur would never consent
to any alterations; he advised him to show the proofs to M.
Conti, Napoleon III's secretary.

"The article cannot appear in the *Moniteur*, but why not
publish it in booklet form?" wrote M. Conti to Pasteur
after having shown these revelations to the Emperor.
Napoleon, talking to Duruy the next day, January 9, showed
great concern at such a state of things.   "Pasteur is right,"
said Duruy, "to expose such deficiencies; it is the best way
to have them remedied.   Is it not deplorable, almost scan-
dalous, that the official world should be so indifferent on
questions of science?"

Duruy felt his combative instincts awakening.   How many
times, in spite of his good humour and almost Roman intre-
pidity, he had asked himself whether he would ever succeed
in causing his ideas on higher education to prevail with his colleagues, the other Ministers, who, carried away by their daily
discussions, hardly seemed to realize that the true supremacy
of a nation does not reside in speeches, but in the silent and
tenacious work of a few men of science and of letters.   Pasteur's
article entitled *Science's Budget* appeared first in the *Revue
des cours scientifiques*, then as as pamphlet.   Pasteur, not content with this, continued his campaign by impetuous speeches
whenever the opportunity offered.   On March 10, he saw himself
nearing his goal, and wrote to Ranlin : "There is now a marked
movement in favour of Science; I think I shall succeed."

Six days later, on March 16, whilst the Court was celebrat-
ing the birthday of the Prince Imperial, Napoleon III, who,
on reading Pasteur's article, had expressed his intention of

consulting not only Pasteur, but also Milne-Edwards, Claude
Bernard, and Henri Sainte Claire Deville, asked the four
scientists to his study to meet Rouher, Marshal Vaillant and
Duruy, perhaps the three men of the Empire who were best
qualified to hear them. The Emperor in his slow, detached
manner, invited each of his guests to express his opinion on
the course to follow. All agreed in regretting that pure
science should be given up. When Rouher said that it was
not to be wondered at that the reign of applied science should
follow that of pure science, " But if the sources of applications
are dried up ! " interposed the Emperor hastily. Pasteur,
asked to express his opinion (he had brought with him notes
of what he wished to say), recalled the fact that the Natural
History Museum and the Ecole Polytechnique, which had had
so great a share in the scientific movement of the early part of
the century, were no longer in that heroic period. For the last
twenty years the industrial prosperity of France had induced
the cleverest Polytechnicians to desert higher studies and
theoretical science, though the source of all applications was to
be found in theory. The Ecole Polytechnique was obliged now
to recruit its teaching staff outside, chiefly among Normaliens.
What was to be done to train future scientists? This : to
maintain in Paris, during two or three years, five or six
graduates chosen from the best students of the large schools as
curators or preparation masters, doing at the Ecole Polytechnique and other establishments what was done at the Ecole
Normale. Thanks to that special institution, science and
higher teaching would have a reserve of men who would become an honour to their country. Next, and this was the
second point, no less important than the first, scientists should
be given resources better appropriated to the pursuit of their
work ; as in Germany, for instance, where a scientist would
leave one university for another on the express condition that
a laboratory should be built for him, " a laboratory," said
Pasteur, " usually magnificent, not in its architecture (though
sometimes that is the case, a proof of the national pride in
scientific glory), but in the number and perfection of its
appliances. Besides," he added, " foreign scientists have their
private homes adjoining their laboratories and collections,"
indeed a most pressing inducement to work.

Pasteur did not suggest that a scientist should give up teaching ; he recognized, on the contrary, that public teaching forces

him to embrace in succession every branch of the science he teaches. "But let him not give too frequent or too varied lectures I they paralyze the faculties," he said, being well aware of the cost of preparing classes. He wished that towns should be interested in the working and success of their scientific establishments. The Universities of Paris, of Lyons, of Strasburg, of Montpellier, of Lille, of Bordeaux, and of Toulouse, forming as a whole the University of France, should be connected to the neighbourhood which they honour in the same way that German universities are connected with their surroundings.

Pasteur had the greatest admiration for the German system : popular instruction liberally provided, and, above it, an intellectually independent higher teaching. Therefore, when the University of Bonn resolved in that year, 1868, to offer him as a great homage the degree of M.D. on acount of his works on micro-organisms, he was proud to see his researches rated at their proper value by a neighbouring nation. He did not then suspect the other side of German nature, the military side, then very differently preoccupied. Those preoccupations were pointed out to the French Government in a spirit of prophecy, and with some patriotic anguish, by two French officers, General Ducrot, commanding since 1865 the 6th Military Division, whose headquarters were at Strasburg, and Colonel Baron Stoffel, military attaché in Prussia since 1866. Their warnings were so little heeded that some Court intrigues were even then on foot to transfer General Ducrot from Strasburg to Bourges, so that he might no longer worry people with his monomania of Prussian ambition.

On March 10, the evening of the day when the Emperor decided upon making improvements, and when Duruy felt assured, thanks to the promised allowances, that he could soon offer to French professors "the necessary appliances with which to compete with their rivals beyond the Rhine," Pasteur started for Alais, where his arrival was impatiently awaited, both by partisans and adversaries of his experiments on silkworm disease. He would much have liked to give the results of his work in his inaugural lecture at the Sorbonne. "But," he wrote to Duruy, "these are but selfishly sentimental reasons, which must be outweighed by the interest of my researches."

On his arrival he found to his joy that those who had prac-

tised seeding according to his rigorous prescriptions had met
with complete success. Other silkworm cultivators, less well
advised, duped by the decoying appearances of certain broods,
had not taken the trouble to examine whether the moths were
corpuscled; they were witnesses and victims of the failure
Pasteur had prophesied. He now looked upon pébrine as conquered; but flachery remained, more difficult to prevent, being
greatly dependent upon the accidents which traverse the life of
a silkworm. Some of those accidents happen in spite of all
precautions, such as a sudden change of temperature or a
stormy day; but at least the leaves of the mulberry tree could be
carefully kept from fermentation, or from contamination by
dusts in the nurseries. Either of those two causes was sufficient to provoke a fatal disorder in silkworms, the feeding of
which is so important that they increase to fifteen thousand
times their own weight during the first month of their life.
Accidental flachery could therefore be avoided by hygienic precautions. In order to prevent it from becoming hereditary,
Pasteur—who had pointed out that the micro-organism which
causes it develops at first in the intestinal canal of the worm
and then becomes localized in the digestive cavity of the chrysalis—advised the following means of producing a healthy
strain of silkworms : "This means," writes M. Gernez,
Pasteur's assiduous collaborator in these studies, "does not
greatly complicate operations, and infallibly ensures healthy
seed. It consists in abstracting with the point of a scalpel a
small portion of the digestive cavity of a moth, then mixing
it with a little water and examining it with a microscope. If
the moths do not contain the characteristic micro-organism, the
strain they come from may unhesitatingly be considered as
suitable for seeding. The flachery micro-organism is as easily
recognized as the pébrine corpuscle."

The seed merchants, made uneasy by these discoveries which
so gravely jeopardized their industry, spread the most slan-
derons reports about them and made themselves the willing
echo of every imposture, however incredible. M. Laurent
wrote to his daughter, Madame Pasteur, in a letter dated from
Lyons (June 6) : "It is being reported here that the failure of
Pasteur's process has excited the population of your neighbourhood so much that he has had to flee from Alais, pursued by
infuriated inhabitants throwing stones after him." Some of
these legends lingered in the minds of ignorant people.

Important news came from Paris to Pasteur in July, and on the 27th he was able to write to Ranlin : " The building of my laboratory is going to be begun ! the orders are given, and the money found. I heard this two days ago from the Minister." 30,000 francs had been allowed for the work by the Minister of Public Instruction, and an equal sum was promised by the Minister of the Emperor's household. Duruy was preparing at the same time a report on two projected decrees concerning laboratories for teaching purposes and for research. " The laboratory for research," wrote Duruy, " will not be useful to the master alone, but more so even to the students, thus ensuring the future progress of science. Students already provided with extensive theoretical knowledge will be initiated in the *teaching laboratories* into the handling of instruments, elementary manipulations, and what I may call classical practice ; this will gather them around eminent masters, from whom they will learn the art of observation and methods of experiment. . . . It is with similar institutions that Germany has succeeded in obtaining the great development of experimental science which we are now watching with an anxious sympathy."

Pasteur returned to Paris with his enthusiastic mind overflowing with plans of all kinds of research. He wanted to be there when the builders began their work on the narrow space in the Rue d'Ulm. He wrote to Raulin on August 10, asking his opinion as he would that of an architect ; then went on to say, planning out his busy holidays : " I shall leave Paris on the 16th with my wife and children to spend three weeks at the seaside, at St. George's, near Bordeaux. If you were free at the end of the month, or at the beginning of September, I wish you could accompany me to Toulon, where experiments on the heating of wines will be made by the Minister of the Navy. Great quantities of heated and of non-heated wine are to be sent to Gabon so as to test the process ; at present our colonial crews have to drink mere vinegar. A commission of very enlightened men is formed and has begun studies with which it seems satisfied. . . . See if you can join me at Bordeaux, where I shall await a notice from the chairman of the Commission, M. de Lapparent, director of naval construction at the Ministry of Marine."

The Commission mentioned by Pasteur had been considering for the last two years the expediency of applying the heating process to wines destined for the fleet and to the colonies. A first trial was made at Brest on the contents of a barrel of 500 litres, half of which was heated. Then the two wines were sealed in different barrels and placed in the ship *Jean Bart*, which remained away from the harbour for ten months. When the vessel returned, the Commission noted the limpidity and mellowness of the heated wine, adding in the official report that the wine had acquired the attractive colour peculiar to mature wines. The non-heated wine was equally limpid, but it had an astringent, almost acid flavour. It was still fit to drink, said the report, but it were better to consume it rapidly, as it would soon be entirely spoilt. Identical results were observed in some bottles of heated and non-heated wines at Rochefort and Orleans.

M. de Lapparent now organized a decisive experiment, to take place under Pasteur's superintendence. The frigate *la Sibylle* started for a tour round the world with a complete cargo of heated wine. Pasteur, who returned to Arbois for a short rest before going back to Paris, wrote from there to his early confidant, Chappuis (September 21, 1868) : "I am quite satisfied with my experiments at Toulon and with the success of the Navy tests. We heated 650 hectolitres in two days; the rapidity of this operation lends itself to quick and considerable commissariat arrangements. Those 650 hectolitres will be taken to the West Coast of Africa, together with 50 hectolitres of the same wine non-heated. If the trial succeeds, that is to say if the 650 hectolitres arrive and can be kept without alteration, and if the 50 hectolitres become spoilt (I feel confident after the experiments I have made that such will be the result), the question will be settled, and, in the future, all the wine for the Navy will be ensured against disease by a preliminary heating. The expense will not be more than five centimes per hectolitre. The result of these experiments will have a great influence on the trade, ever cautious and afraid of innovations. Yet we have seen, at Narbonne in particular, some heating practised on a large scale by several merchants who have spoken to me very favourably about it. The exportation of our French wines will increase enormously, for at present our ordinary table wines lend themselves to trade with England and other countries beyond seas, but only by means of a strong addition of alcohol, which raises their price and tampers with their hygienic qualities."

The experiments were successful. Pasteur's life was now over full. He returned to Paris at the beginning of October, and threw himself into his work, his classes at the Sorbonne, the organization of his laboratory, some further polemics on the subject of silkworm disease, and projected experiments for the following year. This accumulation of mental work brought about extreme cerebral tension.

As soon as he saw M. Gernez, he spoke to him of the coming campaign of sericiculture, of his desire to reduce his adversaries to silence by heaping proof upon proof. Nothing could relieve him from that absorbing preoccupation, not even the gaiety of Bertin, who, living on the same floor at the Ecole Normale, often used to come in after dinner and try to amuse him.

On Monday, October 19, Pasteur, though suffering from a strange tingling sensation of the left side, had a great desire to go and read to the Académie des Sciences a treatise by Salimbeni, an Italian, who, having studied and verified Pasteur's results, declared that the best means of regenerating the culture of silkworms was due to the French scientist. This treatise, the diploma of the Bonn University, the Rumford medal offered by the English, all those testimonials from neighbouring nations were infinitely agreeable to Pasteur, who was proud to lay such homage before the shrine of France. On that day, October 19, 1868, a date which became a bitter memory to his family and friends—in spite of an alarming shivering fit which had caused him to lie down immediately after lunch instead of working as usual—he insisted on going to the Academy sitting at half past two.

Mme. Pasteur, vaguely uneasy, made a pretext of some shopping beyond the Quai Conti and accompanied him as far as the vestibule of the Institute. As she was turning back, she met Balard, who was coming up with the quick step of a young man, stopped him and asked him to walk back with Pasteur, and not to leave him before reaching his own door, though indeed it seemed a curious exchange of parts to ask Balard at sixty years of age to watch over Pasteur still so young. Pasteur read Salimbeni's paper in his usual steady voice, remained until the end of the sitting and walked back with Balard and Sainte Claire Deville. He dined very lightly and went to bed at nine o'clock; he had hardly got into bed when he felt himself attacked by the strange symptoms of the afternoon. He

tried to speak, but in vain; after a few moments he was able to
call for assistance. Mme. Pasteur sent at once for Dr.
Godélier, an intimate friend of the family, an army surgeon,
Clinical Professor at the Ecole du Val-de-Grâce[1]; and Pasteur,
paralysed one moment and free again the next, explained his
own symptoms during the intervals of the dark struggle which
endangered his life.

The cerebral hæmorrhage gradually brought about absence
of movement along the entire left side. When the next morning Dr. Noël Gueneau de Mussy, going his regulation round of
the Ecole Normale students, came into his room and said, so as
not to alarm him, "I heard you were unwell, and thought I
would come to see you," Pasteur smiled the sad smile of a
patient with no illusions. Drs. Godélier and Gueneau de
Mussy decided to call Dr. Andral in consultation, and went to
fetch him at three o'clock at the Académie de Médecine. Somewhat disconcerted by the singular character of this attack of
hemiplegia, Andral prescribed the application of sixteen leeches
behind the ears; blood flowed abundantly, and Dr. Godélier
wrote in the evening bulletin (Tuesday): "Speech clearer,
some movements of the paralysed limbs; intelligence perfect."
Later, at ten o'clock: "Complains of his paralysed arm."
"It is like lead; if it could only be cut off!" groaned Pasteur.
About 2 a.m. Mme Pasteur thought all hope was gone. The
hastily written bulletin reads thus: "Intense cold, anxious
agitation, features depressed, eyes languid." The sleep which
followed was as the sleep of death

At dawn Pasteur awoke from this drowsiness. "Mental
faculties still absolutely intact," wrote M. Godélier at 12.30
on Wednesday, October 21. "The cerebral lesion, whatever
it may be, is not worse; there is an evident pause." Two
hours later the words, "Mind active," were followed by the
startling statement, "Would willingly talk science."

While these periods of calm, agitation, renewed hopes, and
despair were succeeding each other in the course of those
thirty-six hours, Pasteur's friends hastened to his bedside. He
said to Henri Sainte Claire Deville, one of the first to come:
"I am sorry to die; I wanted to do much more for my
country." Sainte Claire Deville, trying to hide his grief under

---

[1] *Val-de-Grâce.* A handsome monument of the seventeenth century,
now a military hospital. [Trans.]

apparent confidence, answered, "Never fear; you will recover, you will make many more marvellous discoveries, you will live happy days; I am your senior, you will survive me. Promise me that you will pronounce my funeral oration. . . . I wish you would; you would say nice things of me," he added between tears and smiles.

Bertin, Gernez, Duclaux, Raulin, Didon, then a curator at the Ecole Normale, Professor Auguste Lamy, the geologist Marcou (the two latter being Franche-comté friends), all claimed the privilege of helping Mme. Pasteur and M. Godélier in nursing one who inspired them all, not merely with an admiring and devoted affection, but with a feeling of tenderness amounting almost to a cult.

A private letter from a cousin, Mme. Cribier, gives an idea of those dark days (October 26, 1868): "The news is rather good this morning; the patient was able to sleep for a few hours last night, which he had not yet done. He had been so restless all day that M. Godélier felt uneasy about him and ordered complete silence in the whole flat; it was only in the study which is farthest away from the bedroom, and which has padded doors, that one was allowed to talk. That room is full from morning till night. All scientific Paris comes to inquire anxiously after the patient; intimate friends take it in turns to watch by him. Dumas, the great chemist, was affectionately insisting on taking his turn yesterday. Every morning the Emperor and Empress send a footman for news, which M. Godélier gives him in a sealed envelope. In fact, every mark of sympathy is given to poor Marie, and I hope that the worst may be spared her in spite of the alarming beginning. His mind seems so absolutely untouched, and he is still so young, that with rest and care he might yet be able to do some work. His stroke is accompanied by symptoms which are now occupying the attention of the whole Academy of Medicine. Paralysis always comes abruptly, whilst for M. Pasteur, it came in little successive fits, twenty or thirty perhaps, and was only complete at the end of twenty-four hours, which completely disconcerted the doctors who watched him, and delayed their having recourse to an active treatment. It seems that this fact is observed for the first time, and is puzzling the whole Faculty."

M. Pasteur's mind remained clear, luminous, dominating his prostrate body; he was evidently afraid that he should die

M

before having thoroughly settled the question of silkworm diseases. " One night that I was alone with him," relates M. Gernez, who hardly left his bedside during that terrible week, " after endeavouring in vain to distract his thoughts, I despairingly gave up the attempt and allowed him to express the ideas which were on his mind ; finding, to my surprise, that they had his accustomed clearness and conciseness, I wrote what he dictated without altering a word, and the next day I brought to his illustrious colleague, Dumas—who hardly credited his senses—the memorandum which appeared in the report of the Académie on October 26, 1868, a week after the stroke which nearly killed him ! It was a note on a very ingenious process for discovering in the earlier tests those eggs which are predisposed to flachery.

The members of the Academy were much cheered by the reading of this note, which seemed to bring Pasteur back into their midst.

The building of the laboratory had been begun, and hoardings erected around the site. Pasteur, from his bed, asked day by day, " How are they getting on? " But his wife and daughter, going to the window of the dining-room which overlooked the Ecole Normale garden, only brought him back vague answers, for, as a matter of fact, the workmen had disappeared from the very first day of Pasteur's illness. All that could be seen was a solitary labourer wheeling a barrow aimlesly about, probably under the orders of some official who feared to alarm the patient.

As Pasteur was not expected to recover, the trouble and expense were deemed unnecessary. Pasteur soon became aware of this, and one day that General Favé had come to see him he gave vent to some bitter feelings as to this cautious interruption of the building works, saying that it would have been simpler and more straightforward to state from the beginning that the work was suspended in the expectation of a probable demise.

Napoleon was informed of this excess of zeal, not only by General Favé, but by Sainte Claire Deville, who was a guest at Compiègne at the beginning of November, 1868. He wrote to the Minister of Public Instruction—

" My dear M. Duruy,—I have heard that—unknown to you probably—the men who were working at M. Pasteur's laboratory were kept away from the very day he became ill; he has been much affected by this circumstance, which seemed to point to his non-recovery. I beg you will issue orders that the work begun should be continued. Believe in my sincere friendship.—Napoleon."

Duruy immediately sent on this note to M. du Mesnil, whose somewhat long title was that of " Chief of the Division of Academic Administration of Scientific Establishments and of Higher Education." M. du Mesnil evidently repudiated the charge for himself or for his Minister, for he wrote in a large hand, on the very margin of the Imperial autograph—

" M. Duruy gave no orders and had to give none. It is at his solicitation that the works were undertaken, but it is the *Direction of Civic Buildings* alone which *can* have interrupted them ; the fact should be verified."

M. de Cardaillac, head of the Direction of Civic Buildings, made an inquiry and the building was resumed.

It was only on November 30 that Pasteur left his bed for the first time and spent an hour in his armchair. He clearly analyzed to himself his melancholy condition, stricken down as he was by hemiplegia in his forty-sixth year ; but having noticed that his remarks saddened his wife and daughter, he spoke no more about his illness, and only expressed his anxiety not to be a trouble, a burden, he said, to his wife, his son and daughter, and the devoted friends who helped to watch him at night.

In the daytime each offered to read to him. General Favé, whose active and inquiring mind was ever on the alert, brought him on one of his almost daily visits an ideal sick man's book, easy to read and offering food for meditation. It was the translation of an English book called *Self-Help*,[1] and it consisted in a series of biographies, histories of lives illustrating the power of courage, devotion or intelligence. The author, glad to expound a discovery, to describe a masterpiece, to relate noble enterprises, to dwell upon the prodigies which energy can achieve, had succeeded in making a homogeneous whole of these unconnected narratives, a sort of homage to Will-power.

Pasteur agreed with the English writer in thinking that the supremacy of a nation resides in " the sum total of private virtues, activities and energy." His thoughts rose higher still ; men of science could wish for a greater glory than that of con-

[1] By Dr. Smiles. [Trans.]

M 2

tributing to the fame and fortune of their country, they might aspire to originating vast benefits to the whole of humanity.

It was indeed a sad and a sublime spectacle, that of the contrast between that ardent, soaring soul and that patient helpless body. It was probably when thinking of those biographies—some of them too succinct, to his mind, Jenner's for instance—that Pasteur wrote : " From the life of men whose passage is marked by a trace of durable light, let us piously gather up every word, every incident likely to make known the incentives of their great soul, for the education of posterity." He looked upon the cult of great men as a great principle of national education, and believed that children, as soon as they could read, should be made acquainted with the heroic or benevolent souls of great men. In his pious patriotism he saw a secret of strength and of hope for a nation in its reverence for the memories of the great, a sacred and intimate bond between the visible and the invisible worlds. His soul was deeply religious. During his illness—a time when the things of this world assume their real proportions—his mind rose far beyond this earth. The Infinite appeared to him as it did to Pascal, and with the same rapture ; he was less attracted by Pascal, when, proud and disdainful, he exposes man's weakness for humiliation's sake, than when he declares that " Man is produced but for Infinity," and " he finds constant instruction in progress." Pasteur believed in material progress as well as in moral improvement ; he invariably marked in the books he was reading—Pascal, Nicole and others—those passages which were both consoling and exalting.

In one of his favourite books, *Of the Knowledge of God and of Self*, he much appreciated the passage where Bossuet ascribes to human nature " the idea of an infinite wisdom, of an absolute power, of an infallible rectitude, in one word, the idea of perfection." Another phrase in the same book seemed to him applicable to experimental method as well as to the conduct of life : " The greatest aberration of the mind consists in believing a thing because it is desirable."

With December, joy began to return to the Ecole Normale : the laboratory was progressing and seemed an embodiment of renewed hopes of further work. M. Godélier's little bulletins now ran : " General condition most satisfactory. Excellent morale ; the progress evidenced daily by the return of action in the paralysed muscles inspires the patient with great confidence.

He is planning out his future sericiculture campaign, receives many callers without too much fatigue, converses brightly and often dictates letters."

One visit was a great pleasure to Pasteur—that of the Minister, his cordial friend, Duruy, who brought him good news of the future of Higher Education. The augmented credit which was granted in the 1869 budget would make it possible to rebuild other laboratories besides that of the Ecole Normale, and also to create in other places new centres of study and research. After so many efforts and struggles, it was at last possible to foresee the day when chemistry, physics, physiology, natural history and mathematics would each have an independent department in a great province, which should be called the Practical School of Higher Studies. There would be no constraint, no hard and fast rules, no curriculum but that of free study : young men who were attracted to pure science, and others who preferred practical application, would find a congenial career before them as well as those who desired to give themselves up to teaching. It can well be imagined with what delight Pasteur heard these good tidings.

The bulletins continued to be favourable : " (December 15) : Progress slow but sure : he has walked from his bed to his armchair with some assistance. (December 22) : he has gone into the dining-room for dinner, leaning on a chair. (29th) : he has walked a few steps without support."

Pasteur saw in his convalescence but the returning means of working, and declared himself ready to start again for the neighbourhood of Alais at once, intead of taking the few months' rest he was advised to have.

He urged that, after certain moths and chrysalides, had been examined through a microscope, complete certainty would be acquired as to the condition of their seed, and that perfect seed would therefore become accessible to all tradesmen both great and small; would it not be absurd and culpable to let reasons of personal health interfere with saving so many poor people from ruin?

His family had to give way, and on January 18, exactly three months after his paralytic stroke, he was taken to the *Gare de Lyon* by his wife and daughter and M. Gernez. He then travelled, lying on the cushions of a *coupé* carriage, as far as Alais, and drove from Alais to St. Hippolyte le Fort, where

tests were being made on forced silkworms by the agricultural
society of Le Vigan.

The house he came into was cold and badly arranged. M.
Gernez improvised a laboratory, with the assistance of Maillot
and Ranlin, who had followed their master down. From his
sofa or from his bed, Pasteur directed certain experiments on
the forced specimens. M. Gernez writes : " The operations,
of which we watched the phases through the microscope, fully
justified his anticipations; and he rejoiced that he had not
given up the game." In the world of the Institute his departure was blamed by some and praised by others; but
Pasteur merely considered that one man's life is worthless if
not useful to others.

Dumas wrote to him early in February : " My dear friend
and colleague,—I have been thinking of you so much! I
dread fatigue for you, and wish I could spare it you, whilst
hoping that you may successfully achieve your great and
patriotic undertaking. I have hesitated to write to you for
fear you should feel obliged to answer. However, I should
like to have direct news of you, as detailed as possible, and,
besides that, I should be much obliged if you could send me a
line to enlighten me on the two following points—

" 1. When are you going back to Alais? And when will
your Alais broods be near enough to their time to be most
interesting to visit?

" 2. What should I say to people who beg for healthy seed
as if my pockets were full of it? I tell them it is too late;
but if you could tell me a means of satisfying them, I should
be pleased, particularly in the case of General Randon and
M. Husson. The Marshal (Vaillant) is full of solicitude for
you, and we never meet but our whole conversation turns upon
you. With me, it is natural. With him less so, perhaps, but
anyhow, he thinks of you as much as is possible, and this gives
me a great deal of pleasure. . . . Please present to Madame
Pasteur our united compliments and wishes. We wish the
South could have the virtues of Achilles' lance—of healing the
wounds it has caused.—Yours affectionately."

Pasteur was reduced to complete helplessness through having slipped and fallen on the stone floor of his uncomfortable
house, and was obliged to dictate the following letter—

" My dear master,—I thank you for thinking of the poor
invalid. I am very much in the same condition as when I

left Paris, my progress having been retarded by a fall on my left side. Fortunately, I sustained no fracture, but only bruises, which were naturally painful and very slow to disappear.

"There are now no remaining traces of that accident, and I am as I was three weeks ago. The improvement in the movements of the leg and arm appears to have begun again, but with excessive slowness. I am about to have recourse to electricity, under the advice and instructions of Dr. Godélier, by means of a small Ruhmkorff apparatus which he has kindly sent me. My brain is still very weak.

"This is how my days are spent : in the morning my three young friends come to see me, and I arrange the day's work. I get up at twelve, after having my breakfast in bed, and having had the newspaper read to me. If fine, I then spend an hour or two in the little garden of this house. Usually, if I am feeling pretty well, I dictate to my dear wife a page, or more frequently half a page, of a little book I am preparing, and in which I intend to give a short account of the whole of my observations. Before dinner, which I have alone with my wife and my little girl in order to avoid the fatigue of conversation, my young collaborators bring me a report of their work. About seven or half past, I always feel terribly tired and inclined to sleep twelve consecutive hours ; but I invariably wake at midnight, not to sleep again until towards morning, when I doze again for an hour or two. What makes me hope for an ultimate cure is the fact that my appetite keeps good, and that those short hours of sleep appear to be sufficient. You see that on the whole I am doing nothing rash, being moreover rigorously watched by my wife and little daughter. The latter pitilessly takes books, pens, papers and pencils away from me with a perseverance which causes me joy and despair.

"It is because I know your affection for your pupils that I venture to give you so many details. I will now answer the other questions in your letter.

"I shall be at Alais from April 1; that will be the time when they will begin hatching seed for the industrial campaign, which will consequently be concluded about May 20 at the latest. Seeding will take place during June, more or less early according to departments. It is indeed very late to obtain seed, especially indigenous seed prepared according to my process. I had foreseen that I should receive demands at

the last moment, and that I should do well to put by a few
ounces; but, about three weeks ago, our energetic Minister
wrote to ask me for some seed to distribute to schoolmasters,
and I promised him what I had. However I will take some
from his share and send you several lots of five grammes. The
director of a most interesting Austrian establishment has also
ordered two ounces, saying he is convinced of the excellence
of my method. His establishment is a most interesting experimental *magnanerie*, founded in a handsome Illyrian property. Lastly, I have also promised two ounces to M. le
Comte de Casabianca. One of my young men is going out to
his place in Corsica to do the seeding.

"I was much touched by what you tell me of Marshal
Vaillant's kind interest in my health, and also by his kind
thought in informing me of the encouragement given to my
studies by the Society of Agriculture. I wish the cultivators
of your South had a little of his scientific and methodical
spirit.

"Madame Pasteur joins with me in sending you and your
family, dear master, the expression of my gratitude and affectionate devotion."

The normal season for the culture of silkworms was now
aproaching, and Pasteur was impatient to accumulate the
proofs which would vouch for the safety of his method; this
had been somewhat doubted by the members of the Lyons
Silks Commission, who possessed an experimental nursery.
Most of those gentlemen averred that too much confidence
should not be placed in the micrographs. "Our Commission," thus ran their report of the preceding year, "con-
siders the examination of corpuscles as a useful indication
which should be consulted, but of which the results cannot
be presented as a fact from which absolute consequences can
be deducted."

"They *are* absolute," answered Pasteur, who did not admit
reservations on a point which he considered as invulnerable.

On March 22, 1869, the Commission asked Pasteur for a
little guaranteed healthy seed. Pasteur not only sent them
this, but also sample lots, of which he thus predicted the future
fate :

1. One lot of healthy seed, which would succeed;

2. One lot of seed, which would perish exclusively from the
corpuscle disease known as pébrine or gattine;

3. One lot of seed, which would perish exclusively from the flachery disease;

4. One lot of seeds, which would perish partly from corpuscle disease and partly from flachery.

"It seems to me," added Pasteur, "that the comparison between the results of those different lots will do more to enlighten the Commission on the certainty of the principles I have established than could a mere sample of healthy seed.

"I desire that this letter should be sent to the Commission at its next meeting, and put down in the minutes."

The Commission accepted with pleasure these unexpected surprise boxes.

About the same time one of his assistants, Maillot, started for Corsica at M. de Casabianca's request. He took with him six lots of healthy seed to Vescovato, a few miles from Bastia.

The rest of the colony returned to the Pont Gisquet, near Alais, that mulberry-planted retreat, where, according to Pasteur, everything was conducive to work. Pasteur now looked forward to his definitive victory, and, full of confidence, organized his pupils' missions. M. Duclaux, who was coming to the Pont Gisquet to watch the normal broods, would afterwards go into the Cévennes to verify the seedings made on the selection system. M. Gernez was to note the results of some seedings made by Pasteur himself the preceding year at M. Raibaud-Lange's, at Paillerols, near Digne (Basses Alpes). Ranlin alone would remain at the Pont Gisquet to study some points of detail concerning the flachery disease. So many results ought surely to reduce contradictors to silence!

"My dear friend and colleague," wrote Dumas to Pasteur, "I need not tell you with what anxiety we are watching the progress of your precious health and of your silkworm campaign. I shall certainly be at Alais at the end of the week, and I shall see, under your kind direction, all that may furnish me with the means of guiding public opinion. You have quacks to fight and envy to conquer, probably a hopeless task; the best is to march right through them, Truth leading the way. It is not likely that they will be converted or reduced to silence."

Whilst these expeditions were being planned, a letter from M. Gressier, the Minister of Agriculture, arrived very inopportunely. M. Gressier was better versed in *sub rosâ* ministerial combinations than in seeding processes, and he asked Pasteur to examine three lots of seeds sent to him by a Mademoiselle Amat, of Brives-la-Gaillarde, who was celebrated in the department of the Corrèze for her good management of silkworms. This *magnanarelle*, having had some successful results, was begging his Excellency to accord to those humble seeds his particular consideration, and to have them developed with every possible care.

At the same time she was sending samples of the same seeds to various places in the Gard, the Bouches du Rhône, etc., etc.

M. Gressier (April 20) asked Pasteur to examine them and to give him a detailed report. Pasteur answered four days afterwards in terms which were certainly not softened by the usual administrative precautions

" Monsieur le Ministre, . . . these three sorts of seed are worthless. If they are developed, even in very small nurseries, they will in every instance succumb to corpuscle disease. If my seeding process had been employed, it would not have required ten minutes to discover that Mademoiselle Amat's cocoons, though excellent for spinning purposes, were absolutely unfit for reproduction. My seeding process gives the means of recognizing those broods which are suitable for seed, whilst opposing the production of the infected eggs which year by year flood the silkworm cultivating departments.

" I shall be much obliged, Monsieur le Ministre, if you will kindly inform the Prefect of the Corrèze of the forecasts which I now impart to you, and if you will ask *him* to report to you the results of Mademoiselle Amat's three lots.

" For my part, I feel so sure of what I now affirm, that I shall not even trouble to test, by hatching them, the samples which you have sent me. I have thrown them into the river. . . ."

J. B. Dumas had come to Alais, Messrs. Gernez and Duclaux now returned from their expeditions. In two hundred broods, each of one or two ounces of seed, coming from three different sources and hatched in various localities, not one failure was recorded. The Lyons Commission, which had made a note of Pasteur's bold prognosis, found it absolutely correct; the excellence of the method was acknowledged by all who had conscientiously tried it. Now that the scourge was really conquered, Pasteur imagined that all he had to do was to set up a table of the results sent to him. But, from the south of France and from Corsica, jealousies were beginning their work of undermining; pseudo-scientists in their vanity proclaimed that everything was illusory that was outside their own affirmations, and the seed merchants, willing to ruin everybody rather than jeopardize their miserable interests, "did not hesitate (we are quoting M. Gernez) to perpetrate the most odious falsehoods."

Instead of being annoyed, saddened, often indignant as he was, Pasteur would have done more wisely to look back upon the history of most great discoveries and of the initial difficulties which beset them. But he could not look upon such things philosophically; stupidity astonished him and he could not easily bring himself to believe in bad faith. His friends in Alais society, M. de Lachadenède, M. Despeyroux, professor of chemistry, might have reminded him, in their evening conversations, of the difficulties ever encountered in the service of mankind. The prejudice against potatoes, for instance, had lasted three hundred years. When they were brought over from Peru in the fifteenth century, it was asserted that they caused leprosy; in the seventeenth century, that accusation was recognized to be absurd, but it was said that they caused fever. One century later, in 1771, the Besançon Academy of Medicine having opened a competition for the answer to the following question of general interest: "What plants can be used to supplement other foods in times of famine?" a military apothecary, named Parmentier, competed and proved victoriously that the potato was quite harmless. After that, he began a propagandist campaign in favour of potatoes. But prejudice still subsisted in spite of his experimental fields and of the dinners in the menu of which potatoes held a large place. Louis XVI had then an inspiration worthy of Henry IV; he appeared in public, wearing in his buttonhole Parmentier's little mauve flower, and thus glorified it in the eyes of the Court and of the crowd.

But such comparisons had no weight with Pasteur; he was henceforth sure of his method and longed to see it adopted, unable to understand why there should be further discussions now that the silkworm industry was saved and the bread of so many poor families assured. He was learning to know all the bitterness of sterile polemics, and the obstacles placed one by one in the way of those who attempt to give humanity anything new and useful. Fortunately he had what so many men of research have lacked, the active and zealous collaboration of pupils imbued with his principles, and the rarer and priceless blessing of a home life mingling with his laboratory life.   His wife and his daughter, a mere child, shared his sericulture labours; they had become *magnanarelles* equal to the most capable in Alais.   Another privilege was the advocacy of some champions quite unknown to him.   Those who loved science and who understood that it would now become, thanks to Pasteur, an important factor in agricultural and sericicultural matters hailed his achievements with joy.   For instance, a letter was published on July 8, 1869, in the *Journal of Practical Agriculture* by a cultivator who had obtained excellent results by applying Pasteur's method; the letter concluded as follows : " We should be obliged, if, through the columns of your paper, you would express to M. Pasteur our feelings of gratitude for his laborious and valuable researches.   We firmly hope that he will one day reap the fruit of his arduous labours, and be amply compensated for the passionate attacks of which he is now the object."

" Monsieur Pasteur," once said the Mayor of Alais, Dr. Pagès, " if what you are showing me becomes verified in current practice, nothing can repay you for your work, but the town of Alais will raise a golden statue to you."

Marshal Vaillant began to take more and more interest in this question, which was not darkened, in his eyes at least, by the dust of polemics.   The old soldier, always scrupulously punctual at the meetings of the Institute and of the Imperial and Central Society of Agriculture, had amused himself by organizing a little silkworm nursery on the Pasteur system, in his own study, in the very centre of Paris.   These experiments, in the Imperial palace might have reminded an erudite reader of Olivier de Serres' *Théâtre d'Agriculture* of the time when the said Olivier de Serres planted mulberry trees in the Tuileries gardens at Henry IV's request, and when, according to the old agricultural writer, a house was arranged at the end of the gardens " accommodated with all things necessary as well for the feeding of the worms as for the preparation of silk."

The Marshal, though calling himself the most modest of sericicultors, had been able to appreciate the safety of a method which produced the same results in Paris as at the Pont Gisquet; the octogenarian veteran dwelt with complacency on the splendid condition of his silkworms in all their phases from the minute worm hatched from the seed-like egg to the splendid cocoon of white or yellow silk.

It occurred to Vaillant to suggest a decisive experiment in favour of Pasteur and of the silkworm industry. The Prince Imperial owned in Illyria, about six leagues from Trieste, a property called Villa Vicentina. One of Napoleon's sisters, Elisa Bonaparte, had lived peacefully there after the fall of the first Empire, and had left it to her daughter, Princess Baciocchi, who bequeathed it to the Prince Imperial, with the rest of her fortune. Vines and mulberry trees grew plentifully on that vast domain, but the produce of cocoons was nil, pébrine and flachery having devastated the place. Marshal Vaillant, Minister of the Emperor's Household, desired to render the princely property once again productive and, at the same time, to give his colleague of the Institute an opportunity of " definitely silencing the opposition created by ignorance and jealousy." In a letter dated October 9, he requested Pasteur to send out 900 ounces of seed to Villa Vicentina, a large quantity, for one ounce produced, on an average, thirty kilogrammes of cocoons. Six days later the Marshal wrote to M. Tisserand, the director of the Crown agricultural establishments, who knew Villa Vicentina : " I have suggested to the Emperor that M. Pasteur should be offered a lodging at Villa Vicentina ; the Emperor acquiesces in the most gracious manner. Tell me whether that is possible."

M. Tisserand, heartily applauding the Marshal's excellent idea, described the domain and the dwelling house, Villa Elisa, a white Italian two-storied house, situated amongst lawns and trees in a park of sixty hectares. " It would indeed be well," continued M. Tisserand, "that M. Pasteur should find peace, rest, and a return of the health he has so valiantly compromised in his devotion to his country, in the midst of the lands which will be the first to profit by the fruit of his splendid discoveries and where his name will be blessed before long."

Pasteur started three weeks later with his family ; the long journey had to be taken in short stages, the state of his health still being very precarious. He stopped at Alais on the way, in order to fetch the selected seed, and on November 25, at 9 p.m., he reached Villa Vicentina. The fifty tenants of the domain did not suspect that the new arrival would bring back with him the prosperity of former years. Ranlin, the " temporizer," joined his master a few weeks later.

This was a period not of rest, but of a great calm, with regular work under a pure sky. Whilst waiting for hatching time, Pasteur continued to dictate to his wife the book he had mentioned to J. B. Dumas in a letter from St. Hippolyte le Fort. But the projected little book was changing its shape and growing into a two-volume work full of facts and documents. It was ready to publish by April, 1870.

When the moment for hatching the seed had arrived, Pasteur distributed twenty-five ounces among the tenants and kept twenty-five ounces for himself. An incident disturbed these days of work : a steward, who had by him an old box of Japanese seed, sold this suspicious seed with the rest. The idea that confiding peasants had thus been swindled sent Pasteur beside himself; in his violent anger he sent for this steward, overwhelmed him with reproaches and forbade him ever to show his face before him again.

" The Marshal," wrote Dumas to Pasteur, "has told me of the swindles you have come across and which have upset you so much. Do not worry unreasonably; if I were you I would merely insert a line in a local-paper : ' M. Pasteur is only answerable for the seeds he himself sells to cultivators.' " Those cultivators soon were duly edified. The results of the seeding process were represented by a harvest of cocoons which brought in, after all expenses were paid, a profit of 22,000 francs, the first profit earned by the property for ten years. This was indeed an Imperial present from Pasteur; the Emperor was amazed and delighted.

The Government then desired to do for Pasteur what had been done for Dumas and Claude Bernard, that is, give him a seat in the Senate. His most decided partisan was the competitor that several political personages suggested against him : Henri Sainte Claire Deville. Deville wrote to Mme. Pasteur in June : " You must know that if Pasteur becomes a Senator, and Pasteur alone, you understand—for they cannot elect two chemists at once !—it will be a triumph for your friend—a triumph and an unmixed pleasure."

The projected decree was one of eighteen then in preparation. The final list—the last under the Emipre—where Emile Augier was to represent French literature was postponed from day to day.

Pasteur left Villa Vicentina on July 6, taking with him the gratitude of the people whose good genius he had been for nearly eight months. In northern Italy, as well as in Austria, his process of cellular seeding was now applied with success.

Before returning to France he went to Vienna and then to Munich : he desired to talk with the German chemist, Liebig, the most determined of his adversaries. He thought it impossible that Liebig's ideas on fermentation should not have been shaken and altered in the last thirteen years. Liebig could not still be affirming that the presence of decomposing animal or vegetable matter should be necessary to fermentation ! That theory had been destroyed by a simple and decisive experiment of Pasteur's : he had sown a trace of yeast in water containing but sugar and mineral crystallized salts, and had seen this yeast multiply itself and produce a regular alcoholic fermentation.

Since all nitrogenized organic matter (constituting the ferment, according to Liebig) was absent, Pasteur considered that he thus proved the life of the ferment and the absence of any action from albuminoid matter in a stage of decomposition. The death phenomenon now appeared as a life phenomenon. How could Liebig deny the independent existence of ferments in their infinite littleness and their power of destroying and transforming everything? What did he think of all these new ideas? would he still write, as in 1845 : " As to the opinion which explains putrefaction of animal substances by the presence of microscopic animalculæ, it may be compared to that of a child who would explain the rapidity of the Rhine current by attributing it to the violent movement of the numerous mill wheels of Mayence? "

Since that ingeniously fallacious paragraph, many results had come to light. Perhaps Liebig, who in 1851 hailed J. B. Dumas as a master, had now come to Dumas' point of view respecting the fruitfulness of the Pastorian theory. That theory was extended to diseases ; the infinitely small appeared as disorganizers of living tissues. The part played by the corpuscles in the contagious and hereditary pébrine led to many reflections on the contagious and hereditary element of human diseases. Even the long-postponed transmission of certain diseases was becoming clearer now that, within the vibrio of flachery, other corpuscles were found, germs of the flachery disease, ready to break out from one year to another.

To convince Liebig, to bring him to acknowledge the triumph of those ideas with the pleasure of a true *savant*, such was Pasteur's desire when he entered Liebig's laboratory. The tall old man, in a long frock coat, received him with kindly courtesy; but when Pasteur, who was eager to come to the object of his visit, tried to approach the delicate subject, Liebig, without losing his amenity, refused all discussion, alleging indisposition. Pasteur did not insist, but promised himself that he would return to the charge.

CHAPTER VII

1870—1872

PASTEUR, on his return, spent forty-eight hours in Strasburg, which was for him full of memories of his laborious days at the Faculty of that town, between 1848 and 1854, at a time when rivalry already existed between France and Germany, a generous rivalry of moral and intellectual effort. He then heard for the first time of the threatening war; all his hopes of progress founded on peace, through scientific discoveries, began to crumble away, and his disappointment was embittered by the recollection of many illusions.

Never was more cruel rebuff given to the generous efforts of a policy of sentiment : after having laid the foundation of the independence and unity of Italy, France had sympathized with Germany's desire for unity, and few of the counsellors, or even the adversaries of the Empire, would not have defended this idea, which was supposed to lead to civilization. During that period of anxious waiting (beginning of July, 1870), when the most alarming news was daily published in Strasburg, it did not occur to any one to look back upon quotations from papers only a few years old, though in that very town a pamphlet might have been found, written by Edmond About in 1860, and containing the following words—

"Let Germany become united! France has no dearer or more ardent desire, for she loves the German nation with a disinterested friendship. France is not alarmed at seeing the formation of an Italian nation of 26,000,000 men in the South : she need not fear to see 32,000,000 Germans found a great people on the Eastern frontier."

Proud to be first to proclaim the rights of nations ; influenced by mingled feelings of kindliness, trustfulness, optimism and a certain vanity of disinterestedness, France, who loves to be loved, imagined that the world would be grateful for her

N

international sociability, and that her smiles were sufficient to maintain peace and joy in Europe.

Far from being alarmed by certain symptoms in her neighbours, she voluntarily closed her eyes to the manœuvres of the Prussian troops, her ears to the roar of the artillery practice constantly heard across her eastern frontier; in 1863 patrols of German cavalry had come as far as Wissemburg. But people thought that Germany was "playing soldiers." Duruy, who shared at that time the general delusion, wrote in some traveller's notes published in 1864: "We have had your German Rhine, and though you have garnished it with bristling fortresses and cannon turning France-wards, we do not wish to have it again, . . . for the time for conquests is past. Conquests shall only now be made with the free consent of nations. Too much blood has been poured into the Rhine! What an immense people would arise if they who were struck down by the sword along its banks could be restored to life!"

After the thunderclap of Sadowa, the French Government, believing, in its infatuation, that it was entitled to a share of gratitude and security, asked for the land along the Rhine as far as Mayence; this territorial aggrandizement might have compensated for Prussia's redoubtable conquests. The refusal was not long in coming. The Rhenish provinces immediately swarmed with Prussian troops. The Emperor, awaking from his dream, hesitating to make war, sent another proposition to Prussia: that the Rhenish provinces should become a buffer State. The same haughty answer was returned. France then hoped for the cession of Luxemburg, a hope all the more natural in that the populations of Luxemburg were willing to vote for annexation to France, and such a policy would have been in accordance with the rights of nations. But this request, apparently entertained at first by Prussia, was presently hampered by intrigues which caused its rejection. Duped, not even treated as an arbiter, but merely as a contemptible witness, France dazzled herself for a moment with the brilliant Exhibition of 1867. But it was a last and splendid flash; the word which is the bane of nations and of sovereigns, "to-morrow," was on the lips of the ageing Emperor. The reform in the French army, which should have been bold and immediate, was postponed and afterwards begun jerkily and unmethodically. Prussia however affected to be alarmed. Then irritation at having been duped, the evidence of a growing peril, a lingering hope in the military fortune of France—everything conspired to give an incident, provoked by Prussia, the proportions of a *casus belli*. But, in spite of so many grievances, people did not yet believe in this sudden return to barbarism. The Imperial policy had indeed been blindly inconsistent; after opening a wide prospect of unity before the German people it had been thought possible to say "No further than the Main," as if the impetuous force of a popular movement could be arrested after once being started. France suddenly opened her eyes to her danger and to the failure of her policy. But if a noble sentiment of generosity had been mingled with the desire to increase her territory without shedding a drop of blood, she had had the honour of being in the vanguard of progress. Were great ideas of peace and human brotherhood about to be engulfed in a war which would throw Europe into an era of violence and brutality?

Pasteur, profoundly saddened, could not bear to realize that his ideal of the peaceful and beneficent destiny of France was about to vanish; he left Strasburg—never to return to it—a prey to the most sombre thoughts.

When he returned to Paris, he met Sainte Claire Deville, who had come back from a scientific mission in Germany, and who had for the first time lost his brightness and optimism. The war appeared to him absolutely disastrous. He had seen the Prussian army, redoubtable in its skilful organization, closing along the frontier; the invasion was certain, and there was nothing to stay it. Everything was lacking in France, even in arsenals like Strasburg. At Toul, on the second line of fortifications, so little attention was paid to defence that the Government had thought that the place could be used as a dépôt for the infantry and cavalry reserves, who could await there the order for crossing the Rhine.

"Ah! my lads, my poor lads!" said Sainte Claire Deville to his Ecole Normale students, "it is all up with us!" And he was seen, between two experiments, wiping his eyes with the corner of his laboratory apron.

The students, with the ordinary confidence of youth, could not believe that an invasion should be so imminent. However, in spite of the privilege which frees *Normaliens* from any military service in exchange for a ten years' engagement at the University, they put patriotic duty above any future University appointments, and entered the ranks as private soldiers. Those who had been favoured by being immediately incorporated in a battalion of *chasseurs à pied* the dépôt of which was at Vincennes, spent their last evening—their vigil as they called it—in the drawing-room of the sub-director of the Ecole, Bertin. Sainte Claire Deville and Pasteur were there, also Duruy, whose three sons had enlisted. Pasteur's son, aged eighteen, was also on the eve of his departure.

Every one of the students at the Ecole Normale enlisted, some as *chasseurs à pied*, some in a line regiment, others with the marines, in the artillery, even with the *franc tireurs*. Pasteur wished to be enrolled in the *garde nationale* with Duruy and Bertin, but he had to be reminded that a half-paralysed man was unfit for service. After the departure of all the students, the Ecole Normale fell into the silence of deserted houses. M. Bouillier, the director, and Bertin decided to turn it into an ambulance, a sort of home for the *Normaliens* who were stationed in various quarters of Paris.

Pasteur, unable to serve his country except by his scientific researches, had the firm intention of continuing his work ; but he was overwhelmed by the reverses which fell upon France, the idea of the bloodshed and of his invaded country oppressed him like a monomania.

"Do not stay in Paris," Bertin said to him, echoed by Dr. Godélier. "You have no right to stay ; you would be a useless mouth during the siege," he added, almost cheerfully, earnestly desiring to see his friend out of harm's way. Pasteur allowed himself to be persuaded, and started for Arbois on September 5, his heart aching for the sorrows of France.

Some notes and letters enable us to follow him there, in the daily detail of his life, amongst his books, his plans of future work, and now and then his outbursts of passionate grief. He tried to return to the books he loved, to feel over again the attraction of "all that is great and beautiful" to quote a favourite phrase. He read at that time Laplace's *Exposition du Système du Monde,* and even copied out some fragments, general ideas, concurring with his own. The vision of a Galileo or a Newton rising through a series of inductions from "particular phenomena to others more far-reaching, and from those to the general laws of Nature," on this earth, "itself so small a part of the solar system, and disappearing entirely in the immensity of the heavens, of which that system is but an unimportant corner,"—that vision enveloped Pasteur

with the twofold feeling with which every man must be imbued : humility before the Great Mystery, and admiration for
those who, raising a corner of the veil, prove that genius is
divinely inspired. Such reading helped Pasteur through the
sad time of anxious waiting, and he would repeat as in brighter
days, " *Laboremus.*"

But sometimes, when he was sitting quietly with his wife
and daughter, the trumpet call would sound, with which the
Arbois crier preceded the proclaiming of news. Then everything was forgotten, the universal order of things of no account,
and Pasteur's anguished soul would concentrate itself on that
imperceptible corner of the universe, France, his suffering
country. He would go downstairs, mix with groups standing
on the little bridge across the Cuisance, listen breathlessly to
the official communication, and sadly go back to the room where
the memories of his father only emphasized the painful contrast
with the present time. In the most prominent place hung
a large medallion of General Bonaparte, by the Franc-Comtoi.
Huguenin, the habit of authority visible in the thin energetic
face; then a larger effigy in bronzed plaster of Napoleon in
profile, in a very simple uniform ; by the mantelpiece a lithograph of the little King of Rome with his curly head; on the
bookshelves, well within reach, books on the Great Epoch,
read over and over again by the old soldier who had died in the
humble room which still reflected some of the Imperial glory.

That glory, that legend had enveloped the childhood and
youth of Pasteur, who, as he advanced in life, still preserved
the same enthusiasm. His imagination pictured the Emperor,
calm in the midst of battles, or reviewing his troops surrounded by an escort of field marshals, entering as a sovereign
a capital not his own, then overwhelmed by numbers at
Waterloo, and finally condemned to exile and inactivity, and
dying in a long drawn agony. Glorious or lugubrious, those
visions came back to him with poignant insistency in those
days of September, 1870. What was Waterloo compared to
Sedan ! The departure for St. Helena had the grandeur of the
end of an epic ; it seemed almost enviable by the side of that
last episode of the Second Empire, when Napoleon III, vanquished, spared by the death which he wooed, left Sedan by
the Donchery road to enter the cottage where Bismarck was to
inform him of the rendezvous given by the King of Prussia.

The Emperor had now but a shadow of power, having made

the Empress Regent before he left Paris; it was therefore not the sword of France, but his own, that he was about to surrender. But he thought he might hope that the King of Prussia would show clemency to the French army and people, having many times declared that he made war on the Emperor and not on France.

"Can it be credited," said Bismarck, speaking afterwards of that interview, "that he actually believed in our generosity!" The chancellor added, speaking of that somewhat protracted *tête-à-tête*, "I felt as I used to in my youth, when my partner in a cotillon was a girl to whom I did not quite know what to say, and whom nobody would fetch away for a turn!"

Napoleon III and the King of Prussia met in the Château of Bellevue, in the neighbourhood of Sedan, opposite a peninsula henceforth known by the sad name of "Camp of Misery." The Emperor looked for the last time upon his 83,000 soldiers, disarmed, starving, waiting in the mud for the Prussian escort which was to convey them as prisoners far beyond the Rhine. Wilhelm did not even pronounce the word peace.

Jules Favre, taking possession on September 6 of the department of Foreign Affairs, recalled to the diplomatic agents the fall of the Empire and the words of the King of Prussia; then in an unaccustomed outburst of eloquence exclaimed: "Does the King of Prussia wish to continue an impious struggle which will be as fatal to him as to us? Does he wish to give to the world in the nineteenth century the cruel spectacle of two nations destroying each other and forgetful of human feelings, of reason and of science, heaping up ruin and death? Let him then assume the responsibility before the world and before posterity!" And then followed the celebrated phrase with which he has been violently and iniquitously reproached, and which expressed the unanimous sentiment of France: "We will not concede one inch of our territory nor a stone of our fortifications."

Bismarck refused the interview Jules Favre asked of him (September 10), under the pretext that the new Government was irregular. The enemy was coming nearer and nearer to Paris. The French city was resolved to resist; thousands upon thousands of oxen were being corralled in the Bois de Boulogne; poor people from the suburbs were coming to take refuge in the city. On the Place de la Concorde, the statue which represents the city of Strasburg was covered with flowers and flags, and seemed to incarnate the idea of the *Patrie* itself.

Articles and letters came to Arbois in that early September, bringing an echo of the sorrows of Paris. Pasteur was then reading the works of General Foy, wherein he found thoughts in accordance with his own, occasionally copying out such passages as the following : " Right and Might struggle for the world ; Right, which constitutes and preserves Society ; Might, which overcomes nations and bleeds them to death."

General Foy fought for France during twenty-five years, and, writing in 1820, recalled with a patriotic shudder the horrors of foreign invasions. Long after peace was signed, by a chance meeting in a street in Paris, General Foy found himself face to face with Wellington. The sight was so odious to him that he spoke of this meeting in the *Chambre* with an accent of sorrowful humiliation which breathed the sadness of Waterloo over the whole assembly. Pasteur could well understand the long continued vibration of that suffering chord, he, who never afterwards could speak without a thrill of sorrow of that war which Germany, in defiance of humanity, was inexcusably pursuing.

It was the fourth time in less than a hundred years that a Prussian invasion overflowed into France. But instead of 42,000 Prussians, scattered in 1792 over the sacred soil of the *Patrie*—Pasteur pronounced the word with the faith and tenderness of a true son of France—there were now 518,000 men to fight 285,000 French.

The thought that they had been armed in secret for the conquest of neighbouring lands, the memory of France's optimism until that diplomatic incident, invented so that France might stumble over it, and the inaction of Europe, inspired Pasteur with reflections which he confided to his pupil Raulin. " What folly, what blindness," he wrote (September 17), " there are in the inertia of Austria, Russia, England ! What ignorance in our army leaders of the respective forces of the two nations ! We *savants* were indeed right when we deplored the poverty of the department of Public Instruction ! The real cause of our misfortunes lies there. It is not with impunity—as it will one day be recognized, too late—that a great nation is allowed to lose its intellectual standard. But, as you say, if we rise again from those disasters, we shall again see our statesmen lose themselves in endless discussions on forms of government and abstract political questions instead of going to the root of the matter. We are paying the penalty of fifty years' forgetfulness of science, of its conditions of development, of its immense influence on the destiny of a great people, and of all that might have assisted the diffusion of light. . . . I cannot go on, all this hurts me. I try to put away all such memories, and also the sight of our terrible distress, in which it seems that a desperate resistance is the only hope we have left. I wish that France may fight to her last man, to her last fortress. I wish that the war may be prolonged until the winter, when, the elements aiding us, all these Vandals may perish of cold and distress. Every one of my future works will bear on its title page the words: ' Hatred to Prussia. Revenge! revenge!'"

There is a passage in the Psalms where the captives of Israel, led to Babylonian rivers, weep at the memory of Jerusalem. After swearing never to forget their country, they wish their enemies every misfortune, and hurl this last imprecation at Babylon: "Blessed shall he be that taketh thy children and throweth them against the stones."[1] One of the most Christlike souls of our time, Henri Perreyve, speaking of Poland, of vanquished and oppressed nations, quoted this Psalm and exclaimed: "O Anger, man's Anger, how difficult it is to drive thee out of man's heart! and how irresistible are the flames kindled by the insolence of injustice!" Those flames were kindled in the soul of Pasteur, full as it was of human tenderness, and they burst out in that sobbing cry of despair.

On that 17th of September, the day before Paris was invested, Jules Favre made another attempt to obtain peace. He published an account of that interview which took place at the Château of Ferrières, near Meaux; this printed account reached every town in France, and was read with grief and anger.

Jules Favre had deluded himself into thinking that victorious Prussia would limit its demands to a war indemnity, probably a formidable one. But Bismarck, besides the indemnity, intended to take a portion of French soil, and claimed Strasburg first of all. "It is the key of the house; I must have it." And with Strasburg he wanted the whole Department of the *Haut-Rhin*, that of the *Bas-Rhin*, Metz, and a part of the Department of *Moselle*. Jules Favre, character-

[1] Ps. cxxxvii. 9.

istically French, exhausted his eloquence in putting sentiment into politics, spoke of European rights, of the right of the people to dispose of themselves, tried to bring out the fact that a brutal annexation was in direct opposition to the progress of civilization. "I know very well," said Bismarck, "that they (meaning the Alsatians and Lorrainers) do not want us; they will give us a deal of trouble, but we must annex them." In the event of a future war Prussia was to have the advantage. All this was said with an authoritative courtesy, an insolent tranquillity, through which contempt for men was visible, evidently the best means of governing them in Bismarck's eyes. As Jules Favre was pleading the cause of heroic Strasburg, whose long resistance was the admiration of Paris, "Strasburg will now fall into our hands," said Bismarck coldly; "it is but a question for engineers; therefore I request that the garrison should surrender as prisoners of war."

Jules Favre "leapt in his grief"—the words are his—but King Wilhelm exacted this condition. Jules Favre, almost breaking down, turning away to hide the tears that welled into his eyes, ended the interview with these words : "It is an indefinite struggle between two nations who should go hand in hand."

Traces of this patriotic anguish are to be found in one of Pasteur's notebooks, as well as a circular addressed by Jules Favre to the diplomatic representatives in answer to certain points disputed by Bismarck. Pasteur admiringly took note of the following passage : "I know not what destinies Fate has in store for us. But I do feel most deeply that if I had to choose between the present situation of France and that of Prussia, I should decide for the former. Better far our sufferings, our perils, our sacrifices, than the cruel and inflexible ambition of our foe."

"We must preserve hope until the end," wrote Pasteur after reading the above, " say nothing to discourage each other, and wish ardently for a prolonged struggle. Let us think of hopeful things; Bazaine may save us." . . . How many French hearts were sharing that hope at the very time when Bazaine was preparing to betray Metz, his troops and his flag !

"Should we not cry : ' Happy are the dead ! ' " wrote Pasteur a few days after the news burst upon France of that army lost without being allowed to fight, of that city of Metz, the strongest in France, surrendered without a struggle !

Through all Pasteur's anxieties about the war, certain observations, certain projected experiments resounded in his mind like the hours that a clock strikes, unheeded but not unheard, in a house visited by death. He could not put them away from him, they were part of his very life.

Any sort of laboratory work was difficult for him in the tanner's house, which had remained the joint property of himself and his sister. His brother-in-law had continued Joseph Pasteur's trade. Pasteur applied his spirit of observation to everything around him, and took the opportunity of studying the fermentation of tan. He would ask endless questions, trying to discover the scientific reason of every process and every routine. Whilst his sister was making bread he would study the raising of the crust, the influence of air in the kneading of the dough, and his imagination rising as usual from a minor point to the greatest problems, he began to seek for a means of increasing the nutritive powers of bread, and consequently of lowering its price.

The *Salut Public* of December 20 contained a notice on that very subject, which Pasteur transcribed. The Central Commission of Hygiene which included among its members Sainte Claire Deville, Wurtz, Bouchardat and Trélat, had tried, when dealing with this question of bread (a vital one during the siege), to prove to the Parisians that bread is the more wholesome for containing a little bran. "With what emotion," wrote Pasteur, "I have just read all those names dear to science, greater now before their fellow-citizens and before posterity. Why could I not share their sufferings and their dangers!" He would have added "and their work" if some of the Académie des Sciences reports had reached him.

The history of the Academy during the war is worthy of brief mention. Moreover it was too deeply interesting to Pasteur, too constantly in his thoughts, not to be considered as forming part of his biography.

During the first period, the Academy, imagining, like the rest of France, that there was no doubt of a favourable issue of the war, continued its purely scientific task. When the first defeats were announced, the habitual communications ceased, and the Academy, unable to think of anything but the war, held sittings of three-quarters of an hour or even less.

One of the correspondents of the Institute, the surgeon Sédillot, who was in Alsace at the head of an ambulance corps, and who himself performed as many as fifteen amputations in one day, addressed two noteworthy letters to the President of the Academy. Those letters mark a date in the history of surgery, and show how restricted was then in France the share of some of Pasteur's ideas at the very time when in other countries they were adopted and followed. Lister, the celebrated English surgeon, having, he said, meditated on Pasteur's theory of germs, and proclaimed himself his follower, convinced that complications and infection of wounds were caused by their giving access to living organisms and infectious germs, elements of trouble, often of death, had already in 1867 inaugurated a method of treatment. He attempted the destruction of germs floating in air by means of a vaporizer filled with a carbolic solution, then isolated and preserved the wound from the contact of the air. Sponges, drainage tubes, etc., were subjected to minute precautions; in one word, he created antisepsis. Four months before the war he had propounded the principles which should guide surgeons, but it occurred to no one in France, in the first battles, to apply the new method. "The horrible mortality amongst the wounded in battle," writes Sédillot, "calls for the attention of all the friends of science and humanity. The surgeon's art, hesitating and disconcerted, pursues a doctrine whose rules seem to flee before research. . . Places where there are wounded are recognizable by the fetor of suppuration and gangrene."

Hundreds and thousands of wounded, their faces pale, but full of hope and desire to live, succumbed between the eighth and tenth day to gangrene and erysipelas. Those failures of the surgery of the past are plain to us now that the doctrine of germs has explained everything; but, at that time, such an avowal of impotence befcre the mysterious *contagium sui generis*, which, the doctors averred, eluded all research, and such awful statistics of mortality embittered the anguish of defeat.

The Academy then attempted to take a share in the national co-operation by making a special study of any subject which interested the public health and defence. A sitting on methods of steering balloons was succeeded by another on various means of preserving meat during the siege. Then came an anxious inquiry into modes of alimentation of infants. At the end of October there were but 20,000 litres of milk per day to be procured in the whole of Paris, and the healthy were implored to abstain from it. It was a question of life and death for young children, and already many little coffins were daily to be seen on the road to the cemetery.

Thus visions of death amongst soldiers in their prime and children in their infancy hung over the Academy meeting hall. It was at one of those mournful sittings, on a dark autumn afternoon, that Chevreul, an octogenarian member of the Institute, who, like Pasteur, had believed in civilization and in the binding together of nations through science, art and letters, looking at the sacks of earth piled outside the windows to save the library from the bursting shells, exclaimed in loud desolate tones—

"And yet we are in the nineteenth century, and a few months ago the French did not even think of a war which has put their capital into a state of siege and traced around its walls a desert zone where he who sowed does not reap! And there are public universities where they teach the Beautiful, the True, and the Right."

"Might goes before Right," Bismarck said. A German journalist invented another phrase which went the round of Europe : "the psychological moment for bombardment." On January 5, one of the first Prussian shells sank into the garden of the Ecole Normale ; another burst in the very ambulance of the Ecole. Bertin, the sub-director, rushed through the suffocating smoke and ascertained that none of the patients was hurt ; he found the breech between two beds. The miserable patients dragged themselves downstairs to the lecture rooms on the ground floor, not a much safer refuge.

From the heights of Châtillon the enemy's batteries were bombarding all the left bank of the Seine, the Prussians, regardless of the white flags bearing the red cross of Geneva, were aiming at the Val-de-Grâce and the Panthéon. "Where is the Germany of our dreams?" wrote Paul de St. Victor on January 9, "the Germany of the poets? Between her and France an abyss of hatred has opened, a Rhine of blood and tears that no peace can ever bridge over."

On that same date, Chevreul read the following declaration to the Academy of Science—

The Garden of Medicinal Plants, founded in Paris
by an edict of King Louis XIII,
dated January, 1826,
Converted into the Museum of Natural History

by a decree of the Convention on June 10, 1793,
was Bombarded,
under the reign of Wilhelm I King of
Prussia, Count von Bismarck, Chancellor,
by the Prussian army, during the night
of January 8–9, 1871.
It had until then been respected by all parties
and all powers, national or
foreign.

Pasteur, on reading this protest, regretted more than ever
that he had not been there to sign it. It then occurred to him
that he too might give vent to the proud plaint of the vanquished from his little house at Arbois. He remembered with
a sudden bitterness the diploma he had received from the University of Bonn. Many years had passed since the time in
the First Empire when one of the 110 French Departments had
been that of Rhine and Moselle, with Coblentz as its *préfecture*
and Bonn and Zimmern as *sous-préfectures*. When, in 1815,
Prussia's iron hand seized again those Rhenish provinces which
had become so French at heart, the Prussian king and his
ministers hit upon the highly politic idea of founding a University on the picturesque banks of the Rhine, thus morally con-
quering the people after reducing them by force. That
University had been a great success and had become most
prosperous. The Strasburg Faculty under the Second Empire,
with its few professors and its general penury, seemed very
poor compared to the Bonn University, with its fifty-three
professors and its vast laboratories of chemistry, physics and
medicine, and even a museum of antiquities. Pasteur and
Duruy had often exchanged remarks on that subject. But that
rivalry between the two Faculties was of a noble nature, animated as it was by the great feeling that science is superior to
national distinctions. King Wilhelm had once said, "Prussia's
conquests must be of the moral kind," and Pasteur had not
thought of any other conquests.
When in 1868 the University of Bonn conferred upon him
the diploma of Doctor of Medicine, saying that "by his very
penetrating experiments, he had much contributed to the knowledge of the history of the generation of micro-organisms, and
had happily advanced the progress of the science of fermentations," he had been much pleased at this acknowledgment of

the future opened to medical studies by his work, and he was proud to show the Degree he had received.

"Now," he wrote (January 18, 1871), to the Head of the Faculty of Medicine, after recalling his former sentiments, "now the sight of that parchment is odious to me, and I feel offended at seeing my name, with the qualification of *Virum clarissimum* that you have given it, placed under a name which is henceforth an object of execration to my country, that of *Rex Gulielmus*.

"While highly asseverating my profound respect for you, Sir, and for the celebrated professors who have affixed their signatures to the decision of the members of your Order, I am called upon by my conscience to ask you to efface my name from the archives of your Faculty, and to take back that diploma, as a sign of the indignation inspired in a French scientist by the barbarity and hypocrisy of him who, in order to satisfy his criminal pride, persists in the massacre of two great nations." Pasteur's protest ended with these words—

"Written at Arbois (Jura) on January 18, 1871, after reading the mark of infamy inscribed on the forehead of your King by the illustrious director of the Museum of Natural History M. Chevreul."

"This letter will not have much weight with a people whose principles differ so totally from those that inspire us," said Pasteur, "but it will at least echo the indignation of French scientists."

He made a collection of stories, of episodes, and letters, which fell in his way; amongst other things we find an open letter from General Chanzy to the commandant of the Prussian troops at Vendôme, denouncing the insults, outrages, and inexcusable violence of the Prussians towards the inhabitants of St. Calais, who had shown great kindness to the enemy's sick and wounded.

"You respond by insolence, destruction and pillage to the generosity with which we treat your prisoners and wounded. I indignantly protest, in the name of humanity and of the rights of men, which you trample under foot."

Pasteur also gathered up tales of bravery, of heroism, and of resignation—that form of heroism so often illustrated by women —during the terrible siege of Paris. And, from all those things, arose the psychology of war in its two aspects : in the invading army a spirit of conquest carried to oppression, and even apart from the thrilling moments of battle, giving to hatred and cruelty a cold-blooded sanction of discipline; in the vanquished nation, an irrepressible revolt, an intoxication of sacrifice. Those who have not seen war do not know what love of the mother country means.

France was the more loved that she was more oppressed; she inspired her true sons with an infinite tenderness. Sully-Prudhomme, the poet of pensive youth, renouncing his love for Humanity in general, promised himself that he would henceforth devote his life to the exclusive love of France. A greater poet than he, Victor Hugo, wrote at that time the first part of his *Année Terrible*, with its mingled devotion and despair.

The death of Henri Regnault was one of the sad episodes of the war. This brilliant young painter—he was only twenty-seven years of age—enlisted as a *garde nationale*, though exempt by law from any military service through being a laureate of the *prix de Rome*.[1] He did his duty valiantly, and on January 19, at the last sortie attempted by the Parisians, at Buzenval, the last Prussian shot struck him in the forehead. The Académie des Sciences, at its sitting of January 23, rendered homage to him whose coffin enclosed such dazzling prospects and some of the glory of France. The very heart of Paris was touched, and a great sadness was felt at the funeral procession of the great artist who seemed an ideal type of all the youth and talent so heroically sacrificed—and all in vain— for the surrender of Paris had just been officially announced.

Regnault's father, the celebrated physicist, a member of the Institute, was at Geneva when he received this terrible blow. Another grief—not however comparable to the despair of a bereaved parent—befell him—an instance of the odious side of war, not in its horrors, its pools of blood and burnt dwellings, but in its premeditated cruelty. Regnault had left his laboratory utensils in his rooms at the Sèvres porcelain manufactory, of which he was the manager. Everything was apparently left in the same place, not a window was broken, no locks forced; but a Prussian, evidently an expert, had been there. "Nothing seemed changed," writes J. B. Dumas, "in that abode of science, and yet everything was destroyed; the glass tubes of barometers, thermometers, etc., were broken; scales

[1] *Prix de Rome.* A competition takes place every year amongst the students of the *Ecole des Beaux Arts* for this prize; the successful competitor is sent to Rome for a year at the expense of the Ecole. [Trans.]

and other similar instruments had been carefully knocked out of
shape with a hammer." In a corner was a heap of ashes; they
were the registers, notes, manuscripts, all Regnault's work of
the last ten years. "Such cruelty," exclaimed J. B. Dumas,
"is unexampled in history. The Roman soldier who butchered
Archimedes in the heat of the onslaught may be excused—he
did not know him; but with what sacrilegious meanness could
such a work of destruction as this be accomplished ! ! ! "

On the very day when the Académie des Sciences was con-
doling with Henri Regnault's sorrowing father, Pasteur,
anxious at having had no news of his son, who had been fighting before Héricourt, determined to go and look for him in the
ranks of the Eastern Army Corps. By Poligny and Lons-le-
Saulnier, the roads were full of stragglers from the various
regiments left several days behind, their route completely lost,
who begged for bread as they marched, barely covered by the
tattered remnants of their uniforms. The main body of the
army was on the way to Besançon, a sad procession of French
soldiers, hanging their heads under the cold grey sky and tramp-
ing painfully in the snow.

Bourbaki, the general-in-chief, a hero of African battlefields,
was becoming more and more unnerved by the combinations
of this war. Whilst the Minister, in a dispatch from Bordeaux,
had ordered him to move back towards Dôle, to prevent the
taking of Dijon, then to hurry to Nevers or Joigny, where
20,000 men would be ready to be incorporated, Bourbaki, overwhelmed by the lamentable spectacle under his eyes, could see
no resource for his corps but a last line of retreat, Pontarlier.

It was among that stream of soldiers that Pasteur attempted
to find his son. His old friend and neighbour, Jules Vercel,
saw him start, accompanied by his wife and daughter, on Tuesday, January 24, in a half broken down old carriage, the last
that was left in the town. After journeying for some hours
in the snow, the sad travellers spent the night in a little way-
side inn near Montrond; the old carriage with its freight of
travelling boxes stood on the roadside like a gipsy's caravan.
The next morning they went on through a pine forest where the
deep silence was unbroken save by the falling masses of snow
from the spreading branches. They slept at Censeau, the next
day at Chaffois, and it was only on the Friday that they reached
Pontarlier, by roads made almost impracticable by the snow,
the carriage now a mere wreck.

The town was full of soldiers, some crouching round fires in the street, others stepping across their dead horses and begging for a little straw to lie on. Many had taken refuge in the church and were lying on the steps of the altar ; a few were attempting to bandage their frozen feet, threatened with gangrene.

Suddenly the news spread that the general-in-chief, Bourbaki, had shot himself through the brain. This did not excite much surprise. He had telegraphed two days before to the Minister of War · '' You cannot have an idea of the sufferings that the army has endured since the beginning of December. It is martyrdom to be in command at such a time,'' he added despairingly.

''The retreat from Moscow cannot have been worse than this,'' said Pasteur to a staff officer, Commandant Bourboulon, a nephew of Sainte Claire Deville, whom he met in the midst of those horrors and who could give him no information as to his son's battalion of *Chasseurs.* '' All that I can tell you,'' said a soldier anxiously questioned by Mme. Pasteur, '' is that out of the 1,200 men of that battalion there are but 300 left.'' As she was questioning another, a soldier who was passing stopped : '' Sergeant Pasteur? Yes, he is alive ; I slept by him last night at Chaffois. He has remained behind ; he is ill. You might meet him on the road towards Chaffois.''

The Pasteurs started again on the road followed the day before. They had barely passed the Pontarlier gate when a rough cart came by. A soldier muffled in his great coat, his hands resting on the edge of the cart, started with surprise. He hurried down, and the family embraced without a word, so great was their emotion.

The capitulation of starving Paris and the proposed armistice are historical events still present in the memory of men who were then beginning to learn the meaning of defeat. The armistice, which Jules Favre thought would be applied without restriction to all the army corps, was interpreted by Bismarck in a peculiar way. He and Jules Favre between them had drawn up a protocol in general terms ; it had been understood in those preliminary confabulations that, before drawing up the limits of the neutral zone applicable to the Eastern Army Corps, some missing information would be awaited, the respective positions of the belligerents being unknown. The information did not come, and Jules Favre in his imprudent trustfulness supposed that the delimitation would be done on the spot by the officers in command. When he heard that the Prussian troops were continuing their march eastwards, he complained to Bismarck, who answered that " the incident cannot have compromised the Eastern Army Corps, as it already was completely routed when the armistice was signed." This calculated reserve on Bismarck's part was eminently characteristic of his moral physiognomy, and this encounter between the two Ministers proved once again the inferiority—when great interests are at stake—of emotional men to hard-hearted business men ; however it must be acknowledged that Bismarck's statement was founded on fact. The Eastern Corps could have fought no more ; its way was blocked. Without food, without clothes, in many cases without arms, nothing remained to the unfortunate soldiers but the refuge offered by Switzerland.

Pasteur went to Geneva with his son, who, after recovering from the illness caused by fatigue and privation, succeeded in getting back to France to rejoin his regiment in the early days of February. Pasteur then went on to Lyons and stayed there with his brother-in-law, M. Loir, Dean of the Lyons Faculty of Science. He intended to go back to Paris, but a letter from Bertin dated February 18 advised him to wait. "This is the present state of the Ecole : south wing : pulled down ; will be built up again ; workmen expected. Third year dormitory : ambulance occupied by eight students. Science dormitory and drawing classroom : ambulance again, forty patients. Ground floor classroom : 120 artillery-men. Pasteur laboratory : 210 gardes nationaux, refugees from Issy. You had better wait." Bertin added, with his indomitable good humour, speaking of the bombardment : " The first day I did not go out, but I took my bearings and found the formula : in leaving the school, walk close along the houses on my left ; on coming back, keep close to them on my right ; with that I went out as usual. The population of Paris has shown magnificent resignation and patience. . . . In order to have our revenge, everything will have to be rebuilt from the top to the bottom, the top especially."

Pasteur also thought that reforms should begin from the top. He prepared a paper dated from Lyons, and entitled "Why France found no superior men in the hours of peril." Amongst the mistakes committed, one in particular had been before his mind for twenty years, ever since he left the Ecole Normale :

"The forgetfulness, disdain even, that France had had for great intellectual men, especially in the realm of exact science." This seemed the more sad to him that things had been very different at the end of the eighteenth century. Pasteur enu- merated the services rendered by science to his threatened country. If in 1792 France was able to face danger on all sides, it was because Lavoisier, Fourcroy, Guyton de Morveau, Chaptal, Berthollet, etc., discovered new means of extracting saltpetre and manufacturing gunpowder ; because Monge found a method of founding cannon with great rapidity ; and because the chemist Clouet invented a quick system of manufacturing steel. Science, in the service of patriotism, made a victorious army of a perturbed nation. If Marat, with his slanderous and injurious insinuations, had not turned from their course the feelings of the mob, Lavoisier never would have perished on the scaffold. The day after his execution, Lagrange said : "One moment was enough for his head to fall, and 200 years may not suffice to produce such another." Monge and Berthollet, also denounced by Marat, nearly shared the same fate : "In a week's time we shall be arrested, tried, condemned and executed," said Berthollet placidly to Monge, who answered with equal composure, thinking only of the country's defence, "All I know is that my gun factories are working admirably."

Bonaparte, from the first, made of science what he would have made of everything—a means of reigning. When he started for Egypt, he desired to have with him a staff of scientists, and Monge and Berthollet undertook to organize that distinguished company. Later, when Bonaparte became Napoleon I, he showed, in the intervals between his wars, so much respect for the place due to science as to proclaim the effacement of national rivalry when scientific discoveries were in question. Pasteur, when studying this side of the Imperial character, found in some pages by Arago on Monge that, after Waterloo, Napoleon, in a conversation he had with Monge at the Elysée, said, "Condemned now to command armies no longer, I can see but Science with which to occupy my mind and my soul . . ."

Alluding to the scientific supremacy of France during the early part of the nineteenth century, Pasteur wrote : "All the other nations acknowledged our superiority, though each could take pride in some great men : Berzelius in Sweden, Davy in England, Volta in Italy, other eminent men in Germany and Switzerland; but in no country were they as numerous as in France . . ." He added these regretful lines : " A victim of her political instability, France has done nothing tc keep up, to propagate and to develop the progress of science in our country; she has merely obeyed a given impulse; she has lived on her past, thinking herself great by the scientific discoveries to which she owed her material prosperity, but not perceiving that she was imprudently allowing the sources of those discoveries to become dry, whilst neighbouring nations, stimulated by her past example, were diverting for their own benefit the course of those springs, rendering them fruitful by their works, their efforts and their sacrifices.

"Whilst Germany was multiplying her universities, establishing between them the most salutary emulation, bestowing honours and consideration on the masters and doctors, creating vast laboratories amply supplied with the most perfect instruments, France, enervated by revolutions, ever vainly seeking for the best form of government, was giving but careless attention to her establishments for higher education . . .

"The cultivation of science in its highest expression is perhaps even more necessary to the moral condition than to the material prosperity of a nation.

" Great discoveries—the manifestations of thought in Art, in Science and in Letters, in a word the disinterested exercise of the mind in every direction and the centres of instruction from which it radiates, introduce into the whole of Society that philosophical or scientific spirit, that spirit of discernment, which submits everything to severe reasoning, condemns ignorance and scatters errors and prejudices. They raise the intellectual level and the moral sense, and through them the Divine idea itself is spread abroad and intensified."

At the very time when Pasteur was preoccupied with the desire of directing the public mind towards the principles of truth, justice and sovereign harmony, Sainte Claire Deville, speaking of the Academy, expressed similar ideas, proclaiming that France had been vanquished by science and that it was now time to free scientific bodies from the tyranny of red tape. Why should not the Academy become the centre of all measures relating to science, independently of government offices or officials?

J. B. Dumas took part in the discussion opened by Sainte Claire Deville, and agreed with his suggestions. He might

have said more, however, on a subject which he often took
up in private : the utility of pure science in daily experience.
With his own special gift of generalization, he could have expounded the progress of all kinds due to the workers who, by
their perseverance in resolving difficult problems, have brought
about so many precious and unexpected results. Few men in
France realized at that time that laboratories could be the
vestibule of farms, factories, etc. ; it was indeed a noble task,
that of proving that science was intended to lighten the burden
of humanity, not merely to be applied to devastation, carnage,
and hatred.

Pasteur was in the midst of these philosophical reflections
when he received the following answer from the principal of
the Faculty of Medicine of Bonn :

"Sir, the undersigned, now Principal of the Faculty of
Medicine of Bonn, is requested to answer the insult which you
have dared to offer to the German nation in the sacred person
of its august Emperor, King Wilhelm of Prussia, by sending
you the expression of its *entire contempt*."—DR. MAURICE
NAUMANN.

"P.S.—Desiring to keep its papers *free from taint*, the
Faculty herewith returns your screed."

Pasteur's reply contained the following : "I have the honour
of informing you, Mr. Principal, that there are times when
the expression of contempt in a Prussian mouth is equivalent
for a true Frenchman to that of *Virum clarissimum* which you
once publicly conferred upon me."

After invoking in favour of Alsace-Lorraine, Truth, of
Justice, and the laws of humanity, Pasteur added in a postscript—

"And now, Mr. Principal, after reading over both your
letter and mine, I sorrow in my heart to think that men who
like yourself and myself have spent a lifetime in the pursuit of
truth and progress, should address each other in such a fashion,
founded on my part on such actions. This is but one of the
results of the character your Emperor has given to this war.
You speak to me of *taint*. Mr. Principal, taint will rest, you
may be assured, until far-distant ages, on the memory of those
who began the bombardment of Paris when capitulation by
famine was inevitable, and who continued this act of savagery
after it had become evident to all men that it would not advance
by one hour the surrender of the heroic city."

Whilst Pasteur thus felt those simple and strong impressions
as a soldier or the man in the street might do, the creative
power of his nature was urging him to great and useful achievements.   He wrote from Lyons in March to M. Duclaux—

"My head is full of splendid projects; the war sent my
brain to grass, but I now· feel ready for further work.   Perhaps I am deluding myself; anyhow I will try   Oh l why
am I not rich, a millionaire?   I would say to you, to Ranlin,
to Gernez, to Van Tieghem, etc., come, we will transform the
world by our discoveries.   How fortunate you are to be young
and strong l   Why can I not begin a new life of study and
work l   Unhappy France, beloved country, if I could only
assist in raising thee from thy disasters l "

A few days later, in a letter to Raulin, this desire for devoted
work was again expressed almost feverishly.   He could foresee, in the dim distance, secret affinities between apparently
dissimilar things.   He had at that time returned to the researches which had absorbed his youth (because those studies
were less materially difficult to organize), and he could perceive
laws and connections between the facts he had observed and
those of the existence of which he felt assured.

"I have begun here some experiments in crystallization
which will open a great prospect if they should lead to positive
results.   You know that I believe that there is a cosmic dis-
symmetric influence which presides constantly and naturally
over the molecular organization of principles immediately essential to life ; and that, in consequence of this, the species of the
three kingdoms, by their structure, by their form, by the disposition of their tissues, have a definite relation to the movements of the universe.   For many of those species, if not for
all, the sun is the *primum movens* of nutrition ; but I believe in
another influence which would affect the whole organization,
for it would be the cause of the molecular dissymmetry proper
to the chemical components of life.   I want to be able by experiment to grasp a few indications as to the nature of this
great cosmic dissymmetrical influence.   It must, it may be
electricity, magnetism. . . . And, as one should always proceed
from the simple to the complex, I am now trying to crystallize
double racemate of soda and ammonia under the influence of a
spiral solenoid.

"I have various other forms of experiment to attempt.   If
one of them should succeed, we shall have work for the rest of

our lives, and in one of the greatest subjects man could approach, for I should not despair of arriving by this means at a very deep, unexpected and extraordinary modification of the animal and vegetable species.

"Good-bye, my dear Ranlin. Let us endeavour to distract our thoughts from human turpitudes by the disinterested search after truth."

In a little notebook where he jotted down some intended experiments we find evidence of those glimpses of divination in a few summary lines : " Show that life is in the germ, that it has been but in a state of transmission since the origin of creation. That the germ possesses possibilities of development, either of intelligence and will, or—and in the same way—of physical organs. Compare these possibilities with those possessed by the germ of chemical species which is in the chemical molecule. The possibilities of development in the germ of the chemical molecule consist in crystallization, in its form, in its physical and chemical properties. Those properties are in power in the germ of the molecule in the same way as the organs and tissues of animals and plants are in their respective germs. Add : nothing is more curious than to carry the comparison of living species with mineral species into the study of the wounds of either, and of their healing by means of nutrition—a nutrition coming from within in living beings, and from without through the medium of crystallization in the others. Here detail facts. . ''

In that same notebook, Pasteur, after writing down the following heading, "Letter to prepare on the species in connection with molecular dissymmetry," added, " I could write that letter to Bernard. I should say that being deprived of a laboratory by the present state of France, I am going to give him the preconceived ideas that I shall try to experiment upon when better times come. There is no peril in expressing ideas *a priori*, when they are taken as such, and can be gradually modified, perhaps even completely transformed, according to the result of the observation of facts."

He once compared those preconceived ideas with searchlights guiding the experimentalist, saying that they only became dangerous when they became fixed ideas.

Civil war had now come, showing, as Renan said, "a sore under the sore, an abyss below the abyss." What were the hopes and projects of Pasteur and of Sainte Claire Deville now that the very existence of the divided country was jeopardized under the eyes of the Prussians? The world of letters and of science, helpless amidst such disorders, had dispersed; Saint Claire Deville was at Gex, Dumas at Geneva. Some were wondering whether lectures could not be organized in Switzerland and in Belgium as they had been under the Empire, thus spreading abroad the influence of French thought. Examples might be quoted of men who had served the glory of their country in other lands, such as Descartes, who took refuge in Holland in order to continue his philosophic meditations. Pasteur might have been tempted to do likewise. Already, before the end of the war, an Italian professor of chemistry, Signor Chiozza, who had applied Pasteur's methods to silkworms in the neighbourhood of Villa Vicentina, got the Italian Government to offer him a laboratory and the direction of a silkworm establishment. Pasteur refused, and a deputy of Pisa, Signor Toscanelli, hearing of this, obtained for Pasteur the offer of what was better still—a professor's chair of Chemistry applied to Agriculture at Pisa; this would give every facility for work and all laboratory resources. "Pisa," Signor Chiozza said, "is a quiet town, a sort of Latin quarter in the middle of the country, where professors and students form the greater part of the population. I think you would be received with the greatest cordiality and quite exceptional consideration . . . I fear that black days of prolonged agitation are in store for France."

Pasteur's health and work were indeed valuable to the whole world, and Signor Chiozza's proposition seemed simple and rational. Pasteur was much divided in his mind: his first impulse was to renew his refusal. He thought but of his vanquished country, and did not wish to forsake it. But was it to his country's real interests that he should remain a helpless spectator of so many disasters? Was it not better to carry French teaching abroad, to try and provoke in young Italian students enthusiasm for French scientists, French achievements? He might still serve his beloved country in that quiet retreat, amidst all those facilities for continuous work. He thought of writing to Raulin, who had relations in Italy, and who might follow his master. Finally, he was offered very great personal advantages, a high salary—and this determined his refusal, for, as he wrote to Signor Chiozza, "I should feel that I deserved a deserter's penalty if I sought, away from my country in distress, a material situation better than it can offer me."

" Nevertheless allow me to tell you, Sir (he wrote to Signor Toscanelli, refusing his offer), in all sincerity, that the memory of your offer will remain in the annals of my family as a title of nobility, as a proof of Italy's sympathy for France, as a token of the esteem accorded to my work. And as far as you, M. le Député, are concerned it will remain in my eyes a brilliant proof of the way in which public men in Italy regard science and its grandeur."

And now what was Pasteur to do—he who could not live away from a laboratory? In April, 1871, he could neither go back to Paris and the Commune nor to Arbois, now trans-formed into a Prussian dépôt. It seemed, indeed, from the letters he received that his fellow citizens were now destined but to feed and serve a victorious foe, whose exactions were all the more rigorous that the invasion of the town on January 25 had been preceded by an attempt at resistance on the part of the inhabitants. On that morning, a few French soldiers who were seeking their regiments and a handful of *franc tireurs* had posted themselves among the vines. About ten o'clock a first shot sounded in the distance ; in a turn of the sinuous Besançon road, when the Prussian vanguard had appeared, a Zouave—who the day before was begging from door to door, shaking with ague, and who had taken refuge in the village of Montigny, two kilometres from Arbois—had in despair fired his last cartridge. A squad of Prussians left the road and rushed to-wards the smoke of the gun. The soldier was seized, shot down on the spot, and mutilated with bayonets. Whilst the main column continued their advance towards the town, de-tachments explored the vines on either side of the road, shoot-ing here and there. An old man who, with a courageous indifference, was working in his vineyard was shot down at his work. A little pastrycook's boy, nicknamed Biscuit by the Arboisians, who, led by curiosity, had come down from the upper town to the big poplar trees at the entrance of Arbois, suddenly staggered, struck by a Prussian bullet. He was just able to creep back to the first house, his eyes already dimmed by death.

Those were but the chances of war, but other crueller episodes thrilled Pasteur to the very depths of his soul. Such things are lost in history, just as a little blood spilt disappears in a river, but, for the witnesses and contemporaries of the facts, the trace of blood remains. An incident will help the reader to understand the lasting indignation the war excited in Pasteur.

One of the Prussian sergeants, who, after the shot fired at Montigny, were leading small detachments of soldiers, thought that a house on the outskirts of Arbois, in the faubourg of Verreux, looked as if it might shelter *franc tireurs*. He directed his men towards it and the house was soon reached.

It was now twelve o'clock, all fighting had ceased, and the first Prussians who had arrived were masters of the town. Others were arriving from various directions; a heavy silence reigned over the town. The mayor, M. Lefort, led by a Prussian officer who covered him with a revolver whenever he addressed him, was treated as a hostage responsible for absolute submission. Every door in the small Town Hall was opened in succession in order to see that there were no arms hidden. The mayor was each time made to pass first, so that he should receive the shot in case of a surprise. In the library, three flags, which General Delort had brought back from the Rhine campaign when he was a captain in the cavalry and given to his native town, were torn down and the general's bust overturned.

The sergeant, violently entering the suspected house with his men, found a whole family peacefully sitting down to their dinner—the husband, wife, a son of nineteen, and two young daughters. The invaders made no search nor asked any questions of those poor people, who had probably done nothing worse than to offer a few glasses of wine to French soldiers as they passed. The sergeant did not even ask the name of the master of the house (Antoine Ducret, aged fifty-nine), but seized him by his coat and ordered his men to seize the son too. The woman, who rushed to the door in her endeavour to prevent her husband and her son from being thus taken from her, was violently flung to the end of the room, her trembling daughters crouching around her as they listened to the heavy Prussian boots going down the wooden stairs. There is a public drinking fountain not far from the house; Ducret was taken there and placed against a wall. He understood, and cried out, "Spare my son!!" "What do you say?" said the sergeant to the boy. "I will stay with my father," he answered simply. The father, struck by two bullets at close range, fell at the feet of his son, who was shot down immediately afterwards. The two corpses, afterwards mutilated with bayonets, remained lying by the water side ; the neighbours succeeded in preventing the mother and her two daughters from leaving their house until the bodies had been placed in a coffin. On the tombs of Antoine and Charles Ducret the equivocal inscription was placed " Fell at Arbois, January 25, 1871, under Prussian fire." For the honour of humanity, a German officer, having heard these details, offered the life of the sergeant to Ducret's widow ; but she entertained no thoughts of revenge. "His death would not give them back to me," she said.

Pasteur could not become resigned to the humiliation of France, and, tearing his thoughts from the nightmare of the war and the Commune, he dwelt continually on the efforts that would be necessary to carry out the great task of raising the country once again to its proper rank. In his mind it was the duty of every one to say, "In what way can I be useful?" Each man should strive not so much to play a great part as to give the best of his ability. He had no patience with those who doubt everything in order to have an excuse for doing nothing.

He had indeed known dark moments of doubt and misgivings, as even the greatest minds must do, but notwithstanding these periods of discouragement he was convinced that science and peace will ultimately triumph over ignorance and war. In spite of recent events, the bitter conditions of peace which tore unwilling Alsace and part of Lorraine away from France, the heavy tax of gold and of blood weighing down future generations, the sad visions of young men in their prime cut down on the battlefield or breathing their last in hospitals all to no apparent purpose ; in spite of all these sad memories he was persuaded that thinkers would gradually awaken in the nations ideas of justice and of concord.

He had now for nine years been following with a passionate interest some work begun in his own laboratory by Raulin, his first curator. Some of the letters he wrote to Raulin during those nine years give us a faint idea of the master that Pasteur was. It had been with great regret that Raulin had left the laboratory in obedience to the then laws of the University in order to take up active work at the Brest college, and Pasteur's letters (December, 1862) brought him joy and encouragement : "Keep up your courage, do not allow the idleness of pro-

vincial life to disturb you.   Teach your pupils to the very best
of your ability and give up your leisure to experiments ; this
was M. Biot's advice to myself." When in July, 1863, he
began to fear that Raulin might allow imagination to lead him
astray in his work, he repeatedly advised him to state
nothing that could not be proved : " Be very strict in
your deductions " ; then, apparently, loth to damp the young
man's ardour : "I have the greatest confidence in your judgment ; do not take too much heed of my observations."

In 1863 Pasteur asked Ranlin to come with him, Gernez and
Duclaux, to Arbois for some studies on wines, etc., but Raulin,
absorbed in the investigations he had undertaken, refused ; in
1865 he refused to come to Alais, still being completely wrapt
up in the same work.   Pasteur sympathized heartily with his
pupil's perseverance, and, when Ranliu was at last able to
announce to his master the results so long sought after, Pasteur
hurried to Caen, where Raulin was now professor of Physics,
and returned full of enthusiasm.   His modesty in all that concerned himself now giving way to delighted pride, he spoke of
Raulin's discoveries to every one.   Yet they concerned an
apparently unimportant subject—a microscopical fungus, a
simple mucor, whose spores, mingled with atmospheric germs,
develop on bread moistened with vinegar or on a slice of lemon ;
yet no precious plant ever inspired more care or solicitude than
that *aspergillus niger*, as it is called.   Raulin, inspired by
Pasteur's studies on cultures in an artificial medium, that is, a
medium exclusively composed of defined chemical substances,
resolved to find for this plant a typical medium capable of giving
its maximum development to the aspergillus niger.   Some of
his comrades looked upon this as upon a sort of laboratory
amusement ; but Raulin, ever a man of one idea, looked upon
the culture of microscopic vegetation as a step towards a greater
knowledge of vegetable physiology, leading to the development
of artificial manure production, and from that to the rational
nutrition of the human organisms.   He started from the conditions indicated by Pasteur for the development of mucedinæ in
general and in particular for a mucor which has some points of
resemblance with the aspergillus niger, the *penicillium glaucum*, which spreads a bluish tint over mouldy bread, jam, and
soft cheeses.   Raulin began by placing pure spores of aspergillus niger on the surface of a saucer containing everything

that seemed necessary to their perfect growth, in a stove heated to a temperature of 20° C.; but in spite of every care, after forty days had passed, the tiny fungus was languishing and unhealthy. A temperature of 30° did not seem more successful; and when the stove was heated to above 38° the result was the same. At 35°, with a moist and changing atmosphere, the result was favourable—very fortunately for Ranlin, for the principal of the college, an economically minded man, did not approve of burning so much gas for such a tiny fungus and with such poor results. This want of sympathy excited Raulin's solemn wrath and caused him to meditate dark projects of revenge, such as ignoring his enemy in the street on some future occasion. In the meanwhile he continued his slow and careful experiments. He succeeded at last in composing a liquid, technically called Raulin's liquid, in which the aspergillus niger grew and flourished within six or even three days. Eleven substances were necessary : water, candied sugar, tartaric acid, nitrate of ammonia, phosphate of ammonia, carbonate of potash, carbonate of magnesia, sulphate of ammonia, sulphate of zinc, sulphate of iron, and silicate of potash. He now studied the part played by each of those elements, varying his quantities, taking away one substance and adding another, and obtained some very curious results. For instance, the aspergillus was extraordinarily sensitive to the action of zinc; if the quantity of zinc was reduced by a few milligrams the vegetation decreased by one-tenth. Other elements were pernicious; if Raulin added to his liquid $\frac{1}{1600000}$ of nitrate of silver, the growth of the fungus ceased. Moreover, if he placed the liquid in a silver goblet instead of a china saucer, the vegetation did not even begin, "though," writes M. Duclaux, analysing this fine work of his fellow student, "it is almost impossible to chemically detect any dissolution of the silver into the liquid. But the fungus proves it by dying."

In this thesis, now a classic, which only appeared in 1870, Raulin enumerated with joyful gratitude all that he owed to his illustrious master—general views, principles and methods, suggestive ideas, advice and encouragement—saying that Pasteur had shown him the road on which he had travelled so far. Pasteur, touched by his pupil's affection, wrote to thank him, saying : "You credit me with too much; it is enough for me that your work should be known as having been begun in my laboratory, and in a direction the fruitfulness of which I was perhaps the first to point out. I had only conceived hopes, and you bring us solid realities."

In April, 1871, Pasteur, preoccupied with the future, and ambitious for those who might come after him, wrote to Claude Bernard : "Allow me to submit to you an idea which has occurred to me, that of conferring on my dear pupil and friend Ranlin the Experimental Physiology prize, for his splendid work on the nutriment of mucors, or rather of a mucor, the excellence of which work has not escaped you. I doubt if you can find anything better. I must tell you that this idea occurred to me whilst reading your admirable report on the progress of General Physiology in France. If therefore my suggestion seems to you acceptable, you will have sown the germ of it in my mind; if you disapprove of it I shall make you partly responsible."

Claude Bernard hastened to reply : " You may depend upon my support for your pupil M. Raulin. It will be for me both a pleasure and a duty to support such excellent work and to glorify the method of the master who inspired it."

In his letter to Claude Bernard, Pasteur had added these words : "I have made up my mind to go and spend a few months at Royat with my family, so as to be near my dear Duclaux. We shall raise a few grammes of silkworm seed."

M. Duclaux was then professor of chemistry at the Faculty of Clermont Ferrand, a short distance from Royat, and Pasteur intended to walk every day to the laboratory of his former pupil. But M. Duclaux did not countenance this plan ; he meant to entertain his master and his master's family in his own house, 25, Rue Montlosier, where he could even have one room arranged as a silkworm nursery. He succeeded in persuading Pasteur, and they organized a delightful home life which recalled the days at Pont Gisquet before the war.

Pasteur was seeking the means of making his seed-selecting process applicable to small private nurseries as well as to large industrial establishments. The only difficulty was the cost of the indispensable microscope ; but Pasteur thought that each village might possess its microscope, and that the village schoolmaster might be entrusted with the examination of the moths.

In a letter written in April, 1871, to M. Bellotti, of the Milan Civic Museum, Pasteur, after describing in a few lines the simple process he had taken five years to study, added—

"If I dared to quote myself, I would recall those words from my book—

"'If I were a silkworm cultivator I never would raise seed from worms I had not observed during the last days of their life, so as to satisfy myself as to their vigour and agility just before spinning. The seed chosen should be that which comes from worms who climbed the twigs with agility, who showed no mortality from flachery between the fourth moulting and climbing time, and whose freedom from corpuscles will have been demonstrated by the microscope. If that is done, any one with the slightest knowledge of silkworm culture will succeed in every case.'"

Italy and Austria vied with each other in adopting the seed selected by the Pasteur system. But it was only when Pasteur was on the eve of receiving from the Austrian Government the great prize offered in 1868 to "whoever should discover a preventive and curative remedy against pébrine" that French sericicultors began to be convinced. The French character offers this strange contrast, that France is often willing to risk her fortune and her blood for causes which may be unworthy, whilst at another moment, in everyday life, she shrinks at the least innovation before accepting a benefit originated on her own soil. The French often wait until other nations have adopted and approved a French discovery before venturing to adopt it in their turn.

Pasteur did not stop to look back and delight in his success, but hastened to turn his mind to another kind of study. His choice of a subject was influenced by patriotic motives. Germany was incontestably superior to France in the manufacture of beer, and he conceived the thought of making France a successful rival in that respect; in order to enable himself to do so, he undertook to study the scientific mechanism of beer manufacture.

There was a brewery at Chamalières, between Clermont and Royat. Pasteur began by visiting it with eager curiosity, inquiring into the minutest details, endeavouring to find out the why and the wherefore of every process, and receiving vague answers with much astonishment. M. Kuhn, the Chamalières brewer, did not know much more about beer than did his fellow brewers in general. Very little was known at that time about the way it was produced; when brewers received complaints from their customers, they procured yeast from a fresh source. In a book of reference which was then much in use, entitled *Alimentary Substances: the Means of Improving and Preserving them, and of Recognizing their Alterations*, six pages were given up to beer by the author, M. Payen, a member of the Institute. He merely showed that germinated barley, called malt, was diluted, then heated and mixed with hops, thus forming beer-wort, which was submitted, when cold, to alcoholic fermentation through the yeast added to the above liquid. M. Payen conceded to beer some nutritive properties, but added, a little disdainfully, " Beer, perhaps on account of the pungent smell of hops, does not seem endowed with stimulating properties as agreeable, or as likely to inspire such bright and cheerful ideas, as the sweet and varied aroma of the good wines of France."

In a paragraph on the alterations of beer—" *spontaneous alterations* "—M. Payen said that it was chiefly during the summer that beer became altered. " It becomes acid, and even noticeably putrid, and ceases to be fit to drink."

Pasteur's hopes of making French beer capable of competing with German beer were much strengthened by faith in his own method. He had, by experimental proof, destroyed the theory of spontaneous generation ; he had shown that chance has no share in fermentations ; the animated nature and the specific characteristics of those ferments, the methods of culture in appropriate media, were so many scientific points gained. The difficulties which remained to be solved were the question of pure yeast and the search for the causes of alteration which make beer thick, acid, sour, slimy or putrid. Pasteur thought that these alterations were probably due to the development of germs in the air, in the water, or on the surface of the numerous utensils used in a brewery.

As he advanced further and further into that domain of the infinitely small which he had discovered, whether the subject was wine, vinegar, or silkworms—this last study already opening before him glimpses of light on human pathology—new and unexpected visions rose before his sight.

Pasteur had formerly demonstrated that if a putrescible liquid, such as beef broth for instance, after being previously boiled, is kept in a vessel with a long curved neck, the air only reaching it after having deposited its germs in the curves of the neck, does not alter it in any way. He now desired to invent an apparatus which would protect the wort against external dusts, against the microscopic germs ever ready to interfere with the course of proper fermentation by the introduction of other noxious ferments. It was necessary to prove that beer remains unalterable whenever it does not contain the organisms which cause its diseases. Many technical difficulties were in the way, but the brewers of Chamalières tried in the most obliging manner to facilitate things for him.

This exchange of services between science and industry was in accordance with Pasteur's plan; though he had been prophesying for fourteen years the great progress which would result from an alliance between laboratories and factories, the idea was hardly understood at that time. Yet the manufacturers of Lille and Orleans, the wine merchants and the silkworm cultivators of the South of France, and of Austria and Italy, might well have been called as enthusiastic witnesses to the advantages of such a collaboration.

Pasteur, happy to make the fortune of others, intended to organize, against the danger of alterations in beer, some experiments which would give to that industry solid notions resting on a scientific basis. "Dear master," wrote he to J. B. Dumas on August 4, 1871, from Clermont, "I have asked the brewer to send you twelve bottles of my beer. . . I hope you will find it compares favourably even with the excellent beer of Paris cafés." There was a postscript to this letter, proving once more Pasteur's solicitude for his pupils. "A thousand thanks for your kind welcome of Raulin's work; Bernard's support has also been promised him. The Academy could not find a better recipient for the prize. It is quite exceptional work."

Pasteur, ever full of praises for his pupil, also found excuses for him. In spite of M. Duclaux's pressing request, Ranlin had again found reasons to refuse an invitation to come to Auvergne for a few days. "I regret very much that you did not come to see us," wrote Pasteur to Ranlin, "especially on account of the beer. . . . Tell me what you think of doing. When are you coming to Paris for good? I shall want you to help me to arrange my laboratory, where everything, as you know, has still to be done; it must be put into working order as soon as possible."

Pasteur would have liked Raulin to come with him to London in September, 1871, before settling down in Paris.

The Chamalières brewery was no longer sufficient for Pasteur; he wished to see one of those great English breweries

P

which produce in one year more than 100,000 hectolitres of beer. The great French *savant* was most courteously received by the managers of one of the most important breweries in London, who offered to show him round the works where 250 men were employed. But Pasteur asked for a little of the barm of the porter which was flowing into a trough from the cask. He examined that yeast with a microscope, and soon recognized a noxious ferment which he drew on a piece of paper and showed to the bystanders, saying, "This porter must leave much to be desired," to the astonished managers, who had not expected this sudden criticism. Pasteur added that surely the defect must have been betrayed by a bad taste, perhaps already complained of by some customers. Thereupon the managers owned that that very morning some fresh yeast had had to be procured from another brewery. Pasteur asked to see the new yeast, and found it incomparably purer, but such was not the case with the barm of the other products then in fermentation—*ale* and *pale ale*.

By degrees, samples of every kind of beer on the premises were brought to Pasteur and put under the microscope. He detected marked beginnings of disease in some, in others merely a trace, but a threatening one. The various foremen were sent for; this scientific visit seemed like a police inquiry. The owner of the brewery, who had been fetched, was obliged to register, one after another, these experimental demonstrations. It was only human to show a little surprise, perhaps a little impatience of wounded feeling. But it was impossible to mistake the authority of the French scientist's words : " Every marked alteration in the quality of the beer coincides with the development of micro-organisms foreign to the nature of true beer yeast." It would have been interesting to a psychologist to study in the expression of Pasteur's hearers those shades of curiosity, doubt, and approbation, which ended in the thoroughly English conclusion that there was profit to be made out of this object lesson.

Pasteur afterwards remembered with a smile the answers he received, rather vague at first, then clearer, and, finally— interest and confidence now obtained—the confession that there was in a corner of the brewery a quantity of spoilt beer, which had gone wrong only a fortnight after it was made, and was not drinkable. " I examined it with a microscope," said Pasteur, " and could not at first detect any ferments of disease; but guessing that it might have become clear through a long rest, the ferments now inert having dropped to the bottom of the reservoirs, I examined the deposit at the bottom of the reservoirs. It was entirely composed of filaments of disease unmixed with the least globule of alcoholic yeast. The complementary fermentation of that beer had therefore been exclusively a morbid fermentation.''

When he visited the same brewery again, a week later, he found that not only had a microscope been procured immediately, but the yeast of all the beer then being brewed had been changed.

Pasteur was happy to offer to the English, who like to call themselves practical men, a proof of the usefulness of disinterested science, persuaded as he was that the moral debt incurred to a French scientist would in some measure revert to France herself. "We must make some friends for our beloved France," he would say. And if in the course of conversation an Englishman gave expression to any doubt concerning the future of the country, Pasteur, his grave and powerful face full of energy, would answer that every Frenchman, after the horrible storm which had raged for so many months, was valiantly returning to his daily task, whether great or humble, each one thinking of retrieving the national fall.

Every morning, as he left his hotel to go to the various breweries which he was now privileged to visit in their smallest details, he observed this English people, knowing the value of time, seeing its own interests in all things, consistent in its ideas and in its efforts, respectful of established institutions and hierarchy; and he thought with regret how his own countrymen lacked these qualities. But if the French are rightly taxed with a feverish love of change, should not justice be rendered to that generous side of the French character, so gifted, capable of so much, and which finds in self-sacrifice the secret of energy, for whom hatred is a real suffering? "Let us work!" Pasteur's favourite phrase ever ended those philosophical discussions.

He wanted to do two years' work in one, regardless of health and strength. Beyond the diseases of beer, avoidable since they come from outside, he foresaw the application of the doctrine of exterior germs to other diseases. But he did not allow his imagination to run away with him, and resolutely fixed his mind on his present object, which was the application of science to the brewing industry.

" The interest of those visits to English breweries," wrote Pasteur to Ranlin, " and of the information I am able to collect (I hear that I ought to consider this as a great favour) causes me to regret very much that you should be in want of rest, for I am sure you would have been charmed to acquire so much instruction *de visu.* Why should you not come for a day or two if your health permits? Do as you like about that, but in any case prepare for immediate work on my return. We need not wait for the new laboratory; we can settle down in the old one and in a Paris brewery."

When Pasteur returned to Paris, Bertin, who had not seen him since the recent historic events, welcomed him with a radiant delight. School friendships are like those favourite books which always open at the page we prefer; time has no hold on certain affections; ever new, ever young, they never show signs of age. Bertin's love was very precious to Pasteur, though the two friends were as different from each other as possible. Pasteur, ever preoccupied, seemed to justify the Englishman who said that genius consists in an infinite capacity for taking pains; whilst Bertin, with his merry eyes, was the very image of a smiling philosopher. In spite of his position as sub-director, which he most conscientiously filled, he was not afraid to whistle or to sing popular songs as he went along the passages of the Ecole Normale. He came round to Pasteur's rooms almost every evening, bringing with him joy, lightness of heart, and a rest and relaxation for the mind, brightening up his friend by his amusing way of looking at things in general, and—at that time—beer in particular.

Whilst Pasteur saw but pure yeast, and thought but of spores of disease, ferments, and parasitic invasions, Bertin would dilate on certain cafés in the Latin quarter, where, without regard to great scientific principles, experts could be asked to pronounce between the beer on the premises and laboratory beer, harmless and almost agreeable, but lacking in the refinement of taste of which Bertin, who had spent many years in Strasburg, was a competent judge. Pasteur, accustomed to an absolutely infallible method, like that which he had invented for the seeding of silkworms, heard Bertin say to him, " First of all, give me a good *bock,* you can talk learnedly afterwards." Pasteur acknowledged, however, the improvements obtained by certain brewers, who, thanks to the experience of years, knew how to choose yeast which gave a particular taste, and also how to employ preventive measures against accidental and pernicious ferments (such as the use of ice, or of hops in a larger quantity). But, though laughing at Bertin's jokes, Pasteur was convinced that great progress in the brewer's art would date from his studies.

He was now going through a series of experiments, buying at Bertin's much praised cafés samples of various famous beers Strasburg, Nancy, Vienna, Burton's, etc. After letting the samples rest for twenty-four hours he decanted them and sowed one drop of the déposit in vessels full of pure wort, which he placed in a temperature of 20° C. After fifteen or eighteen days he studied and tasted the yeasts formed in the wort, and found them all to contain ferments of diseases. He sowed some pure yeast in some other vessels, with the same precautions, and all the beers of this series remained pure from strange ferments and free from bad taste; they had merely become *flat*.

He was eagerly seeking the means of judging how his laboratory tests would work in practice. He spent some time at Tantonville, in Lorraine, visiting an immense brewery, of which the owners were the brothers Tourtel. Though very carefully kept, the brewery was yet not quite clean enough to satisfy him. It is true that he was more than difficult to please in that respect; a small detail of his everyday life revealed this constant preoccupation. He never used a plate or a glass without examining them minutely and wiping them carefully; no microscopic speck of dust escaped his shortsighted eyes. Whether at home or with strangers he invariably went through this preliminary exercise, in spite of the anxious astonishment of his hostess, who usually feared that some negligence had occurred, until Pasteur, noticing her slight dismay, assured her that this was but an inveterate scientist's habit. If he carried such minute care into daily life, we can imagine how strict was his examination of scientific things and of brewery tanks.

After those studies at Tantonville with his curator, M. Grenet, Pasteur laid down three great principles—

1. Every alteration either of the wort or of the beer itself depends on the development of micro-organisms which are ferments of diseases.

2. These germs of ferments are brought by the air, by the ingredients, or by the apparatus used in breweries.

3. Whenever beer contains no living germs it is unalterable.

When once those principles were formulated and proved they were to triumph over all professional uncertainties. And in the same way that wines could be preserved from various causes of alteration by heating, bottled beer could escape the development of disease ferments by being brought to a temperature of 50° to 55°. The application of this process gave rise to the new word " *pasteurized* " beer, a neologism which soon became current in technical language.

Pasteur foresaw the distant consequences of these studies, and wrote in his book on beer—

"When we see beer and wine subjected to deep alterations because they have given refuge to micro-organisms invisibly introduced and now swarming within them, it is impossible not to be pursued by the thought that similar facts may, *must*, take place in animals and in man. But if we are inclined to believe that it is so because we think it likely and possible, let us endeavour to remember, before we affirm it, that the greatest disorder of the mind is to allow the will to direct the belief."

This shows us once more the strange duality of this inspired man, who associated in his person the faith of an apostle with the inquiring patience of a scientist.

He was often disturbed by tiresome discussions from the researches to which he would gladly have given his whole time. The heterogenists had not surrendered; they would not admit that alterable organic liquids could be indefinitely preserved from putrefaction and fermentation when in contact with air freed from dusts.

Pouchet, the most celebrated of them, who considered that part of a scientist's duty consists in vulgarizing his discoveries, was preparing for the New Year, 1872, a book called *The Universe: the Infinitely Great and the Infinitely Small.* He enthusiastically recalled the spectacle revealed at the end of the seventeenth century by the microscope, which he compared to a sixth sense. He praised the discoveries made in 1838 by Ehrenberg on the prodigious activity of infusories, but he never mentioned Pasteur's name, leaving entirely on one side the immense work accomplished by the infinitely small and ever active agents of putrefaction and fermentation.

He owned that "a few microzoa did fly about here and there," but he called the theory of germs a "ridiculous fiction"

At the same time Liebig, who, since the interview in July, 1870, had had time to recover his health, published a long treatise disputing certain facts put forward by Pasteur.

Pasteur had declared that, in the process of vinegar-making known as the German process, the chips of beech-wood placed in the barrels were but supports for the *mycoderma aceti.* Liebig, after having, he said, consulted at Munich the chief of one of the largest vinegar factories, who did not believe in the presence of the mycoderma, affirmed that he himself had not seen a trace of the fungus on chips which had been used in that factory for twenty-five years.

In order to bring this debate to a conclusion Pasteur suggested a very simple experiment, which was to dry some of those chips rapidly in a stove and to send them to Paris, where a commission, selected from the members of the Académie des Sciences, would decide on this conflict. Pasteur undertook to demonstrate to the Commission the presence of the mycoderma on the surface of the chips. Or another means might be used : the Munich vinegar maker would be asked to scald one of his barrels with boiling water and then to make use of it again. "According to Liebig's theory," said Pasteur, "that barrel should work as before, but I affirm that no vinegar will form in it for a long time, not until new mycoderma have grown on the surface of the chips." In effect, the boiling water would destroy the little fungus. With the usual clear directness which increased the interest of the public in this scientific discussion, Pasteur formulated once more his complete theory of acetification : "The principle is very simple : whenever wine is transformed into vinegar, it is by the action of the layer of *mycoderma aceti* developed on its surface." Liebig, however, refused the suggested test.

Immediately after that episode a fresh adversary, M. Frémy, a member of the Académie des Sciences, began with Pasteur a discussion, which was destined to be a long one, on the question of the origin of ferments. M. Frémy alluded to the fact that he had given many years to that subject, having published a notice on lactic fermentation as far back as 1841, "at a time," he said, "when our learned colleague—M. Pasteur—was barely entering into science." . . . " In the production of wine," said M. Frémy, " it is the juice of the fruit itself, which, put in contact with air, gives birth to grains of yeast by the transformation of albuminous matter, whilst M. Pasteur declares that the grains of yeast are produced by germs." According to M. Frémy, ferments did not come from atmospheric dusts, but were created by organic bodies. And, inventing for his own use the new word *hemiorganism*, M. Frémy explained the word and the action by saying that there are some *hemiorganized* bodies which, by reason of the vital force with which they are endowed, go through successive decompositions and give birth to new derivatives; thus are ferments engendered.

Another colleague, M. Trécul, a botanist and a genuine truth-seeking *savant*, arose in his turn. He said he had witnessed a whole transformation of microscopic species each into the other, and in support of this theory he invoked the names of the three inseparables—Pouchet, Musset and Joly. Himself a heterogenist, he had in 1867 given a definition to which he willingly alluded : "Heterogenesis is a natural operation by which life, on the point of abandoning an organized body, concentrates its action on some particles of that body and forms thereof beings quite different from that of the substance which has been borrowed."

Old arguments and renewed negations were brought forward, and Pasteur knew well that this was but a reappearance of the old quarrel; he therefore answered by going straight to the point. At the Académie des Sciences, on December 26, 1871, he addressed M. Trécul in these words : "I can assure our learned colleague that he might have found in the treatises I have published decisive answers to most of the questions he has raised. I am really surprised to see him tackle the question of so-called spontaneous generation, without having more at his disposal than doubtful facts and incomplete observations. My astonishment was not less than at our last sitting, when M. Frémy entered upon the same debate with nothing to produce but superannuated opinions and not one new positive fact."

In his passion for truth and his desire to be convincing Pasteur threw out this challenge : "Would M. Frémy confess his error if I were to demonstrate to him that the natural juice of the grape, exposed to the contact of air, deprived of its germs, can neither ferment nor give birth to organized yeasts?" This interpellation was perhaps more violent than was usual in the meetings of the solemn Academy, but scientific truth was in question. And Pasteur, recognizing the old arguments under M. Frémy's hemiorganism and M. Trécul's transformations, referred his two contradictors to the experiments by which he had proved that alterable liquids, such as blood or urine, could be exposed to the contact of air deprived of its germs without undergoing the least fermentation or putrefaction. Had not this fact been the basis on which Lister had founded "his marvellous surgical method"? And in the bitterness given to his speech by his irritation against error, the epithet "marvellous" burst out with a visible delight in rendering homage to Lister.

Pasteur, then in full possession of all the qualities of his genius, was feeling the sort of fever known to great scientists, great artists, great writers : the ardent desire of finding, of discovering something he could leave to posterity. Interrupted by these belated contradictors when he wanted to be going forward, he only restrained his impatience with difficulty.

His old master, Balard, appealed to him in the Académie itself (January 22, 1872), in the name of their old friendship, to disregard the attacks of his adversaries, instead of wasting his time and his strength in trying to convince them. He reminded him of all he had achieved, of the benefits he had brought to the industries of wine, beer, vinegar, silkworms, etc., and alluded to the possibility foreseen by Pasteur himself of preserving mankind from some of the mysterious diseases which were perhaps due to germs in atmospheric air. He ended by urging him to continue his studies peacefully in the laboratory built for him, and to continue the scientific education of young pupils who might one day become worthy successors of Van Tieghem, Duclaux, Gernez, Raulin, etc.   thus forming a whole generation of young scientists instructed in Pasteur's school.

M. Duclaux wrote to him in the same sense : "I see very well what you may lose in that fruitless struggle—your rest, your time and your health ; I try in vain to see any possible advantage."

But nothing stopped him ; neither Balard's public advice, his pupils' letters, even J. B. Dumas' imploring looks. He could not keep himself from replying. Sometimes he regretted his somewhat sharp language, though—in his own words— he never associated it with feelings of hostility towards his contradictors as long as he believed in their good faith; what he wanted was that truth should have the last word. "What *you* lack, M. Frémy, is familiarity with a microscope, and you, M. Trécul, are not accustomed to laboratories!" "M. Frémy is always trying to displace the question," said Pasteur, ten months after M. Balard's appeal.

Whilst M. Frémy disputed, discussed, and filled the Académie with his objections, M. Trécul, whose life was somewhat misanthropical and whose usually sad and distrustful face was seen nowhere but at the Institute, insisted slowly, in a mournful voice, on certain transformations of divers cells or spores from one into the other. Pasteur declared that those ideas of transformation were erroneous; but—and there lay the interest of the debate—there was one of those transformations that Pasteur himself had once believed possible : that of the *mycoderma vini*, or wine flower, into an alcoholic ferment under certain conditions of existence.

A modification in the life of the mycoderma when submerged had led him to believe in a transformation of the mycoderma cells into yeast cells. It was on this question, which had been left in suspense, that the debate with Trécul came to an end, leaving to the witnesses of it a most vivid memory of Pasteur's personality—inflexible when he held his proofs, full of scruples and reserve when seeking those proofs, and accepting no personal praise if scientific truth was not recognized and honoured before everything else.

On November 11 Pasteur said : "Four months ago doubts suddenly appeared in my mind as to the truth of the fact in question, and which M. Trécul still looks upon as indisputable. . . . In order to disperse those doubts I have instituted the most numerous and varied experiments and I have not succeeded through those four months in satisfying myself by irrefragable proofs; I still have my doubts. Let this example show to M. Trécul how difficult it is to conclude definitely in such delicate studies."

Pasteur studied the scientific point for a long time, for he never abandoned a subject, but was ever ready to begin again after a failure. He modified the disposition of his first tests, and by the use of special vessels and slightly complicated apparatus succeeded in eliminating the only imaginable cause of error—the possible fall, during the manipulations, of exterior germs, that is, the fortuitous sowing of yeast cells. After that he saw no more yeast and no more active alcoholic fermentation; he had therefore formerly been the dupe of a delusion. In his *Studies on Beer* Pasteur tells of his error and its rectification : "At a time when ideas on the transformations of species are so readily adopted, perhaps because they dispense with rigorous experimentation, it is somewhat interesting to consider that in the course of my researches on microscopic plants in a state of purity I once had occasion to believe in the transformation of one organism into another, the transformation of the *mycoderma vini* or *cerevisiae* into yeast, and that this time I was in error ; I had not avoided the cause of illusion which my confirmed confidence in the theory of germs had so often led me to discover in the observations of others."

"The notion of species," writes M. Duclaux, who was narrowly associated with those experiments, " was saved for the present from the attacks directed against it, and it has not been seriously contested since, at least not on that ground."

Some failures are blessings in disguise. When discovering his mistake, Pasteur directed his attention to a strange phenomenon. We find in his book on beer—a sort of laboratory diary—the following details on his observation of the growth of some mycoderma seed which he had just scattered over some sweetened wine or beer-wort in small china saucers.

" When the cells or articles of the mycoderma vini are in full germinating and propagating activity in contact with air on a sweetened substratum, they live at the expense of that sugar and other subjacent materials absolutely like the animals who also utilize the oxygen in the air while freeing carbonic acid gas, consuming this and that, and correlatively increasing, regenerating themselves and creating new materials.

"Under those conditions not only does the mycoderma vini form no alcohol appreciable by analysis, but if alcohol exists in the subjacent liquid the mycoderma reduces it to water and carbonic acid gas by the fixation of the oxygen in the air." Pasteur, having submerged the mycoderma and studied it to see how it would accommodate itself to the new conditions offered to it, and whether it would die like an animal asphyxiated by the sudden deprivation of oxygen, saw that life was continued in the submerged cells, slow, difficult, of a short duration, but undoubtedly life, and that this life was accompanied by alcoholic fermentation. This time fermentation was due to the fungus itself. The mycoderma, originally an aërobia—that is, a being to the life and development of which air was necessary—became, after being submerged, an anaërobia, that is, a creature living without air in the depths of the liquid, and behaving after the manner of ferments.

This extended the notions on aërobiæ and anaërobiæ which Pasteur had formerly discovered whilst making researches concerning the vibrio which is the butyric ferment, and those vibriones which are entrusted with the special fermentation known as putrefaction. Between the aërobiæ who require air to live and the anaërobiæ which perish when exposed to air, there was a class of organisms capable of living for a time outside the influence of air. No one had thought of studying the mouldiness which develops so easily when in contact with air; Pasteur was curious to see what became of it when submitted like the mycoderma to that unexpected *régime*. He saw the penicillium, the aspergillus, the mucor-mucedo take the character of ferments when living without air, or with a quantity of air too small to surround their organs as completely as was necessary to their aërobia-plant life. The mucor, when submerged and thus forced to become an anaërobia, offers budding cells, and there again it seemed as if they were yeast globules. "But," said Pasteur, "this change of form merely corresponds to a change of function, it is but a self-adaptation to the new life of an anaërobia." And then, generalizing again and seeking for laws under the accumulation of isolated facts, he thought it probable that ferments had, "but in a higher degree, a character common to most mucors if not to all, and probably possessed more or less by all living cells, viz., to be alternately aërobic or anaërobic, according to conditions of environment."

Fermentation, therefore, no longer appeared as an isolated and mysterious act; it was a general phenomenon, subordinate however to the small number of substances capable of a decomposition accompanied by a production of heat and of being used for the alimentation of inferior beings outside the presence and action of air. Pasteur put the whole theory into this concise formula, "Fermentation is life without air."

"It will be seen," wrote M. Duclaux, "to what heights he had raised the debate; by changing the mode of interpretation of known facts he brought out a new theory."

But this new theory raised a chorus of controversy. Pasteur held to his proofs; he recalled what he had published concerning the typical ferment, the yeast of beer, an article inserted in the reports of the Académie des Sciences for 1861, and entitled, *The Influence of Oxygen on the Development of Yeast and on Alcoholic Fermentation.* In this article Pasteur, à propos of the chemical action connected with vegetable life, explained in the most interesting manner the two modes of life of the yeast of beer.

1. The yeast, placed in some sweet liquid in contact with air, assimilates oxygen gas and develops abundantly; under those conditions, it practically works for itself only, the production of alcohol is insignificant, and the proportion between the weight of sugar absorbed and that of the yeast is infinitesimal. 2. But, in its second mode of life, if yeast is made to act upon sugar without the action of atmospheric air, it can no longer freely assimilate oxygen gas, and is reduced to abstracting oxygen from the fermentescible matter.

" It seems therefore natural," wrote Pasteur, " to admit that when yeast is a ferment, acting out of the reach of atmospheric air, it takes oxygen from sugar, that being the origin of its fermentative character." It is possible to put the fermentative power of yeast through divers degrees of intensity by introducing free oxygen in variable quantities.

After comparing the yeast of beer to an ordinary plant, Pasteur added that " the analogy would be complete if ordinary plants had an affinity for oxygen so strong as to breathe, by withdrawing that element from unstable components, in which case they would act as ferments on those substances." He suggested that it might be possible to meet with conditions which would allow certain inferior plants to live away from atmospheric air in the presence of sugar, and to provoke fermentation of that substance after the manner of beer yeast.

He was already at that time scattering germs of ideas, with the intention of taking them up later on and experimenting on them, or, if time should fail him, willingly offering them to any attentive scientist. These studies on beer had brought him back to his former studies, to his great delight.

" What a sacrifice I made for you," he could not help saying to Dumas, with a mixture of affection and deference, and some modesty, for he apparently forgot the immense service rendered to sericiculture, " when I gave up my studies on ferments for five whole years in order to study silkworms ! l l "

No doubt a great deal of time was also wasted by the endless discussions entered into by his scientific adversaries; but those discussions certainly brought out and evidenced many guiding facts which are now undisputed, as for instance the following—1. Ferments are living beings. 2. There is a special ferment corresponding to each kind of fermentation. 3. Ferments are not born spontaneously.

Liebig and his partisans had looked upon fermentation as a phenomenon of death; they had thought that beer yeast, and in general all animal and vegetable matter in a state of putrefaction, extended to other bodies its own state of decomposition.

Pasteur, on the contrary, had seen in fermentation a phenomenon correlative with life; he had provoked the complete fermentation of a sweet liquid which contained mineral substances only, by introducing into it a trace of yeast, which, instead of dying, lived, flourished and developed.

To those who, believing in spontaneous generation, saw in fermentations but a question of chance, Pasteur by a series of experimental proofs had shown the origin of their delusion by indicating the door open to germs coming from outside. He had moreover taught the method of pure cultures. Finally, in those recent renewals of old quarrels on the transformations into each other of microscopic species, Pasteur, obliged by the mycoderma vini to study closely its alleged transformation, which he had himself believed possible, had thrown ample light on the only dark spot of his luminous domain.

"It is enough to think," writes M. Duclaux concerning that long discussion, "we have but to remember that those who denied the specific nature of the germ would now deny the specific nature of disease, in order to understand the darkness in which such opinions would have confined microbian pathology; it was therefore important that they should be uprooted from every mind."

CHAPTER VIII

PASTEUR had glimpses of another world beyond the phenomena of fermentation—the world of virus ferments. Two centuries earlier, an English physicist, Robert Boyle, had said that he who could probe to the bottom the nature of ferments and fermentation would probably be more capable than any one of explaining certain morbid phenomena. These words often recurred to the mind of Pasteur, who had, concerning the problem of contagious diseases, those sudden flashes of light wherein genius is revealed. But, ever insisting on experimental proofs, he constrained his exalted imagination so as to follow calmly and patiently the road of experimental method. He could not bear the slightest error, or even hasty interpretation, in the praises addressed to him. One day, during the period of the most ardent polemics, in the midst of the struggle on spontaneous generation, a medical man named Déclat, who declared that Pasteur's experiments were "the glory of our century and the salvation of future generations," gave a lecture on "The Infinitesimally Small and their Rôle in the World." "After the lecture," relates Dr. Déclat himself, "M. Pasteur, whom I only knew by name, came to me, and, after the usual compliments, condemned the inductions I had drawn from his experiments. 'The arguments,' he said, 'by which you support my theories, are most ingenious, but not founded on demonstrated facts; analogy is no proof.'"

Pasteur used to speak very modestly of his work. He said, in a speech to some Arbois students, that it was "through assiduous work, with no special gift but that of perseverance joined to an attraction towards all that is great and good," that he had met with success in his researches. He did not add that an ardent kindness of heart was ever urging him forward. After the services rendered within the last ten years to vinegar

makers, silkworm cultivators, vine growers, and brewers, he
now wished to tackle what he had had in his mind since 1861
—the study of contagious diseases. Thus, with the consistent
logic of his mind, showing him as it did the possibility of
realizing in the future Robert Boyle's prophecy, he associated
the secret power of his feelings ; not to give those feelings their
share would be to leave one side of his nature entirely in the
shade. He had himself revealed this great factor in his character when he had said, " It would indeed be a grand thing to
give the heart its share in the progress of science." He was
ever giving it a greater share in his work.

His sorrows had only made him incline the more towards
the griefs of others. The memory of the children he had lost,
the mournings he had witnessed, caused him to passionately
desire that there might be fewer empty places in desolate
homes, and that this might be due to the application of methods
derived from his discoveries, of which he foresaw the immense
bearings on pathology. Beyond this, patriotism being for him
a ruling motive, he thought of the thousands of young men lost
to France every year, victims of the tiny germs of murderous
diseases. And, at the thought of epidemics and the heavy tax
they levy on the whole world, his compassion extended itself
to all human suffering.

He regretted that he was not a medical man, fancying that
it might have facilitated his task. It was true that, at every
incursion on the domain of Medicine, he was looked upon as
a chemist—a *chymiaster*, some said—who was poaching on the
preserves of others. The distrust felt by the physicians in the
chemists was of a long standing. In the *Traité de Thérapeu-
tique*, published in 1855 by Trousseau and Pidoux, we find
this passage : "When a chemist has seen the chemical conditions of respiration, of digestion, or of the action of some drug,
he thinks he has given the theory of those functions and
phenomena. It is ever the same delusion which chemists will
never get over. We must make up our minds to that, but let
us beware of trying to profit by the precious researches which
they would probably never undertake if they were not stimulated by the ambition of explaining what is outside their
range." Pidoux never retrenched anything from two other
phrases, also to be found in that same treatise : "Between a
physiological fact and a pathological fact there is the same difference as between a mineral and a vegetable "; and : "It is

not within the power of physiology to explain the simplest pathological affection." Trousseau, on the other hand, was endowed with the far-seeing intelligence of a great physician attentive to the progress of science. He was greatly interested in Pasteur's work, and fully appreciated the possibilities opened by each of his discoveries.

Pasteur, with the simplicity which contrasted with his extraordinary powers, supposed that, if he were armed with diplomas, he would have greater authority to direct Medicine towards the study of the conditions of existence of phenomena, and—correlatively to the traditional method of observation, which consists in knowing and describing exactly the course of the disease—to inspire practitioners with the desire to prevent and to determine its cause. An unexpected offer went some way towards filling what he considered as a blank. At the beginning of the year 1873, a place was vacant in the section of the Free Associates of the Academy of Medicine. He was asked to stand for it, and hastened to accept. He was elected with a majority of only one vote, though he had been first on the section's list. The other suffrages were divided between Messrs. Le Roy de Méricourt, Brochin, Lhéritier, and Bertillon.

Pasteur, as soon as he was elected, promised himself that he would be a most punctual academician. It was on a Tuesday in April that he attended his first meeting. As he walked towards the desk allotted to him, his paralyzed left leg dragging a little, no one among his colleagues suspected that this quiet and unassuming new member would become the greatest revolutionary ever known in Medicine.

One thing added to Pasteur's pleasure in being elected—the fact that he would join Claude Bernard. The latter had often felt somewhat forlorn in that centre, where some hostility was so often to be seen towards all that was outside the Clinic. This was the time when the "princes of science," or those who were considered as such, were all physicians. Every great physician was conscious of being a ruling power. The almost daily habit of advising and counselling was added to that idea of haughty or benevolent superiority to the rest of the world; and, accustomed to dictate his wishes, the physician frequently adopted an authoritative tone and became a sort of personage. "Have you noticed," said Claude Bernard to Pasteur with a smile under which many feelings were hidden, "that, when a

Q

doctor enters a room, he always looks as if he was going to say,
' I have just been saving a fellow-man ' ? "

Pasteur knew not those harmless shafts which are a revenge
for prolonged pomposity. Why need Claude Bernard trouble
to wonder what So-and-so might think? He had the consciousness of the work accomplished and the esteem and
admiration of men whose suffrage more than satisfied him.
Whilst Pasteur was already desirous of spreading in the
Académie de Médecine the faith which inspired him, Claude
Bernard remembered the refractory state of mind of those who,
at the time of his first lectures on experimental physiology
applied to medicine, affirmed that " physiology can be of no
practical use in medicine ; it is but a *science de luxe* which could
well be dispensed with." He energetically defended this
science de luxe as the very science of life. In his opening
lecture at the Museum in 1870, he said that " descriptive
anatomy is to physiology as geography to history ; and, as it
is not sufficient to understand the topography of a country to
know its history, so is it not enough to know the anatomy of
an organ to understand its functions." Méry, an old surgeon,
familiarly compared anatomists to those errand boys in large
towns, who know the names of the streets and the numbers of
the houses, but do not know what goes on inside. There are
indeed in tissues and organs physico-chemical phenomena for
which anatomy cannot account.

Claude Bernard was convinced that Medicine would gradually
emerge from quackery, and this by means of the experimental
method, like all other science. " No doubt," he said, " we
shall not live to see the blossoming out of scientific medicine,
but such is the fate of humanity ; those that sow on the field
of science are not destined to reap the fruit of their labours."
And so saying, Claude Bernard continued to sow.

It is true that here and there flashes of light had preceded
Pasteur ; but, instead of being guided by them, most doctors
continued to advance majestically in the midst of darkness.
Whenever murderous diseases, scourges of humanity, were in
question, long French or Latin words were put forward, such
as " Epidemic genius," *fatum, quid ignotum quid divinum*, etc.
Medical constitution was also a useful word, elastic and applicable to anything.

When the Vale de Grâce physician, Villemin—a modest,
gentle-voiced man, who, under his quiet exterior, hid a veritable

thirst for scientific truth—after experimental researches carried on from 1865 to 1869, brought the proof that tuberculosis is a disease which reproduces itself, and cannot be reproduced but by itself; in a word, specific, inoculable, and contagious, he was treated almost as a perturber of medical order.

Dr. Pidoux, an ideal representative of traditional medicine, with his gold-buttoned blue coat and his reputation equally great in Paris and at the Eaux-Bonnes, declared that the idea of specificity was a fatal thought.   Himself a pillar of the doctrine of diathesis and of the morbid spontaneity of the organism, he exclaimed in some much applauded speeches : " Tuberculosis ! but that is the common result of a quantity of divers external and internal causes, not the product of a specific agent ever the same ! "   Was not this disease to be looked upon as " one and multiple at the same time, bringing the same final conclusion, the necrobiotic and infecting destruction of the plasmatic tissue of an organ by a number of roads which the hygienist and physician must endeavour to close?"   Where would these specificity doctrines lead to?   " Applied to chronic diseases, these doctrines condemn us to the research of specific remedies or vaccines, and all progress is arrested.   . . Specificity immobilizes medicine."   These phrases were reproduced by the medical press.

The bacillus of tuberculosis had not been discovered by Villemin ; it was only found and isolated much later, in 1882, by Dr. Koch ; but Villemin suspected the existence of a virus.   In order to demonstrate the infectious nature of tuberculosis, he experimented on animals, multiplying inoculations ; he took the sputum of tuberculous patients, spread it on cotton wool, dried it, and then made the cotton wool into a bed for little guineapigs, who became tuberculous.   Pidoux answered these precise facts by declaring that Villemin was fascinated by inoculation, adding ironically, " Then all we doctors have to do is to set out nets to catch the sporules of tuberculosis, and find a vaccine."

That sudden theory of phthisis, falling from the clouds, resembled Pasteur's theory of germs floating in air.   Was it not better, urged Pidoux the heterogenist, to remain in the truer and more philosophical doctrine of spontaneous generation?   " Let us believe, until the contrary is proved, that we are right, we partisans of the common etiology of phthisis, partisans of the spontaneous tuberculous degeneration of the organism under the influence of accessible causes, which we seek everywhere in order to cut down the evil in its roots."

A reception somewhat similar to that given to Villemin was reserved for Davaine, who, having meditated on Pasteur's works on butyric ferment and the part played by that ferment, compared it and its action with certain parasites visible with a microscope and observed by him in the blood of animals which had died of charbon disease. By its action and its rapid multiplication in the blood, this agent endowed with life probably acted, said Davaine, after the manner of ferments. The blood was modified to that extent that it speedily brought about the death of the infected animal. Davaine called those filaments found in anthrax "bacteria," and added, "They have a place in the classification of living beings." But what was that animated virus to many doctors? They answered experimental proofs by oratorical arguments.

At the very time when Pasteur took his seat at the Academy of Medicine, Davaine was being violently attacked; his experiments on septicæmia were the cause, or the pretext. But the mere tone of the discussions prepared Pasteur for future battles. The theory of germs, the doctrine of virus ferments, all this was considered as a complete reversal of acquired notions, a heresy which had to be suppressed. A well-known surgeon, Dr. Chassaignac, spoke before the Académie de Médecine of what he called "laboratory surgery, which has destroyed very many animals and saved very few human beings." In order to remind experimentalists of the distance between them and practitioners, he added : " Laboratory results should be brought out in a circumspect, modest and reserved manner, as long as they have not been sanctioned by long clinical researches, a sanction without which there is no real and practical medical science." Everything, he said, could not be resolved into a question of bacteria ! And, ironically, far from realizing the truth of his sarcastic prophecy, he exclaimed, " Typhoid fever, bacterization ! Hospital miasma, bacterization !"

Every one had a word to say. Dr. Piorry, an octogenarian, somewhat weighed down with the burden of his years and reputation, rose to speak with his accustomed solemnity. He had found for Villemin's experiments the simple explanation that " the tuberculous matter seems to be no other than pus, which, in consequence of its sojourn in the organs, has undergone varied and numerous modifications "; and he now im-

agined that one of the principal causes of fatal accidents due
to septicæmia after surgical operations was the imperfect ventilation of hospital wards. It was enough, he thought, that
putrid odours should not be perceptible, for the rate of mortality to be decreased.

It was then affirmed that putrid infection was not an organized ferment, that inferior organisms had in themselves
no toxic action, in fact, that they were the result and not
the cause of putrid alteration; whereupon Dr. Bouillaud, a
contemporary of Dr. Piorry, called upon their new colleague
to give his opinion on the subject.

It would have been an act of graceful welcome to Pasteur, and
a fitting homage to the memory of the celebrated Trousseau, who
had died five years before, in 1867, if any member present had
then quoted one of the great practitioner's last lectures at the
Hôtel Dieu, wherein he predicted a future for Pasteur's works:

"The great theory of ferments is therefore now connected
with an organic function; every ferment is a germ, the life
of which is manifested by a special secretion. It may be
that it is so for morbid viruses; they may be ferments, which,
deposited within the organism at a given moment and under
determined circumstances, manifest themselves by divers products. So will the variolous ferment produce variolic fermentation, giving birth to thousands of pustules, and likewise
the virus of glanders, that of sheep pox, etc

"Other viruses appear to act locally, but, nevertheless, they
ultimately modify the whole organism, as do gangrene, malignant pustula, contagious erysipelas, etc. May it not be
supposed, under such circumstances, that the ferment or organized matter of those viruses can be carried about by the
lancet, the atmosphere or the linen bandages?"

But it occurred to no one in the Academy to quote those
forgotten words.

Pasteur, answering Bouillaud, recalled his own researches
on lactic and butyric fermentations and spoke of his studies
on beer. He stated that the alteration of beer was due to
the presence of filiform organisms; if beer becomes altered,
it is because it contains germs of organized ferments. "The
correlation is certain, indisputable, between the disease and
the presence of organisms." He spoke those last words with
so much emphasis that the stenographer who was taking down
the extempore speeches underlined them.

A few months later, on November 17, 1873, he read to the
Academy a paper containing further developments of his principles. "In order that beer should become altered and become
sour, putrid, slimy, 'ropy,' acid or lactic, it is necessary that
foreign organisms should develop within it, and those organisms only appear and multiply when those germs are
already extant in the liquid mass." It is possible to oppose
the introduction of those germs; Pasteur drew on the blackboard the diagram of an apparatus which only communicated
with the outer air by means of tubes fulfilling the office of
the sinuous necks of the glass vessels he had used for his
experiments on so-called spontaneous generation. He entered
into every detail, demonstrating that as long as pure yeast
alone had been sown, the security was absolute. "That which
has been put forward on the subject of a possible transformation of yeast into bacteria, vibriones, *mycoderma aceti* and
vulgar mucors, or vice versa, is mistaken."

He wrote in a private letter on the subject: "These simple
and clear results have cost me many sleepless nights before
presenting themselves before me in the precise form I have
now given them."

But his own conviction had not yet penetrated the minds
of his adversaries, and M. Trécul was still supporting his
hypothesis of transformations, the so-called proofs of which,
according to Pasteur, rested on a basis of confused facts tainted
with involuntary errors due to imperfect experiments.

In December, 1873, at a sitting of the Academy, he presented M. Trécul with a few little flagons, in which he had
sown some pure seed of *penicillium glaucum*, begging him to
accept them and to observe them at his leisure, assuring him
that it would be impossible to find a trace of any transformation
of the spores into yeast cells.

"When M. Trécul has finished the little task which I am
soliciting of his devotion to the knowledge of truth," continued Pasteur, "I shall give him the elements of a similar
work on the *mycoderma vini*; in other words, I shall bring to
M. Trécul some absolutely pure *mycoderma vini* with which
he can reproduce his former experiments and recognize the
exactness of the facts which I have lately announced."

Pasteur concluded thus: "The Academy will allow me to
make one last remark. It must be owned that my contradictors have been peculiarly unlucky in taking the occasion

of my paper on the diseases of beer to renew this discussion. How is it they did not understand that my process for the fabrication of inalterable beer could not exist if beer wort in contact with air could present all the transformations of which they speak? And that work on beer, entirely founded as it is on the discovery and knowledge of some microscopic beings, has it not followed my studies on vinegar, on the mycoderma aceti and on the new process of acetification which I have invented? Has not that work been followed by my studies on the causes of wine diseases and the means of preventing them, still founded on the discovery and knowledge of non-spontaneous microscopic beings? Have not these last researches been followed by the discovery of means to prevent the silkworm disease, equally deducted from the study of non-spontaneous microscopic beings?

"Are not all the researches I have pursued for seventeen years, at the cost of many efforts, the product of the same ideas, the same principles, pushed by incessant toil into consequences ever new? The best proof that an observer is in the right track lies in the uninterrupted fruitfulness of his work."

This fruitfulness was evidenced, not only by Pasteur's personal labours, but by those he inspired and encouraged. Thus, in that same period, M. Gayon, a former student of the Ecole Normale, whom he had chosen as curator, started on some researches on the alteration of eggs. He stated that when an egg is stale, rotten, this is due to the presence and multiplication of infinitesimally small beings; the germs of those organisms and the organisms themselves come from the oviduct of the hen and penetrate even into the points where the shell membrane and the albumen are formed "The result is," concluded M. Gayon, "that, during the formation of those various elements, the egg may or may not, according to circumstances, gather up organisms or germs of organisms, and consequently bear within itself, as soon as it is laid, the cause of ulterior alterations. It will be seen at the same time that the number of eggs susceptible of alteration may vary from one hen to another, as well as between the eggs of one hen, for the organisms to be observed on the oviduct rise to variable heights."

If the organisms which alter the eggs and cause them to rot "were formed," said Pasteur, "by the spontaneous self-organization of the matter within the egg into those small beings, all eggs should putrefy equally, whereas they do not." At the end of M. Gayon's thesis—which had not taken so long as Raulin's to prepare, only three years—we find the following conclusion : " Putrefaction in eggs is correlative with the development and multiplication of beings which are bacteria when in contact with air and vibriones when away from the contact of air. Eggs, from that point of view, do not depart from the general law discovered by M. Pasteur."

Pasteur's influence was now spreading beyond the Laboratory of Physiological Chemistry, as the small laboratory at the Ecole Normale was called.

In the treatise he had published in 1862, criticizing the doctrine of spontaneous generation, he had mentioned, among the organisms produced by urine in putrefaction, the existence of a torulacea in very small-grained chaplets. A physician, Dr. Traube, in 1864, had demonstrated that Pasteur was right in thinking that ammoniacal fermentation was due to this torulacea, whose properties were afterwards studied with infinite care by M. Van Tieghem, a former student of the Ecole Normale, who had inspired Pasteur with a deep affection. Pasteur, in his turn, completed his own observations and assured himself that this little organized ferment was to be found in every case of ammoniacal urine. Finally, after proving that boracic acid impeded the development of that ammoniacal ferment, he suggested to M. Guyon, the celebrated surgeon, the use of boracic acid for washing out the bladder ; M. Guyon put the advice into practice with success, and attributed the credit of it to Pasteur.

In a letter written at the end of 1873, Pasteur wrote : "How I wish I had enough health and sufficient knowledge to throw myself body and soul into the experimental study of one of our infectious diseases ! " He considered that his studies on fermentations would lead him in that direction ; he thought that when it should be made evident that every serious alteration in beer was due to the micro-organisms which find in that liquid a medium favourable to their development, when it should be seen that—in contradiction to the old ideas by which those alterations are looked upon as spontaneous, inherent in those liquids, and depending on their nature and composition—the cause of those diseases is not interior but exterior, then would indeed be defeated the doctrine of men like Pidoux, who à propos of diseases, said : "Disease is in us, of us, by us," and who, à propos of small-pox, even said that he was not certain that it could only proceed from inoculation and contagion.

Though the majority of physicians and surgeons considered that it was waste of time to listen to "a mere chemist," there was a small group of young men, undergraduates, who, in their thirst for knowledge, assembled at the Académie de Médecine every Tuesday, hoping that Pasteur might bring out one of his communications concerning a scientific method "which resolves each difficulty by an easily interpreted experiment, delightful to the mind, and at the same time so decisive that it is as satisfying as a geometrical demonstration, and gives an impression of security."

Those words were written by one of those who came to the Académie sittings, feeling that they were on the eve of some great revelations. He was a clinical assistant of Dr. Bébier's, and, busy as he was with medical analysis, he was going over Pasteur's experiments on fermentations for his own edification. He was delighted with the sureness of the Pastorian methods, and was impatient to continue the struggle now begun. Enthusiasm was evinced in his brilliant eyes, in the timbre of his voice, clear, incisive, slightly imperious perhaps, and in his implacable desire for logic. Of solitary habits, with no ambition for distinction or degrees, he worked unceasingly for sheer love of science. The greatest desire of that young man of twenty-one, quite unknown to Pasteur, was to be one day admitted, in the very humblest rank, to the Ecole Normale laboratory. His name was Roux.

Was not that medical student, that disciple lost in the crowd, an image of the new generation hungering for new ideas, more convinced than the preceding one had been of the necessity of proofs? Struck by the unstable basis of medical theories, those young men divined that the secret of progress in hospitals was to be found in the laboratories. Medicine and surgery in those days were such a contrast to what they are now that it seems as if centuries divided them. No doubt one day some professor, some medical historian, will give us a full account of that vast and immense progress. But, whilst awaiting a fully competent work of that kind, it is possible, even in a book such as this (which is, from many causes, but a hasty epitome of many very different things spread over a very simple

biography), to give to a reader unfamiliar with such studies a
certain idea of one of the most interesting chapters in the history
of civilization, affecting the preservation of innumerable human
lives.

"A pin-prick is a door open to Death," said the surgeon
Velpeau. That open door widened before the smallest operation ; the lancing of an abscess or a whitlow sometimes had such
serious consequences that surgeons hesitated before the slightest
use of the bistoury. It was much worse when a great surgical
intervention was necessary, though, through the irony of things,
the immediate success of the most difficult operations was now
guaranteed by the progress of skill and the precious discovery
of anæsthesia. The patient, his will and consciousness suspended, awoke from the most terrible operation as from a
dream. But at that very moment when the surgeon's art was
emboldened by being able to disregard pain, it was arrested,
disconcerted, and terrified by the fatal failures which supervened after almost every operation. The words pyæmia,
gangrene, erysipelas, septicæmia, purulent infection, were
bywords in those days.

In the face of those terrible consequences, it had been
thought better, about forty years ago, to discourage and even
to prohibit a certain operation, then recently invented and practised in England and America, ovariotomy, "even," said
Velpeau, " if the reported cures be true." In order to express
the terror inspired by ovariotomy, a physician went so far as
to say that it should be " classed among the attributes of the
executioner."

As it was supposed that the infected air of the hospitals
might be the cause of the invariably fatal results of that operation, the Assistance Publique [1] hired an isolated house in the
Avenue de Meudon, near Paris, a salubrious spot. In 1863,
ten women in succession were sent to that house ; the neighbouring inhabitants watched those ten patients entering the
house, and a short time afterwards their ten coffins being taken
away. In their terrified ignorance they called that house the
House of Crime.

Surgeons were asking themselves whether they did not
carry death with them, unconsciously scattering virus and
subtle poisons.

---

[1] *Assistance Publique,* official organization of the charitable works
supported by the State. [Trans.]

Since the beginning of the nineteenth century, surgery had positively retrograded; the mortality after operations was infinitely less in the preceding centuries, because antisepsis was practised unknowingly, though cauterizations by fire, boiling liquids and disinfecting substances. In a popular handbook published in 1749, and entitled *Medicine and Surgery for the Poor*, we read that wounds should be kept from the contact of air; it was also recommended not to touch the wound with fingers or instruments. "It is very salutary, when uncovering the wound in order to dress it, to begin by applying over its whole surface a piece of cloth dipped into hot wine or brandy." Good results had been obtained by the great surgeon Larrey, under the first Empire, by hot oil, hot brandy, and unfrequent dressings. But, under the influence of Broussais, the theory of inflammation caused a retrogression in surgery. Then came forth basins for making poultices, packets of charpie (usually made of old hospital sheets merely washed), and rows of pots of ointment. It is true that, during the second half of the last century, a few attempts were made to renew the use of alcoholized water for dressings. In 1868, at the time when the mortality after amputation in hospitals was over sixty per cent., Surgeon Léon Le Fort banished sponges, exacted from his students scrupulous cleanliness and constant washing of hands and instruments before every operation, and employed alcoholized water for dressings. But though he obtained such satisfactory results as to lower, in his wards at the Hôpital Cochin, the average of mortality after amputations to twenty-four per cent., his colleagues were very far from suspecting that the first secret for preventing fatal results after operations consisted in a reform of the dressings.

Those who visited an ambulance ward during the war of 1870, especially those who were medical students, have preserved such a recollection of the sight that they do not, even now, care to speak about it. It was perpetual agony, the wounds of all the patients were suppurating, a horrible fetor pervaded the place, and infectious septicæmia was everywhere. "Pus seemed to germinate everywhere," said a student of that time (M. Landouzy, who became a professor at the Faculty of Medicine), "as if it had been sown by the surgeon." M. Landouzy also recalled the words of M. Denonvilliers, a surgeon of the Charité Hospital, whom he calls "a splendid

operator. . . . a virtuoso, and a dilettante in the art of operating," who said to his pupils : " When an amputation seems
necessary, think ten times about it, for too often, when we
decide upon an operation, we sign the patient's death-war-
rant." Another surgeon, who must have been profoundly
discouraged in spite of his youthful energy, M. Verneuil, exclaimed : " There were no longer any precise indications, any
rational provisions ; nothing was successful, neither abstention,
conservation, restricted or radical mutilation, early or postponed extraction of the bullets, dressings rare or frequent,
emollient or excitant, dry or moist, with or without drainage ;
we tried everything in vain ! " During the siege of Paris, in
the Grand Hôtel, which had been turned into an ambulance,
Nélaton, in despair at the sight of the death of almost every
patient who had been operated on, declared that he who should
conquer purulent infection would deserve a golden statue.

It was only at the end of the war that it occurred to Alphonse
Guérin—(who to his intense irritation was so often confounded
with another surgeon, his namesake and opponent, Jules
Guérin)—that " the cause of purulent infection may perhaps
be due to the germs or ferments discovered by Pasteur to
exist in the air." Alphonse Guérin saw, in malarial fever,
emanations of putrefied vegetable matter, and, in purulent
infection, animal emanations, septic, and capable of causing
death.

" I thought more firmly than ever," he declared, " that
the miasms emanating from the pus of the wounded were
the real cause of this frightful disease, to which I had the
sorrow of seeing the wounded succumb—whether their wounds
were dressed with charpie and cerate or with alcoholized and
carbolic lotions, either renewed several times a day or impregnating linen bandages which remained applied to the wounds.
In my despair—ever seeking some means of preventing these
terrible complications—I bethought me that the miasms, whose
existence I admitted, because I could not otherwise explain
the production of purulent infection—and which were only
known to me by their deleterious influence—might well be
living corpuscles, of the kind which Pasteur had seen in
atmospheric air, and, from that moment, the history of mias-
matic poisoning became clearer to me. If," I said, " miasms
are ferments, I might protect the wounded from their fatal
influence by filtering the air, as Pasteur did. I then con-

ceived the idea of cotton-wool dressings, and I had the satisfaction of seeing my anticipations realized."

After arresting the bleeding, ligaturing the blood vessels
and carefully washing the wound with carbolic solution or
camphorated alcohol, Alphonse Guérin applied thin layers of
cotton wool, over which he placed thicker masses of the same,
binding the whole with strong bandages of new linen. This
dressing looked like a voluminous parcel and did not require
to be removed for about twenty days. This was done at
the St. Louis Hospital to the wounded of the Commune from
March till June, 1871. Other surgeons learnt with amaze-
ment that, out of thirty-four patients treated in that way,
nineteen had survived operation. Dr. Reclus, who could not
bring himself to believe it, said : "We had grown to look
upon purulent infection as upon an inevitable and necessary
disease, an almost Divinely instituted consequence of any
important operation."

There is a much greater danger than that of atmospheric
germs, that of the contagium germ, of which the surgeon's
hands ; sponges and tools are the receptacle, if minute and
infinite precautions are not taken against it. Such precautions were not even thought of in those days ; charpie, odious
charpie, was left lying about on hospital and ambulance
tables, in contact with dirty vessels. It had, therefore, been
sufficient to institute careful washing of the wounds, and especially to reduce the frequency of dressings, and so diminish
the chances of infection to obtain—thanks to a reform inspired
by Pasteur's labours—this precious and unexpected remedy
to fatalities subsequent to operations. In 1873, Alphonse
Guérin, now a surgeon at the Hôtel Dieu, submitted to Pasteur
all the facts which had taken place at the hospital St. Louis
where surgery was more " active," he said, than at the
Hôtel Dieu ; he asked him to come and see his cotton-wool
dressings, and Pasteur gladly hastened to accept the invitation. It was with much pleasure that Pasteur entered upon
this new period of visits to hospitals and practical discussions
with his colleagues of the Académie de Médecine. His joy
at the thought that he had been the means of awakening in
other minds ideas likely to lead to the good of humanity was
increased by the following letter from Lister, dated from
Edinburgh, February 13, 1874, which is here reproduced in
the original—

" My dear Sir—allow me to beg your acceptance of a pamphlet, which I send by the same post, containing an account of some investigations into the subject which you have done so much to elucidate, the germ theory of fermentative changes. I flatter myself that you may read with some interest what I have written on the organism which you were the first to describe in your *Mémoire sur la fermentation appelée lactique.*

"I do not know whether the records of British *Surgery* ever meet your eye. If so, you will have seen from time to time notices of the antiseptic system of treatment, which I have been labouring for the last nine years to bring to perfection.

"Allow me to take this opportunity to tender you my most cordial thanks for having, by your brilliant researches, demonstrated to me the truth of the germ theory of putrefaction, and thus furnished me with the principle upon which alone the antiseptic system can be carried out. Should you at any time visit Edinburgh, it would, I believe, give you sincere gratification to see at our hospital how largely mankind is being benefited by your labours.

"I need hardly add that it would afford me the highest gratification to show you how greatly surgery is indebted to you.

"Forgive the freedom with which a common love of science inspires me, and

"Believe me, with profound respect,

"Yours very sincerely,

"JOSEPH LISTER."

In Lister's wards, the instruments, sponges and other articles used for dressings were first of all purified in a strong solution of carbolic acid. The same precautions were taken for the hands of the surgeon and of his assistants. During the whole course of each operation, a vaporizer of carbolic solution created around the wound an antiseptic atmosphere; after it was over, the wound was again washed with the carbolic solution. Special articles were used for dressing: a sort of gauze, similar to tarlatan and impregnated with a mixture of resin, paraffin and carbolic, maintained an antiseptic atmosphere around the wound. Such was —in its main lines— Lister's method.

A medical student, M. Just Lucas-Championnière—who later on became an exponent in France of this method, and who described it in a valuable treatise published in 1876—had already in 1869, after a journey to Glasgow, stated in the *Journal de médecine et de chirurgie pratique* what were those first principles of defence against gangrene—"extreme and minute care in the dressing of wounds." But his isolated voice was not heard; neither was any notice taken of a celebrated lecture given by Lister at the beginning of 1870 on the penetrating of germs into a purulent centre and on the utility of antisepsis applied to clinical practice. A few months before the war, Tyndall, the great English physicist, alluded to this lecture in an article entitled "Dusts and Diseases," which was published by the *Revue des cours scientifiques*. But the heads of the profession in France had at that time absolute confidence in themselves, and nobody took any interest in the rumour of success attained by the antiseptic method. Yet, between 1867 and 1869, thirty-four of Lister's patients out of forty had survived after amputation. It is impossible on reading of this not to feel an immense sadness at the thought of the hundreds and thousands of young men who perished in ambulances and hospitals during the fatal year, and who might have been saved by Lister's method. In his own country, Lister had also been violently criticized. "People turned into ridicule Lister's minute precautions in the dressing of wounds," writes a competent judge, Dr. Auguste Reaudin, a professor at the Geneva Faculty of Medicine, "and those who lost nearly all their patients by poulticing them had nothing but sarcasms for the man who was so infinitely superior to them." Lister, with his calm courage and smiling kindliness, let people talk, and endeavoured year by year to perfect his method, testing it constantly and improving it in detail. No one, however sceptical, whom he invited to look at his results, could preserve his scepticism in the face of such marked success.

Some of his opponents thought to attack him on another point by denying him the priority of the use of carbolic acid. Lister never claimed that priority, but his enemies took pleasure in recalling that Jules Lemaire, in 1860, had proposed the use of weak carbolic solution for the treatment of open wounds, and that the same had been prescribed by Dr. Déclat in 1861, and also by Maisonneuve, Demarquay and others. The fact that should have been proclaimed was that Lister had created a surgical method which was in itself an immense and beneficial progress; and Lister took pleasure in declaring that he owed to Pasteur the principles which had guided him.

At the time when Pasteur received the letter above quoted, which gave him deep gratification, people in France were so far from all that concerned antisepsis and asepsis, that, when he advised surgeons at the Académie de Médecine to put their instruments through a flame before using them, they did not understand what he meant, and he had to explain—

"I mean that surgical instruments should merely be put through a flame, not really heated, and for this reason : if a sound were examined with a microscope, it would be seen that its surface presents grooves where dusts are harboured, which cannot be completely removed even by the most careful cleansing. Fire entirely destroys those organic dusts; in my laboratory, where I am surrounded by dust of all kinds, I never make use of an instrument without previously putting it through a flame."

Pasteur was ever ready to help others, giving them willing advice or information. In November, 1874, when visiting the Hôtel Dieu with Messrs. Larrey and Gosselin, he had occasion to notice that a certain cotton-wool dressing had been very badly done by a student in one of Guérin's wards. A wound on the dirty hand of a labouring man had been bandaged with cotton wool without having been washed in any way. When the bandaging was removed in the presence of Guérin, the pus exhaled a repugnant odour, and was found to swarm with vibriones. Pasteur in a sitting of the Académie des Sciences, entered into details as to the precautions which are necessary to get rid of the germs originally present on the surface of the wound or of the cotton wool; he declared that the layers of cotton wool should be heated to a very high temperature. He also suggested the following experiment : "In order to demonstrate the evil influence of ferments and proto-organisms in the suppuration of wounds, I would make two identical wounds on the two symmetrical limbs of an animal under chloroform; on one of those wounds I would apply a cotton-wool dressing with every possible precaution ; on the other, on the contrary, I would cultivate, so to speak, micro-organisms abstracted from a strange sore, and offering, more or less, a septic character.

"Finally, I should like to cut open a wound on an animal

under chloroform in a very carefully selected part of the body
for the experiment would be a very delicate one—and in
absolutely pure air, that is, air absolutely devoid of any kind
of germs, afterwards maintaining a pure atmosphere around
the wound, and having recourse to no dressing whatever. I
am inclined to think that perfect healing would ensue under
such conditions, for there would be nothing to hinder the work
of repair and reorganization which must be accomplished on
the surface of a wound if it is to heal."

He explained in that way the advantage accruing to
hygiene, in hospitals and elsewhere, from infinite precautions
of cleanliness and the destroying of infectious germs. Himself
a great investigator of new ideas, he intended to compel his
colleagues at the Académie de Médecine to include the pathogenic share of the infinitesimally small among matters de-
manding the attention of medicine and surgery. The struggle
was a long, unceasing and painful one. In February, 1875,
his presence gave rise to a discussion on ferments, which
lasted until the end of March. In the course of this discussion he recalled the experiments he had made fifteen years
before, describing how—in a liquid composed of mineral
elements, apart from the contact of atmospheric air and
previously raised to ebullition—vibriones could be sown and
subsequently seen to flourish and multiply, offering the sight
of those two important phenomena : life without air, and
fermentation.

"They are far behind us now," he said; "they are now
relegated to the rank of chimeras, those theories of fermentation imagined by Berzelius, Mitscherlich, and Liebig, and re-
edited with an accompaniment of new hypotheses by Messrs.
Pouchet, Frémy, Trécul, and Béchamp. Who would now
dare to affirm that fermentations are contact phenomena,
phenomena of motion, communicated by an altering albuminoid
matter, or phenomena produced by semi-organized materia,
transforming themselves into this or into that? All those
creations of fancy fall to pieces before this simple and decisive
experiment."

Pasteur ended up his speech by an unexpected attack on
the pompous etiquette of the Academy's usual proceedings,
urging his colleagues to remain within the bounds of a
scientific discussion instead of making flowery speeches. He
was much applauded, and his exhortation taken in good part.

His colleagues also probably sympathized with his irritation
in hearing a member of the assembly, M. Poggiale, formerly
apothecary in chief to the Val de Grâce, give a somewhat
sceptical dissertation on such a subject as spontaneous generation, saying disdainfully—

" M. Pasteur has told us that he had looked for spontaneous
generation for twenty years without finding it; he will long
continue to look for it, and, in spite of his courage, perseverance and sagacity, I doubt whether he ever will find it.
It is almost an unsolvable question. However those who, like
me, have no fixed opinion on the question of spontaneous
generation reserve the right of verifying, of sifting and of
disputing new facts, as they appear, one by one and wherever
they are produced."

" What ! " cried Pasteur, wrathful whenever those great
questions were thoughtlessly tackled, " what ! I have been for
twenty years engaged in one subject and I am not to have an
opinion ! and the right of verifying, sifting, and disputing the
facts is to belong to him who does nothing to become enlightened but merely to read our works more or less attentively,
his feet on his study fender ! ! !

" You have no opinion on spontaneous generation, my dear
colleague; I can well believe that, while regretting it. I am
not speaking, of course, of those sentimental opinions that
everybody has, more or less, in questions of this nature, for
in this assembly we do not go in for sentiment. You say that,
in the present state of science, it is wiser to have no opinion :
well, I have an opinion, not a sentimental one, but a rational
one, having acquired a right to it by twenty years of assiduous
labour, and it would be wise in every impartial mind to share
it. My opinion—nay, more, my conviction—is that, in the
present state of science, as you rightly say, spontaneous generation is a chimera; and it would be impossible for you to
contradict me, for my experiments all stand forth to prove
that spontaneous generation is a chimera. What is then
your judgment on my experiments? Have I not a hundred
times placed organic matter in contact with pure air in the
best conditions for it to produce life spontaneously? Have
I not practised on those organic materia which are most
favourable, according to all accounts, to the genesis of spontaneity, such as blood, urine, and grape juice? How is it
that you do not see the essential difference between my op-

ponents and myself? Not only have I contradicted, proof in hand, every one of their assertions, while they have never dared to seriously contradict one of mine, but, for them, every cause of error benefits their opinion. For me, affirming as I do that there are no spontaneous fermentations, I am bound to eliminate every cause of error, every perturbing influence, I can maintain my results only by means of most irreproachable experiments; their opinions, on the contrary, profit by every insufficient experiment and that is where they find their support."

Pasteur having been abruptly addressed by a colleague, who remarked that there were yet many unexplained facts in connection with fermentation, he answered by thus apostrophizing his adversaries—

"What is then your idea of the progress of Science? Science advances one step, then another, and then draws back and meditates before taking a third. Does the impossibility of taking that last step suppress the success acquired by the two others? Would you say to an infant who hesitated before a third step, having ventured on two previous ones : 'Thy former efforts are of no avail ; never shalt thou walk'?

"You wish to upset what you call my theory, apparently in order to defend another ; allow me to tell you by what signs these theories are recognized : the characteristic of erroneous theories is the impossibility of ever foreseeing new facts ; whenever such a fact is discovered, those theories have to be grafted with further hypotheses in order to account for them. True theories, on the contrary, are the expression of actual facts and are characterized by being able to predict new facts, a natural consequence of those already known. In a word, the characteristic of a true theory is its fruitfulness."

"Science," said he again at the following sitting of the Academy, "should not concern itself in any way with the philosophical consequences of its discoveries. If through the development of my experimental studies I come to demonstrate that matter can organize itself of its own accord into a cell or into a living being, I would come here to proclaim it with the legitimate pride of an inventor conscious of having made a great discovery, and I would add, if provoked to do so, 'All the worse for those whose doctrines or systems do not fit in with the truth of the natural facts.'

"It was with similar pride that I defied my opponents to

contradict me when I said, '·In the present state of science the doctrine of spontaneous generation is a chimera.' And I add, with similar independence, ' All the worse for those whose philosophical or political ideas are hindered by my studies.'

" This is not to be taken to mean that, in my beliefs and in the conduct of my life, I only take account of acquired science : if I would, I could not do so, for I should then have to strip myself of a part of myself. There are two men in each one of us : the scientist, he who starts with a clear field and desires to rise to the knowledge of Nature through observation, experimentation and reasoning, and the man of senti-ment, the man of belief, the man who mourns his dead children, and who cannot, alas, prove that he will see them again, but who believes that he will, and lives in that hope, the man who will not die like a vibrio, but who feels that the force that is within him cannot die. The two domains are distinct, and woe to him who tries to let them tresspass on each other in the so imperfect state of human knowledge."

And that separation, as he understood it, caused in him none of those conflicts which often determine a crisis in a human soul. As a scientist, he claimed absolute liberty of research ; he considered, with Claude Bernard and Littré, that it was a mistaken waste of time to endeavour to penetrate primary causes ; " we can only note correlations," he said. But, with the spiritual sentiment which caused him to claim for the inner moral life the same liberty as for scientific re-search, he could not understand certain givers of easy explana-tions who affirm that matter has organized itself, and who, considering as perfectly simple the spectacle of the Universe of which Earth is but an infinitesimal part, are in no wise moved by the Infinite Power who created the worlds. With his whole heart he proclaimed the immortality of the soul.

His mode of looking upon human life, in spite of sorrows, of struggles, of heavy burdens, had in it a strong element of consolation : " No effort is wasted," he said, giving thus a most virile lesson of philosophy to those inferior minds who only see immediate results in the work they undertake and are discouraged by the first disappointment. In his respect for the great phenomenon of Conscience, by which almost all men, enveloped as they are in the mystery of the Universe, have the prescience of an Ideal, of a God, he considered that

" the greatness of human actions can be measured by the inspi-
rations which give them birth." He was convinced that there
are no vain prayers. If all is simple to the simple, all is
great to the great; it was through "the Divine regions of
Knowledge and of Light" that he had visions of those who are
no more.

It was very seldom that he spoke of such things, though
he was sometimes induced to do so in the course of a discussion so as to manifest his repugnance for vainglorious
negations and barren irony ; sometimes too he would enter into
such feelings when speaking to an assembly of young men.

Those discussions at the Academy of Medicine had the
advantage of inciting medical men to the research of the
infinitesimally small, described by the Annual Secretary
Roger as "those subtle artisans of many disorders in the
living economy."

M. Roger, at the end of a brief account of his colleague's
work, wrote, " To the signal services rendered by M. Pasteur
to science and to our country, it was but fair that a signal recompense should be given : the National Assembly has undertaken that care."

That recompense, voted a few months previously, was the
third national recompense accorded to French scientists since
the beginning of the century. In 1837, Arago, before the
Chamber of Deputies, and Gay Lussac, before the Chamber
of Peers, had otained a glorious recognition of the services
rendered by Daguerre and Niepce. In 1845 another national
recompense was accorded, to M. Vicat, the engineer. In 1874,
Paul Bert, a member of the National Assembly, gladly reporting on the projected law tending to offer a national
recompense to Pasteur, wrote quoting those precedents :

" Such an assurance of gratitude, given by a nation to men
who have made it richer and more illustrious, honours it at
least as much as it does them.   ." Paul Bert continued
by enumerating Pasteur's discoveries, and spoke of the millions
Pasteur had assured to France, " without retaining the least
share of them for himself." In sericiculture alone, the losses
in twenty years, before Pasteur's interference, rose to 1,500
millions of francs.

" M. Pasteur's discoveries, gentlemen," concluded Paul
Bert, " after throwing a new light on the obscure question of
fermentations and of the mode of appearance of microscopic

beings, have revolutionized certain branches of industry, of agriculture, and of pathology. One is struck with admiration when seeing that so many, and such divers results, proceed through an unbroken chain of facts, nothing being left to hypothesis—from theoretical studies on the manner in which tartaric acid deviates polarized light. Never was the famous saying, 'Genius consists in sufficient patience,' more amply justified. The Government now proposes that you should honour this admirable combination of theoretical and practical study by a national recompense; your Commission unanimously approves of this proposition.

"The suggested recompense consists in a life annuity of 12,000 francs, which is the approximate amount of the salary of the Sorbonne professorship, which M. Pasteur's ill health has compelled him to give up. It is indeed small when compared with the value of the services rendered, and your Commission much regrets that the state of our finances does not allow us to increase that amount. But the Commission agrees with its learned chairman (M. Marès) ' that the economic and hygienic results of M. Pasteur's discoveries will presently become so considerable that the French nation will desire to increase later on its testimony of gratitude towards him and towards Science, of which he is one of the most glorious representatives.'"

Half the amount of the annuity was to revert to Pasteur's widow. The Bill was passed by 532 votes against 24.

"Where is the government which has secured such a majority?" wrote Pasteur's old friend Chappuis, now Rector of the Grenoble Academy. The value of the recompense was certainly much enhanced by the fact that the Assembly, divided upon so many subjects, had been almost unanimous in its feeling of gratitude towards him who had laboured so hard for Science, for the country and for Humanity.

"Bravo, my dear Pasteur : I am glad for you and for myself, and proud for us all. Your devoted friend, Sainte Claire Deville."

" You are going to be a happy scientist," wrote M. Duclaux, " for you can already see, and you will see more and more, the triumph of your doctrines and of your discoveries."

Those who imagined that this national recompense was the close of a great chapter, perhaps even the last chapter of the book of his life, gave him, in their well-meaning ignorance, some advice which highly irritated him : they advised him to rest. It is true that his cerebral hæmorrhage had left him with a certain degree of lameness and a slight stiffness of the left hand, those external signs reminding him only too well of the threatening possibility of another stroke ; but his mighty soul was more than ever powerful to master his infirm body. It was therefore evident that Nisard, usually very subtle in his insight into character, did not thoroughly understand Pasteur when he wrote to him, "Now, dear friend, you must give up your energies to living for your family, for all those who love you, and a little too for yourself."

In spite of his deep, even passionate tenderness for his family, Pasteur had other desires than to limit his life to such a narrow circle. Every man who knows he has a mission to fulfil feels that there are rays of a light purer and more exalted than that proceeding from the hearth. As to the suggestion that Pasteur should take care of his own health, it was as useless as it would be to advise certain men to take care of that of others.

Dr. Andral had vainly said and written that he should forbid Pasteur any assiduous labour. Pasteur considered that not to work was to lose the object of living at all. If, however, a certain equilibrium was established between the anxious solicitude of friends, the prohibitions of medical advisers and the great amount of work which Pasteur insisted on doing, it was owing to her who with a discreet activity watched in silence to see that nothing outside his work should complicate Pasteur's life, herself his most precious collaborator, the confidante of every experiment.

Everything was subordinate to the laboratory ; Pasteur never accepted an invitation to those large social gatherings which are a tax laid by those who have nothing to do on the time of those who are busy, especially if they be celebrated. Pasteur's name, known throughout the world, was never mentioned in fashionable journals ; he did not even go to theatres. In the evening, after dinner, he usually perambulated the hall and corridor of his rooms at the Ecole Normale, cogitating over various details of his work. At ten o'clock, he went to bed, and at eight the next morning, whether he had had a good night or a bad one, he resumed his work in the laboratory.

That regular life, preserving its even tenor through so many polemics and discussions, was momentarily perturbed by

politics in January, 1876. Pasteur, who, in his extraordinary, almost disconcerting modesty, believed that a medical diploma would have facilitated his scientific revolution,
imagined—after the pressing overtures made to him by some
of his proud compatriots—that he would be able to serve more
usefully the cause of higher education if he were to obtain a
seat at the Senate.

He addressed from Paris a letter to the senatorial electors
of the department of Jura. "I am not a political man," he
said, "I am bound to no party; not having studied politics I
am ignorant of many things, but I do know this, that I love
my country and have served her with all my strength." Like
many good citizens, he thought that a renewal of the national
grandeur and prosperity might be sought in a serious experimental trial of the Republic. If honoured with the suffrages
of his countrymen, he would "represent in the Senate, Science
in all its purity, dignity and independence." Two Jura
newspapers, of different opinions, agreed in regretting that
Pasteur should leave "the peaceful altitudes of science,"
and come down into the Jura to solicit the electors' suffrages.

In his answers to such articles, letters dictated to his son—
who acted as his secretary during that electoral campaign and
accompanied him to Lons-le-Saulnier, where they spent a
week, published addresses, posters, etc.—Pasteur invoked the
following motto, "*Science et Patrie.*" Why had France been
victorious in 1792? "Because Science had given to our
fathers the material means of fighting." And he recalled the
names of Monge, of Carnot, of Fourcroy, of Guyton de Morveau, of Berthollet, that concourse of men of science, thanks
to whom it had been possible—during that grandiose epoch—
to hasten the working of steel and the preparation of leather
for soldiers' boots, and to find means of extracting saltpetre
for gunpowder from plaster rubbish, of making use of recon-
noitring balloons and of perfecting telegraphy.

The senatorial electors numbered 650. Jules Grévy came
to Lons-le-Saulnier to support the candidature of MM. Tamisier and Thurel. In a meeting which took place the day before
the election he said, "You will give them your suffrage to-
morrow, and in so doing you will have deserved well of the
Republic and of France." He mentioned, incidentally, that
" M. Pasteur's character and scientific work entitle him to
universal respect and esteem ; but Science has its natural place

at the Institute," he added, insisting on the Senate's political attributes. Grévy's intervention in favour of his two candidates was decisive. M. Tamisier obtained 446 votes, M. Thurel 445, General Picard 113, M. Besson, a monarchist, 153, Pasteur 62 only.

He had received on that very morning a letter from his daughter, wishing him a failure—a bright, girlish letter, frankly expressing the opinion that her father could be most useful to his country by confining himself to laboratory work, and that politics would necessarily hinder such work.

It was easy to be absolutely frank with Pasteur, who willingly accepted every truthful statement. No man was ever more beloved, more admired and less flattered in his own home than he was.

"What a wise judge you are, my dearest girl!" answered Pasteur the same evening; "you are perfectly right. But I am not sorry to have seen all this, and that your brother should have seen it; all knowledge is useful."

That little incursion into the domain of politics was rendered insignificant in Pasteur's life by the fact that his long-desired object was almost reached. Three months later, at the distribution of prizes of the *Concours Général*, the Minister of Public Instruction pronounced a speech, of which Pasteur preserved the text, underlining with his own hand the following passages : " Soon, I hope, we shall see the Schools of Medicine and of Pharmacy reconstructed; the Collège de France provided with new laboratories; the Faculty of Medicine transferred and enlarged, and the ancient Sorbonne itself restored and extended."

And while the Minister spoke of " those higher studies of Philosophy, of History, of disinterested Science which are the glory of a nation and an honour to the human mind . . . which must retain the first rank to shed their serene light over inferior studies, and to remind men of the true goal and the true grandeur of human intelligence. . . ." Pasteur could say to himself that the great cause which he had pleaded since he was made Dean of Faculty at Lille in 1854, which he had supported in 1868 and again on the morrow of the war, was at last about to be won in 1876.

He had a patriotic treat during the summer holidays of that same year. A great international congress of sericiculture was gathered at Milan; there were delegates from Russia, Austria,

Italy and France, and Pasteur represented France.   He was
accompanied by his former pupils, his associates in his silkworm studies, Duclaux and Ranlin, both of whom had become
professors at the Lyons Faculty of Sciences, and Maillot, who
was then manager of the silkworm establishment of Montpellier.   The members of the Congress had been previously
informed of the programme of questions, and each intending
speaker was armed with facts and observations.   The open
discussions allowed Duclaux, Ranlin and Maillot to demonstrate the strictness and perfection of the experimental method
which they had learned from their master and which they were
teaching in their turn.

Excursions formed a delightful interlude ; one on the lake of
Como was an enchantment.   Then the French delegates were
offered the pleasant surprise of a visit to an immense seeding
establishment in the neighbourhood of Milan, which had been
named after Pasteur.   We have an account of this visit in a
letter to J. B. Dumas (September 17).

" My dear Master . . . I very much regret that you are not
here : you would have shared my satisfaction.   I am dating
my letter from Milan, but in reality, the congress being ended,
we are staying at Signor Susani's country house for a few days.
Here, from July 4, sixty or seventy women are busy for ten
hours every day with microscopic examinations of absolute
accuracy.   I never saw a better arranged establishment.
400,000 moth cells are put under the microscope every day.
The order and cleanliness are admirable ; any error is made
impossible by the organization of a second test following the
first.

" I felt, in seeing my name in large letters on the façade of
that splendid establishment, a joy which compensates for much
of the frivolous opposition I have encountered from some of
my countrymen these last few years ; it is a spontaneous
homage from the proprietor to my studies.   Many sericicultors
do their seeding themselves, by selection, or have it done by
competent workers accustomed to the operation.   The harvest
from that excellent seed depends on the climate only ; in a
moderately favourable season the production often reaches fifty
or seventy kilogrammes per ounce of twenty-five grammes."

Signor Susani was looking forward to producing for that one
year 30,000 ounces of seed.   In the presence of the prodigious
activity of this veritable factory- -where, besides the microscope

women, more than one hundred persons were occupied in various ways, washing the mortars with which the moths are pounded before being put under the microscopes, cleansing the slides, etc. ; in fact, doing those various delicate but simple operations which had formerly been pronounced to be impracticable—Pasteur's thoughts went back to his experiments in the Pont-Gisquet greenhouse, to the modest beginnings of his process, now so magnificently applied in Italy. A month before this, J. B. Dumas, presiding at a scientific meeting at Clermont Ferrand, had said—

"The future belongs to Science ; woe to the nations who close their eyes to this fact. . . . Let us call to our aid on this neutral and pacific ground of Natural Philosophy, where defeats cost neither blood nor tears, those hearts which are moved by their country's grandeur ; it is by the exaltation of science that France will recover her prestige."

Those same ideas were expressed in a toast given by Pasteur in the name of France at a farewell banquet, when the 300 members of the Sericiculture Congress were present.

"Gentlemen, I propose a toast—To the peaceful strife of Science. It is the first time that I have the honour of being present on foreign soil at an international congress ; I ask myself what are the impressions produced in me, besides these courteous discussions, by the brilliant hospitality of the noble Milanese city, and I find myself deeply impressed by two propositions. First, that Science is of no nationality ; and secondly, in apparent, but only in apparent, contradiction, that Science is the highest personification of nationality. Science has no nationality because knowledge is the patrimony of humanity, the torch which gives light to the world. Science should be the highest personification of nationality because, of all the nations, that one will always be foremost which shall be first to progress by the labours of thought and of intelligence.

"Let us therefore strive in the pacific field of Science for the pre-eminence of our several countries. Let us strive, for strife is effort, strife is life when progress is the goal.

"You Italians, try to multiply on the soil of your beautiful and glorious country the Tecchi, the Brioschi, the Tacchini, the Sella, the Cornalia. . . You, proud children of Austria-Hungary, follow even more firmly than in the past the fruitful impulse which an eminent statesman, now your representative at the Court of England, has given to Science and Agriculture.

We, who are here present, do not forget that the first sericiculture establishment was founded in Austria. As to you,
Japanese, may the cultivation of Science be numbered among
the chief objects of your care in the amazing social and political
transformation of which you are giving the marvellous spectacle to the world. We Frenchmen, bending under the sorrow
of our mutilated country, should show once again that great
trials may give rise to great thoughts and great actions.

"I drink to the peaceful strife of Science."

"You will find," wrote Pasteur to Dumas, telling him of
this toast, which had been received with enthusiastic applause,
"an echo of the feelings with which you have inspired your
pupils on the grandeur and the destiny of Science in modern
society."

The tender and delicate side of this powerful spirit was thus
once again apparent in this deference to his master in the midst
of acclamations, and in those deep and noble ideas expressed
in the middle of a noisy banquet. But it was chiefly in his
private life that his open-heartedness, his desire to love and
to be loved, became apparent. That great genius had a childlike heart, and the charm of this was incomparable.

He once said : "The recompense and the ambition of a
scientist is to conquer the approbation of his peers and of the
masters whom he venerates." He had already known that
recompense and could satisfy that ambition. Dumas had
known and appreciated him for thirty years; Lister had proclaimed his gratitude; Tyndall—an indefatigable excursionist,
who loved to survey wide horizons, and who in his celebrated
classes was wont to make use of comparisons with altitudes
and heights and everything which opens a clear and vast out-
look—had a great admiration for the wide development of Pasteur's work. Now, Pasteur's experiments had been strongly
attacked by a young English physician, Dr. Bastian, who had
excited in the English and American public a bitter prejudice
against the results announced by Pasteur on the subject of
spontaneous generation.

"The confusion and uncertainty," wrote Tyndall to Pasteur, "have finally become such that, six months ago, I thought
that it would be rendering a service to Science, at the same
time as justice to yourself, if the question were subjected to a
fresh investigation.

"Putting into practice an idea which 1 had entertained six

years ago—the details of which are set out in the article in the *British Medical Journal* which I had the pleasure to send you— I went over a large portion of the ground on which Dr. Bastian had taken up his stand, and refuted, I think, many of the fallacies which had misled the public.

" The change which has taken place since then in the tone of the English medical journals is quite remarkable, and I am disposed to think that the general confidence of the public in the accuracy of Dr. Bastian's experiments has been considerably shaken.

" In taking up these investigations, I have had the opportunity of refreshing my memory about your labours; they have reawakened in me all the admiration which I felt for them when I first read of them. I intend to continue these investigations until I have dispersed all the doubts which may have arisen as to the indisputable accuracy of your conclusions."

And Tyndall added a paragraph for which Pasteur modestly substituted asterisks in communicating this letter to the Academy.

" For the first time in the history of Science we have the right to cherish the sure and certain hope that, as regards epidemic diseases, medicine will soon be delivered from quackery and placed on a real scientific basis. When that day arrives, Humanity, in my opinion, will know how to recognize that it is to you that will be due the largest share of her gratitude."

Tyndall was indeed qualified to sign this passport to immortality. But in the meanwhile a struggle was necessary, and Pasteur did not wish to leave the burden of the discussion even on such shoulders as Tyndall's ! Moreover he was interested in his opponent.

" Dr. Bastian," writes M. Duclaux, " had some tenacity, a fertile mind, and the love, if not the gift, of the experimental method." The discussion was destined to last for months. In general (according to J. B. Dumas' calculation) "at the end of ten years, judgment on a great thing is usually formed; it is by then an accomplished fact, an idea adopted by Science or irrevocably repudiated." Pasteur, on the morrow of the Milan Congress, might feel that it had been so for the adoption of his system of cellular seeding, but such was not the case in this question of spontaneous generation. The quarrel had started again at the Academy of Sciences and at the Academy of Medicine ; it was now being revived in England, and Bastian proposed to come himself and experiment in the laboratory of the Ecole Normale.

"For nearly twenty years," said Pasteur, "I have pursued, without finding it, a proof of life existing without an anterior and similar life. The consequences of such a discovery would be incalculable; natural science in general, and medicine and philosophy in particular, would receive therefrom an impulse which cannot be foreseen. Therefore, whenever I hear that this discovery has been made, I hasten to verify the assertions of my fortunate rival. It is true that I hasten towards him with some degree of mistrust, so many times have I experienced that, in the difficult art of experimenting, the very cleverest stagger at every step, and that the interpretation of facts is no less perilous."

Dr. Bastian operated on acid urine, boiled and neutralized by a solution of potash heated to a temperature of 120° C. If, after the flask of urine had cooled down, it was heated to a temperature of 50° C. in order to facilitate the development of germs, the liquid in ten hours' time swarmed with bacteria. "Those facts prove spontaneous generation," said Dr. Bastian.

Pasteur invited him to replace his boiled solution of potash by a fragment of solid potash, after heating it to 110° C., in order to avoid the bacteria germs which might be contained in the aqueous solution. This question of the germs of inferior organisms possibly contained in water was—during the course of that protracted discussion—studied by Pasteur with the assistance of M. Joubert, Professor of Physics at the Collège Rollin. Such germs were to be found even in the distilled water of laboratories; it was sufficient that the water should be poured in a thin stream through the air to become contaminated. Spring water, if slowly filtered through a solid mass of ground, alone contained no germs.

There was also the question of the urine and that of the recipient. The urine, collected by Dr. Bastian in a vase and placed into a retort, neither of which had been put through a flame, might contain spores of a bacillus called *bacillus subtilis*, which offer a great resistance to the action of heat. Those spores do not develop in notably acid liquids, but the liquid having been neutralized or rendered slightly alkaline by the potash, the development of germs took place. The thing therefore to be done was to collect the urine in a vase and introduce it into a retort both of which had been put through a flame. After that, no organisms were produced, as was stated in the thesis of M. Chamberland, then a curator at the laboratory, and who took an active part in these experiments.

A chapter might well have been written by a moralist '' On the use of certain opponents ''; for it was through that discussion with Bastian that it was discovered how it was that—at the time of the celebrated discussions on spontaneous generation--the heterogenists, Pouchet, Joly, and Musset, operating as Pasteur did, but in a different medium, obtained results apparently contradictory to Pasteur's. If their flasks, filled with a decoction of hay, almost constantly showed germs, whilst Pasteur's, full of yeast water, were always sterile, it was because the hay water contained spores of the bacillus subtilis. The spores remained inactive as long as the liquid was preserved from the contact of air, but as soon as oxygen re-entered the flask they were able to develop.

The custom of raising liquids to a temperature of 120° C. in order to sterilize them dates from that conflict with Bastian. '' But,'' writes M. Duclaux, ''the heating to 120° of a flask half filled with liquid can sterilize the liquid part only, allowing life to persist in those regions which are not in contact with the liquid. In order to destroy everything, the dry walls must be heated to 180° C.''

A former pupil of the Ecole Normale, who had been a curator in Pasteur's laboratory since October, 1876, Boutroux by name, who witnessed all these researches, wrote in his thesis : '' The knowledge of these facts makes it possible to obtain absolutely pure neutral culture mediums, and, in consequence, to study as many generations as are required of one unmixed microorganism, whenever pure seed has been procured.''

Pasteur has defined what he meant by putting tubes, cotton, vases, etc., through a flame. '' In order to get rid of the microscopic germs which the dusts of air and of the water used for the washing of vessels deposit on every object, the best means is to place the vessels (their openings closed with pads of cotton wool) during half an hour in a gas stove, heating the air in which the articles stand to a temperature of about 150° C. to 200° C. The vessels, tubes, etc., are then ready for use. The cotton wool is enclosed in tubes or in blotting-paper.''

What Pasteur had recommended to surgeons, when he advised them to pass through a flame all the instruments they used, had become a current practice in the laboratory ; the least pad of cotton wool used as a stopper was previously sterilized. Thus was an entirely new technique rising fully armed and ready to repel new attacks and ensure new victories.

If Pasteur was so anxious to drive Dr. Bastian to the wall, it was because he saw behind that so-called experiment on spontaneous generation a cause of perpetual conflict with physicians and surgeons. Some of them desired to repel purely and simply the whole theory of germs. Others, disposed to admit the results of Pasteur's researches, as laboratory work, did not admit his experimental incursions on clinical ground. Pasteur therefore wrote to Dr. Bastian in the early part of July, 1877—

" Do you know why I desire so much to fight and conquer you? it is because you are one of the principal adepts of a medical doctrine which I believe to be fatal to progress in the art of healing—the doctrine of the spontaneity of all diseases. . . That is an error which, I repeat it, is harmful to medical progress. From the prophylactic as well as from the therapeutic point of view, the fate of the physician and surgeon depends upon the adoption of the one or the other of these two doctrines."

CHAPTER IX

THE confusion of ideas on the origin of contagious and epidemic diseases was about to be suddenly enlightened; Pasteur had now taken up the study of the disease known as charbon or splenic fever. This disease was ruining agriculture; the French provinces of Beauce, Brie, Burgundy, Nivernais, Berry, Champagne, Dauphiné and Auvergne, paid a formidable yearly tribute to this mysterious scourge. In the Beauce, for instance, twenty sheep out of every hundred died in one flock; in some parts of Auvergne the proportion was ten or fifteen per cent., sometimes even twenty-five, thirty-five, or fifty per cent. At Provins, at Meaux, at Fontainebleau, some farms were called *charbon farms*; elsewhere, certain fields or hills were looked upon as accursed and an evil spell seemed to be thrown over flocks bold enough to enter those fields or ascend those hills. Animals stricken with this disease almost always died in a few hours; sheep were seen to lag behind the flock, with drooping head, shaking limbs and gasping breath; after a rigor and some sanguinolent evacuations, occurring also through the mouth and nostrils, death supervened, often before the shepherd had had time to notice the attack. The carcase rapidly became distended, and the least rent in the skin gave issue to a flow of black, thick and viscid blood, hence the name of *anthrax* given to the disease. It was also called splenic fever, because necropsy showed that the spleen had assumed enormous dimensions; if that were opened, it presented a black and liquid pulp. In some places the disease assumed a character of extreme virulence; in the one district of Novgorod, in Russia, 56,000 head of cattle died of splenic infection between 1867 and 1870. Horses, oxen, cows, sheep, everything succumbed, as did also 528 persons, attacked by the contagion under divers forms; a

s

pin prick or a scratch is sufficient to inoculate shepherds, butchers, knackers or farmers with the malignant pustule.

Though a professor at the Alfort Veterinary School, M. Delafond, did point out to his pupils as far back as 1838 that charbon blood contained "little rods," as he called them; it was only looked upon by himself and them as a curiosity with no scientific importance. Davaine, when he—and Rayer as well—recognized in 1850 those little filiform bodies in the blood of animals dying of splenic fever, he too merely mentioned the fact, which seemed to him of so little moment that he did not even report it in the first notice of his works edited by himself.

It was only eleven years later that Davaine—struck, as he himself gladly acknowledged, by reading Pasteur's paper on the butyric ferment, the little cylindrical rods of which offer all the characteristics of vibriones or bacteria—asked himself whether the filiform corpuscles seen in the blood of the charbon victims might not act after the manner of ferments and be the cause of the disease. In 1863, a medical man at Dourdan, whose neighbour, a farmer, had lost twelve sheep of charbon in a week, sent blood from one of these sheep to Davaine, who hastened to inoculate some rabbits with this blood. He recognized the presence of those little transparent and motionless rods which he called bacteridia (a diminutive of bacterium, or rod-shaped vibriones). It might be thought that the cause of the evil was found, in other words that the relation between those bacteridia and the disease which had caused death could not be doubted. But two professors of the Val de Grâce, Jaillard and Leplat, refuted these experiments.

They had procured, in the middle of the summer, from a knacker's yard near Chartres, a little blood from a cow which had died of anthrax, and they inoculated some rabbits with it. The rabbits died, but without presenting any bacteridia. Jaillard and Leplat therefore affirmed that splenic fever was not an affection caused by parasites, that the bacteridium was an epiphenomenon of the disease and could not be looked upon as the cause of it.

Davaine, on repeating Jaillard and Leplat's experiments, found a new interpretation; he alleged that the disease they had inoculated was not anthrax. Then Jaillard and Leplat obtained a little diseased sheep's blood from M. Boutet, a veterinary surgeon at Chartres, and tried that instead of cow's

blood. The result was identical : death ensued, but no bacteridia. Were there then two diseases?

Others made observations in their turn. It occurred to a
young German physician, Dr. Koch, who in 1876 was beginning his career in a small village in Germany, to seek a culture
medium for the bacteridium. A few drops of aqueous humour,
collected in the eyes of oxen or of rabbits, seemed to him
favourable. After a few hours of this nutrition the rods seen
under the microscope were ten or twenty times larger than at
first; they lengthened immoderately, so as to cover the whole
slide of the microscope, and might have been compared to a
ball of tangled thread. Dr. Koch examined those lengths, and
after a certain time noticed little spots here and there looking
like a punctuation of spores. Tyndall, who knew how to secure
continuous attention by a variety of comparisons, said at a scientific conference in Glasgow a few months later that those little
ovoid bodies were contained within the envelope of the filament
like peas in their pods. It is interesting to note that Pasteur,
when he studied, in connection with silkworm diseases, the
mode of reproduction of the vibriones of flachery, had seen
them divide into spores similar to shining corpuscles ; he had
demonstrated that those spores, like seeds of plants, could revive after a lapse of years and continue their disastrous work.
The bacterium of charbon, or *bacillus anthracis* as it now began
to be called, reproduced itself in the same way, and, when
inoculated by Dr. Koch into guinea-pigs, rabbits and mice, provoked splenic fever as easily and inevitably as blood from the
veins of an animal that had died of the disease. Bacilli and
spores therefore yielded the secret of the contagion, and it
seemed that the fact was established, when Paul Bert, in
January, 1877, announced to the *Société de Biologie* that it was
" possible to destroy the bacillus anthracis in a drop of blood by
compressed oxygen, to inoculate what remained, and to re
produce the disease and death without any trace of the bac
teridium.   . Bacteridia," he added, " are therefore neither
the cause nor the necessary effect of splenic fever, which must
be due to a virus."

Pasteur tackled the subject. A little drop of the blood of an
animal which had died of anthrax—a microscopic drop—was
laid, sown, after the usual precautions to ensure purity, in a
sterilized balloon which contained neutral or slightly alkaline
urine. The culture medium might equally be common house-

hold broth, or beer-yeast water, either of them neutralized by potash. After a few hours, a sort of flake was floating in the liquid; the bacteridia could be seen, not under the shape of short broken rods, but with the appearance of filaments, tangled like a skein; the culture medium being highly favourable, they were rapidly growing longer. A drop of that liquid, abstracted from the first vessel, was sown into a second vessel, of which one drop was again placed into a third, and so on, until the fortieth flask; the seed of each successive culture came from a tiny drop of the preceding one. If a drop from one of those flasks was introduced under the skin of a rabbit or guinea-pig, splenic fever and death immediately ensued, with the same symptoms and characteristics as if the original drop of blood had been inoculated. In the presence of the results from those successive cultures, what became of the hypothesis of an inanimate substance contained in the first drop of blood? It was now diluted in a proportion impossible to imagine. It would therefore be absurd, thought Pasteur, to imagine that the last virulence owed its power to a virulent agent existing in the original drop of blood; it was to the bacteridium, multiplied in each culture, and to the bacteridium alone, that this power was due; the life of the bacteridium had made the virulence. "Anthrax is therefore," Pasteur declared, "the disease of the bacteridium, as trichinosis is the disease of the trichina, as itch is the disease of its special acarus, with this circumstance, however, that, in anthrax, the parasite can only be seen through a microscope, and very much enlarged." After the bacteridium had presented those long filaments, within a few hours, two days at the most, another spectacle followed; amidst those filaments, appeared the oval shapes, the germs, spores or seeds, pointed out by Dr. Koch. Those spores, sown in broth, reproduced in their turn the little packets of tangled filaments, the bacteridia. Pasteur reported that "one single germ of bacteridium in the drop which is sown multiplies during the following hours and ends by filling the whole liquid with such a thickness of bacteridia that, to the naked eye, it seems that carded cotton has been mixed with the broth."

M. Chamberland, a pupil who became intimately associated with this work on anthrax, has defined as follows what Pasteur had now achieved: "By his admirable process of culture outside organism, Pasteur shows that the rods which exist in the blood, and for which he has preserved the name of bacteridia given them by Davaine, are living beings capable of being indefinitely reproduced in appropriate liquids, after the manner of a plant multiplied by successive cuttings. The bacterium does not reproduce itself only under the filamentous form, but also through spores or germs, after the manner of many plants which present two modes of reproduction, by cuttings and by seeds." The first point was therefore settled. The ground suspected and indicated by Davaine was now part of the domain of science, and preserved from any new attacks.

Yet Jaillard and Leplat's experiments remained to be explained : how had they provoked death through the blood of a splenic fever victim and found no bacteridia afterwards? It was then that Pasteur, guided, as Tyndall expressed it, by "his extraordinary faculty of combining facts with the reasons of those facts," placed himself, to begin with, in the conditions of Jaillard and Leplat, who had received, during the height of the summer, some blood from a cow and a sheep which had died of anthrax, that blood having evidently been abstracted more than twenty-four hours before the experiment. Pasteur, who had arranged to go to the very spot, the knacker's yard near Chartres, and himself collect diseased blood, wrote to ask that the carcases of animals which had died of splenic fever should be kept for him for two or three days.

He arrived on June 13, 1877, accompanied by the veterinary surgeon, M. Boutet. Three carcases were awaiting him : that of a sheep which had been dead sixteen hours, that of a horse whose death dated from the preceding day, and that of a cow which must have been dead for two or three days, for it had been brought from a distant village. The blood of the recently diseased sheep contained bacteridia of anthrax only. In the blood of the horse, putrefaction vibriones were to be found, besides the bacteridia, and those vibriones existed in a still greater proportion in the blood of the cow. The sheep's blood, inoculated into guinea-pigs, provoked anthrax with pure bacteridia ; that of the cow and of the horse brought a rapid death with no bacteridia.

Henceforth what had happened in Jaillard and Leplat's experiments, and in the incomplete and uncertain experiments of Davaine, became simple and perfectly clear to Pasteur, as well as the confusion caused by another experimentalist who had said his say ten years after the discussions of Jaillard, Leplat and Davaine.

This was a Paris veterinary surgeon, M. Signol. He had written to the Academy of Sciences that it was enough that a healthy animal should be felled, or rather asphyxiated, for its blood, taken from the deeper veins, to become violently virulent within sixteen hours. M. Signol thought he had seen motionless bacteridia similar to the bacillus anthracis; but those bacteridia, he said, were incapable of multiplying in the inoculated animals. Yet the blood was so very virulent that animals rapidly succumbed in a manner analogous to death by splenic fever. A Commission was nominated to ascertain the facts; Pasteur was made a member of it, as was also his colleague Bouillaud—still so quick and alert, in spite of his eighty years, that he looked less like an old man than like a wrinkled young man—and another colleague, twenty years younger, Bouley, the first veterinary surgeon in France who had a seat at the Institute. The latter was a tall, handsome man, with a somewhat military appearance, and an expression of energetic good humour which his disposition fully justified. He was eager to help in the propagation of new ideas and discoveries, and soon, with eager enthusiasm, placed his marked talents as a writer and orator at Pasteur's disposal.

On the day when the Commission met, M. Signol showed the carcase of a horse, which he had sacrificed for this experiment, having asphyxiated it when in excellent health. Pasteur uncovered the deep veins of the horse and showed to Bouley, and also to Messrs. Joubert and Chamberland, a long vibrio, so translucid as to be almost invisible, creeping, flexible, and which, according to Pasteur's comparison, slipped between the globules of the blood as a serpent slips between high grasses; it was the septic vibrio. From the peritoneum, where it swarms, that vibrio passes into the blood a few hours after death; it represents the vanguard of the vibriones of putrefaction. When Jaillard and Leplat had asked for blood infected with anthrax, they had received blood which was at the same time septic. It was septicæmia (so prompt in its action that inoculated rabbits or sheep perish in twenty-four or thirty-six hours) that had killed Jaillard and Leplat's rabbits. It was also septicæmia, provoked by this vibrio (or its germs, for it too has germs), that M. Signol had unknowingly inoculated into the animals upon which he experimented. Successive cultures of that septic vibrio enabled Pasteur to show, as he had done for the bacillus anthracis, that one drop of those cultures caused septicæmia in an animal. But, while the bacillus anthracis is aërobic, the septic vibrio, being anaërobic, must be cultivated in a vacuum, or in carbonic acid gas. And, cultivating those bacteridia and those vibriones with at least as much care as a Dutchman might give to rare tulips, Pasteur succeeded in parting the bacillus anthracis and the septic vibrio when they were temporarily associated. In a culture in contact with air, only bacteridia developed, in a culture preserved from air, only the septic vibrio.

What Pasteur called "the Paul Bert fact" now alone remained to be explained; this also was simple. The blood Paul Bert had received from Chartres was of the same quality as that which Jaillard and Leplat had had; that is to say already septic. If filaments of bacillus anthracis and of septic vibriones perish under compressed oxygen, such is not the case with the germs, which are extremely tenacious; they can be kept for several hours at a temperature of 70° C., and even of 95° C. Nothing injures them, neither lack of air, carbonic acid gas nor compressed oxygen. Paul Bert, therefore, killed filamentous bacteridia under the influence of high pressure; but, as the germs were none the worse, those germs revived the splenic fever. Paul Bert came to Pasteur's laboratory, ascertained facts and watched experiments. On June 23, 1877, he hastened to the Société de Biologie and proclaimed his mistake, acting in this as a loyal Frenchman, Pasteur said.

In spite of this testimony, and notwithstanding the admiration conceived for Pasteur by certain medical men—notably H. Gueneau de Mussy, who published in that very year (1877) a paper on the theory of the contagium germ and the application of that theory to the etiology of typhoid fever—the struggle was being continued between Pasteur and the current medical doctrines. In the long discussion which began at that time in the Académie de Médecine on typhoid fever, some masters of medical oratory violently attacked the germ theory, proclaiming the spontaneity of living organism. Typhoid fever, they said, is engendered by ourselves within ourselves. Whilst Pasteur was convinced that the day would come—and that was indeed the supreme goal of his life work—when contagiou√ and virulent diseases would be effaced from the preoccupation√, mournings and anxieties of humanity, and when the infinitesimally small, known, isolated and studied, would at last be vanquished, his ideas were called Utopian dream√.

The old professors, whose career had been built on a combination of theories which they were pleased to call medical
truth, dazed by such startling novelties, endeavoured, as did
Piorry, to attract attention to their former writings. "It is
not the disease, an abstract being," said Piorry, "which we
have to treat, but the patient, whom we must study with the
greatest care by all the physical, chemical and clinical means
which Science offers."

The contagion which Pasteur showed, appearing clearly in
the disorders visible in the carcases of inoculated guinea-pigs,
was counted as nothing. As to the assimilation of a laboratory
experiment on rabbits and guinea-pigs to what occurred in
human pathology, it may be guessed that it was quite out of
the question for men who did not even admit the possibility of a
comparison between veterinary medicine and the other. It
would be interesting to reconstitute these hostile surroundings
in order to appreciate the efforts of will required of Pasteur to
enable him to triumph over all the obstacles raised before him
in the medical and the veterinary world.

The Professor of Alfort School, Colin, who had, he said,
made 500 experiments on anthrax within the last twelve years,
stated, in a paper of seventeen pages, read at the Academy of
Medicine on July 31, that the results of Pasteur's experiments
had not the importance which Pasteur attributed to them.
Among many other objections, one was considered by Colin as
a fatal one—the existence of a virulent agent situated in the
blood, besides the bacteridia.

Bouley, who had just communicated to the Academy of
Sciences some notes by M. Toussaint, professor at the Toulouse
veterinary school, whose experiments agreed with those of
Pasteur, was nevertheless a little moved by Colin's reading.
He wrote in that sense to Pasteur, who was then spending his
holidays in the Jura. Pasteur addressed to him an answer as
vigorous as any of his replies at the Academy.

"Arbois, August 18, 1877.—My dear colleague . . . I
hasten to answer your letter. I should like to accept literally
the honour which you confer upon me by calling me 'your
master,' and to give you a severe reprimand, you faith-
less man, who would seem to have been shaken by M.
Colin's reading at the Académie des Sciences, since you are
still holding forth on the possibility of a virulent agent,
and since your uncertainties seem to be appeased by a new

notice, read by yourself, last Monday, at the Académie des Sciences.

"Let me tell you frankly that you have not sufficiently imbibed the teaching contained in the papers I have read, in my own name and in that of M. Joubert, at the Académie des Sciences and at the Academy of Medicine. Can you believe that I should have read those papers if they had wanted the confirmation you mention, or if M. Colin's contradictions could have touched them? You know what my situation is, in these grave controversies; you know that, ignorant as I am of medical and veterinary knowledge, I should immediately be taxed with presumption if I had the boldness to speak without being armed for struggle and for victory! All of you, physicians and veterinary surgeons, would quite reasonably fall upon me if I brought into your debates a mere semblance of proof.

"How is it that you have not noticed that M. Colin has travestied—I should even say suppressed—because it hindered his theory, the important experiment of the successive cultures of the bacteridium in urine?

"If a drop of blood, infected with anthrax, is mixed with water, with pure blood or with humour from the eye, as was done by Davaine, Koch and M. Colin himself, and some of that mixture is inoculated and death ensues, doubt may remain in the mind as to the cause of virulence, especially since Davaine's well-known experiments on septicæmia. Our experiment is very different . . ."

And Pasteur showed how, from one artificial culture to another, he reached the fiftieth, the hundredth, and how a drop of this hundredth culture, identical with the first, could bring about death as certainly as a drop of infected blood.

Months passed, and—as Pasteur used to wish in his youth that it might be—few passed without showing one step forward. In a private letter to his old Arbois school-fellow, Jules Vercel, he wrote (February 11, 1878) : " I am extremely busy; at no epoch of my scientific life have I worked so hard or been so much interested in the results of my researches, which will, I hope, throw a new and a great light on certain very important branches of medicine and of surgery."

In the face of those successive discoveries, every one had a word to say. This accumulation of facts was looked down upon by that category of people who borrow assurance from a mixture of ignorance and prejudice. Others, on the other hand, amongst whom the greatest were to be found, proclaimed that Pasteur's work was immortal and that the word "theory" used by him should be changed into that of " doctrine." One of those who thus spoke, with the right given by full knowledge, was Dr. Sédillot, whose open and critical mind had kept him from becoming like the old men described by Sainte Beuve as stopping their watch at a given time and refusing to recognize further progress. He was formerly Director of the Army Medical School at Strasburg, and had already retired in 1870, but had joined the army again as volunteer surgeon. It will be remembered that he had written from the Hagueneau ambulance to the Académie des Sciences—of which he was a corresponding member—to call the attention of his colleagues to the horrors of purulent infection, which defied his zeal and devotion.

No one followed Pasteur's work with greater attention than this tall, sad-looking old man of seventy-four; he was one of those who had been torn away from his native Alsace, and he could not get over it. In March, 1878, he read a paper to the Academy, entitled " On the Influence of M. Pasteur's Work on Medicine and Surgery."

Those discoveries, he said, which had deeply modified the state of surgery, and particularly the treatment of wounds, could be traced back to one principle. This principle was applicable to various facts, and explained Lister's success, and the fact that certain operations had become possible, and that certain cases, formerly considered hopeless, were now being recorded on all sides. Real progress lay there. Sédillot's concluding paragraph deserves to be handed down as a comment precious from a contemporary : " We shall have seen the conception and birth of a new surgery, a daughter of Science and of Art, which will be one of the greatest wonders of our century, and with which the names of Pasteur and Lister will remain gloriously connected."

In that treatise, Sédillot invented a new word to characterize all that body of organisms and infinitely small vibriones, bacteria, bacteridia, etc.; he proposed to designate them all under the generic term of *microbe*. This word had, in Sédillot's eyes, the advantage of being short and of having a general signification. He however felt some scruple before using it, and consulted Littré. who replied on February 26,

1878 : "Dear colleague and friend, *microbe* and *microbia* are very good words. To designate the animalculæ I should give the preference to *microbe*, because, as you say, it is short, and because it leaves microbia, a feminine noun, for the designation of the state of a microbe."

Certain philologists criticized the formation of the word in the name of the Greek language. Microbe, they said, means an animal with a short life, rather than an infinitesimally small animal. Littré gave a second testimonial to the word microbe—

"It is true," he wrote to Sédillot, "that μικρόβιος and μακρόβιος probably mean in Greek *short-lived* and *long-lived*. But, as you justly remark, the question is not what is most purely Greek, but what is the use made in our language of the Greek roots. Now the Greek has βίος, life, βιοῦν, to live, βιούς, living, the root of which may very well figure under the form of *bi*, *bia* with the sense *living*, in *aërobia*, *anaërobia* and *microbe*. I should advise you not to trouble to answer criticisms, but let the word stand for itself, which it will no doubt do." Pasteur, by adopting it, made the whole world familiar with it.

Though during that month of March, 1878, Pasteur had had the pleasure of hearing Sédillot's prophetic words at the Académie des Sciences, he had heard very different language at the Académie de Médecine. Colin of Alfort, from the isolated corner where he indulged in his misanthropy, had renewed his criticisms of Pasteur. As he spoke unceasingly of a state of virulent anthrax devoid of bacteridia, Pasteur, losing patience, begged of the Académie to nominate a Commission of Arbitration.

"I desire expressly that M. Colin should be urged to demonstrate what he states to be the fact, for his assertion implies another, which is that an organic matter, containing neither bacteridia nor germs of bacteridia, produces within the body of a living animal the bacteridia of anthrax. This would be the spontaneous generation of the bacillus anthracis !"

Colin's antagonism to Pasteur was such that he contradicted him in every point and on every subject. Pasteur having stated that birds, and notably hens, did not take the charbon disease, Colin had hastened to say that nothing was easier than to give anthrax to hens; this was in July, 1877. Pasteur, who was at that moment sending Colin some samples of bacteridia culture which he had promised him, begged that he would kindly bring him in exchange a hen suffering from that disease, since it could contract it so easily.

Pasteur told the story of this episode in March, 1878; it was an amusing interlude in the midst of those technical discussions. "At the end of the week, I saw M. Colin coming into my laboratory, and, even before I shook hands with him, I said to him : ' Why, you have not brought me that diseased hen ? ' —'Trust me,' answered M. Colin, 'you shall have it next week.'—I left for the vacation ; on my return, and at the first meeting of the Academy which I attended, I went to M. Colin and said, ' Well, where is my dying hen?' 'I have only just begun experimenting again,' said M. Colin ; ' in a few days I will bring you a hen suffering from charbon.'—Days and weeks went by, with fresh insistence on my part and new promises from M. Colin. One day, about two months ago, M. Colin owned to me that he had been mistaken, and that it was impossible to give anthrax to a hen. ' Well, my dear colleague,' I said to him, ' I will show you that it is possible to give anthrax to hens ; in fact, I will one day myself bring you at Alfort a hen which shall die of charbon.'

" I have told the Academy this story of the hen M. Colin had promised in order to show that our colleague's contradiction of our observations on charbon had never been very serious."

Colin, after speaking about several other things, ended by saying : "I regret that I have not until now been able to hand to M. Pasteur a hen dying or dead of anthrax. The two that I had bought for that purpose were inoculated several times with very active blood, but neither of them has fallen ill. Perhaps the experiment might have succeeded afterwards, but, one fine day, a greedy dog prevented that by eating up the two birds, whose cage had probably been badly closed." On the Tuesday which followed this incident, the passers-by were somewhat surprised to see Pasteur emerging from the Ecole Normale, carrying a cage, within which were three hens, one of them dead. Thus laden, he took a fiacre, and drove to the Académie de Médecine, where, on arriving, he deposited this unexpected object on the desk. He explained that the dead hen had been inoculated with charbon two days before, at twelve o'clock on the Sunday, with five drops of yeast water employed as a nutritive liquid for pure bacteridium germs, and that it had died on the Monday at five o'clock, twenty-nine hours after the inoculation. He also explained, in his own name, and in the names of Messrs. Joubert and Chamberland, how in the presence of the curious fact that hens were refractory to charbon, it had occurred to them to see whether that singular and hitherto mysterious preservation did not have its cause in the temperature of a hen's body, "higher by several degrees than the temperature of the body of all the animal species which can be decimated by charbon."

This preconceived idea was followed by an ingenious experiment. In order to lower the temperature of an inoculated hen's body, it was kept for some time in a bath, the water covering one-third of its body. When treated in that way, said Pasteur, the hen dies the next day. "All its blood, spleen, lungs, and liver are filled with bacilli anthracis susceptible of ulterior cultures either in inert liquids or in the bodies of animals. We have not met with a single exception."

As a proof of the success of the experiment, the white hen lay on the floor of the cage. As people might be forthcoming, even at the Academy, who would accuse the prolonged bath of having caused death, one of the two living hens, a gray one, who was extremely lively, had been placed in the same bath, at the same temperature and during the same time. The third one, a black hen, also in perfect health, had been inoculated at the same time as the white hen, with the same liquid, but with ten drops instead of five, to make the comparative result more convincing ; it had not been subjected to the bath treatment. "You can see how healthy it is," said Pasteur ; "it is therefore impossible to doubt that the white hen died of charbon ; besides, the fact is proved by the bacteridia which fill its body."

A fourth experiment remained to be tried on a fourth hen, but the Academy of Medicine did not care to hold an all-night sitting. Time lacking, it was only done later, in the laboratory. Could a hen, inoculated of charbon and placed in a bath, recover and be cured merely by being taken out of its bath? A hen was taken, inoculated and held down a prisoner in a bath, its feet fastened to the bottom of the tub, until it was obvious that the disease was in full progress. The hen was then taken out of the water, dried, and wrapped up in cotton wool and placed in a temperature of 35° C. The bacteridia were reabsorbed by the blood, and the hen recovered completely.

This was, indeed, a most suggestive experiment, proving that the mere fall of temperature from 42° C. (the temperature of hens) to 38° C. was sufficient to cause a receptive condition; the hen, brought down by immersion to the temperature of rabbits or guinea-pigs, became a victim like them.

Between Sédillot's enthusiasm and Colin's perpetual contradiction, many attentive surgeons and physicians were taking a middle course, watching for Pasteur's results and ultimately accepting them with admiration. Such was the state of mind of M. Lereboullet, an editor of the *Weekly Gazette of Medicine and Surgery*, who wrote in an account of the Académie de Médecine meeting that " those facts throw a new light on the theory of the genesis and development of the bacillus anthracis. They will be ascertained and verified by other experimentalists, and it seems very probable that M. Pasteur, who never brings any premature or conjectural assertion to the academic tribune, will deduce from them conclusions of the greatest interest concerning the etiology of virulent diseases."

But even to those who admired Pasteur as much as did M. Lereboullet, it did not seem that such an important part should immediately be attributed to microbes. Towards the end of his report (dated March 22, 1878) he reminded his readers that a discussion was open at the Académie de Médecine, and that the surgeon, Léon Le Fort, did not admit the germ theory in its entirety. M. Le Fort recognized " all the services rendered to surgery by laboratory studies, chiefly by calling attention to certain accidents of wounds and sores, and by provoking new researches with a view to improving methods of dressing and bandaging." " Like all his colleagues at the Academy, and like our eminent master, M. Sédillot," added M. Lereboullet, " M. Le Fort renders homage to the work of M. Pasteur; but he remains within his rights as a practitioner and reserves his opinion as to its general application to surgery."

This was a mild way of putting it; M. Le Fort's words were, " That theory, in its applications to clinical surgery, is absolutely inacceptable." For him, the original purulent infection, though coming from the wound, was born under the influence of general and local phenomena *within* the patient, and not *outside* him. He believed that the economy had the power, under various influences, to produce purulent infection. A septic poison was created, born spontaneously, which was afterwards carried to other patients by such medicines as the tools and bandages and the hands of the surgeon. But, originally, before the propagation of the contagium germ, a purulent infection was spontaneously produced and developed. And, in order to put his teaching into forcible words, M. Le Fort declared to the Académie de Médecine : " I believe in the *interiority* of the principle of purulent infection in certain patients ; that is why I oppose the extension to surgery of the germ theory which proclaims the constant *exteriority* of that principle."

Pasteur rose, and with his firm, powerful voice, exclaimed : " Before the Academy accepts the conclusion of the paper we have just heard, before the application of the germ theory to pathology is condemned, I beg that I may be allowed to make a statement of the researches I am engaged in with the collahoration of Messrs. Joubert and Chamberland."

His impatience was so great that he formulated then and there some headings for the lecture he was preparing, propositions on septicæmia or putrid infection, on the septic vibrio itself, on the germs of that vibrio carried by wind in the shape of dust, or suspended in water, on the vitality of those germs, etc. He called attention to the mistakes which might be made if, in that new acquaintance with microbes, their morphologic aspect alone was taken account of. " The septic vibrio, for instance, varies so much in its shape, length and thickness, according to the media wherein it is cultivated, that one would think one was dealing with beings specifically distinct from each other."

It was on April 30, 1878, that Pasteur read that celebrated lecture on the germ theory, in his own name and in that of Messrs. Joubert and Chamberland. It began by a proud exordium : " All Sciences gain by mutual support. When, subsequently to my early communications on fermentations, in 1857-1858, it was admitted that ferments, properly so called, are living beings; that germs of microscopical organisms abound on the surface of all objects in the atmosphere and in water; that the hypothesis of spontaneous generation is a chimera; that wines, beer, vinegar, blood, urine and all the liquids of the economy are preserved from their common changes when in contact with pure air—Medicine and Surgery cast their eyes towards these new lights. A French physician, M. Davaine, made a first successful application of those principles to medicine in 1863."

Pasteur himself, elected to the Académie des Sciences as a mineralogist, proved by the concatenation of his studies within the last thirty years that Science was indeed one and all embracing. Having thus called his audience's attention to the bonds which connect one scientific subject with another, Pasteur proceeded to show the connection between his yesterday's researches on the etiology of Charbon to those he now pursued on septicæmia. He hastily glanced back on his successful cultures of the bacillus anthracis, and on the certain, indisputable proof that the last culture acted equally with the first in producing charbon within the body of animals. He then owned to the failure, at first, of a similar method of cultivating the septic vibrio : " All our first experiments failed in spite of the variety of culture media that we used ; beer-yeast water, meat broth, etc., etc. . . ."

He then expounded, in the most masterly manner : (1) the idea which had occurred to him that this vibrio might be an exclusively anaërobic organism, and that the sterility of the liquids might proceed from the fact that the vibrio was killed by the oxygen held in a state of solution by those liquids ; (2) the similarity offered by analogous facts in connection with the vibrio of butyric fermentation, which not only lives without air, but is killed by air ; (3) the attempts made to cultivate the septic vibrio in a vacuum or in the presence of carbonic acid gas, and the success of both those attempts ; and, finally, as the result of the foregoing, the proof obtained that the action of the air kills the septic vibriones, which are then seen to perish, under the shape of moving threads, and ultimately to disappear, as if burnt away by oxygen.

"If it is terrifying," said Pasteur, " to think that life may be at the mercy of the multiplication of those infinitesimally small creatures, it is also consoling to hope that Science will not always remain powerless before such enemies, since it is already now able to inform us that the simple contact of air is sometimes sufficient to destroy them. But," he continued, meeting his hearers' possible arguments, "if oxygen destroys vibriones, how can septicæmia exist, as it does, in the constant presence of atmospheric air? How can those facts be reconciled with the germ theory? How can blood exposed to air become septic through the dusts contained in air? All is dark.

obscure and open to dispute when the cause of the phenomena is not known; all is light when it is grasped."

In a septic liquid exposed to the contact of air, vibriones die and disappear; but, below the surface, in the depths of the liquid (one centimetre of septic liquid may in this case be called depths), "the vibriones are protected against the action of oxygen by their brothers, who are dying above them, and they continue for a time to multiply by division; they afterwards produce germs or spores, the filiform vibriones themselves being gradually reabsorbed. Instead of a quantity of moving threads, the length of which often extends beyond the field of the microscope, nothing is seen but a dust of isolated, shiny specks, sometimes surrounded by a sort of amorphous gangue hardly visible. Here then is the septic dust, living the latent life of germs, no longer fearing the destructive action of oxygen, and we are now prepared to understand what seemed at first so obscure : the sowing of septic dust into putrescible liquids by the surrounding atmosphere, and the permanence of putrid diseases on the surface of the earth."

Pasteur continued from this to open a parenthesis on diseases "transmissible, contagious, infectious, of which the cause resides essentially and solely in the presence of microscopic organisms. It is the proof that, for a certain number of diseases, we must for ever abandon the ideas of spontaneous virulence, of contagious and infectious elements suddenly produced within the bodies of men or of animals and originating diseases afterwards propagated under identical shapes ; all those opinions fatal to medical progress and which are engendered by the gratuitous hypotheses of the spontaneous generation of albuminoid-ferment materia, of hemiorganism, of archebiosis, and many other conceptions not founded on observation."

Pasteur recommended the following experiment to surgeons. After cutting a fissure into a leg of mutton, by means of a bistoury, he introduced a drop of septic vibrio culture; the vibrio immediately did its work. "The meat under those conditions becomes quite gangrened, green on its surface, swollen with gases, and is easily crushed into a disgusting, sanious pulp." And addressing the surgeons present at the meeting : "The water, the sponge, the charpie with which you wash or dress a wound, lay on its surface germs which, as you see, have an extreme facility of propagating within the tissues, and which

T

would infallibly bring about the death of the patients within a very short time if life in their limbs did not oppose the multiplication of germs. But how often, alas, is that vital resistance powerless! how often do the patient's constitution, his weakness, his moral condition, the unhealthy dressings, oppose but an insufficient barrier to the invasion of the Infinitesimally Small with which you have covered the injured part! If I had the honour of being a surgeon, convinced as I am of the dangers caused by the germs of microbes scattered on the surface of every object, particularly in the hospitals, not only would I use absolutely clean instruments, but, after cleansing my hands with the greatest care and putting them quickly through a frame (an easy thing to do with a little practice), I would only make use of charpie, bandages, and sponges which had previously been raised to a heat of 130° C. to 150° C.; I would only employ water which had been heated to a temperature of 110° C. to 120° C. All that is easy in practice, and, in that way, I should still have to fear the germs suspended in the atmosphere surrounding the bed of the patient; but observation shows us every day that the number of those germs is almost insignificant compared to that of those which lie scattered on the surface of objects, or in the clearest ordinary water.''

He came down to the smallest details, seeing in each one an application of the rigorous principles which were to transform Surgery, Medicine and Hygiene. How many human lives have since then been saved by the dual development of that one method! The defence against microbes afforded by the substances which kill them or arrest their development, such as carbolic acid, sublimate, iodoform, salol, etc., etc., constitutes *antisepsis*; then the other progress, born of the first, the obstacle opposed to the arrival of the microbes and germs by complete disinfection, absolute cleanliness of the instruments and hands, of all which is to come into contact with the paient; in one word, *asepsis*.

It might have been prophesied at that date that Pasteur's surprised delight at seeing his name gratefully inscribed on the great Italian establishment of sericiculture would one day be surpassed by his happiness in living to see realized some of the progress and benefits due to him, his name invoked in all operating theatres, engraved over the doors of medical and surgical wards, and a new era inaugurated.

A presentiment of the future deliverance of Humanity from

those redoubtable microscopic foes gave Pasteur a fever for work, a thirst for new research, and an immense hope. But once again he constrained himself, refrained from throwing himself into varied studies, and, continuing what he had begun, reverted to his studies on splenic fever.

The neighbourhood of Chartres being most afflicted, the Minister of Agriculture, anticipating the wish of the Conseil Général of the department of Eure et Loir, had entrusted Pasteur with the mission of studying the causes of so-called spontaneous charbon, that which bursts out unexpectedly in a flock, and of seeking for curative and preventive means of opposing the evil. Thirty-six years earlier, the learned veterinary surgeon, Delafond, had been sent to seek, particularly in the Beauce country, the causes of the charbon disease. Bouley, a great reader, said that there was no contrast more instructive than that which could be seen between the reasoning method followed by Delafond and the experimental method practised by Pasteur. It was in 1842 that Delafond received from M. Cunin Gridaine, then Minister of Agriculture, the mission of "going to study that malady on the spot, to seek for its causes, and to examine particularly whether those causes did not reside in the mode of culture in use in that part of the country." Delafond arrived in the Beauce, and, having seen that the disease struck the strongest sheep, it occurred to him that it came from "an excess of blood circulating in the vessels." He concluded from that that there might be a correlation between the rich blood of the Beauce sheep and the rich nitrogenous pasture of their food.

He therefore advised the cultivators to diminish the daily ration ; and he was encouraged in his views by noting that the frequency of the disease diminished in poor, damp, or sandy soils.

Bouley, in order to show up Delafond's efforts to make facts accord with his reasoning, added that to explain "a disease, of which the essence is general plethora, becoming contagious and expressing itself by charbon symptoms in man," Delafond had imagined that the atmosphere of the pens, into which the animals were crowded, was laden with evil gases and putrefying emanations which produced an alteration of the blood " due at the same time to a slow asphyxia and to the introduction through the lungs of septic elements into the blood."

It would have been but justice to recall other researches connected with Delafond's name. In 1863, Delafond had collected some blood infected with charbon, and, at a time when such experiments had hardly been thought of, he had attempted some experiments on the development of the bacteridium, under a watch glass, at the normal blood temperature. He had seen the little rods grow into filaments, and compared them to a "very remarkable mycelium." "I have vainly tried to see the mechanism of fructification," added Delafond, "but I hope I still may." Death struck down Delafond before he could continue his work.

In 1869 a scientific congress was held at Chartres; one of the questions examined being this : "What has been done to oppose splenic fever in sheep?" A veterinary surgeon enumerated the causes which contributed, according to him, to produce and augment mortality by splenic fever : bad hygienic conditions; tainted food, musty or cryptogamized; heated and vitiated air in the crowded pens, full of putrid manure; paludic miasma or effluvia; damp soil flooded by storms, etc., etc. A well-known veterinary surgeon, M. Boutet, saw no other means to preserve what remained of a stricken flock but to take it to another soil, which, in contradiction with his colleague, he thought should be chosen cool and damp. No conclusion could be drawn. The disastrous loss caused by splenic fever in the Beauce alone was terrible; it was said to have reached 20,000,000 francs in some particularly bad years. The migration of the tainted flock seemed the only remedy, but it was difficult in practice and offered danger to other flocks, as carcases of dead sheep were wont to mark the road that had been followed.

Pasteur, starting from the fact that the charbon disease is produced by the bacteridium, proposed to prove that, in a department like that of Eure et Loir, the disease maintained itself by itself. When an animal dies of splenic fever in a field, it is frequently buried in the very spot where it fell; thus a focus of contagion is created, due to the anthrax spores mixed with the earth where other flocks are brought to graze. Those germs, thought Pasteur, are probably like the germs of the flachery vibrio, which survive from one year to another and transmit the disease. He proposed to study the disease on the spot.

It almost always happened that, when he was most anxious to give himself up entirely to the study of a problem, some

new discussion was started to hinder him. He had certainly
thought that the experimental power of giving anthrax to hens
had been fully demonstrated, and that that question was dead,
as dead as the inoculated and immersed hen.

Colin, however, returned to the subject, and at an Academy
meeting of July 9 said somewhat insolently, "I wish we could
have seen the bacteridia of that dead hen which M. Pasteur
showed us without taking it out of its cage, and which he
took away intact instead of making us witness the necropsy
and microscopical examination." "I will take no notice,"
said Pasteur at the following meeting, "of the malevolent
insinuations contained in that sentence, and only consider M.
Colin's desire to hold in his hands the body of a hen dead of
anthrax, full of bacteridia. I will, therefore, ask M. Colin if
he will accept such a hen under the following condition : the
necropsy and microscopic examination shall be made by himself, in my presence, and in that of one of our colleagues of this
Academy, designated by himself or by this Academy, and an
official report shall be drawn up and signed by the persons
present. So shall it be well and duly stated that M. Colin's
conclusions, in his paper of May 14, are null and void. The
Academy will understand my insistence in rejecting M. Colin's
superficial contradictions.

"I say it here with no sham modesty : I have always considered that my only right to a seat in this place is that given
me by your great kindness, for I have no medical or veterinary
knowledge. I therefore consider that I must be more scrupulously exact than any one else in the presentations which I have
the honour to make to you ; I should promptly lose all credit if I
brought you erroneous or merely doubtful facts. If ever I am
mistaken, a thing which may happen to the most scrupulous,
it is because my good faith has been greatly surprised.

"On the other hand, I have come amongst you with a programme to follow which demands accuracy at every step. I
can tell you my programme in two words : I have sought for
twenty years, and I am still seeking, spontaneous generation
properly so called.

"If God permit, I shall seek for twenty years and more the
spontaneous generation of transmissible diseases.

"In these difficult researches, whilst sternly deprecating
frivolous contradiction, I only feel esteem and gratitude
towards those who may warn me if I should be in error."

The Academy decided that the necropsy and microscopic examination of the dead hen which Pasteur was to bring to Colin should take place in the presence of a Commission composed of Pasteur, Colin, Davaine, Bouley, and Vulpian. This Commission met on the following Saturday, July 20, in the Council Chamber of the Academy of Medicine. M. Armand Moreau, a member of the Academy, joined the five members present, partly out of curiosity, and partly because he had special reasons for wishing to speak to Pasteur after the meeting.

Three hens were lying on the table, all of them dead. The first one had been inoculated under the thorax with five drops of yeast water slightly alkalized, which had been given as a nutritive medium to some bacteridia anthracis; the hen had been placed in a bath at 25° C., and had died within twenty-two hours. The second one, inoculated with ten drops of a culture liquid, had been placed in a warmer bath, 30° C., and had died in thirty-six hours. The third hen, also inoculated and immersed, had died in forty-six hours.

Besides those three dead hens, there was a living one which had been inoculated in the same way as the first hen. This one had remained for forty-three hours with one-third of its body immersed in a barrel of water. When it was seen in the laboratory that its temperature had gone down to 36° C., that it was incapable of eating and seemed very ill, it was taken out of the tub that very Saturday morning, and warmed in a stove at 42° C. It was now getting better, though still weak, and gave signs of an excellent appetite before leaving the Academy council chamber.

The third hen, which had been inoculated with ten drops, was dissected then and there. Bouley, after noting a serous infiltration at the inoculation focus, showed to the judges sitting in this room, thus suddenly turned into a testing laboratory, numerous bacteridia scattered throughout every part of the hen.

" After those ascertained results," wrote Bouley, who drew up the report, " M. Colin declared that it was useless to proceed to the necropsy of the two other hens, that which had just been made leaving no doubt of the presence of bacilli anthracis in the blood of a hen inoculated with charbon and then placed under the conditions designated by M. Pasteur as making inoculation efficacious.

" The hen No. 2 has been given up to M. Colin to be used for any examination or experiment which he might like to try at Alfort.

" Signed : G. Colin, H. Bouley, C. Davaine, L. Pasteur, A. Vulpian."

" This is a precious autograph, headed as it is by M. Colin's signature ! " gaily said Bouley. But Pasteur, pleased as he was with this conclusion, which put an end to all discussion on that particular point, was already turning his thoughts into another channel. The Academician who had joined the members of the Commission was showing him a number of the *Revue Scientifique* which had appeared that morning, and which contained an article of much interest to Pasteur.

In October, 1877, Claude Bernard, staying for the last time at St. Julien, near Villefranche, had begun some experiments on fermentations. He had continued them on his return to Paris, alone, in the study which was above his laboratory at the Collège de France.

When Paul Bert, his favourite pupil, M. d'Arsonval, his curator, M. Dastre, a former pupil, and M. Armand Moreau, his friend, came to see him, he said to them in short, enigmatical sentences, with no comment or experimental demonstration, that he had done some good work during the vacation. " Pasteur will have to look out . . . Pasteur has only seen one side of the question . . . I make alcohol without cells . . . There is no life without air . "

Bernard's and Pasteur's seats at the Academy of Sciences were next to each other, and they usually enjoyed interchanging ideas. Claude Bernard had come to the November and December sittings, but, with a reticence to which he had not accustomed Pasteur, he had made no allusion to his October experiments. In January, 1878, he became seriously ill ; in his conversations with M. d'Arsonval, who was affectionately nursing him, Claude Bernard talked of his next lecture at the Museum, and said that he would discuss his ideas with Pasteur before handling the subject of fermentations. At the end of January M. d'Arsonval alluded to these incomplete revelations "It is all in my head," said Claude Bernard, "but I am too tired to explain it to you." He made the same weary answer two or three days before his death. When he succumbed, on February 10, 1878, Paul Bert, M. d'Arsonval and M. Dastre thought it their duty to ascertain whether their master had left any notes relative to the work which embodied his last thoughts. M. d'Arsonval, after a few days' search, discovered some notes, carefully hidden in a cabinet in Claude Bernard's bedroom; they were all dated from the 1st to the 20th of October, 1877; of November and December there was no record. Had he then not continued his experiments during that period? Paul Bert thought that these notes did not represent a work, not even a sketch, but a sort of programme. "It was all condensed into a series of masterly conclusions," said Paul Bert, "which evidenced certitude, but there were no means of discussing through which channel that certitude had come to his prudent and powerful mind." What should be done with those notes? Claude Bernard's three followers decided to publish them. "We must," said Paul Bert, "while telling the conditions under which the manuscript was found, give it its character of incomplete notes, of confidences made to itself by a great mind seeking its way, and marking its road indiscriminately with facts and with hypotheses in order to arrive at that feeling of certainty which, in the mind of a man of genius, often precedes proof." M. Berthelot, to whom the manuscript was brought, presented these notes to the readers of the *Revue Scientifique.* He pointed to their character, too abbreviated to conclude with a rigorous demonstration, but he explained that several friends and pupils of Claude Bernard had "thought that there would be some interest for Science in preserving the trace of the last subjects of thought, however incomplete, of that great mind."

Pasteur, after the experiment at the Académie de Médecine, hurried back to his laboratory and read with avidity those last notes of Claude Bernard. Were they a precious find, explaining the secrets Claude Bernard had hinted at? "Should I," said Pasteur, "have to defend my work, this time against that colleague and friend for whom I professed deep admiration, or should I come across unexpected revelations, weakening and discrediting the results I thought I had definitely established?"

His reading reassured him on that point, but saddened him on the other hand. Since Claude Bernard had neither desired nor even authorized the publication of those notes, why, said Pasteur, were they not accompanied by an experimental commentary? Thus Claude Bernard would have been credited with what was good in his MSS., and he would not have been held responsible for what was incomplete or defective.

" As for me, personally," wrote Pasteur in the first pages of his *Critical Examination of a Posthumous Work of Claude Bernard on Fermentation*, " I found myself cruelly puzzled; had I the right to consider Claude Bernard's MS. as the expression of his thought, and was I free to criticize it thoroughly? " The table of contents and headings of chapters in Claude Bernard's incomplete MS. condemned Pasteur's work on alcoholic fermentation. The non-existence of life without air; the ferment *not* originated by exterior germs; alcohol formed by a soluble ferment outside life . . . such were Claude Bernard's conclusions. " If Claude Bernard was convinced," thought Pasteur, " that he held the key to the masterly conclusions with which he ended his manuscript, what could have been his motive in withholding it from me ? I looked back upon the many marks of kindly affection which he had given me since I entered on a scientific career, and I came to the conclusion that the notes left by Bernard were but a programme of studies, that he had tackled the subject, and that, following in this a method habitual to him, he had, the better to discover the truth, formed the intention of trying experiments which might contradict my opinions and results."

Pasteur, much perplexed, resolved to put the case before his colleagues, and did so two days later. He spoke of Bernard's silence, his abstention from any allusion at their weekly meetings. " It seems to me almost impossible," he said, " and I wonder that those who are publishing these notes have not perceived that it is a very delicate thing to take upon oneself, with no authorization from the author, the making public of private notebooks ! Which of us would care to think it might be done to him ! . . . Bernard must have put before himself that leading idea, that I was in the wrong on every point, and taken that method of preparing the subject he intended to study." Such was also the opinion of those who remembered that Claude Bernard's advice invariably was that every theory should be doubted at first and only trusted when found capable of resisting objections and attacks.

" If then, in the intimacy of conversation with his friends and the yet more intimate secret of notes put down on paper and carefully put away, Claude Bernard develops a plan of research with a view to judging of a theory—if he imagines experiments—he is resolved not to speak about it until those experiments have been clearly checked; we should therefore

not take from his notes the most expressly formulated propositions without reminding ourselves that all that was but a
project, and that he meant to go once again through the experiments he had already made."

Pasteur declared himself ready to answer any one who would
defend those experiments which he looked upon as doubtful,
erroneous, or wrongly interpreted. "In the opposite case,"
he said, "out of respect for Claude Bernard's memory, I will
repeat his experiments before discussing them."

Some Academicians discoursed on these notes as on simple
suggestions and advised Pasteur to continue his studies without allowing himself to be delayed by mere control experiments. Others considered these notes as the expression of
Claude Bernard's thought. "That opinion," said Pasteur—
man of sentiment as he was—"that opinion, however, does
not explain the enigma of his silence towards me. But why
should I look for that explanation elsewhere than in my intimate knowledge of his fine character ? Was not his silence
a new proof of his kindness, and one of the effects of our
mutual esteem ? Since he thought that he held in his hands
a proof that the interpretation I had given to my experiments
was fallacious, did he not simply wish to wait to inform me
of it until the time when he thought himself ready for a definite
statement ? I prefer to attribute high motives to my friend's
actions, and, in my opinion, the surprise caused in me by his
reserve towards the one colleague whom his work most interested should give way in my heart to feelings of pious gratitude.
However, Bernard would have been the first to remind me that
scientific truth soars above the proprieties of friendship, and
that my duty lies in discussing views and opinions in my turn
with full liberty."

Pasteur having made this communication to the Academy on
July 22, hastily ordered three glass houses, which he intended
to take with him into the Jura, "where I possess," he told his
colleagues, "a vineyard occupying some thirty or forty square
yards."

Two observations expounded in a chapter of his *Studies on
Beer* tend to establish that yeast can only appear about the
time when grapes ripen, and that it disappears in the winter
only to show itself again at the end of the summer." Therefore "germs of yeast do not yet exist on green grapes." "We
are," he added, "at an epoch in the year when, by reason of

the lateness of vegetation due to a cold and rainy season, grapes are still in the green stage in the vineyards of Arbois. If I choose this moment to enclose some vines in almost hermetically closed glass houses, I shall have in October during the vintage some vines bearing ripe grapes without the exterior germs of wine yeast. Those grapes, crushed with precautions which will not allow of the introduction of yeast germs, will neither ferment nor produce wine. I shall give myself the pleasure of bringing some back to Paris, to present them to the Academy and to offer a few bunches to those of our colleagues who are still able to believe in the spontaneous generation of yeast."

In the midst of the agitation caused by that posthumous work some said, or only insinuated, that if Pasteur was announcing new researches on the subject, it was because he felt that his work was threatened.

"I will not accept such an interpretation of my conduct," he wrote to J. B. Dumas on August 4, 1878, at the very time when he was starting for the Jura; "I have clearly explained this in my notice of July 22, when I said I would make new experiments solely from respect to Bernard's memory."

As soon as Pasteur's glass houses arrived, they were put up in the little vineyard he possessed, two kilometres from Arbois. While they were being put together, he examined whether the yeast germs were really absent from the bunches of green grapes; he had the satisfaction of seeing that it was so, and that the particular branches which were about to be placed under glass did not bear a trace of yeast germs. Still, fearing that the closing of the glass might be insufficient and that there might thus be a danger of germs, he took the precaution, "while leaving some bunches free, of wrapping a few on each plant with cotton wool previously heated to 150° C."

He then returned to Paris and his studies on anthrax, whilst patiently waiting for the ripening of his grapes.

Besides M. Chamberland, Pasteur had enrolled M. Roux, the young man who was so desirous of taking part in the work at the laboratory. He and M. Chamberland were to settle down at Chartres in the middle of the summer. A recent student of the Alfort Veterinary School, M. Vinsot, joined them at his own request. M. Roux has told of those days in a paper on *Pasteur's Medical Work*:

"Our guide was M. Boutet, who had unrivalled knowledge

of the splenic fever country, and we sometimes met M. Toussaint, who was studying the same subject as we were. We
have kept a pleasant memory of that campaign against charbon
in the Chartres neighbourhood. Early in the morning, we
would visit the sheepfolds scattered on that wide plateau of the
Beauce, dazzling with the splendour of the August sunshine;
then necropsies took place in M. Rabourdin's knacker's yard
or in the farmyards. In the afternoon, we edited our experiment notebooks, wrote to Pasteur, and arranged for new
experiments. The day was well filled, and how interesting
and salutary was that bacteriology practised in the open
air !

"On the days when Pasteur came to Chartres, we did not
linger over our lunch at the Hôtel de France; we drove off to
St. Germain, where M. Maunoury had kindly put his farm
and flocks at our disposal. During the drive we talked of the
week's work and of what remained to be done.

"As soon as Pasteur left the carriage he hurried to the folds.
Standing motionless by the gate, he would gaze at the lots
which were being experimented upon, with a careful attention
which nothing escaped; he would spend hours watching one
sheep which seemed to him to be sickening. We had to remind
him of the time and to point out to him that the towers of
Chartres Cathedral were beginning to disappear in the falling
darkness before we could prevail upon him to come away. He
questioned farmers and their servants, giving much credit to
the opinions of shepherds, who on account of their solitary life,
give their whole attention to their flocks and often become
sagacious observers."

When again at Arbois, on September 17, Pasteur began to
write to the Minister of Agriculture a note on the practical
ideas suggested by this first campaign. A few sheep, bought
near Chartres and gathered in a fold, had received, amongst
the armfuls of forage offered them, a few anthrax spores.
Nothing had been easier than to bring these from the laboratory, in a liquid culture of bacteria, and to scatter them on the
field where the little flock grazed. The first meals did not give
good scientific results, death was not easily provoked. But
when the experimental menu was completed by prickly plants,
likely to wound the sheep on their tongue or in their pharynx,
such, for instance, as thistles or ears of barley, the mortality
began. It was perhaps not as considerable as might have

been wished for demonstration purposes, but nevertheless it was sufficient to explain how charbon could declare itself, for necropsy showed the characteristic lesions of the so-called spontaneous splenic fever. It was also to be concluded therefrom that the evil begins in the mouth, or at the back of the throat, supervening on meals of infected food, alone or mixed with prickly plants likely to cause abrasion.

It was therefore necessary, in a department like that of Eure et Loir, which must be full of anthrax germs,—particularly on the surface of the graves containing carcases of animals which had fallen victims to the disease,—that sheep farmers should keep from the food of their animals plants such as thistles, ears of barley, and sharp pieces of straw; for the least scratch, usually harmless to sheep, became dangerous through the possible introduction of the germs of the disease.

"It would also be necessary," wrote Pasteur, "to avoid all probable diffusion of charbon germs through the carcases of animals dying of that disease, for it is likely that the department of Eure et Loir contains those germs in greater quantities than the other departments; splenic fever having long been established there, it always goes on, dead animals not being disposed of so as to destroy all germs of ulterior contagion."

After finishing this report, Pasteur went to his little vineyard on the Besançon road, where he met with a disappointment; his precious grapes had not ripened, all the strength of the plant seemed to have gone to the wood and leaves. But the grapes had their turn at the end of September and in October, those bunches that were swathed in cotton wool as well as those which had remained free under the glass; there was a great difference of colour between them, the former being very pale. Pasteur placed grapes from the two series in distinct tubes. On October 10, he compared the grapes of the glass houses, free or swathed, with the neighbouring open-air grapes. "The result was beyond my expectations; the tubes of open-air grapes fermented with grape yeast after a thirty-six or forty-eight hours' sojourn in a stove from 25° C. to 30° C.; not one, on the contrary, of the numerous tubes of grapes swathed in cotton wool entered into alcoholic fermentation, neither did any of the tubes containing grapes ripened free under glass. It was the experiment described in my *Studies on Beer*. On the following days I repeated these experiments with the same results." He went on to another experiment. He cut some of the swathed bunches and hung them to the vines grown in the open air, thinking that those bunches—exactly similar to those which he had found in-capable of fermentation—would thus get covered with the germs of alcoholic ferments, as did the bunches grown in the open air and their wood. After that, the bunches taken from under the glass and submitted to the usual régime would fer-ment under the influence of the germs which they would receive as well as the others; this was exactly what happened.

The difficulty now was to bring to the Académie des Sciences these branches bearing swathed bunches of grapes; in order to avoid the least contact to the grapes, these vine plants, as precious as the rarest orchids, had to be held upright all the way from Arbois to Paris. Pasteur came back to Paris in a coupé carriage on the express train, accompanied by his wife and daughter, who took it in turns to carry the vines. At last, they arrived safely at the Ecole Normale, and from the Ecole Normale to the Institute, and Pasteur had the pleasure of bringing his grapes to his colleagues as he had brought his hens. "If you crush them while in contact with pure air," he said, "I defy you to see them ferment." A long discussion then ensued with M. Berthelot, which was prolonged until February, 1879.

"It is a characteristic of exalted minds," wrote M. Roux, "to put passion into ideas. . . . For Pasteur, the alcoholic fermentation was correlative with the life of the ferment; for Bernard and M. Berthelot, it was a chemical action like any other, and could be accomplished without the participation of living cells." "In alcoholic fermentation," said M. Berthelot, "a soluble alcoholic ferment may be produced, which perhaps consumes itself as its production goes on."

M. Roux had seen Pasteur try to "extract the soluble alco-holic ferment from yeast cells by crushing them in a mortar, by freezing them until they burst, or by putting them into concentrated saline solutions, in order to force by osmose the succus to leave its envelope." Pasteur confessed that his efforts were vain. In a communication to the Académie des Sciences on December 30, 1878, he said—

"It ever is an enigma to me that it should be believed that the discovery of soluble ferments in fermentations properly so called, or of the formation of alcohol by means of sugar, inde-

pendently of cells would hamper me. It is true—I own it
without hesitation, and I am ready to explain myself more
lengthily if desired—that at present I neither see the necessity
for the existence of those ferments, nor the usefulness of their
action in this order of fermentations. Why should actions of
diastase, which are but phenomena of hydration, be confused
with those of organized ferments, or vice versâ? But I do not
see that the presence of those soluble substances, if it were
ascertained, could change in any way the conclusions drawn
from my labours, and even less so if alcohol were formed by
electrolysis.

"They agree with me who admit ·

"Firstly. That fermentations, properly so called, offer as
an essential condition the presence of microscopic organisms.

"Secondly. That those organisms have not a spontaneous
origin.

"Thirdly. That the life of every organism which can exist
away from free oxygen is suddenly concomitant with acts of
fermentation ; and that it is so with every cell which continues
to produce chemical action without the contact of oxygen."

When Pasteur related this discussion, and formed of it an
appendix to his book, *Critical Examination of a Posthumous
Work of Claude Bernard on Fermentations*, his painful feelings
in opposing a friend who was no more were so clearly evidenced
that Sainte Claire Deville wrote to him (June 9, 1879) : "My
dear Pasteur, I read a few passages of your new book yesterday to a small party of professors and *savants*. We all were
much moved by the expressions with which you praise our
dear Bernard, and by your feelings of friendship and pure
fraternity."

Sainte Claire Deville often spoke of his admiration for
Pasteur's precision of thought, his forcible speech, the clearness
of his writings. As for J. B. Dumas, he called the attention
of his colleagues at the Académie Française to certain pages
of that *Critical Examination*. Though unaccustomed to those
particular subjects, they could not but be struck by the sagacity
and ingenuity of Pasteur's researches, and by the eloquence
inspired by his genius. A propos of those ferment germs, which
turn grape juice into wine, and from which he had preserved
his swathed bunches, Pasteur wrote—

"What meditations are induced by those results ! It is
impossible not to observe that, the further we penetrate into the

experimental study of germs, the more we perceive sudden
lights and clear ideas on the knowledge of the causes of contagious diseases! Is it not worthy of attention that, in that
Arbois vineyard (and it would be true of the million *hectares*
of vineyards of all the countries in the world), there should not
have been, at the time when I made the aforesaid experiments,
one single particle of earth which would not have been capable
of provoking fermentation by a grape yeast, and that, on the
other hand, the earth of the glass houses I have mentioned
should have been powerless to fulfil that office? And why?
Because, at a given moment, I covered that earth with some
glass. The death, if I may so express it, of a bunch of grapes
thrown at that time on any vineyard, would infallibly have
occurred through the *saccharomyces* parasites of which I speak;
that kind of death would have been impossible, on the contrary,
on the little space enclosed by my glass houses. Those few
cubic yards of air, those few square yards of soil, were there,
in the midst of a universal possible contagion, and they were
safe from it."

And suddenly looking beyond those questions of yeast and
vintage, towards the germs of disease and of death: "Is it
not permissible to believe, by analogy, that a day will come
when easily applied preventive measures will arrest those
scourges which suddenly desolate and terrify populations; such
as the fearful disease (yellow fever) which has recently invaded
Senegal and the valley of the Mississippi, or that other (bubonic
plague), yet more terrible perhaps, which has ravaged the banks
of the Volga."

Pasteur, with his quick answers, his tenacious refutations,
was looked upon as a great fighter by his colleagues at the
Academy, but in the laboratory, while seeking Claude Bernard's soluble ferment, he tackled subjects from which he drew
conclusions which were amazing to physiciàns.

A worker in the laboratory had had a series of furuncles.
Pasteur, whose proverb was "Seek the microbe," asked himself whether the pus of furuncles might not have an organism,
which, carried to and fro,—for it may be said that a furuncle
never comes alone—would explain the centre of inflammation
and the recurrence of the furuncles. After abstracting—with
the usual purity precautions—some pus from three successive
furuncles, he found in some sterilized broth a microbe, formed
of little rounded specks which clustered to the sides of the

culture vessel. The same was observed on a man whom Dr. Maurice Raynaud, interested in those researches on furuncles, had sent to the laboratory, and afterwards on a female patient of the Lariboisière Hospital, whose back was covered with furuncles. Later on, Pasteur, taken by Dr. Lannelongue to the Trousseau Hospital, where a little girl was about to be operated on for that disease of the bones and marrow called *osteomyelitis*, gathered a few drops of pus from the inside and the outside of the bone, and again found clusters of microbes. Sown into a culture liquid, this microbe seemed so identical with the furuncle organism that "it might be affirmed at first sight," said Pasteur, "that osteomyelitis is the furuncle of bones."

The hospital now took as much place in Pasteur's life as the laboratory. "Chamberland and I assisted him in those studies," writes M. Roux. "It was to the Hôpital Cochin or to the Maternité that we went most frequently, taking our culture tubes and sterilized pipets into the wards or operating theatres. No one knows what feelings of repulsion Pasteur had to overcome before visiting patients and witnessing post-mortem examinations. His sensibility was extreme, and he suffered morally and physically from the pains of others ; the cut of the bistoury opening an abscess made him wince as if he himself had received it. The sight of corpses, the sad business of necropsies, caused him real disgust ; we have often seen him go home ill from those operating theatres. But his love of science, his desire for truth were the stronger ; he returned the next day."

He was highly interested in the study of puerperal fever, which was still enveloped in profound darkness. Might not the application of his theories to the progress of surgery be realized in obstetrics? Could not those epidemics be arrested which passed like scourges over lying-in hospitals? It was still remembered with horror how, in the Paris Maternity Hospital, between April 1 and May 10, 1856, 64 fatalities had taken place out of 347 confinements. The hospital had to be closed, and the survivors took refuge at the Lariboisière Hospital, where they nearly all succumbed, pursued, it was thought, by the epidemic.

Dr. Tarnier, a student residing at the Maternité during that disastrous time, related afterwards how the ignorance of the causes of puerperal fever was such that he was sometimes called

U

away, by one of his chiefs, from some post-mortem business, to assist in the maternity wards; nobody being struck by the thought of the infection which might thus be carried from the theatre to the bed of the patient.

The discussion which arose in 1858 at the Académie de Médecine lasted four months, and hypotheses of all kinds were brought forward. Trousseau alone showed some prescience of the future by noticing an analogy between infectious surgical accidents and infectious puerperal accidents; the idea of a ferment even occurred to him. Years passed; women of the lower classes looked upon the Maternité as the vestibule of death. In 1864, 310 deaths occurred out of 1,350 confinement cases; in 1865, the hospital had to be closed. Works of cleansing and improvements gave rise to a hope that the "epidemic genius" might be driven away. "But, at the very beginning of 1866," wrote Dr. Trélat, then surgeon-in-chief at the Maternité, "the sanitary condition seemed perturbed, the mortality rose in January, and in February we were overwhelmed." Twenty-eight deaths had occurred out of 103 cases.

Trélat enumerated various causes, bad ventilation, neighbouring wards, etc., but where was the origin of the evil?

"Under the influence of causes which escape us," wrote M. Léon Le Fort about that time, "puerperal fever develops in a recently delivered woman; she becomes a centre of infection, and, if that infection is freely exercised, the epidemic is constituted."

Tarnier, who took Trélat's place at the Maternité, in 1867, had been for eleven years so convinced of the infectious nature of puerperal fever that he thought but of arresting the evil by every possible means of defence, the first of which seemed to him isolation of the patients.

In 1874, Dr. Budin, then walking the hospitals, had noted in Edinburgh the improvement due to antisepsis, thanks to Lister. Three or four years later, in 1877 and 1878, after having seen that, in the various maternity hospitals of Holland, Germany, Austria, Russia and Denmark, antisepsis was practised with success, he brought his impressions with him to Paris. Tarnier hastened to employ carbolic acid at the Maternité with excellent results, and his assistant, M. Bar, tried sublimate. While that new period of victory over fatal cases was beginning, Pasteur came to the Académie de Médecine, having found, in certain puerperal infections, a microbe in the shape of a chain or chaplet, which lent itself very well to culture.

"Pasteur," wrote M. Roux, "does not hesitate to declare that that microscopic organism is the most frequent cause of infection in recently delivered women. One day, in a discussion on puerperal fever at the Academy, one of his most weighty colleagues was eloquently enlarging upon the causes of epidemics in lying-in hospitals; Pasteur interrupted him from his place. 'None of those things cause the epidemic; it is the nursing and medical staff who carry the microbe from an infected woman to a healthy one.' And as the orator replied that he feared that microbe would never be found, Pasteur went to the blackboard and drew a diagram of the chain-like organism, saying : 'There, that is what it is like!' His conviction was so deep that he could not help expressing it forcibly. It would be impossible now to picture the state of surprise and stupefaction into which he would send the students and doctors in hospitals, when, with an assurance and simplicity almost disconcerting in a man who was entering a lying-in ward for the first time, he criticized the appliances, and declared that all the linen should be put into a sterilizing stove."

Pasteur was not satisfied with offering advice and criticism, making for himself irreconcilable enemies amongst those who were more desirous of personal distinction than of the progress of Science. In order the better to convince those who still doubted, he affirmed that, in a badly infected patient—what he usually and sorrowfully called an *invaded* patient—he could bring the microbe into evidence by a simple pin prick on the finger tip of the unhappy woman doomed to die the next day.

"And he did so," writes M. Roux. "In spite of the tyranny of medical education which weighed down the public mind, some students were attracted, and came to the laboratory to examine more closely those matters, which allowed of such precise diagnosis and such confident prognosis."

What struggles, what efforts, were necessary before it could be instilled into every mind that a constant watch must be kept in the presence of those invisible foes, ready to invade the human body through the least scratch—that surgeons, dressers and nurses may become causes of infection and propagators of death through forgetfulness! and before the theory of germs and the all powerfulness of microbes could be put under a full light à propos of that discussion on puerperal fever !

But Pasteur was supported and inspired during that period, perhaps the most fruitful of his existence, by the prescience that those notions meant the salvation of human lives, and that mothers need no longer be torn by death from the cradle of their new-born infants.

"I shall force them to see; they will have to see!" he repeated with a holy wrath against doctors who continued to talk, from their study or at their clubs, with some scepticism, of those newly discovered little creatures, of those ultra-microscopic parasites, trying to moderate enthusiasm and even confidence.

An experimental fact which occurred about that time was followed with interest, not only by the Académie des Sciences, but by the general public, whose attention was beginning to be awakened. A professor at the Nancy Faculty, M. Feltz, had announced to the Académie des Sciences in March, 1879, that, in the blood abstracted from a woman, who had died at the Nancy Hospital of puerperal fever, he had found motionless filaments, simple or articulated, transparent, straight or curved, which belonged, he said, to the genus *leptothrix*. Pasteur, who in his studies on puerperal fever had seen nothing of the kind, wrote to Dr. Feltz, asking him to send him a few drops of that infected blood. After receiving and examining the sample, Pasteur hastened to inform M. Feltz that that leptothrix was no other than the bacillus anthracis. M. Feltz, much surprised and perplexed, declared himself ready to own his error and to proclaim it if he were convinced by examining blood infected by charbon, and which, he said, he should collect wherever he could find it. Pasteur desired to save him that trouble, and offered to send him three little guinea-pigs alive, but inoculated, the one with the deceased woman's blood, the other with the bacteridia of charbon-infected blood from Chartres, the third with some charbon-infected blood from a Jura cow.

The three rodents were inoculated on May 12, at three o'clock in the afternoon, and arrived, living, at Nancy, on the morning of the thirteenth. They died on the fourteenth, in the laboratory of M. Feltz, who was thus able to observe them with particular attention until their death.

"After carefully examining the blood of the three animals after their death, I was unable," said M. Feltz, "to detect the least difference; not only the blood, but the internal organs, and notably the spleen, were affected in the same manner."

'It is a certainty to my mind," he wrote to Pasteur, " that the contaminating agent has been the same in the three cases, and that it was the bacteridium of what you call anthrax."

There was therefore no such thing as a leptothrix puerperalis. And it was at a distance, without having seen the patient, that Pasteur said : " That woman died of charbon." With an honourable straightforwardness, M. Feltz wrote to the Académie des Sciences relating the facts.

" It is doubly regrettable," he concluded, " that I should not have known charbon already last year, for, on the one hand, I might have diagnosed the redoubtable complication presented by the case, and, on the other hand, sought for the mode of contamination, which at present escapes me almost completely." All he had been able to find was that the woman, a charwoman, lived in a little room near a stable belonging to a horse dealer. Many animals came there; the stable might have contained diseased ones; M. Feltz had been unable to ascertain the fact. " I must end," he added, " with thanks to M. Pasteur for the great kindness he has shown me during my intercourse with him. Thanks to him, I was able to convince myself of the identity between the bacillus anthracis and the bacteridium found in the blood of a woman who presented all the symptoms of grave puerperal fever."

At the time when that convincing episode was taking place, other experiments equally precise were being undertaken concerning splenic fever. The question was to discover whether it would be possible to find germs of charbon in the earth of the fields which had been contaminated purposely, fourteen months before, by pouring culture liquids over it. It seemed beyond all probability that those germs might be withdrawn and isolated from the innumerable other microbes contained in the soil. It was done, however; 500 grammes of earth were mixed with water, and infinitesimal particles of it isolated. The spore of the bacillus anthracis resists a temperature of 80° C. or 90° C., which would kill any other microbe; those particles of earth were accordingly raised to that degree of heat and then injected into some guinea-pigs, several of which died of splenic fever. It was therefore evident that flocks were exposed to infection merely by grazing over certain fields in that land of the Beauce.

For it was sufficient that some infected blood should have remained on the ground, for germs of bacteridia to be found there, perhaps years later. How often was such blood spilt as a dead animal was being taken to the knacker's yard or buried on the spot! Millions of bacteridia, thus scattered on and below the surface of the soil, produced their spores, seeds of death ready to germinate.

And yet negative facts were being opposed to these positive facts, and the theory of spontaneity invoked! "It is with deep sorrow," said Pasteur at the Académie de Médecine on November 11, 1873, "that I so frequently find myself obliged to answer thoughtless contradiction; it also grieves me much to see that the medical Press speaks of these discussions in apparent ignorance of the true principles of experimental method. . . .

" That aimlessness of criticism seems explicable to me, however, by this circumstance—that Medicine and Surgery are, I think, going through a crisis, a transition. There are two opposite currents, that of the old and that of the new-born doctrine; the first, still followed by innumerable partisans, rests on the belief in the spontaneity of transmissible diseases; the second is the theory of germs, of the living contagium with all its legitimate consequences. "

The better to point out that difference between epochs, Pasteur respectfully advised M. Bouillaud, who was taking part in the discussion, to read over Littré's *Medicine and Physicians*, and to compare with present ideas the chapter on epidemics written in 1836, four years after the cholera which had spread terror over Paris and over France. "Poisons and venoms die out on the spot after working the evil which is special to them," wrote Littré, " and are not reproduced in the body of the victim, but virus and miasmata are reproduced and propagated. Nothing is more obscure to physiologists than those mysterious combinations of organic elements; but there lies the dark room of sickness and of death which we must try to open." "Among epidemic diseases," said Littré in another passage equally noted by Pasteur, " some occupy the world and decimate nearly all parts of it, others are limited to more or less wide areas. The origin of the latter may be sought either in local circumstances of dampness, of marshy ground, of decomposing animal or vegetable matter, or in the changes which take place in men's mode of life."

"If I had to defend the novelty of the ideas introduced into medicine by my labours of the last twenty years," wrote Pasteur from Arbois in September, 1879, "I should invoke the significant spirit of Littré's words. Such was then the state of Science in 1836, and those ideas on the etiology of great epidemies were those of one of the most advanced and penetrating minds of the time. I would observe, contrarily to Littré's opinion, that nothing proves the spontaneity of great epidemics ! As we have lately seen the phylloxera, imported from America, invade Europe, so it might be that the causes of great pests were originated, unknowingly to stricken countries, in other countries which had had fortuitous contact with the latter. Imagine a microscopic being, inhabiting some part of Africa and existing on plants, on animals, or even on men, and capable of communicating a disease to the white race ; if brought to Europe by some fortuitous circumstance, it may become the occasion of an epidemic. .   "

And, writing later, about the same passage : "Nowadays, if an article had to be written on the same subject, it would certainly be the idea of living ferments and microscopic beings and germs which would be mentioned and discussed as a cause. That is the great progress," added Pasteur with legitimate pride, "in which my labours have had so large a share. But it is characteristic of Science and Progress that they go on opening new fields to our vision ; the scientist, who is exploring the unknown, resembles the traveller who perceives further and higher summits as he reaches greater altitudes. In these days, more infectious diseases, more microscopic beings appear to the mind as things to be discovered, the discovery of which will render a wonderful account of pathological conditions and of their means of action and propagation, of self-multiplication within and destruction of the organism. The point of view is very different from Littré's ! ! "

On his return to Paris, Pasteur, his mind overflowing with ideas, had felt himself impelled to speak again, to fight once more the fallacious theory of the spontaneity of transmissible diseases. He foresaw the triumph of the germ theory arising from the ruin of the old doctrines—at the price, it is true, of many efforts, many struggles, but those were of little consequence to him.

The power of his mind, the radiating gifts that he possessed, were such that his own people were more and more interested

in the laboratory, every one trying day by day to penetrate further into Pasteur's thoughts.   His family circle had widened ;
his son and his daughter had married, and the two new-comers
had soon been initiated into past results and recent experiments.   He had, in his childhood and youth, been passionately
loved by his parents and sisters, and now, in his middle age, his
tenderness towards his wife and children was eagerly repaid by
the love they bore him.   He made happiness around him whilst
he gave glory to France.

CHAPTER X

1880—1882.

A NEW microbe now became the object of the same studies of culture and inoculation as the bacillus anthracis. Readers of this book may have had occasion to witness the disasters caused in a farmyard by a strange and sudden epidemic. Hens, believed to be good sitters, are found dead on their nests. Others, surrounded by their brood, allow the chicks to leave them, giving them no attention; they stand motionless in the centre of the yard, staggering under a deadly drowsiness. A young and superb cock, whose triumphant voice was yesterday heard by all the neighbours, falls into a sudden agony, his beak closed, his eyes dim, his purple comb drooping limply. Other chickens, respited till the next day, come near the dying and the dead, picking here and there grains soiled with excreta containing the deadly germs : it is chicken cholera.

An Alsatian veterinary surgeon of the name of Moritz had been the first to notice, in 1869, some " granulations " in the corpses of animals struck down by this lightning disease, which sometimes kills as many as ninety chickens out of a hundred, those who survive having probably recovered from a slight attack of the cholera. Nine years after Moritz, Perroncito, an Italian veterinary surgeon, made a sketch of the microbe, which has the appearance of little specks. Toussaint studied it, and demonstrated that this microbe was indeed the cause of virulence in the blood. He sent to Pasteur the head of a cock that had died of cholera. The first thing to do, after isolating the microbe, was to try successive cultures; Toussaint had used neutralized urine. This, though perfect for the culture of the bacillus anthracis, proved a bad culture medium for the microbe of chicken cholera; its multiplication soon became arrested. If sown in a small flask of yeast water, equally favourable to bacteridia, the result was worse still : the microbe disappeared in forty-eight hours.

"Is not that," said Pasteur—with the gift of comparison which made him turn each failure into food for reflection—" an image of what we observe when a microscopic organism proves to be harmless to a particular animal species? It is harmless because it does not develop within the body, or because its development does not reach the organs essential to life."

After trying other culture mediums, Pasteur found that the one which answered best was a broth of chicken gristle, neutralized with potash and sterilized by a temperature of 110° C. to 115° C.

" The facility of multiplication of the micro-organism in that culture medium is really prodigious," wrote Pasteur in a duplicate communication to the Academies of Sciences and of Medicine (February, 1880), entitled *Of Virulent Diseases, and in particular that commonly called Chicken Cholera.* " In a few hours, the most limpid broth becomes turgid and is found to be full of little articles of an extreme tenuity, slightly strangled in their middle and looking at first sight like isolated specks ; they are incapable of locomotion. Within a few days, those beings, already so small, change into a multitude of specks so much smaller, that the culture liquid, which had at first become turgid, almost milky, becomes nearly clear again, the specks being of such narrow diameter as to be impossible to measure, even approximately.

" This microbe certainly belongs to quite another group than that of the vibriones. I imagine that it will one day find a place with the still mysterious virus, when the latter are successfully cultivated, which will be soon, I hope."

Pasteur stated that the virulence of this microbe was such that the smallest drop of recent culture, on a few crumbs, was sufficient to kill a chicken. Hens fed in this way contracted the disease by their intestinal canal, an excellent culture medium for the micro-organism, and perished rapidly. Their infected excreta became a cause of contagion to the hens which shared with them the laboratory cages. Pasteur thus described one of these sick hens

" The animal suffering from this disease is powerless, staggering, its wings droop and its bristling feathers give it the shape of a ball ; an irresistible somnolence overpowers it. If its eyes are made to open, it seems to awake from a deep sleep, and death frequently supervenes after a dumb agony, before the animal has stirred from its place; sometimes there is a faint fluttering of the wings for a few seconds."

Pasteur tried the effect of this microbe on guinea-pigs which had been brought up in the laboratory, and found it but rarely mortal; in general it merely caused a sore, terminating in an abscess, at the point of inoculation. If this abscess were opened, instead of being allowed to heal of its own accord, the little microbe of chicken cholera was to be found in the pus, preserved in the abscess as it might be in a phial.

"Chickens or rabbits," remarked Pasteur, "living in the society of guinea-pigs presenting these abscesses, might suddenly become ill and die without any alteration being seen in the guinea-pigs' health. It would suffice for this purpose that those abscesses should open and drop some of their contents on the food of the chickens and rabbits.

"An observer witnessing those facts, and ignorant of the above-mentioned cause, would be astonished to see hens and rabbits decimated without apparent cause, and would believe in the spontaneity of the evil; for he would be far from supposing that it had its origin in the guinea-pigs, all of them in good health. How many mysteries in the history of contagions will one day be solved as simply as this ! ! ! "

A chance, such as happens to those who have the genius of observation, was now about to mark an immense step in advance and prepare the way for a great discovery. As long as the culture flasks of chicken-cholera microbe had been sown without interruption, at twenty-four hours' interval, the virulence had remained the same; but when some hens were inoculated with an old culture, put away and forgotten a few weeks before, they were seen with surprise to become ill and then to recover. These unexpectedly refractory hens were then inoculated with some new culture, but the phenomenon of resistance recurred. What had happened? What could have attenuated the activity of the microbe ?   Researches proved that oxygen was the cause; and, by putting between the cultures variable intervals of days, of one, two or three months, variations of mortality were obtained, eight hens dying out of ten, then five, then only one out of ten, and at last, when, as in the first case, the culture had had time to get stale, no hens died at all, though the microbe could still be cultivated.

"Finally," said Pasteur, eagerly explaining this phenomenon, "if you take each of these attenuated cultures as a starting-point for successive and uninterrupted cultures, all this series of cultures will reproduce the attenuated virulence of that which served as the starting-point; in the same way non-virulence will reproduce non-virulence."

And, while hens who had never had chicken-cholera perished when exposed to the deadly virus, those who had undergone attenuated inoculations, and who afterwards received more than their share of the deadly virus, were affected with the disease in a benign form, a passing indisposition, sometimes even they remained perfectly well; they had acquired immunity. Was not this fact worthy of being placed by the side of that great fact of vaccine, over which Pasteur had so often pondered and meditated?

He now felt that he might entertain the hope of obtaining, through artificial culture, some vaccinating-virus against the virulent diseases which cause great losses to agriculture in the breeding of domestic animals, and, beyond that, the greater hope of preserving humanity from those contagious diseases which continually decimate it. This invincible hope led him to wish that he might live long enough to accomplish some new discoveries and to see his followers step into the road he had marked out.

Strong in his experimental method which enabled him to produce proofs and thus to demonstrate the truth; able to establish the connection between a virulent and a microbian disease; finally, ready to reproduce by culture, in several degrees of attenuation, a veritable vaccine, could he not now force those of his opponents who were acting in good faith to acknowledge the evidence of facts? Could he not carry all attentive minds with him into the great movement which was about to replace old ideas by new and precise notions, more and more accessible?

Pasteur enjoyed days of incomparable happiness during that period of enthusiasm, joys of the mind in its full power, joys of the heart in all its expansion; for good was being done. He felt that nothing could arrest the course of his doctrine, of which he said—"The breath of Truth is carrying it towards the fruitful fields of the future." He had that intuition which makes a great poet of a great scientist. The innumerable ideas surging through his mind were like so many bees all trying to issue from the hive at the same time. So many plans and preconceived ideas only stimulated him to further researches; but, when he was once started on a road, he distrusted each step and only progressed in the train of precise, clear and irrefutable experiments.

A paper of his on the plague, dated April, 1880, illustrates his train of thought. The preceding year the Academy of Medicine had appointed a commission composed of eight members, to draw up a programme of research relative to the plague. The scourge had appeared in a village situated on the right bank of the Volga, in the district of Astrakhan. There had been one isolated case at first, followed ten days later by another death ; the dread disease had then invaded and devoured the whole village, going from house to house like an inextinguishable fire ; 370 deaths had occurred in a population of 1,372 inhabitants ; thirty or forty people died every day. In one of those sinister moments when men forget everything in their desire to live, parents and relations had abandoned their sick and dying among the unburied dead, with 20° C. of frost ! ! The neighbouring villages were contaminated ; but, thanks to the Russian authorities, who had established a strict sanitary cordon, the evil was successfully localized. Some doctors, meeting in Vienna, declared that that plague was no other than the Black Death of the fourteenth century, which had depopulated Europe. The old pictures and sculptures of the time, which represent Death pressing into his lugubrious gang children and old men, beggars and emperors, bear witness to the formidable ravages of such a scourge. In France, since the epidemic at Marseilles in 1720, it seemed as if the plague were but a memory, a distant nightmare, almost a horrible fairy tale. Dr. Rochard, in a report to the Académie de Médecine, recalled how the contagion had burst out in May, 1720 ; a ship, having lost six men from the plague on its journey, had entered Marseilles harbour. The plague, after an insidious first phase, had raged in all its fury in July.

" Since the plague is a disease," wrote Pasteur (whose paper was a sort of programme of studies), "the cause of which is absolutely unknown, it is not illogical to suppose that it too is perhaps produced by a special microbe. All experimental research must be guided by some preconceived ideas, and it would probably be very useful to tackle the study of that disease with the belief that it is due to a parasite.

" The most decisive of all the proofs which can be invoked in favour of the possible correlation between a determined affection and the presence of a micro-organism, is that afforded by the method of cultures of organisms in a state of purity; a method by which I have solved, within the last twenty-two years, the chief difficulties relative to fermentations properly so called; notably the important question, much debated formerly, of the correlation which exists between those fermentations and their particular ferments."

He then pointed out that if, after gathering either blood or pus immediately before or immediately after the death of a plague patient, one could succeed in discovering the microorganism, and then in finding for that microbe an appropriate culture medium, it would be advisable to inoculate with it animals of various kinds, perhaps monkeys for preference, and to look for the lesions capable of establishing relations from cause to effect between that organism and the disease in mankind.

He did not hide from himself the great difficulties to be met with in experimenting; for, after discovering and isolating the organism, there is nothing to indicate *a priori* to the experimentalist an appropriate culture medium. Liquids which suit some microbes admirably are absolutely unsuitable to others. Take, for instance, the microbe of chicken-cholera, which will not develop in beer yeast; a hasty experimentalist might conclude that the chicken-cholera is not produced by a microorganism, and that it is a spontaneous disease with unknown immediate causes. "The fallacy would be a fatal one," said Pasteur, "for in another medium, say, for instance, in chicken-broth, there would be a virulent culture."

In these researches on the plague, then, various mediums should be tried; also the character, either aërobic or anaërobic, of the microbe should be present to the mind.

"The sterility of a culture liquid may come from the presence of air and not from its own constitution; the septic vibrio, for instance, is killed by oxygen in air. From this last circumstance it is plain that culture must be made not only in the presence of air but also in a vacuum or in the presence of pure carbonic acid gas. In the latter case, immediately after sowing the blood or humour to be tested, a vacuum must be made in the tubes, they must be sealed by means of a lamp, and left in a suitable temperature, usually between 30° C. and 40° C." Thus he prepared landmarks for the guidance of scientific research on the etiology of the plague.

Desiring as Pasteur did that the public in general should take an interest in laboratory research, he sent to his friend Nisard the number of the *Bulletin of the Académie de Médecine* which contained a first communication on chicken-cholera, and also his paper on the plague.

" Read them if you have time," he wrote (May 3, 1880) : " they may interest you, and *there should be no blanks in your education*. They will be followed by others.

" To-day at the Institute, and to-morrow at the Académie de Médecine, I shall give a new lecture.

" Do repeat to me every criticism you hear ; I much prefer them to praise, barren unless encouragement is wanted, which is certainly not my case ; I have a lasting provision of faith and fire."

Nisard answered on May 7 : " My very dear friend, I am almost dazed with the effort made by my ignorance to follow your ideas, and dazzled with the beauty of your discoveries on the principal point, and the number of secondary discoveries enumerated in your marvellous paper. You are right not to care for barren praise ; but you would wrong those who love you if you found no pleasure in being praised by them when they have no other means of acknowledging your notes.

" I am reading the notice on chicken-cholera for the second time, and I observe that the writer is following the discoverer, and that your language becomes elevated, supple and coloured, in order to express the various aspects of the subject.

" It gives me pleasure to see the daily growth of your fame, and I am indeed proud of enjoying your friendship."

Amidst his researches on a vaccine for chicken-cholera, the etiology of splenic fever was unceasingly preoccupying Pasteur. Did the splenic germs return to the surface of the soil, and how ? One day, in one of his habitual excursions with Messrs. Roux and Chamberland to the farm of St. Germain, near Chartres, he suddenly perceived an answer to that enigma. In a field recently harvested, he noticed a place where the colour of the soil differed a little from the neighbouring earth. He questioned M. Maunoury, the proprietor of the farm, who answered that sheep dead of anthrax had been buried there the preceding year. Pasteur drew nearer, and was interested by the mass of little earth cylinders, those little twists which earth-worms deposit on the ground. Might that be, he wondered, the explanation of the origin of the germs which reappear on the surface ? Might not the worms, returning from their subterranean journeys in the immediate neighbourhood of graves, bring back with them splenic spores, and thus scatter the germs so exhumed? That would again be a singular revelation, un-expected but quite simple, due to the germ theory. He wasted no time in dreaming of the possibilities opened by that precon-ceived idea, but, with his usual impatience to get at the truth, decided to proceed to experiment.

On his return to Paris Pasteur spoke to Bouley of this pos-sible part of germ carriers played by earthworms, and Bouley caused some to be gathered which had appeared on the surface of pits where animals dead of splenic fever had been buried some years before. Villemin and Davaine were invited as well as Bouley to come to the laboratory and see the bodies of these worms opened; anthrax spores were found in the earth cylinders which filled their intestinal tube.

At the time when Pasteur revealed this pathogenic action of the earthworm, Darwin, in his last book, was expounding their share in agriculture. He too, with his deep attention and force of method, able to discover the hidden importance of what seemed of little account to second-rate minds, had seen how earthworms open their tunnels, and how, by turning over the soil, and by bringing so many particles up to the surface by their "castings," they ventilate and drain the soil, and, by their incessant and continuous work, render great services to agriculture. These excellent labourers are redoubtable grave-diggers; each of those two tasks, the one beneficent and the other full of perils, was brought to light by Pasteur and Darwin, unknowingly to each other.

Pasteur had gathered earth from the pits where splenic cows had been buried in July, 1878, in the Jura. "At three different times within those two years," he said to the Académie des Sciences and to the Académie de Médecine in July, 1880, "the surface soil of those same pits has presented charbon spores." This fact had been confirmed by recent experiments on the soil of the Beauce farm; particles of earth from other parts of the field had no power of provoking splenic fever.

Pasteur, going on to practical advice, showed how grazing animals might find in certain places the germs of charbon, freed by the loosening by rain of the little castings of earth-worms. Animals are wont to choose the surface of the pits, where the soil, being richer in humus, produces thicker growth,

and in so doing risk their lives, for they become infected, somewhat in the same manner as in the experiments when their
forage was poisoned with a few drops of splenic culture liquid.
Septic germs are brought to the surface of the soil in the same
way.

"Animals," said Pasteur, "should never be buriĕd in
fields intended for pasture or the growing of hay. Whenever it is possible, burying-grounds should be chosen in sandy
or chalky soils, poor, dry, and unsuitable to the life of earthworms."

Pasteur, like a general with only two aides de camp, was
obliged to direct the efforts of Messrs. Chamberland and Roux
simultaneously in different parts of France. Sometimes facts
had to be checked which had been over-hastily announced by
rash experimentalists. Thus M. Roux went, towards the end
of the month of July, to an isolated property near Nancy, called
Bois le Duc Farm, to ascertain whether the successive deaths
of nineteen head of cattle were really, as affirmed, due to
splenic fever. The water of this pasture was alleged to be
contaminated; the absolute isolation of the herd seemed to
exclude all idea of contagion. After collecting water and
earth from various points on the estate M. Roux had returned
to the laboratory with his tubes and pipets. He was much
inclined to believe that there had been septicæmia and not
splenic fever.

M. Chamberland was at Savagna, near Lons-le-Saulnier,
where, in order to experiment on the contamination of the surface of pits, he had had a little enclosure traced out and
surrounded by an open paling in a meadow where victims of
splenic fever had been buried two years previously. Four
sheep were folded in this enclosure. Another similar fold, also
enclosing four sheep, was placed a few yards above the first
one. This experiment was intended to occupy the vacation,
and Pasteur meant to watch it from Arbois.

A great sorrow awaited him there. "I have just had the
misfortune of losing my sister," he wrote to Nisard at the
beginning of August, "to see whom (as also my parents' and
children's graves) I returned yearly to Arbois. Within forty-
eight hours I witnessed life, sickness, death and burial; such
rapidity is terrifying. I deeply loved my sister, who, in difficult times, when modest ease even did not reign in our home,
carried the heavy burden of the day and devoted herself to the

little ones of whom I was one. I am now the only survivor of my paternal and maternal families."

In the first days of August, Toussaint, the young professor of the Toulouse Veterinary School, declared that he had succeeded in vaccinating sheep against splenic fever. One process of vaccination (which consisted in collecting the blood of an animal affected with charbon just before or immediately after death, defibrinating it and then passing it through a piece of linen and filtering it through ten or twelve sheets of paper) had been unsuccessful; the bacteridia came through it all and killed instead of preserving the animal. Toussaint then had recourse to heat to kill the bacteridia : " I raised," he said, "the defibrinated blood to a heat of 55° C. for ten minutes; the result was complete. Five sheep inoculated with three cubic cent. of that blood, and afterwards with very active charbon blood, have not felt it in the least." However, several successive inoculations had to be made.

"All ideas of holidays must be postponed; we must set to work in Jura as well as in Paris," wrote Pasteur to his assistants. Bouley, who thought that the goal was reached, did not hide from himself the difficulties of interpretation of the alleged fact. He obtained from the Minister of Agriculture permission to try at Alfort this so-called vaccinal liquid on twenty sheep.

"Yesterday," wrote Pasteur to his son-in-law on August 13, "I went to give M. Chamberland instructions so that I may verify as soon as possible the Toussaint fact, which I will only believe when I have seen it, seen it with my own eyes. I am having twenty sheep bought, and I hope to be satisfied as to the exactitude of this really extraordinary observation in about three weeks' time. Nature may have mystified M. Toussaint, though his assertions seem to attest the existence of a very interesting fact."

Toussaint's assertion had been hasty, and Pasteur was not long in clearing up that point. The temperature of 55° C. prolonged for ten minutes was not sufficient to kill the bacteridia in the blood; they were but weakened and retarded in their development; even after fifteen minutes' exposure to the heat, there was but a numbness of the bacteridium. Whilst these experiments were being pursued in the Jura and in the laboratory of the Ecole Normale, the Alfort sheep were giving Bouley great anxiety. One died of charbon one day after inoculation, three two days later. The others were so ill that

M. Nocard wanted to sacrifice one in order to proceed to immediate necropsy; Bouley apprehended a complete disaster. But the sixteen remaining sheep recovered gradually and became ready for the counter test of charbon inoculation.

Whilst Pasteur was noting the decisive points, he heard from Bouley and from Roux at the same time, that Toussaint now obtained his vaccinal liquid, no longer by the action of heat, but by the measured action of carbolic acid on splenic fever blood. The interpretation by weakening remained the same.

"What ought we to conclude from that result?" wrote Bouley to Pasteur. "It is evident that Toussaint does not vaccinate as he thought, with a liquid destitute of bacteridia, since he gives charbon with that liquid; but that he uses a liquid in which the power of the bacteridium is reduced by the diminished number and the attenuated activity. His vaccine must then only be charbon liquid of which the intensity of action may be weakened to the point of not being mortal to a certain number of susceptible animals receiving it. But it may be a most treacherous vaccine, in that it might be capable of recuperating its power with time. The Alfort experiment makes it probable that the vaccine tested at Toulouse and found to be harmless, had acquired in the lapse of twelve days before it was tried at Alfort, a greater intensity, because the bacteridium, numbed for a time by carbolic acid, had had time to awaken and to swarm, in spite of the acid."

Whilst Toussaint had gone to Rheims (where sat the French Association for the Advancement of Science) to state that it was not, as he had announced, the liquid which placed the animal into conditions of relative immunity and to epitomize Bouley's interpretation, to wit, that it was a bearable charbon which he had inoculated, Pasteur wrote rather a severe note on the subject. His insisting on scrupulous accuracy in experiment sometimes made him a little hard; though the process was unreliable and the explanation inexact, Toussaint at least had the merit of having noted a condition of transitory attenuation in the bacteridium. Bouley begged Pasteur to postpone his communication out of consideration for Toussaint.

One of the sheep folded over splenic-fever pits had died on August 25, its body, full of bacteridia, proving once more the error of those who believed in the spontaneity of transmissible diseases. Pasteur informed J. B. Dumas of this, and at the same time expressed his opinion on the Toussaint fact. This letter was read at the Académie des Sciences.

"Allow me, before I finish, to tell you another secret. I have hastened, again with the assistance of Messrs. Chamberland and Roux, to verify the extraordinary facts recently announced to the Academy by M. Toussaint, professor at the Toulouse Veterinary School.

"After numerous experiments leaving no room for doubt, I can assure you that M. Toussaint's interpretations should be gone over again. Neither do I agree with M. Toussaint on the identity which he affirms as existing between acute septicæmia and chicken-cholera; those two diseases differ absolutely."

Bouley was touched by this temperate language after all the verifying experiments made at the Ecole Normale and in the Jura. When relating the Alfort incidents, and while expressing a hope that some vaccination against anthrax would shortly be discovered, he revealed that Pasteur had had "the delicacy of abstaining from a detailed criticism, so as to leave M. Toussaint the care of checking his own results."

The struggle against virulent diseases was becoming more and more the capital question for Pasteur. He constantly recurred to the subject, not only in the laboratory, but in his home conversations, for he associated his family with all the preoccupations of his scientific life. Now that the oxygen of air appeared as a modifying influence on the development of a microbe in the body of animals, it seemed possible that there might be a general law applicable to every virus! What a benefit it would be if the vaccine of every virulent disease could thus be discovered! And in his thirst for research, considering that the scientific history of chicken-cholera was more advanced than that of variolic and vaccinal affections—the great fact of vaccination remaining isolated and unexplained—he hastened on his return to Paris (September, 1880) to press physicians on this special point—the relations between small-pox and vaccine. "From the point of view of physiological experimentation," he said, "the identity of the variola virus with the vaccine virus has never been demonstrated." When Jules Guérin—a born fighter, still desirous at the age of eighty to measure himself successfully with Pasteur—declared that "human vaccine is the product of animal variola (cow pox and horse pox) inoculated into man and humanised by its successive transmissions on man," Pasteur answered ironically that he might as well say, " Vaccine is—vaccine."

Those who were accustomed to speak to Pasteur with absolute sincerity advised him not to let himself be dragged further into those discussions when his adversaries, taking words for ideas, drowned the debate in a flood of phrases. Of what good were such debates to science, since those who took the first place among veterinary surgeons, physicians and surgeons, loudly acknowledged the debt which science owned to Pasteur? Why be surprised that certain minds, deeply disturbed in their habits, their principles, their influence, should feel some difficulty, some anger even in abandoning their ideas? If it is painful to tenants to leave a house in which they have spent their youth, what must it be to break with one's whole education?

Pasteur, who allowed himself thus to be told that he lacked philosophical serenity, acknowledged this good advice with an affectionate smile. He promised to be calm ; but when once in the room, his adversaries' attacks, their prejudices and insinuations, enervated and irritated him. All his promises were forgotten.

" To pretend to express the relation between human variola and vaccine by speaking but of vaccine and its relations with cow pox and horse pox, without even pronouncing the word small-pox, is mere equivocation, done on purpose to avoid the real point of the debate." Becoming excited by Guérin's antagonism, Pasteur turned some of Guérin's operating processes into ridicule with such effect that Guérin started from his place and rushed at him. The fiery octogenarian was stopped by Baron Larrey; the sitting was suspended in confusion. The following day, Guérin sent two seconds to ask for reparation by arms from Pasteur. Pasteur referred them to M. Béclard, Permanent Secretary to the Académie de Médicine, and M. Bergeron, its Annual Secretary, who were jointly responsible for the *Official Bulletin of the Academy*. " I am ready," said Pasteur, " having no right to act otherwise, to modify whatever the editors may consider as going beyond the rights of criticism and legitimate defence."

In deference to the opinion of Messrs. Béclard and Bergeron, Pasteur consented to terminate the quarrel by writing to the chairman of the Academy that he had no intention of offending a colleague, and that in all discussions of that kind, he never thought of anything but to defend the exactitude of his own work.

The *Journal de la Médecine et de la Chimie*, edited by M. Lucas-Championniére, said à propos of this very reasonable letter—" We, for our part, admire the meekness of M. Pasteur, who is so often described as combative and ever on the war-path.   Here we have a scientist, who now and then makes short, substantial and extremely interesting communications. He is not a medical man, and yet, guided by his genius, he opens new paths across the most arduous studies of medical science.   Instead of being offered the tribute of attention and admiration which he deserves, he meets with a raging opposition from some quarrelsome individuals, ever inclined to contradict after listening as little as possible.   If he makes use of a scientific expression not understood by everybody, or if he uses a medical expression slightly incorrectly, then rises before him the spectre of endless speeches, intended to prove to him that all was for the best in medical science before it was assisted by the precise studies and resources of chemistry and experimentation. . . . Indeed, M. Pasteur's expression of *equivocation* seemed to us moderate l "

How many such futile incidents, such vain quarrels, traverse the life of a great man l   Later on, we only see glory, apotheosis, and the statues in public places; the demi-gods seemed to have marched in triumph towards a grateful posterity.   But how many obstacles and oppositions are there to retard the progress of a free mind desirous of bringing his task to a successful conclusion and incited by the fruitful thought of Death, ever present to spirits preoccupied with interests of a superior order?   Pasteur looked upon himself as merely a passing guest of those homes of intellect which he wished to enlarge and fortify for those who would come after him.

Confronted with the hostility, indifference and scepticism which he found in the members of the Medical Academy, he once appealed to the students who sat on the seats open to the public.

"Young men, you who sit on those benches, and who are perhaps the hope of the medical future of the country, do not come here to seek the excitement of polemics, but come and learn Method."

His method, as opposed to vague conceptions and *a priori* speculations, went on fortifying itself day by day. Artificial attenuation, that is, virus modified by the oxygen of air, which weakens and abates virulence; vaccination by the attenuated virus—those two immense steps in advance were announced by Pasteur at the end of 1880. But would the same process apply to the microbe of charbon? That was a great problem. The vaccine of chicken-cholera was easy to obtain; by leaving pure cultures to themselves for a time in contact with air, they soon lost their virulence. But the spores of charbon, very indifferent to atmospheric air, preserved an indefinitely prolonged virulence. After eight, ten or twelve years, spores found in the graves of victims of splenic fever were still in full virulent activity. It was therefore necessary to turn the difficulty by a culture process which would act on the filament-shaped bacteridium before the formation of spores. What may now be explained in a few words demanded long weeks of trials, tests and counter tests.

In neutralized chicken broth, the bacteridium can no longer be cultivated at a temperature of 45° C.; it can still be cultivated easily at a temperature of 42° C. or 43° C., but the spores do not develop.

"At that extreme temperature," explains M. Chamberland, "the bacteridia yet live and reproduce themselves, but they never give any germs. Thenceforth, when trying the virulence of the phials after six, eight, ten or fifteen days, we have found exactly the same phenomena as for chicken-cholera. After eight days, for instance, our culture, which originally killed ten sheep out of ten, only kills four or five; after ten or twelve days it does not kill any; it merely communicates to animals a benignant malady which preserves them from the deadly form.

" A remarkable thing is that the bacteridia whose virulence has been attenuated may afterwards be cultivated in a temperature of 30° C. to 35° C., at which temperature they give germs presenting the same virulence as the filaments which formed them."

Bouley, who was a witness of all these facts, said, in other words, that " if that attenuated and degenerated bacteridium is translated to a culture medium in a lower temperature, favourable to its activity, it becomes once again apt to produce spores. But those spores born of weakened bacteridia, will only produce bacteridia likewise weakened in their swarming faculties."

Thus is obtained and enclosed in inalterable spores a vaccine ready to be sent to every part of the world to preserve animals by vaccination against splenic fever.

On the day when he became sure of this discovery, Pasteur, returning to his rooms from his laboratory, said to his family, with a deep emotion—"Nothing would have consoled me if this discovery, which my collaborators and I have made, had not been a French discovery."

He desired to wait a little longer before proclaiming it. Yet the cause of the evil was revealed, the mode of propagation indicated, prophylaxis made easy; surely, enough had been achieved to move attentive minds to enthusiasm and to deserve the gratitude of sheep owners!

So thought the *Society of French Agricultors*, when it decided, on February 21, 1881, to offer to Pasteur a medal of honour. J. B. Dumas, detained at the Académie des Sciences, was unable to attend the meeting. He wrote to Bouley, who had been requested to enumerate Pasteur's principal discoveries at that large meeting—"I had desired to make public by my presence my heartfelt concurrence in your admiration for him who will never be honoured to the full measure of his merits, of his services and of his passionate devotion to truth and to our country."

On the following Monday, Bouley said to Dumas, as they were walking to the Académie des Sciences, "Your letter assures me of a small share of immortality."

"See," answered Dumas, pointing to Pasteur, who was preceding them, "there is he who will lead us both to immortality."

On that Monday, February 28, Pasteur made his celebrated communication on the vaccine of splenic fever and the whole graduated scale of virulence. The secret of those returns to virulence lay entirely in some successive cultures through the body of certain animals. If a weakened bacteridium was inoculated into a guinea-pig a few days old it was harmless; but it killed a new-born guinea-pig.

"If we then go from one new-born guinea-pig to another," said Pasteur, "by inoculation of the blood of the first to the second, from the second to a third, and so on, the virulence of the bacteridium—that is: its adaptability to development within the economy—becomes gradually strengthened. It becomes by degrees able to kill guinea-pigs three or four days old, then a week, a month, some years old, then sheep themselves; the bacteridium has returned to its original virulence. We may affirm, without hesitation, though we have not had the opportunity of testing the fact, that it would be capable of killing cows and horses; and it preserves that virulence indefinitely if nothing is done to attenuate it again.

" As to the microbe of chicken-cholera, when it has lost its power of action on hens, its virulence may be restored to it by applying it to small birds such as sparrows or canaries, which it kills immediately. Then by successive passages through the bodies of those animals, it gradually assumes again a virulence capable of manifesting itself anew on adult hens.

" Need I add, that, during that return to virulence, by the way, virus-vaccines can be prepared at every degree of virulence for the bacillus anthracis and for the chicken-cholera microbe.

"This question of the return to virulence is of the greatest interest for the etiology of contagious diseases."

Since charbon does not recur, said Pasteur in the course of that communication, each of the charbon microbes attenuated in the laboratory constitutes a vaccine for the superior microbe. " What therefore is easier than to find in those successive virus, virus capable of giving splenic fever to sheep, cows and horses, without making them perish, and assuring them of ulterior immunity from the deadly disease? We have practised that operation on sheep with the greatest success. When the season comes for sheep-folding in the Beauce, we will try to apply it on a large scale."

The means of doing this were given to Pasteur before long; assistance was offered to him by various people for various reasons; some desired to see a brilliant demonstration of the truth; others whispered their hopes of a signal failure. The promoter of one very large experiment was a Melun veterinary surgeon, M. Rossignol.

In the *Veterinary Press*, of which M. Rossignol was one of the editors, an article by him might have been read on the 31st January, 1881, less than a month before that great discovery on charbon vaccine, wherein he expressed himself as follows · " Will you have some microbe ? There is some everywhere. Microbiolatry is the fashion, it reigns undisputed; it is a doctrine which must not even be discussed, especially when its Pontiff, the learned M. Pasteur, has pronounced the sacramental words, *I have spoken.* The microbe alone is and shall be the characteristic of a disease; that is understood and settled; henceforth the germ theory must have precedence of pure clinics; the Microbe alone is true, and Pasteur is its prophet.''

At the end of March, M. Rossignol began a campaign, begging for subscriptions, pointing out how much the cultivators of the Brie—whose cattle suffered almost as much as that of the Beauce—were interested in the question. The discovery, *if it were genuine*, should not remain confined to the Ecole Normale laboratory, or monopolized by the privileged public of the Académie des Sciences, who had no use for it. M. Rossignol soon collected about 100 subscribers. Did he believe that Pasteur and his little phials would come to a hopeless fiasco in a farmyard before a public of old practitioners who had always been powerless in the presence of splenic fever? Microbes were a subject for ceaseless joking; people had hilarious visions of the veterinary profession confined some twenty years hence in a model laboratory assiduously cultivating numberless races, sub-races, varieties and subvarieties of microbes.

It is probable that, if light comes from above, a good many practitioners would not have been sorry to see a strong wind from below putting out Pasteur's light.

M. Rossignol succeeded in interesting every one in this undertaking. When the project was placed before the Melun Agricultural Society on the 2nd April, they hastened to approve of it and to accord their patronage.

The chairman, Baron de la Rochette, was requested to approach Pasteur and to invite him to organize public experiments on the preventive vaccination of charbon in the districts of Melun, Fontainebleau and Provins.

''The noise which those experiments will necessarily cause,'' wrote M. Rossignol, ''will strike every mind and convince those who may still be doubting; the evidence of facts will have the result of ending all uncertainty.''

Baron de la Rochette was a typical old French gentleman; his whole person was an ideal of old-time distinction and courtesy. Well up to date in all agricultural progress, and justly priding himself, with the ease of a great landowner, that he made of agriculture an art and a science, he could speak in any surroundings with knowledge of his subject and a winning grace of manner. When he entered the laboratory, he was at once charmed by the simplicity of the scientist, who hastened to accept the proposal of an extensive experiment.

At the end of April, Pasteur wrote out the programme which was to be followed near Melun at the farm of Pouilly le Fort. M. Rossignol had a number of copies of that programme printed, and distributed them, not only throughout the Department of Seine et Marne, but in the whole agricultural world. This programme was so decidedly affirmative that some one said to Pasteur, with a little anxiety : " You remember what Marshal Gouyion St. Cyr said of Napoleon, that ' he liked hazardous games with a character of grandeur and audacity.' It was neck or nothing with him ; you are going on in the same way ! "

" Yes," answered Pasteur, who meant to compel a victory.

And as his collaborators, to whom he had just read the precise and strict arrangements he had made, themselves felt a little nervous, he said to them, " What has succeeded in the laboratory on fourteen sheep will succeed just as well at Melun on fifty."

This programme left him no retreat. The Melun Agricultural Society put sixty sheep at Pasteur's disposal ; twenty-five were to be vaccinated by two inoculations, at twelve or fifteen days' interval, with some attenuated charbon virus. Some days later those twenty-five and also twenty-five others would be inoculated with some very virulent charbon culture.

" The twenty-five unvaccinated sheep will all perish," wrote Pasteur, " the twenty-five vaccinated ones will survive." They would afterwards be compared with the ten sheep which had undergone no treatment at all. It would thus be seen that vaccination did not prevent sheep from returning to their normal state of health after a certain time.

Then came other prescriptions, for instance, the burying of the dead sheep in distinct graves, near each other and enclosed within a paling.

" In May, 1882," added Pasteur, " twenty new sheep, that is, sheep never before used for experimentation, will be shut within that paling."

And he predicted that the following year, 1882, out of those twenty-five sheep fed on the grass of that little enclosure or on forage deposited there, several would become infected by the charbon germs brought to the surface by earthworms, and that they would die of splenic fever. Finally, twenty-five other sheep might be folded in a neighbouring spot, where no charbon victims had ever been buried, and under these conditions none would contract the disease.

M. de la Rochette having expressed a desire that cows should be included in the programme, Pasteur answered that he was willing to try that new experiment, though his tests on vaccine for cows were not as advanced as those on sheep vaccine. Perhaps, he said, the results may not be as positive, though he thought they probably would be. He was offered ten cows; six were to be vaccinated and four not vaccinated. The experiments were to begin on the Thursday, 5th May, and would in all likelihood terminate about the first fortnight in June.

At the time when M. Rossignol declared that all was ready for the fixed time, an editor's notice in the *Veterinary Press* said that the laboratory experiments were about to be repeated *in campo*, and that Pasteur could thus "demonstrate that he had not been mistaken when he affirmed before the astonished Academy that he had discovered the vaccine of splenic fever, a preventative to one of the most terrible diseases with which animals and even men could be attacked." This notice ended thus, with an unexpected classical reminiscence: "These experiments are solemn ones, and they will become memorable if, as M. Pasteur asserts, with such confidence, they confirm all those he has already instituted. We ardently wish that M. Pasteur may succeed and remain the victor in a tournament which has now lasted long enough. If he succeeds, he will have endowed his country with a great benefit, and his adversaries should, as in the days of antiquity, wreathe their brows with laurel leaves and prepare to follow, chained and prostrate, the chariot of the immortal Victor. But he must succeed: such is the price of triumph. Let M. Pasteur not forget that the Tarpeian Rock is near the Capitol."

On May 5 a numerous crowd arriving from Melun station or from the little station of Cesson, was seen moving towards the yard of Pouilly le Fort farm; it looked like a mobilisation of *Conseillers Généraux*, agricultors, physicians, apothecaries, and especially veterinary surgeons. Most of these last were full of scepticism—as was remarked by M. Thierry, who represented the Veterinary Society of the Yonne, and one of his colleagues, M. Biot, of Pont-sur-Yonne. They were exchanging jokes and looks to the complete satisfaction of Pasteur's adversaries. They were looking forward to the last and most virulent inoculation.

Pasteur, assisted not only by Messrs. Chamberland and Roux, but also by a third pupil of the name of Thuillier, proceeded to the arrangement of the subjects. At the last moment, two goats were substituted for two of the sheep.

Vaccination candidates and unvaccinated test sheep were divided under a large shed. For the injection of the vaccinal liquid, Pravaz's little syringe was used; those who have experienced morphia injections know how easily the needle penetrates the subcutaneous tissues. Each of the twenty-five sheep received, on the inner surface of the right thigh, five drops of the bacteridian culture which Pasteur called the first vaccine. Five cows and one ox substituted for the sixth cow were vaccinated in their turn, behind the shoulder. The ox and the cows were marked on the right horn, and the sheep on the ear.

Pasteur was, after this, asked to give a lecture on splenic fever in the large hall of the Pouilly farm. Then, in clear, simple language, meeting every objection half-way, showing no astonishment at ignorance or prejudice, knowing perfectly well that many were really hoping for a failure, he methodically described the road already travelled, and pointed to the goal he would reach. For nearly an hour he interested and instructed his mixed audience; he made them feel the genuineness of his faith, and, besides his interest in the scientific problem, his desire to spare heavy losses to cultivators. After the lecture, some, better informed than others, were admiring the logical harmony of that career, mingling with pure science results of incalculable benefit to the public, an extraordinary alliance which gave a special moral physiognomy to this man of prodigious labours.

An appointment was made for the second inoculation. In the interval—on May 6, 7, 8 and 9—Messrs. Chamberland and Roux came to Pouilly le Fort to take the temperature of the vaccinated animals, and found nothing abnormal. On May 17 a second inoculation was made with a liquid which, though still attenuated, was more virulent than the first. If that liquid had been inoculated to begin with it would have caused a mortality of 50 per 100.

"On Tuesday, May 31," wrote Pasteur to his son-in-law,

" the third and last inoculation will take place—this time with fifty sheep and ten cows. I feel great confidence—for the two first, on the 5th and the 17th, have been effected under the best conditions without any mortality amongst the twenty-five vaccinated subjects. On June 5 at latest the final result will be known, and should be twenty-five survivors out of twenty-five vaccinated, and six cows. If the success is complete, this will be one of the finest examples of applied science in this century, consecrating one of the greatest and most fruitful discoveries."

This great experiment did not hinder other studies being pursued in the laboratory. The very day of the second inoculation at Pouilly le Fort, Mme. Pasteur wrote to her daughter, " One of the laboratory dogs seems to be sickening for hydrophobia ; it seems that that would be very lucky, in view of the interesting experiment it would provide."

On May 25, another letter from Mme. Pasteur shows how deeply each member of the family shared Pasteur's preoccupations and hopes and was carried away with the stream of his ideas · " Your father has just brought great news from the laboratory. The new dog which was trephined and inoculated with hydrophobia died last night after nineteen days' incubation only. The disease manifested itself on the fourteenth day, and this morning the same dog was used for the trephining of a fresh dog, which was done by Roux with unrivalled skill. All this means that we shall have as many mad dogs as will be required for experiments, and those experiments will become extremely interesting.

" Next month one of the *master's* delegates will go to the south of France to study the ' rouget ' of swine, which ordinarily rages at this time.

" It is much hoped that the vaccine of that disease will be found."

The trephining of that dog had much disturbed Pasteur He, who was described in certain anti-vivisectionist quarters as a laboratory executioner, had a great horror of inflicting suffering on any animal.

" He could assist without too much effort," writes M. Roux, " at a simple operation such as a subcutaneous inoculation, and even then, if the animal screamed at all, Pasteur was immediately filled with compassion, and tried to comfort and encourage the victim, in a way which would have seemed ludicrous if it had not been touching. The thought of having a dog's cranium perforated was very disagreeable to him; he very much wished that the experiment should take place, and yet he feared to see it begun. I performed it one day when he was out. The next day, as I was telling him that the intercranial inoculation had presented no difficulty, he began pitying the dog. 'Poor thing! His brain is no doubt injured, he must be paralysed!' I did not answer, but went to fetch the dog, whom I brought into the laboratory. Pasteur was not fond of dogs, but when he saw this one, full of life, curiously investigating every part of the laboratory, he showed the keenest pleasure, and spoke to the dog in the most affectionate manner. Pasteur was infinitely grateful to this dog for having borne trephining so well, thus lessening his scruples for future trephining."

As the day was approaching for the last experiments at Pouilly le Fort, excitement was increasing in the veterinary world. Every chance meeting led to a discussion; some prudent men said "Wait." Those that believed were still few in number.

One or two days before the third and decisive inoculation, the veterinary surgeon of Pont-sur-Yonne, M. Biot, who was watching with a rare scepticism the Pouilly le Fort experiments, met Colin on the road to Maisons-Alfort. "Our conversation"—M. Biot dictated the relation of this episode to M. Thierry, his colleague, also very sceptical and expecting the Tarpeian Rock—"our conversation naturally turned on Pasteur's experiments. Colin said: 'You must beware, for there are two parts in the bacteridia-culture broth: one upper part which is inert, and one deep part very active, in which the bacteridia become accumulated, having dropped to the bottom because of their weight. The vaccinated sheep will be inoculated with the upper part of the liquid, whilst the others will be inoculated with the bottom liquid, which will kill them.'" Colin advised M. Biot to seize at the last moment the phial containing the virulent liquid and to shake it violently, "so as to produce a perfect mixture rendering the whole uniformly virulent."

If Bouley had heard such a thing, he would have lost his temper, or he would have laughed heartily. A year before this, in a letter to M. Thierry, who not only defended but extolled Colin, Bouley had written:

" No doubt Colin is a man of some value, and he has cleverly taken advantage of his position of Chief of the Anatomy department at Alfort to accomplish some important labours. But it is notable that his negative genius has ever led him to try and demolish really great work. He denied Davaine, Marey, Claude Bernard, Chauveau; now he is going for Pasteur." Bouley, to whom Colin was indebted for his situation at Alfort, might have added, "And he calls me his persecutor!" But Biot refused to believe in Colin's hostility and only credited him with scruples on the question of experimental physiology. Colin did not doubt M. Pasteur's bona fides, M. Biot said, but only his aptitude to conduct experiments *in anima vili*.

On May 31, every one was at the farm. M. Biot executed Colin's indications and shook the virulent tube with real veterinary energy. He did more : still acting on advice from Colin, who had told him that the effective virulence was in direct proportion to the quantity injected, he asked that a larger quantity of liquid than had been intended should be inoculated into the animals. A triple dose was given. Other veterinary surgeons desired that the virulent liquid should be inoculated alternatively into vaccinated and unvaccinated animals. Pasteur lent himself to these divers requests with impassive indifference and without seeking for their motives.

At half-past three everything was done, and a rendezvous fixed for June 2 at the same place. The proportion between believers and unbelievers was changing. Pasteur seemed so sure of his ground that many were saying "He can surely not be mistaken." One little group had that very morning drunk to a *fiasco*. But, whether from a sly desire to witness a failure, or from a generous wish to be present at the great scientific victory, every man impatiently counted the hours of the two following days.

On June 4, Messrs. Chamberland and Roux went back to Pouilly le Fort to judge of the condition of the patients. Amongst the lot of unvaccinated sheep, several were standing apart with drooping heads, refusing their food. A few of the vaccinated subjects showed an increase of temperature ; one of them even had 40° C. (104° Fahrenheit) ; one sheep presented a slight œdéma of which the point of inoculation was the centre ; one lamb was lame, another manifestly feverish, but all, save one, had preserved their appetite. All the unvaccinated sheep were getting worse and worse. " In all of them," noted M. Rossignol, "breathlessness is at its maximum; the heaving of the sides is now and then interrupted by groans. If the most sick are forced to get up and walk, it is with great difficulty that they advance a few steps, their limbs being so weak and vacillating." Three had died by the time M. Rossignol left Pouilly le Fort. "Everything leads me to believe," he wrote, "that a great number of sheep will succumb during the night."

Pasteur's anxiety was great when Messrs. Chamberland and Roux returned, having noticed a rise in the temperature of certain vaccinated subjects. It was increased by the arrival of a telegram from M. Rossignol announcing that he considered one sheep as lost. By a sudden reaction, Pasteur, who had drawn up such a bold programme, leaving no margin for the unexpected, and who the day before seemed of an imperturbable tranquillity among all those sheep, the life or death of whom was about to decide between an immortal discovery and an irremediable failure, now felt himself beset with doubts and anguish.

Bouley, who had that evening come to see his *master*, as he liked to call him, could not understand this reaction—the result of too much strain on the mind, said M. Roux, whom it did not astonish. Pasteur's emotional nature, strangely allied to his fighting temperament, was mastering him. "His faith staggered for a time," writes M. Roux, "as if the experimental method could betray him." The night was a sleepless one.

"This morning, at eight o'clock," wrote Mme. Pasteur to her daughter, "we were still very much excited and awaiting the telegram which might announce some disaster. Your father would not let his mind be distracted from his anxiety. At nine o'clock the laboratory was informed, and the telegram handed to me five minutes later. I had a moment's emotion, which made me pass through all the colours of the rainbow. Yesterday, a considerable rise of temperature had been noticed with terror in one of the sheep; this morning that same sheep was well again."

On the arrival of the telegram Pasteur's face lighted up; his joy was deep, and he desired to share it immediately with his absent children. Before starting for Melun, he wrote them this letter :

" *June* 2, 1881.

" It is only Thursday, and I am already writing to you ; it is because a great result is now acquired. A wire from Melun has just announced it. On Tuesday last, 31st May, we inoculated all the sheep, vaccinated and non-vaccinated, with very virulent splenic fever. It is not forty-eight hours ago. Well, the telegram tells me that, when we arrive at two o'clock this afternoon, all the non-vaccinated subjects will be dead ; eighteen were already dead this morning, and the others dying. As to the vaccinated ones, they are all well ; the telegram ends by the words ' *stunning success* ' ; it is from the veterinary surgeon, M. Rossignol.

"It is too early yet for a final judgment ; the vaccinated sheep might yet fall ill. But when I write to you on Sunday, if all goes well, it may be taken for granted that they will henceforth preserve their good health, and that the success will indeed have been startling. On Tuesday, we had a foretaste of the final results. On Saturday and Sunday, two sheep had been abstracted from the lot of twenty-five vaccinated sheep, and two from the lot of twenty-five non-vaccinated ones, and inoculated with a very virulent virus. Now, when on Tuesday all the visitors arrived, amongst whom were M. Tisserand, M. Patinot, the Prefect of Seine et Marne, M. Foucher de Careil, Senator, etc., we found the two unvaccinated sheep dead, and the two others in good health. I then said to one of the veterinary surgeons who were present, 'Did I not read in a newspaper, signed by you, à propos of the virulent little organism of saliva, "There ! one more microbe ; when there are 100 we shall make a cross "?' 'It is true,' he immediately answered, honestly. 'But I am a converted and repentant sinner.' 'Well,' I answered, ' allow me to remind you of the words of the Gospel : Joy shall be in heaven over one sinner that repenteth, more than over ninety and nine just persons which need no repentance.' Another veterinary surgeon who was present said, ' I will bring you another, M. Colin.' ' You are mistaken,' I replied. ' M. Colin contradicts for the sake of contradicting, and does not believe because he will not believe. You would have to cure a case of neurosis, and you cannot do that ! ' Joy reigns in the laboratory and in the house. Rejoice, my dear children."

When Pasteur arrived, at two o'clock in the afternoon, at the farmyard of Pouilly le Fort, accompanied by his young collaborators, a murmur of applause arose, which soon became loud acclamation, bursting from all lips. Delegates from the Agricultural Society of Melun, from medical societies, veterinary societies, from the Central Council of Hygiene of Seine et Marne, journalists, small farmers who had been divided in their minds by laudatory or injurious newspaper articles all were there. The carcases of twenty-two unvaccinated sheep were lying side by side; two others were breathing their last; the last survivors of the sacrificed lot showed all the characteristic symptoms of splenic fever. All the vaccinated sheep were in perfect health.

Bouley's happy face reflected the feelings which were so characteristic of his attractive personality : enthusiasm for a great cause, devotion to a great man. M. Rossignol, in one of those loyal impulses which honour human nature, disowned with perfect sincerity his first hasty judgment; Bouley congratulated him. He himself, many years before, had allowed himself to judge too hastily, he said, of certain experiments of Davaine's, of which the results then appeared impossible. After having witnessed these experiments, Bouley had thought it a duty to proclaim his error at the Académie de Médecine, and to render a public homage to Davaine. "That, I think," he said, "is the line of conduct which should always be observed ; we honour ourselves by acknowledging our mistakes and by rendering justice to neglected merit."

No success had ever been greater than Pasteur's. The veterinary surgeons, until then the most incredulous, now convinced, desired to become the apostles of his doctrine. M. Biot spoke of nothing less than of being himself vaccinated and afterwards inoculated with the most active virus. Colin's absence was much regretted. Pasteur was not yet satisfied. "We must wait until the 5th of June," he said, "for the experiment to be complete, and the proof decisive."

M. Rossignol and M. Biot proceeded on the spot to the necropsy of two of the dead sheep. An abundance of bacteridia was very clearly seen in the blood through the microscope.

Pasteur was accompanied back to the station by an enthusiastic crowd, saluting him—with a luxury of epithets contrasting with former ironies—as the immortal author of the magnificent discovery of splenic fever vaccination, and it was decided that the farm of Pouilly le Fort would henceforth bear the name of *Clos Pasteur.*

The one remaining unvaccinated sheep died that same night. Amongst the vaccinated lot one ewe alone caused some anxiety. She was pregnant, and died on the 4th of June, but from an accident due to her condition, and not from the consequences of the inoculation, as was proved by a post-mortem examination.

Amongst the cattle, those which had been vaccinated showed no sign whatever of any disturbance; the others presented enormous œdemata.

Pasteur wrote to his daughter : " Success is definitely confirmed ; the vaccinated animals are keeping perfectly well, the test is complete. On Wednesday a report of the facts and results will be drawn up which I shall communicate to the Académie des Sciences on Monday, and on Tuesday to the Académie de Médecine."

And, that same day, he addressed a joyful telegram to Bouley, who, in his quality of General Inspector of Veterinary Schools, had been obliged to go to Lyons. Bouley answered by the following letter :

" Lyons, June 5, 1881. Dearest Master, your triumph has filled me with joy. Though the days are long past now when my faith in you was still somewhat hesitating, not having sufficiently impregnated my mind with your spirit, as long as the event—which has just been realized in a manner so rigorously in conformity with your predictions—was still in the future, I could not keep myself from feeling a certain anxiety, of which you were yourself the cause, since I had seen you also a prey to it, like all inventors on the eve of the day which reveals their glory. At last your telegram, *for which I was pining,* has come to tell me that the world has found you faithful to all your promises, and that you have inscribed one more great date in the *annals of Science,* and particularly in those of Medicine, for which you have opened a new era.

"I feel the greatest joy at your triumph ; in the first place, for you, who are to-day receiving the reward of your noble efforts in the pursuit of Truth ; and—shall I tell you?—for myself too, for I have so intimately associated myself with your work that I should have felt your failure absolutely as if it had been personal to me. All my teaching at the Museum consists in relating your labours and predicting their fruitfulness."

Those experiments at Pouilly le Fort caused a tremendous

sensation; the whole of France burst out in an explosion of enthusiasm. Pasteur now knew fame under its rarest and purest form; the loving veneration, the almost worship with which he inspired those who lived near him or worked with him, had become the feeling of a whole nation.

On June 13, at the Académie des Sciences, he was able to state as follows his results and their practical consequences: "We now possess virus vaccines of charbon, capable of preserving from the deadly disease, without ever being themselves deadly—living vaccines, to be cultivated at will, transportable anywhere without alteration, and prepared by a method which we may believe susceptible of being generalized, since it has been the means of discovering the vaccine of chicken-cholera. By the character of the conditions I am now enumerating, and from a purely scientific point of view, the discovery of the vaccine of anthrax constitutes a marked step in advance of that of Jenner's vaccine, since the latter has never been experimentally obtained."

On all sides, it was felt that something very great, very unexpected, justifying every sort of hope, had been brought forth. Ideas of research were coming up. On the very morrow of the results obtained at Pouilly le Fort, Pasteur was asked to go to the Cape to study a contagious disease raging among goats.

"Your father would like to take that long journey," wrote Mme. Pasteur to her daughter, "passing on his way through Senegal to gather some good germs of pernicious fever; but I am trying to moderate his ardour. I consider that the study of hydrophobia should suffice him for the present."

He was at that time "at boiling point," as he put it—going from his laboratory work to the Academies of Sciences and Medicine to read some notes; then to read reports at the Agricultural Society; to Versailles, to give a lecture to an Agronomic Congress, and to Alfort to lecture to the professors and students. His clear and well-arranged words, the connection between ideas and the facts supporting them, the methodical recital of experiments, allied to an enthusiastic view of the future and its prospects—especially when addressing a youthful audience—deeply impressed his hearers. Those who saw and heard him for the first time were the more surprised that, in certain circles, a legend had formed round Pasteur's name. He had been described as of an irritable, intolerant temper, domineering and authoritative, almost despotic; and people now saw a man of perfect simplicity, so modest that he did not seem to realize his own glory, pleased to answer—even to provoke—every objection, only raising his voice to defend Truth, to exalt Work, and to inspire love for France, which he wished to see again in the first rank of nations. He did not cease to repeat that the country must regain her place through scientific progress. Boys and youths—ever quick to penetrate the clever calculations of those who seek their own interest instead of accomplishing a duty—listened to him eagerly and, very soon conquered, enrolled themselves among his followers. In him they recognized the three rarely united qualities which go to form true benefactors of humanity : a mighty genius, great force of character, and genuine goodness.

The Republican Government, desirous of recognizing this great discovery of splenic fever vaccination, offered him the Grand Cordon of the Legion of Honour. Pasteur put forward one condition ; he wanted, at the same time, the red ribbon for his two collaborators. " What I have most set my heart upon is to obtain the Cross for Chamberland and Roux," he wrote to his son-in-law on June 26 ; " only at that price will I accept the Grand Cross. They are taking such trouble ! Yesterday they went to a place fifteen kilometres from Senlis, to vaccinate ten cows and 250 sheep. On Thursday we vaccinated 300 sheep at Vincennes. On Sunday they were near Coulommiers. On Friday we are going to Pithiviers. What I chiefly wish is that the discovery should be consecrated by an exceptional distinction to two devoted young men, full of merit and courage. I wrote yesterday to Paul Bert, asking him to intervene most warmly in their favour."

One of Pasteur's earliest friends, who, in 1862, had greeted with joy his election to the Académie des Sciences, and who had never ceased to show the greatest interest in the progress due to the experimental method, entered the Ecole Normale laboratory with a beaming face. Happy to bring good tidings, he took his share of them like the devoted, hardworking, kindly man that he was. " M. Grandeau," wrote Mme. Pasteur to her children, " has just brought to the laboratory the news that Roux and Chamberland have the Cross and M. Pasteur the Grand Cross of the Legion of Honour. Hearty congratulations were exchanged in the midst of the rabbits and guinea-pigs."

Those days were darkened by a great sorrow. Henri Sainte

Claire Deville died. Pasteur was then reminded of the words
of his friend in 1868 : " You will survive me, I am your senior ;
promise that you will pronounce my funeral oration." When
formulating this desire, Sainte Claire Deville had no doubt been
desirous of giving another direction to the presentiments of
Pasteur, who believed himself death-stricken. But, whether
it was from a secret desire, or from an affectionate impulse, he
felt that none understood him better than Pasteur. Both loved
Science after the same manner ; they gave to patriotism its
real place ; they had hopes for the future of the human mind ;
they were moved by the same religious feelings before the
mysteries of the Infinite.

Pasteur began by recalling his friend's wish : "And here
am I, before thy cold remains, obliged to ask my memory what
thou wert in order to repeat it to the multitude crowding around
thy coffin. But how superfluous ! Thy sympathetic countenance, thy witty merriment and frank smile, the sound of thy
voice remain with us and live within us. The earth which
bears us, the air we breathe, the elements, often interrogated
and ever docile to answer thee, could speak to us of thee. Thy
services to Science are known to the whole world, and every
one who has appreciated the progress of the human mind is now
mourning for thee."

He then enumerated the scientist's qualities, the inventive
precision of that eager mind, full of imagination, and at the
same time the strictness of analysis and the fruitful teaching so
delightedly recognized by those who had worked with him,
Debray, Troost, Fouqué, Grandeau, Hautefeuille, Gernez,
Lechartier. Then, showing that, in Sainte Claire Deville,
the man equalled the scientist :

"Shall I now say what thou wert in private life? Again,
how superfluous ! Thy friends do not want to be reminded
of thy warm heart. Thy pupils want no proofs of thy affection
for them and thy devotion in being of service to them ! See
their sorrow.

"Should I tell thy sons, thy five sons, thy joy and pride, of
the preoccupations of thy paternal and prudent tenderness?
And can I speak of thy smiling goodness to her, the companion of thy life, the mere thought of whom filled thy eyes
with a sweet emotion?

"Oh ! I implore thee, do not now look down upon thy weep-
ing wife and afflicted sons : thou wouldst regret this life too

much ! Wait for them rather in those divine regions of knowledge and full light, where thou knowest all now, where thou
canst understand the Infinite itself, that terrible and bewildering
notion, closed for ever to man in this world, and yet the eternal
source of all Grandeur, of all Justice and all Liberty."

Pasteur's voice was almost stifled by his tears, as had been
that of J. B. Dumas speaking at Péclet's tomb. The emotions
of savants are all the deeper that they are not enfeebled, as in
so many writers or speakers, by the constant use of words
which end by wearing out the feelings.

Little groups slowly walking away from a country church-
yard seem to take with them some of the sadness they have
been feeling, but the departure from a Paris cemetery gives a
very different impression. Life immediately grasps again and
carries away in its movement the mourners, who now look as if
they had been witnessing an incident in which they were not
concerned. Pasteur felt such bitter contrasts with all his
tender soul, he had a cult for dear memories; Sainte Claire
Deville's portrait ever remained in his study.

The adversaries of the new discovery now had recourse to a
new mode of attack. The virus which had been used at Pouilly
le Fort to show how efficacious were the preventive vaccinations was, they said, a culture virus—some even said a
Machiavellian preparation of Pasteur's. Would vaccinated
animals resist equally well the action of the charbon blood
itself, the really malignant and infallibly deadly blood? Those
sceptics were therefore impatiently awaiting the result of some
experiments which were being carried out near Chartres in the
farm of Lambert. Sixteen Beauceron sheep were joined to a
lot of nineteen sheep brought from Alfort and taken from the
herd of 300 sheep vaccinated against charbon three weeks
before, on the very day of the lecture at Alfort. On July 16,
at 10 o'clock in the morning, the thirty-five sheep, vaccinated
and non-vaccinated, were gathered together. The corpse of a
sheep who had died of charbon four hours before, in a neighbouring farm, was brought into the field selected for the experiments. After making a post-mortem examination and noting
the characteristic injuries of splenic fever, ten drops of the
dead sheep's blood were injected into each of the thirty-five
sheep, taking one vaccinated at Alfort and one non-vaccinated
Beauceron alternately. Two days later, on July 18, ten of the

latter were already dead, most of the others were prostrated. The vaccinated sheep were perfectly well.

While the ten dead sheep were being examined, two more died, and three more on the 19th. Bouley, informed by the veterinary surgeon, Boutet, of those successive incidents, wrote on the 20th to Pasteur: "My dear Master, Boutet has just informed me of the Chartres event. All has been accomplished according to the master's words; your vaccinated sheep have triumphantly come through the trial, and all the others save one are dead. That result is of special importance in a country-side where incredulity was being maintained in spite of all the demonstrations made. It seems that the doctors especially were refractory. They said it was too good to be true, and they counted on the strength of the natural charbon to find your method in default. Now they are converted, Boutet writes, and the veterinary surgeon too—one amongst others, whose brain, it seems, was absolutely *iron-clad*—also the agricultors. There is a general Hosannah in your honour."

After congratulating Pasteur on the Grand Cross, he added, "I was also very glad of the reward you have obtained for your two young collaborators, so full of your spirit, so devoted to your work and your person, and whose assistance is so self-sacrificing and disinterested. The Government has honoured itself by so happily crowning with that distinction the greatness of the discovery in which they took part."

Henceforth, and for a time, systematic opposition ceased. Thousands and thousands of doses were used of the new vaccine, which afterwards saved millions to agriculture.

A few days later, came a change in Pasteur's surroundings. He was invited by the Organizing Committee to attend the International Medical Congress in London, and desired by the Government of the Republic to represent France.

On August 3, when he arrived in St. James' Hall, filled to overflowing, from the stalls to the topmost galleries, he was recognized by one of the stewards, who invited him to come to the platform reserved for the most illustrious members of the Congress. As he was going towards the platform, there was an outburst of applause, hurrahs and acclamations. Pasteur turned to his two companions, his son and his son-in-law, and said, with a little uneasiness: "It is no doubt the Prince of Wales arriving; I ought to have come sooner."

"But it is you that they are all cheering," said the President of the Congress, Sir James Paget, with his grave, kindly smile.

A few moments later, the Prince of Wales entered, accompanying his brother-in-law, the German Crown Prince.

In his speech, Sir James Paget said that medical science should aim at three objects : novelty, utility and charity. The only scientist named was Pasteur; the applause was such that Pasteur, who was sitting behind Sir James Paget, had to rise and bow to the huge assembly.

" I felt very proud," wrote Pasteur to Mme. Pasteur in a letter dated that same day, " I felt inwardly very proud, not for myself—you know how little I care for triumph !—but for my country, in seeing that I was specially distinguished among that immense concourse of foreigners, especially of Germans, who are here in much greater numbers than the French, whose total, however, reaches two hundred and fifty. Jean Baptiste and René were in the Hall; you can imagine their emotion.

" After the meeting, we lunched at Sir James Paget's house; he had the Prussian Crown Prince on his right and the Prince of Wales on his left. Then there was a gathering of about twenty-five or thirty guests in the drawing-room. Sir James presented me to the Prince of Wales, to whom I bowed, saying that I was happy to salute a friend to France. ' Yes,' he answered, ' a great friend.' Sir James Paget had the good taste not to ask me to be presented to the Prince of Prussia; though there is of course room for nothing but courtesy under such circumstances, I could not have brought myself to appear to wish to be presented to him. But he himself came up to me and said, ' M. Pasteur, allow me to introduce myself to you, and to tell you that I had great pleasure in applauding you just now,' adding some more pleasant things."

In the midst of the unexpected meetings brought about by that Congress, it was an interesting thing to see this son of a King and Emperor, the heir to the German crown, thus going towards that Frenchman whose conquests were made over disease and death. Of what glory might one day dream this Prince, who became Frederic III !

His tall and commanding stature, the highest position in the Prussian army conferred on him by his father, King William, in a solemn letter dated from Versailles, October, 1870—everything seemed to combine in making a warlike man of this powerful-looking prince. And yet was it not said in France

that he had protested against certain barbarities, coldly
executed by some Prussian generals during that campaign of
1870? Had he not considered the clauses of the Treaty of
Frankfort as Draconian and dangerous? If he had been sole
master, would he have torn Alsace away from France? What
share would his coming reign bear in the history of civilization? . . . Fate had already marked this Prince, only fifty
years old, for an approaching death. In his great sufferings,
before the inexorable death which was suffocating him, he was
heroically patient. His long agony began at San Remo,
amongst the roses and sunshine; he was an Emperor for less
than one hundred days, and, on his death-bed, words of peace,
peace for his people, were on his lips.

As Pasteur, coming to this Congress, was not only curious to
see what was the place held in medicine and surgery by the
germ-theory, but also desirous to learn as much as possible, he
never missed a discussion and attended every meeting. It was
in a simple sectional meeting that Bastian attempted to refute
Lister. After his speech, the President suddenly said, "I call
on M. Pasteur," though Pasteur had not risen. There was
great applause; Pasteur did not know English; he turned to
Lister and asked him what Bastian had said.

"He said," whispered Lister, "that microscopic organiza-
tions in disease were formed by the tissues themselves."

"That is enough for me," said Pasteur. And he then
invited Bastian to try the following experiment:

"Take an animal's limb, crush it, allow blood and other
normal or abnormal liquids to spread around the bones, only
taking care that the skin should neither be torn nor opened in
any way, and I defy you to see any micro-organism formed
within that limb as long as the illness will last."

Pasteur, desired to do so by Sir James Paget at one of the
great General Meetings of the Congress, gave a lecture on the
principles which had led him to the attenuation of virus, on
the methods which had enabled him to obtain the vaccines of
chicken-cholera and of charbon, and, finally, on the results
obtained. "In a fortnight," he said, "we vaccinated, in the
Departments surrounding Paris, nearly 20,000 sheep, and a
great many oxen, cows and horses

"Allow me," he continued, "not to conclude without telling
you of the great joy that I feel in thinking that it is as a
member of the International Medical Congress sitting in

London that I have made known to you the vaccination of a disease more terrible perhaps for domestic animals than is small-pox for man. I have given to the word vaccination an extension which I hope Science will consecrate as a homage to the merit and immense services rendered by your Jenner, one of England's greatest men. It is a great happiness to me to glorify that immortal name on the very soil of the noble and hospitable city of London ! "

" Pasteur was the greatest success of the Congress," wrote the correspondent of the *Journal des Débats*, Dr. Daremberg, glad as a Frenchman and as a physician to hear the unanimous hurrahs which greeted the delegate of France. " When M. Pasteur spoke, when his name was mentioned, a thunder of applause rose from all benches, from all nations. An indefatigable worker, a sagacious seeker, a precise and brilliant experimentalist, an implacable logician, and an enthusiastic apostle, he has produced an invincible effect on every mind."

The English people, who chiefly look in a great man for power of initiative and strength of character, shared this admiration. One group only, alone in darkness, away from the Congress, was hostile to the general movement and was looking for an opportunity for direct or indirect revenge ; it was the group of anti-vaccinators and anti-vivisectionists. The influence of the latter was great enough in England to prevent experimentation on animals. At a general meeting of the Congress, Virchow, the German scientist, spoke on the use of experimenting in pathology.

Already at a preceding Congress held in Amsterdam, Virchow had said amid the applause of the Assembly : " Those who attack vivisection have not the faintest idea of Science, and even less of the importance and utility of vivisection for the progress of medicine." But to this just argument, the international leagues for the protection of animals—very powerful, like everything that is founded on a sentiment which may be exalted—had answered by combative phrases. The physiological laboratories were compared to chambers of torture. It seemed as if, through caprice or cruelty, quite uselessly at any rate, this and that man of science had the unique desire of inflicting on bound animals, secured on a board, sufferings of which death was the only limit. It is easy to excite pity towards animals; an audience is conquered as soon as dogs are mentioned. Which of us, whether a cherished child, a neglected old maid, a man in the prime of his youth or a misanthrope weary of everything, has not, holding the best place in his recollections, the memory of some example of fidelity, courage or devotion given by a dog? In order to raise the revolt, it was sufficient for anti-vivisectionists to evoke amongst the ghosts of dog martyrs the oft-quoted dog who, whilst undergoing an experiment, licked the hand of the operator. As there had been some cruel abuses on the part of certain students, those abuses alone were quoted. Scientists did not pay much heed to this agitation, partly a feminine one : they relied on the good sense of the public to put an end to those doleful declamations. But the English Parliament voted a Bill prohibiting vivisection ; and, after 1876, English experimentalists had to cross the Channel to inoculate a guinea-pig.

Virchow did not go into details ; but, in a wide exposé of Experimental Physiological Medicine, he recalled how, at each new progress of Science—at one time against the dissection of dead bodies and now against experiments on living animals—the same passionate criticisms had been renewed. The Interdiction Bill voted in England had filled a new Leipzig Society with ardour; it had asked the Reichstag in that same year, 1881, to pass a law punishing cruelty to animals under pretext of scientific research, by imprisonment, varying between five weeks and two years, and deprivation of civil rights. Other societies did not go quite so far, but asked that some of their members should have a right of entrance and inspection into the laboratories of the Faculties.

"He who takes more interest in animals than in Science and in the knowledge of truth is not qualified to inspect officially things pertaining to Science," said Virchow. With an ironical gravity on his quizzical wrinkled face, he added, "Where shall we be if a scientist who has just begun a bonâ fide experiment finds himself, in the midst of his researches, obliged to answer questions from a new-comer and afterwards to defend himself before some magistrate for the crime of not having chosen another method, other instruments, perhaps another experiment? . . .

"We must prove to the whole world the soundness of our cause," concluded Virchow, uneasy at those "leagues" which grew and multiplied, and scattered through innumerable lecture halls the most fallacious judgments on the work of scientists.

Pasteur might have brought him, to support his statements relative to certain deviations of ideas and sentiments, number-less letters which reached him regularly from England—letters full of threats, insults and maledictions, devoting him to eternal torments for having multiplied his crimes on the hens, guinea-pigs, dogs and sheep of the laboratory. Love of animals carries some women to such lengths!

It would have been interesting, if, after Virchow's speech, some French physician had in his turn related a series of facts, showing how prejudices equally tenacious had had to be struggled against in France, and how savants had succeeded in enforcing the certainty that there can be no pathological science if Physiology is not progressing, and that it can only progress by means of the experimental method. Claude Bernard had expressed this idea under so many forms that it would almost have been enough to give a few extracts from his works.

In 1841, when he was Magendie's curator, he was one day attending a lesson on experimental physiology, when he saw an old man come in, whose costume—a long coat with a straight collar and a hat with a very wide brim—indicated a Quaker.

"Thou hast no right," he said, addressing Magendie, "to kill animals or to make them suffer. Thou givest a wicked example and thou accustomest thy fellow creatures to cruelty."

Magendie replied that it was a pity to look at it from that point of view, and that a physiologist, when moved by the thought of making a discovery useful to Medicine, and conse-quently useful to his fellow creatures, did not deserve that reproach.

"Your countryman Harvey," said he, hoping to convince him, "would not have discovered the circulation of the blood if he had not made some experiments in vivisection. That discovery was surely worth the sacrifice of a few deer in Charles the First's Park?"

But the Quaker stuck to his idea; his mission, he said, was to drive three things from this world : war, hunting and shoot-ing, and experiments on live animals. Magendie had to show him out.

Three years later, Claude Bernard, in his turn, was taxed

with barbarity by a Police Magistrate. In order to study the digestive properties of gastric juice, it had occurred to him to collect it by means of a cannula, a sort of silver tap which he adapted to the stomach of live dogs. A Berlin surgeon, M. Dieffenbach, who was staying in Paris, expressed a wish to see this application of a cannula to the stomach. M. Pelouze, the chemist, had a laboratory in the Rue Dauphine; he offered it to Claude Bernard. A stray dog was used as a subject for the experiment and shut up in the yard of the house, where Claude Bernard wished to keep a watch on him. But, as the treatment in no wise hindered the dog from running about, the door of the yard was hardly opened when he escaped, cannula and all.

"A few days later," writes Claude Bernard in the course of an otherwise grave report concerning the progress of general physiology in France (1867), "I was still in bed, early one morning, when I received a visit from a man who came to tell men that the Police Commissary of the Medicine School District wished to speak to me, and that I must go round to see him. I went in the course of the day to the Police Commissariat of the Rue du Jardinet; I found a very respectable-looking little old man, who received me very coldly at first and without saying anything. He took me into another room and showed me, to my great astonishment, the dog on whom I had operated in M. Pelouze's laboratory, asking me if I confessed to having fixed that instrument in his stomach. I answered affirmatively, adding that I was delighted to see my cannula, which I thought I had lost. This confession, far from satisfying the Commissary, apparently provoked his wrath, for he gave me an admonition of most exaggerated severity, accompanied with threats for having had the audacity to steal his dog to experiment on it.

"I explained that I had not stolen his dog, but that I had bought it of some individuals who sold dogs to physiologists, and who claimed to be employed by the police in picking up stray dogs. I added that I was sorry to have been the involuntary cause of the grief occasioned in his household by the misadventure to the dog, but that the animal would not die of it; that the only thing to do was to let me take away my silver cannula and let him keep his dog. Those last words altered the Commissary's language and completely calmed his wife and daughter. I removed my instrument and left, promising to return, which I did the next and following days. The dog was perfectly cured in a day or two, and I became a friend of the family, completely securing the Commissary's future protection. It was on that account that I soon after set up my laboratory in his District, and for many years continued my private classes of experimental physiology, enjoying the protection and warnings of the Commissary and thus avoiding much unpleasantness, until the time when I was at last made an assistant to Magendie at the Collége de France."

The London Society for the Protection of Animals had the singular idea of sending to Napoleon III complaints, almost remonstrances, on the vivisection practised within the French Empire. The Emperor simply sent on those English lamentations to the Academy of Medicine. The matter was prolonged by academical speeches. In a letter addressed to M. Grandeau, undated, but evidently written in August, 1863, Claude Bernard showed some irritation, a rare thing with him. Declaring that he would not go to the Academy and listen to the " nonsense " of " those who protect animals in hatred of mankind" he gave his concluding epitome : "You ask me what are the principal discoveries due to vivisection, so that you can mention them as arguments for that kind of study. All the knowledge possessed by experimental physiology can be quoted in that connection ; there is not a single fact which is not the direct and necessary consequence of vivisection. From Galen, who, by cutting the laryngeal nerves, learnt their use for respiration and the voice, to Harvey, who discovered circulation ; Pecquet and Aselli, the lymphatic vessels ; Haller, muscular irritability ; Bell and Magendie, the nervous functions, and all that has been learnt since the extension of that method of vivisection, which is the only experimental method ; in biology, all that is known on digestion, circulation, the liver, the sympathetic system, the bones, Development—all, absolutely all, is the result of vivisection, alone or combined with other means of study."

In 1875, he again returned to this idea in his experimental medicine classes at the Collége de France : " It is to experimentation that we owe all our precise notions on the functions of the viscera and *a fortiori* on the properties of such organs as muscles, nerves, etc."

One more interesting quotation might have been offered to the members of the Congress. A Swede had questioned

Darwin on vivisection, for the anti-vivisectionist propaganda was spreading on every side. Darwin, who, like Pasteur, did not admit that useless suffering should be inflicted on animals (Pasteur carried this so far that he would never, he said, have had the courage to shoot a bird for sport)—Darwin, in a letter dated April 14th, 1881, approved any measures that could be taken to prevent cruelty, but he added : " On the other hand, I know that physiology can make no progress if experiments on living animals are suppressed, and I have an intimate conviction that to retard the progress of physiology is to commit a crime against humanity. . . . Unless one is absolutely ignorant of all that Science has done for humanity, one must be convinced that physiology is destined to render incalculable benefits in the future to man and even to animals. See the results obtained by M. Pasteur's work on the germs of contagious diseases : will not animals be the first to profit thereby? How many lives have been saved, how much suffering spared by the discovery of parasitic worms following on experiments made by Virchow and others on living animals ! "

The London Congress marked a step on the road of progress. Besides the questions which were discussed and which were capable of precise solution, the scientific spirit showed itself susceptible of permeating other general subjects. Instead of remaining the impassive Sovereign we are wont to fancy her, Science—and this was proved by Pasteur's discoveries and their consequences, as Paget, Tyndall, Lister, and Priestley loudly proclaimed—Science showed herself capable of associating with pure research and perpetual care for Truth a deep feeling of compassion for all suffering and an ever-growing thirst for self-sacrifice.

Pasteur's speech at the London Medical Congress was printed at the request of an English M.P. and distributed to all the members of the House of Commons. Dr. H. Gueneau de Mussy, who had spent part of his life in England, having followed the Orleans family into exile, wrote to Pasteur on August 15, " I have been very happy in witnessing your triumph ; you are raising us up again in the eyes of foreign nations."

Applause was to Pasteur but a stimulus to further efforts. He was proud of his discoveries, but not vain of the effect they produced ; he said in a private letter : " The *Temps* again

z

refers, in a London letter, to my speech at the Congress. What an unexpected success ! "

Having heard that yellow fever had just been brought into the Gironde, at the Pauillac lazaretto by the vessel *Condé* from Senegal, Pasteur immediately started for Bordeaux. He hoped to find the microbe in the blood of the sick or the dead, and to succeed in cultivating it. M. Roux hastened to join his master.

If people spoke to Pasteur of the danger of infection, "What does it matter?" he said. "Life in the midst of danger ·is *the* life, the real life, the life of sacrifice, of example, of fruitfulness."

He was vexed to find his arrival notified in the newspapers ; it worried him not to be able to work and to travel *incognito*.

On September 17, he wrote to Mme. Pasteur : ". . . We rowed out to a great transport ship which is lying in the Pauillac roads, having just arrived. From our boat, we were able to speak to the men of the crew. Their health is good, but they lost seven persons at St. Louis, two passengers and five men of the crew. Save the captain and one engineer, they are all Senegalese negroes on that ship. We have been near another large steamboat, and yet another ; their health is equally good. . . .

" The most afflicted ship is the *Condé*, which is in quarantine in the Pauillac roads, and near which we have not been able to go. She has lost eighteen persons, either at sea or at the lazaretto.   "

No experiment could be attempted—the patients were convalescent. "But," he wrote the next day, "the *Richelieu* will arrive between the 25th and 28th, I think with some passengers. . . . It is more than likely that there will have been deaths during the passage, and patients for the lazaretto. I am therefore awaiting the arrival of that ship with the hope —God forgive a scientist's passion ! !—that I may attempt some researches at the Pauillac lazaretto, where I will arrange things in consequence. You may be sure I shall take every precaution. In the meanwhile, what shall I do in Bordeaux?

" I have made the acquaintance of the young librarian of the town library, which is a few doors from the Hôtel Richelieu, in the Avenues of Tourny. The library is opened to me at all hours : I am there even now, alone and very comfortably seated, surrounded with more Littré than I can possibly get through.''

For some months, several members of the Académie Française—according to the traditions of the Society which has ever thought it an honour to number among its members scientists such as Cuvier, Flourens, Biot, Claude Bernard, J. B. Dumas—had been urging Pasteur to become a candidate to the place left vacant by Littré. Pasteur was anxious to know not only the works, but the life of him whose place he might be called upon to fill. It was with some emotion that he first came upon the following lines printed on the title-page of the translation of the works of Hippocrates; they are a dedication by Littré to the memory of his father, a sergeant-major in the Marines under the Revolution.

'' . . . Prepared by his lessons and by his example, I have been sustained through this long work by his ever present memory. I wish to inscribe his name on the first page of this book, in the writing of which he has had so much share from his grave, so that the work of the father should not be forgotten in the work of the son, and that a pious and just gratitude should connect the work of the living with the heritage of the dead. . . .''

Pasteur in 1876 had obeyed a similar filial feeling when he wrote on the first page of his *Studies on Beer*—

'' To the memory of my father, a soldier under the first Empire, and a knight of the Legion of Honour. The more I have advanced in age, the better I have understood thy love and the superiority of thy reason. The efforts I have given to these Studies and those which have preceded them are the fruit of thy example and advice. Wishing to honour these pious recollections, I dedicate this work to thy memory.''

The two dedications are very similar. Those two soldiers' sons had kept the virile imprint of the paternal virtues. A great tenderness was also in them both; Littré, when he lost his mother, had felt a terrible grief, comparable to Pasteur's under the same circumstances.

In spite of Pasteur's interest in studying Littré in the Bordeaux library, he did not cease thinking of yellow fever. He often saw M. Berchon, the sanitary director, and inquired of him whether there were any news of the *Richelieu*. A young physician, Dr. Talmy, had expressed a desire to join Pasteur at Bordeaux and to obtain permission, when the time came, to be shut up with the patients in the lazaretto. Pasteur wrote on December 25 to Mme. Pasteur : " There is nothing new save the Minister's authorization to Dr. Talmy to enter the lazaretto ; I have just telegraphed to him that he might start. The owners of the *Richelieu* still suppose that she will reach Pauillac on Tuesday. M. Berchon, who is the first to be informed of what takes place in the roads, will send me a telegram as soon as the *Richelieu* is signalled, and we shall then go—M. Talmy, Roux and I—to ascertain the state of the ship, of course without going on board, which we should not be allowed to do if it has a suspicious bill of health."

And, as Mme. Pasteur had asked what happened when a ship arrived, he continued in the same letter : " From his boat to windward, M. Berchon receives the ship's papers, giving the sanitary state of the ship day by day. Before passing from the hands of the captain of the vessel to those of the sanitary director, the papers are sprinkled over with chloride of lime.

" If there are cases of illness, all the passengers are taken to the lazaretto ; only a few men are left on board the ship, which is henceforth in quarantine, no one being allowed to leave or enter it.

" God permit that, in the body of one of those unfortunate victims of medical ignorance, I may discover some specific microscopic being. And after that? Afterwards, it would be really beautiful to make that agent of disease and death become its own vaccine. Yellow fever is one of the three great scourges of the East—bubonic plague, cholera, and yellow fever. Do you know that it is already a fine thing to be able to put the problem in those words ! "

The *Richelieu* arrived, but she was free from fever. The last passenger had died during the crossing and his body had been thrown into the sea.

Pasteur left Bordeaux and returned to his laboratory.

CHAPTER XI

PASTEUR was in the midst of some new experiments when he heard that the date of the election to the Académie Française was fixed for December 8. Certain candidates spent half their time in *fiacres*, paying the traditional calls, counting the voters, calculating their chances, and taking every polite phrase for a promise. Pasteur, with perfect simplicity, contented himself with saying to the Academicians whom he went to see, "I had never in my life contemplated the great honour of entering the Académie Française. People have been kind enough to say to me, 'Stand and you will be elected.' It is impossible to resist an invitation so glorious for Science and so flattering to myself."

One member of the Académie, Alexandre Dumas, refused to let Pasteur call on him. "I will not allow him to come and see me," he said; "I will myself go and thank him for consenting to become one of us." He agreed with M. Grandeau, who wrote to Pasteur that "when Claude Bernard and Pasteur consent to enter the ranks of a Society, all the honour is for the latter."

When Pasteur was elected, his youthfulness of sentiment was made apparent; it seemed to him an immense honour to be one of the Forty. He therefore prepared his reception speech with the greatest care, without however allowing his scientific work to suffer. The life of his predecessor interested him more and more; to work in the midst of family intimacy had evidently been Littré's ideal of happiness.

Few people, beyond Littré's colleagues, know that his wife and daughter collaborated in his great work; they looked out the quotations necessary to that Dictionary, of which, if laid end to end, the columns would reach a length of thirty-seven kilometres. The Dictionary, commenced in 1857, when

Littré was almost sixty years old, was only interrupted twice : in 1861, when Auguste Comte's widow asked Littré for a biography of the founder of positive philosophy ; and in 1870, when the life of France was compromised and arrested during long months.

Littré, poor and disinterested as he was, had been able to realize his only dream, which was to possess a house in the country. Pasteur, bringing to bear in this, as in all things, his habits of scrupulous accuracy, left his laboratory for one day, and visited that villa, situated near Maisons-Laffitte.

The gardener who opened the door to him might have been the owner of that humble dwelling ; the house was in a bad state of repair, but the small garden gave a look of comfort to the little property. It had been the only luxury of the philosopher, who enjoyed cultivating vegetables while quoting Virgil, Horace or La Fontaine, and listened to the nightingale when early dawn found him still sitting at his work.

After visiting this house and garden, reflecting as they did the life of a sage, Pasteur said sadly, " Is it possible that such a man should have been so misjudged ! "

A crucifix, hanging in the room where Littré's family were wont to work, testified to his respect for the beliefs of his wife and daughter. " I know too well," he said one day, "what are the sufferings and difficulties of human life, to wish to take from any one convictions which may comfort them."

Pasteur also studied the Positivist doctrine of which Auguste Comte had been the pontiff and Littré the prophet. This scientific conception of the world affirms nothing, denies nothing, beyond what is visible and easily demonstrated. It suggests altruism, a "subordination of personality to sociability," it inspires patriotism and the love of humanity. Pasteur, in his scrupulously positive and accurate work, his constant thought for others, his self-sacrificing devotion to humanity, might have been supposed to be an adept of this doctrine. But he found it lacking in one great point. " Positivism," he said, "does not take into account the most important of positive notions, that of the Infinite." He wondered that Positivism should confine the mind within limits ; with an impulse of deep feeling, Pasteur, the scientist, the slow and precise observer, wrote the following passage in his speech : " What is beyond? the human mind, actuated by an invincible force, will never cease to ask itself : What is

beyond? . . . It is of no use to answer : Beyond is limitless
space, limitless time or limitless grandeur ; no one understands
those words. He who proclaims the existence of the Infinite
—and none can avoid it—accumulates in that affirmation more
of the supernatural than is to be found in all the miracles of
all the religions ; for the notion of the Infinite presents that
double character that it forces itself upon us and yet is incomprehensible. When this notion seizes upon our understanding, we can but kneel. . . I see everywhere the inevitable
expression of the Infinite in the world ; through it, the supernatural is at the bottom of every heart. The idea of God is a
form of the idea of the Infinite. As long as the mystery of the
Infinite weighs on human thought, temples will be erected
for the worship of the Infinite, whether God is called Brahma,
Allah, Jehovah, or Jesus ; and on the pavement of those
temples, men will be seen kneeling, prostrated, annihilated in
the thought of the Infinite."

At that time, when triumphant Positivism was inspiring
many leaders of men, the very man who might have given himself up to what he called " the enchantment of Science " proclaimed the Mystery of the universe ; with his intellectual
humility, Pasteur bowed before a Power greater than human
power. He continued with the following words, worthy of
being preserved for ever, for they are of those which pass over
humanity like a Divine breath : "Blessed is he who carries
within himself a God, an ideal, and who obeys it ; ideal of art,
ideal of science, ideal of the gospel virtues, therein lie the
springs of great thoughts and great actions ; they all reflect
light from the Infinite."

Pasteur concluded by a supreme homage to Littré. " Often
have I fancied him seated by his wife, as in a picture of early
Christian times : he, looking down upon earth, full of compassion for human suffering ; she, a fervent Catholic, her eyes
raised to heaven : he, inspired by all earthly virtues ; she, by
every Divine grandeur ; uniting in one impulse and in one
heart the twofold holiness which forms the aureole of the Man-
God, the one proceeding from devotion to humanity, the other
emanating from ardent love for the Divinity : she a saint in
the canonic sense of the word, he a lay-saint. This last word
is not mine ; I have gathered it on the lips of all those that
knew him."

The two colleagues whom Pasteur had chosen for his

Academic sponsors were J. B. Dumas and Nisard. Dumas, who appreciated more than any one the scientific progress due to Pasteur, and who applauded his brilliant success, was touched by the simplicity and modesty which his former pupil showed, now as in the distant past, when the then obscure young man sat taking notes on the Sorbonne benches.

Their mutual relationship had remained unchanged when Pasteur, accompanied by one of his family, rang at Dumas' door in March, 1882, with the manuscript of his noble speech in his pocket; he seemed more like a student, respectfully calling on his master, than like a savant affectionately visiting a colleague.

Dumas received Pasteur in a little private study adjoining the fine drawing-room where he was accustomed to dispense an elegant hospitality. Pasteur drew a stool up to a table and began to read, but in a shy and hurried manner, without even raising his eyes towards Dumas, who listened, enthroned in his armchair, with an occasional murmur of approbation. Whilst Pasteur's careworn face revealed some of his ardent struggles and persevering work, nothing perturbed Dumas' grave and gentle countenance. His smile, at most times prudently affable and benevolent in varying degree, now frankly illumined his face as he congratulated Pasteur. He called to mind his own reception speech at the Academy when he had succeeded Guizot, and the fact that he too had concluded by a confession of faith in his Creator.

Pasteur's other sponsor, Nisard, almost an octogenarian, was not so happy as Dumas; death had deprived him of almost all his old friends. It was a great joy to him when Pasteur came to see him on the wintry Sunday afternoons; he fancied himself back again at the Ecole Normale and the happy days when he reigned supreme in that establishment. Pasteur's deference, greater even perhaps than it had been in former times, aided the delightful delusion. Though Nisard was ever inclined to bring a shade of patronage into every intimacy, he was a conversationalist of the old and rare stamp. Pasteur enjoyed hearing Nisard's recollections and watching for a smile lighting up the almost blind face. Those Sunday talks reminded him of the old delightful conversations with Chappuis at the Besançon College when, in their youthful fervour, they read together André Chénier's and Lamartine's verses. Eighteen years later, Pasteur had not missed one of Sainte

Beuve's lectures to the Ecole Normale students; he liked that varied and penetrating criticism, opening sidelights on every point of the literary horizon. Nisard understood criticism rather as a solemn treaty, with clauses and conditions; with his taste for hierarchy, he even gave different ranks to authors as if they had been students before his chair. But, when he spoke, the rigidity of his system was enveloped in the grace of his conversation. Pasteur had but a restricted corner of his mind to give to literature, but that corner was a privileged one; he only read what was really worth reading, and every writer worthy of the name inspired him with more than esteem, with absolute respect. He had a most exalted idea of Literature and its influence on society; he was saying one day to Nisard that Literature was a great educator : " The mind alone can if necessary suffice to Science; both the mind and the heart intervene in Literature, and that explains the secret of its superiority in leading the general train of thought." This was preaching to an apostle : no homage to literature ever seemed too great in the eyes of Nisard.

He approved of the modest exordium in Pasteur's speech—

" At this moment when presenting myself before this illustrious assembly, I feel once more the emotion with which I first solicited your suffrages. The sense of my own inadequacy is borne in upon me afresh, and I should feel some confusion in finding myself in this place, were it not my duty to attribute to Science itself the honour—so to speak, an impersonal one—which you have bestowed upon me."

The Permanent Secretary, Camille Doucet, well versed in the usages of the Institute, and preoccupied with the effect produced, thought that the public would not believe in such self-effacement, sincere as it was, and sent the following letter to Pasteur with the proof-sheet of his speech—

" Dear and honoured colleague, allow me to suggest to you a modification of your first sentence; your modesty is excessive."

Camille Doucet had struck out *the sense of my own inadequacy is borne in upon me afresh,* and further *so to speak, an impersonal one.* Pasteur consulted Nisard, and *the sense of my own inadequacy* was replaced by *the sense of my deficiencies,* while Pasteur adhered energetically to *so to speak, an impersonal one*; he saw in his election less a particular distinction than a homage rendered to Science in general.

A reception at the Académie Française is like a sensational

first night at a theatre; a special public is interested days
beforehand in every coming detail. Wives, daughters, sisters
of Academicians, great ladies interested in coming candidates,
widows of deceased Academicians, laureates of various
Academy prizes—the whole literary world agitates to obtain
tickets. Pasteur's reception promised to be full of interest,
some even said piquancy, for it fell to Renan to welcome him.

In order to have a foretaste of the contrast between the two
men it was sufficient to recall Renan's opening speech three
years before, when he succeeded Claude Bernard. His thanks
to his colleagues began thus—

" Your cenaculum is only reached at the age of Ecclesiastes,
a delightful age of serene cheerfulness, when after a laborious
prime, it begins to be seen that all is but vanity, but also that
some vain things are worthy of being lingeringly enjoyed."

The two minds were as different as the two speeches;
Pasteur took everything seriously, giving to words their absolute sense; Renan, an incomparable writer, with his supple,
undulating style, slipped away and hid himself within the
sinuosities of his own philosophy. He disliked plain statements, and was ever ready to deny when others affirmed, even
if he afterwards blamed excessive negation in his own followers.
He religiously consoled those whose faith he destroyed, and,
whilst invoking the Eternal, claimed the right of finding fault
even there. When applauded by a crowd, he would willingly
have murmured *Noli me tangere*, and even added with his joyful
mixture of disdain and good-fellowship, " Let infinitely witty
men come unto me."

On that Thursday, April 27, 1882, the Institute was crowded.
When the noise had subsided, Renan, seated at the desk as
Director of the Academy between Camille Doucet, the Permanent Secretary, and Maxime du Camp, the Chancellor,
declared the meeting opened. Pasteur, looking paler than
usual, rose from his seat, dressed in the customary green-
embroidered coat of an Academician, wearing across his breast
the Grand Cordon of the Legion of Honour. In a clear, grave
voice, he began by expressing his deep gratification, and, with
the absolute knowledge and sincerity which always compelled
the attention of his audience, of whatever kind, he proceeded
to praise his predecessor. There was no artifice of composition, no struggle after effect, only a homage to the man, followed almost immediately by a confession of dissent on

philosophic questions. He was listened to with attentive emotion, and when he showed the error of Positivism in attempting to do away with the idea of the Infinite, and proclaimed the instinctive and necessary worship by Man of the great Mystery, he seemed to bring out all the weakness and the dignity of Man—passing through this world bowed under the law of Toil and with the prescience of the Ideal—into a startling and consolatory light.

One of the privileges of the Academician who receives a new member is to remain seated in his armchair before a table, and to comfortably prepare to read his own speech, in answer, often in contradiction, to the first. Renan, visibly enjoying the presidential chair, smiled at the audience with complex feelings, understood by some who were his assiduous readers. Respect for so much work achieved by a scientist of the first rank in the world; a gratified feeling of the honour which reverted to France; some personal pleasure in welcoming such a man in the name of the Académie, and, at the same time, in the opportunity for a light and ironical answer to Pasteur's beliefs—all these sensations were perceptible in Renan's powerful face, the benevolence of whose soft blue eyes was corrected by the redoubtable keenness of the smile.

He began in a caressing voice by acknowledging that the Academy was somewhat incompetent to judge of the work and glory of Pasteur. "But," he added, with graceful eloquence, "apart from the ground of the doctrine, which is not within our attributions, there is, Sir, a greatness on which our experience of the human mind gives us a right to pronounce an opinion; something which we recognize in the most varied applications, which belongs in the same degree to Galileo, Pascal, Michael-Angelo, or Moliére; something which gives sublimity to the poet, depth to the philosopher, fascination to the orator, divination to the scientist.

"That common basis of all beautiful and true work, that divine fire, that indefinable breath which inspires Science, Literature, and Art—we have found it in you, Sir—it is Genius. No one has walked so surely through the circles of elemental nature; your scientific life is like unto a luminous tract in the great night of the Infinitesimally Small, in that last abyss where life is born."

After a brilliant and rapid enumeration of the Pastorian discoveries, congratulating Pasteur on having touched through

his art the very confines of the springs of life, Renan went
on to speak of truth as he would have spoken of a woman :
" Truth, Sir, is a great coquette ; she will not be sought with
too much passion, but often is most amenable to indifference.
She escapes when apparently caught, but gives herself up
if patiently waited for ; revealing herself after farewells have
been said, but inexorable when loved with too much fervour."
And further : " Nature is plebeian, and insists upon work,
preferring horny hands and careworn brows."

He then commenced a courteous controversy. Whilst
Pasteur, with his vision of the Infinite, showed himself as
religious as Newton, Renan, who enjoyed moral problems,
spoke of Doubt with delectation. " The answer to the enigma
which torments and charms us will never be given to us.
    What matters it, since the imperceptible corner of
reality which we see is full of delicious harmonies, and since
life, as bestowed upon us, is an excellent gift, and for each of
us a revelation of infinite goodness ? "

Legend will probably hand to posterity a picture of Renan
as he was in those latter days, ironically cheerful and
unctuously indulgent. But, before attaining the quizzical
tranquillity he now exhibited to the Academy, he had gone
through a complete evolution. When about the age of forty-
eight, he might bitterly have owned that there was not one
basis of thought which in him had not crumbled to dust.
Beliefs, political ideas, his ideal of European civilization, all
had fallen to the ground. After his separation from the
Church, he had turned to historical science ; Germany had
appeared to him, as once to Madame de Staël and so many
others, as a refuge for thinkers. It had seemed to him
that a collaboration between France, England, and Germany
would create " An invincible trinity, carrying the world along
the road of progress through reason." But that German
façade which he took for that of a temple hid behind it the
most formidable barracks which Europe had ever known, and
beside it were cannon foundries, death-manufactories, all the
preparations of the German people for the invasion of France.
His awakening was bitter ; war as practised by the Prussians,
with a method in their cruelty, filled him with grief.

Time passed and his art, like a lily of the desert growing
amongst ruins, gave flowers and perfumes to surrounding
moral devastation. A mixture of disdain and nobility now

made him regard as almost imperceptible the number of men
capable of understanding his philosophical elevation. Pasteur
had bared his soul; Renan took pleasure in throwing light on
the intellectual antithesis of certain minds, and on their points
of contact.

" Allow me, Sir, to recall to you your fine discovery of right
and left tartaric acids.   There are some minds which
it is as impossible to bring together as it is impossible, according to your own comparison, to fit two gloves one into the
other. And yet both gloves are equally necessary; they complete each other. One's two hands cannot be superposed, they
may be joined. In the vast bosom of nature, the most diverse
efforts, added to each other, combine with each other, and
result in a most majestic unity."

Renan handled the French language, "this old and admirable language, poor but to those who do not know it," with a
dexterity, a choice of delicate shades, of tasteful harmonies
which have never been surpassed. Able as he was to define
every human feeling, he went on from the above comparison,
painting divergent intellectual capabilities, to the following
imprecation against death : " Death, according to a thought
admired by M. Littré, is but a function, the last and quietest
of all. To me it seems odious, hateful, insane, when it lays
its cold blind hand on virtue and on genius. A voice is in
us, which only great and good souls can hear, and that voice
cries unceasingly ' Truth and Good are the ends of thy life;
sacrifice all to that goal '; and when, following the call of that
siren within us, claiming to bear the promises of life, we
reach the place where the reward should await us, the deceit-
ful consoler fails us. Philosophy, which had promised us the
secret of death, makes a lame apology, and the ideal which
had brought us to the limits of the air we breathe disappears
from view at the supreme hour when we look for it. Nature's
object has been attained ; a powerful effort has been realized,
and then, with characteristic carelessness, the enchantress
abandons us and leaves us to the hooting birds of the night."

Renan, save in one little sentence in his answer to Pasteur—
" The divine work accomplishes itself by the intimate tendency
to what is Good and what is True in the universe "—did not
go further into the statement of his doctrines. Perhaps he
thought them too austere for his audience; he was wont to
eschew critical and religious considerations when in a world

which he looked upon as frivolous.   Moreover, he thought his
own century amusing, and was willing to amuse it further.
If he raised his eyes to Heaven, he said that we owe virtue
to the Eternal, but that we have the right to add to it irony.
Pasteur thought it strange that irony should be applied to
subjects which have beset so many great minds and which so
many simple hearts solve in their own way.

The week which followed Pasteur's reception at the Académie Française brought him a manifestation of applause
in the provinces. The town of Aubenas in the Ardèche
was erecting a statue to Olivier de Serres, and desired to associate with the name of the founder of the silk industry in
France in the sixteenth century that of its preserver in the
nineteenth.

This was the second time that a French town proclaimed
its gratitude towards Pasteur. A few months before, the
Melun Agricultural Society had held a special meeting in his
honour, and had decided " to strike a medal with Pasteur's
effigy on it, in commemoration of one of the greatest services
ever rendered by Science to Agriculture."

But amidst this pæan of praise, Pasteur, instead of dwelling
complacently on the recollection of his experiments at Pouilly
le Fort, was absorbed in one idea, characteristic of the man :
he wanted to at once begin some experiments on the peripneumonia of horned cattle.   The veterinary surgeon,
Rossignol, had just been speaking on this subject to the meeting.   Pasteur, who had recently been asked by the Committee
of Epizootic Diseases to inquire into the mortality often caused
by the inoculation of the peripneumonia virus, reminded his
hearers in a few words of the variable qualities of virus and
how the slightest impurity in a virus may exercise an influence
on the effects of that virus.

He and his collaborators had vainly tried to cultivate the
virus of peripneumonia in chicken-broth, veal-broth, yeast-
water, etc.   They had to gather the virus from the lung of a
cow which had died of peripneumonia, by means of tubes
previously sterilized; it was injected, with every precaution
against alteration, under the skin of the tail of the animal,
this part being chosen on account of the thickness of the skin
and of the cellular tissue.   By operating on other parts,
serious accidents were apt to occur, the virus being extremely

violent, so much so in fact that the local irritation sometimes went so far as to cause the loss of part of the tail. At the end of the same year (1882), Pasteur published in the *Recueil de la Médecine Vétérinaire* a paper indicating the following means of preserving the virus in a state of purity—

"Pure virus remains virulent for weeks and months. One lung is sufficient to provide large quantities of it, and its purity can easily be tested in a stove and even in ordinary temperature. From one lung only, enough can be procured to be used for many animals. Moreover, without having recourse to additional lungs, the provision of virus could be maintained in the following manner; it would suffice, before exhausting the first stock of virus, to inoculate a young calf behind the shoulder. Death speedily supervenes, and all the tissues are infiltrated with a serosity, which in its turn becomes virulent. This also can be collected and preserved in a state of purity." It remained to be seen whether virus thus preserved would become so attenuated as to lose all degree of virulence.

Aubenas, then, wished to follow the example of Melun. In deference to the unanimous wish of the inhabitants of the little town, Pasteur went there on the 4th of May. His arrival was a veritable triumph; there were decorations at the station, floral arches in the streets, brass and other bands, speeches from the Mayor, presentation of the Municipal Council, of the Chamber of Commerce, etc., etc. Excitement reigned everywhere, and the music of the bands was almost drowned by the acclamations of the people. At the meeting of the Agricultural Society, Pasteur was offered a medal with his own effigy, and a work of art representing genii around a cup, their hands full of cocoons. A little microscope—that microscope which had been called an impracticable instrument, fit for scientists only—figured as an attribute.

"For us all," said the President of the Aubenas Spinning Syndicate, "you have been the kindly magician whose intervention conjured away the scourge which threatened us; in you we hail our benefactor."

Pasteur, effacing his own personality as he had done at the Académie, laid all this enthusiasm and gratitude as an offering to Science.

"I am not its object, but rather a pretext for it," he said, and continued: "Science has been the ruling passion of my life. I have lived but for Science, and in the hours of difficulty

which are inherent to protracted efforts, the thought of France
upheld my courage. I associated her greatness with the greatness of Science.

"By erecting a statue to Olivier de Serres, the illustrious
son of the Vivarais, you give to France a noble example; you
show to all that you venerate great men and the great things
they have accomplished. Therein lies fruitful seed; you have
gathered it, may your sons see it grow and fructify. I look
back upon the time, already distant, when, desirous of respond-
ing to the suggestions of a kind and illustrious friend, I left
Paris to study in a neighbouring Department the scourge which
was decimating your *magnaneries*. For five years I struggled
to obtain some knowledge of the evil and the means of preventing it; and, after having found it, I still had to struggle
to implant in other minds the convictions I had acquired.

"All that is past and gone now, and I can speak of it with
moderation. I am not often credited with that characteristic,
and yet I am the most hesitating of men, the most fearful of
responsibility, so long as I am not in possession of a proof.
But when solid scientific proofs confirm my convictions, no
consideration can prevent me from defending what I hold to
be true.

"A man whose kindness to me was truly paternal (Biot)
had for his motto : *Per vias rectas*. I congratulate myself that
I borrowed it from him. If I had been more timid or more
doubtful in view of the principles I had established, many
points of science and of application might have remained
obscure and subject to endless discussion. The hypothesis of
spontaneous generation would still throw its veil over many
questions. Your nurseries of silkworms would be under the
sway of charlatanism, with no guide to the production of good
seed. The vaccination of charbon, destined to preserve agriculture from immense losses, would be misunderstood and
rejected as a dangerous practice.

"Where are now all the contradictions? They pass away,
and Truth remains. After an interval of fifteen years, you
now render it a noble testimony. I therefore feel a deep joy
in seeing my efforts understood and celebrated in an impulse
of sympathy which will remain in my memory and in that of
my family as a glorious recollection."

Pasteur was not allowed to return at once to his laboratory.
The agricultors and veterinary surgeons of Nîmes, who had

taken an interest in all the tests on the vaccination of charbon, had, in their turn, drawn up a programme of experiments.

Pasteur arrived at a meeting of the Agricultural Society of the Gard in time to hear the report of the veterinary surgeons and to receive the congratulations of the Society. The President expressed to him the gratitude of all the cattle-owners and breeders, hitherto powerless to arrest the progress of the disease which he had now vanquished. Whilst a com-memoration medal was being offered to him and a banquet being prepared—for Southern enthusiasm always implies a series of toasts—Pasteur thanked these enterprising men who were contemplating new experiments in order to dispel the doubts of a few veterinary surgeons, and especially the characteristic distrust, felt by some of the shepherds, of every-thing that did not come from the South. Sheep, oxen, and horses, some of them vaccinated, others intact, were put at Pasteur's disposal; he, with his usual energy, fixed the experi-ments for the next morning at eight o'clock. After inoculating all the animals with the charbon virus, Pasteur announced that those which had been vaccinated would remain unharmed, but that the twelve unvaccinated sheep would be dead or dying within forty-eight hours. An appointment was made for next day but one, on May 11, at the town knacker's, near the Bridge of Justice, where post-mortem examinations were made. Pasteur then went on to Montpellier, where he was expected by the Hérault Central Society of Agriculture, who had also made some experiments and had asked him to give a lecture at the Agricultural School. He entered the large hall, feeling very tired, almost ill, but his face lighted up at the sight of that assembly of professors and students who had hurried from all the neighbouring Faculties, and those agricultors crowding from every part of the Department, all of them either full of scientific curiosity or moved by their agricultural interests. His voice, at first weak and showing marks of weariness, soon became strengthened, and, forgetting his fatigue, he threw himself into the subject of virulent and contagious diseases. He gave himself up, heart and soul, to this audience for two whole hours, inspiring every one with his own enthusiasm. He stopped now and then to invite questions, and his answers to the objectors swept away the last shred of resistance.

" We must not," said the Vice-President of the Agricultural Society, M. Vialla, " encroach further on the time of M.

Pasteur, which belongs to France itself. Perhaps, however he will allow me to prefer a last request : he has delivered us from the terrible scourge of splenic fever ; will he now turn to a no less redoubtable infection, viz. rot, which is, so to speak, endemic in our regions? He will surely find the remedy for it."

"I have hardly finished my experiments on splenic fever," answered Pasteur gently, "and you want me to find a remedy for rot! Why not for phylloxera as well ? " And, while regretting that the days were not longer, he added, with the energy of which he had just given a new proof : " As to efforts, I am yours *usque ad mortem.*"

He afterwards was the honoured guest at the banquet prepared for him. It was now not only Sericiculture, but also Agriculture, which proclaimed its infinite gratitude to him ; he was given an enthusiastic ovation, in which, as usual, he saw no fame for himself, but for work and science only.

On May 11, at nine o'clock in the morning, he was again at Nîmes to meet the physicians, veterinary surgeons, cattle-breeders, and shepherds at the Bridge of Justice. Of the twelve sheep, six were already dead, the others dying ; it was easy to see that their symptoms were the same as are characteristic of the ordinary splenic fever. "M. Pasteur gave all necessary explanations with his usual modesty and clearness," said the local papers.

"And now let us go back to work ! " exclaimed Pasteur, as he stepped into the Paris express ; he was impatient to return to his laboratory.

In order to give him a mark of public gratitude greater still than that which came from this or that district, the Académie des Sciences resolved to organize a general movement of Scientific Societies. It was decided to present him with a medal, engraved by Alphée Dubois, and bearing on one side Pasteur's profile and on the other the inscription : "To Louis Pasteur, his colleagues, his friends, and his admirers."

On June 25, a Sunday, a delegation, headed by Dumas, and composed of Boussingault, Bouley, Jamin, Daubrée, Bertin, Tisserand and Davaine arrived at the Ecole Normale and found Pasteur in the midst of his family.

"My dear Pasteur," said Dumas, in his deep voice, " forty years ago, you entered this building as a student. From the very first, your masters foresaw that you would be an honour to it, but no one would have dared to predict the startling services which you were destined to render to science, France, and the world."

And after summing up in a few words Pasteur's great career, the sources of wealth which he had discovered or revived, the benefits he had acquired to medicine and surgery : " My dear Pasteur," continued Dumas, with an affectionate emotion, " your life has known but success. The scientific method which you use in such a masterly manner owes you its greatest triumphs. The Ecole Normale is proud to number you amongst its pupils ; the Académie des Sciences is proud of your work ; France ranks you amongst its glories.

"At this time, when marks of public gratitude are flowing towards you from every quarter, the homage which we have come to offer you, in the name of your admirers and friends, may seem worthy of your particular attention. It emanates from a spontaneous and universal feeling, and it will preserve for posterity the faithful likeness of your features.

" May you, my dear Pasteur, long live to enjoy your fame, and to contemplate the rich and abundant fruit of your work. Science, agriculture, industry, and humanity will preserve eternal gratitude towards you, and your name will live in their annals amongst the most illustrious and the most revered."

Pasteur, standing with bowed head, his eyes full of tears, was for a few moments unable to reply, and then, making a violent effort, he said in a low voice—

" My dear master—it is indeed forty years since I first had the happiness of knowing you, and since you first taught me to love science.

" I was fresh from the country ; after each of your classes, I used to leave the Sorbonne transported, often moved to tears. From that moment, your talent as a professor, your immortal labours and your noble character have inspired me with an admiration which has but grown with the maturity of my mind.

" You have surely guessed my feelings, my dear master. There has not been one important circumstance in my life or in that of my family, either happy or painful, which you have not, as it were, blessed by your presence and sympathy.

" Again to-day, you take the foremost rank in the expression of that testimony, very excessive, I think, of the esteem of my masters, who have become my friends. And what you have done for me, you have done for all your pupils; it is one of the distinctive traits of your nature. Behind the individual, you have always considered France and her greatness.

"What shall I do henceforth? Until now, great praise had inflamed my ardour, and only inspired me with the idea of making myself worthy of it by renewed efforts; but that which you have just given me in the names of the Académie and of the Scientific Societies is in truth beyond my courage."

Pasteur, who for a year had been applauded by the crowd, received on that June 25, 1882, the testimony which he rated above every other : praise from his master.

Whilst he recalled the beneficent influence which Dumas had had over him, those who were sitting in his drawing-room at the Ecole Normale were thinking that Dumas might have evoked similar recollections with similar charm. He too had known enthusiasms which had illumined his youth. In 1822, the very year when Pasteur was born, Dumas, who was then living in a student's attic at Geneva, received the visit of a man about fifty, dressed Directoire fashion, in a light blue coat with steel buttons, a white waistcoat and yellow breeches. It was Alexander von Humboldt, who had wished, on his way through Geneva, to see the young man who, though only twenty-two years old, had just published, in collaboration with Prévost, treatises on blood and on urea. That visit, the long conversations, or rather the monologues, of Humboldt had inspired Dumas with the feelings of surprise, pride, gratitude and devotion with which the first meeting with a great man is wont to fill the heart of an enthusiastic youth. When Dumas heard Humboldt speak of Laplace, Berthollet, Gay-Lussac, Arago, Thenard, Cuvier, etc., and describe them as familiarly accessible, instead of as the awe-inspiring personages he had imagined, Dumas became possessed with the idea of going to Paris, knowing those men, living near them and imbibing their methods. "On the day when Humboldt left Geneva," Dumas used to say, "the town for me became empty." It was thus that Dumas' journey to Paris was decided on, and his dazzling career of sixty years begun.

He was now near the end of his scientific career, closing peacefully like a beautiful summer evening, and he was happy in the fame of his former pupil. As he left the Ecole Normale, on that June afternoon, he passed under the windows of the laboratory, where a few young men, imbued with Pasteur's doctrines, represented a future reserve for the progress of science.

That year 1882 was the more interesting in Pasteur's life, in that though victory on many points was quite indisputable, partial struggles still burst out here and there, and an adversary often arose suddenly when he had thought the engagement over.

The sharpest attacks came from Germany. The Record of the Works of the German Sanitary Office had led, under the direction of Dr. Koch and his pupils, a veritable campaign against Pasteur, whom they declared incapable of cultivating microbes in a state of purity. He did not even, they said, know how to recognize the septic vibrio, though he had discovered it. The experiments by which hens contracted splenic fever under a lowered temperature after inoculation signified nothing. The share of the earthworms in the propagation of charbon, the inoculation into guinea-pigs of the germs found in the little cylinders produced by those worms followed by the death of the guinea-pigs, all this they said was pointless and laughable. They even contested the preserving influence of vaccination.

Whilst these things were being said and written, the Veterinary School of Berlin asked the laboratory of the Ecole Normale for some charbon vaccine. Pasteur answered that he wished that experiments should be made before a commission nominated by the German Government. It was constituted by the Minister of Agriculture and Forests, and Virchow was one of the members of it. A former student of the Ecole Normale—who, after leaving the school first on the list of competitors for the *agrégation* of physical science, had entered the laboratory—one in whom Pasteur founded many hopes, Thuillier, left for Germany with his little tubes of attenuated virus. Pasteur was not satisfied; he would have liked to meet his adversaries face to face and oblige them publicly to own their defeat. An opportunity was soon to arise. He had come to Arbois, as usual, for the months of August and September, and was having some alterations made in his little house. The tannery pits were being filled up. "It will not improve the house itself," he wrote to his son, "but it will be made brighter and more comfortable by having a tidy yard and a garden along the riverside."

The Committee of the International Congress of Hygiene,

which was to meet at Geneva, interrupted these peaceful holidays by inviting Pasteur to read a paper on attenuated virus. As a special compliment, the whole of one meeting, that of Tuesday, September 5, was to be reserved for his paper only. Pasteur immediately returned to work; he only consented under the greatest pressure to go for a short walk on the Besançon road at five o'clock every afternoon. After spending the whole morning and the whole afternoon sitting at his writing table over laboratory registers, he came away grumbling at being disturbed in his work. If any member of his family ventured a question on the proposed paper, he hastily cut them short, declaring that he must be let alone. It was only when Mme. Pasteur had copied out in her clear handwriting all the little sheets covered with footnotes, that the contents of the paper became known.

When Pasteur entered the Congress Hall, great applause greeted him on every side. The seats were occupied, not only by the physicians and professors who form the usual audience of a congress, but also by tourists, who take an interest in scientific things when they happen to be the fashion.

Pasteur spoke of the invitation he had received. "I hastened to accept it," he said, "and I am pleased to find myself the guest of a country which has been a friend to France in good as in evil days. Moreover, I hoped to meet here some of the contradictors of my work of the last few years. If a congress is a ground for conciliation, it is in the same degree a ground for courteous discussion. We all are actuated by a supreme passion, that of progress and of truth."

Almost always, at the opening of a congress, great politeness reigns in a confusion of languages. Men are seen offering each other pamphlets, exchanging visiting cards, and only lending an inattentive ear to the solemn speeches going on. This time, the first scene of the first act suspended all private conversation. Pasteur stood above the assembly in his full strength and glory. Though he was almost sixty, his hair had remained black, his beard alone was turning grey. His face reflected indomitable energy; if he had not been slightly lame, and if his left hand had not been a little stiff, no one could have supposed that he had been struck with paralysis fourteen years before. The feeling of the place France should hold in an International Congress gave him a proud look and an imposing accent of authority. He was visibly ready to meet his adversaries and to make of this assembly a tribunal of judges. Except for a few diplomats who at the first words exchanged anxious looks at the idea of possible polemics, Frenchmen felt happy at being better represented than any other nation. Men eagerly pointed out to each other Dr. Koch, twenty-one years younger than Pasteur, who sat on one of the benches, listening, with impassive eyes behind his gold spectacles.

Pasteur analysed all the work he had done with the collaboration of MM. Chamberland, Roux, and Thuillier. He made clear to the most ignorant among his hearers his ingenious experiments either to obtain, preserve or modify the virulence of certain microbes. "It cannot be doubted," he said, "that we possess a general method of attenuation. . . . The general principles are found, and it cannot be disbelieved that the future of those researches is rich with the greatest hopes. But, however obvious a demonstrated truth may be, it has not always the privilege of being easily accepted. I have met in France and elsewhere with some obstinate contradictors.

Allow me to choose amongst them the one whose personal merit gives him the greatest claims to our attention, I mean Dr Koch, of Berlin."

Pasteur then summed up the various criticisms which had appeared in the Record of the Works of the German Sanitary Office. "Perhaps there may be some persons in this assembly," he went on, "who share the opinions of my contradictors. They will allow me to invite them to speak; I should be happy to answer them."

Koch, mounting the platform, declined to discuss the subject, preferring, he said, to make answer in writing later on. Pasteur was disappointed; he would have wished the Congress, or at least a Commission designated by Koch, to decide on the experiments. He resigned himself to wait. On the following days, as the members of the Congress saw him attending meetings on general hygiene, school hygiene, and veterinary hygiene, they hardly recognized in the simple, attentive man, anxious for instruction, the man who had defied his adversary. Outside the arena, Pasteur became again the most modest of men, never allowing himself to criticize what he had not thoroughly studied. But, when sure of his facts, he showed himself full of a violent passion, the passion of truth · when truth had triumphed, he preserved not the least bitterness of former struggles.

That day of the 5th September was remembered in Geneva. "All the honour was for France," wrote Pasteur to his son; "that was what I had wished."

He was already keen in the pursuit of another malady which caused great damage, the "rouget" disease or swine fever. Thuillier, ever ready to start when a demonstration had to be made or an experiment to be attempted, had ascertained, in March, 1882, in a part of the Department of the Vienne, the existence of a microbe in the swine attacked with that disease.

In order to know whether this microbe was the cause of the evil, the usual operations of the sovereign method had to be resorted to. First of all, a culture medium had to be found which was suitable to the micro-organism (veal broth was found to be very successful); then a drop of the culture had to be abstracted from the little phials where the microbe was developing and sown into other flasks; lastly the culture liquid had to be inoculated into swine. Death supervened with all the symptoms of swine fever; the microbe was therefore the cause of the evil? Could it be attenuated and a vaccine obtained? Being pressed to study that disease, and to find the remedy for it, by M. Maucuer, a veterinary surgeon of the Department of Vaucluse, living at Bolléne, Pasteur started, accompanied by his nephew, Adrien Loir, and M. Thuillier. The three arrived at Bolléne on September 13.

"It is impossible to imagine more obliging kindness than that of those excellent Maucuers," wrote Pasteur to his wife the next day. "Where, in what dark corner they sleep, in order to give us two bedrooms, mine and another with two beds, I do not like to think. They are young, and have an eight-year-old son at the Avignon College, for whom they have obtained a half-holiday to-day in order that he may be presented to ' M. Pasteur.' The two men and I are taken care of in a manner you might envy. It is colder here and more rainy than in Paris. I have a fire in my room, that green oak-wood fire that you will remember we had at the Pont Gisquet.

"I was much pleased to hear that the swine fever is far from being extinguished. There are sick swine everywhere, some dying, some dead, at Bolléne and in the country around; the evil is disastrous this year. We saw some dead and dying yesterday afternoon. We have brought here a young hog who is very ill, and this morning we shall attempt vaccination at a

M. de Ballincourt's, who has lost all his pigs, and who has just bought some more in the hope that the vaccine will be preservative. From morning till night we shall be able to watch the disease and to try to prevent it. This reminds me of the pébrine, with pigsties and sick pigs instead of nurseries full of dying silkworms. Not ten thousand, but at least twenty thousand swine have perished, and I am told it is worse still in the Ardèche."

On the 17th, the day was taken up by the inoculation of some pigs on the estate of M. de la Gardette, a few kilometres from Bolléne. In the evening, a former State Councillor, M. de Gaillard, came at the head of a delegation to compliment Pasteur and invite him to a banquet. Pasteur declined this honour, saying he would accept it when the swine fever was conquered. They spoke to him of his past services, but he had no thought for them; like all progress-seeking men, he saw but what was before him. Experiments were being carried out —he had hastened to have an experimental pigsty erected near M. Maucuer's house—and already, on the 21st, he wrote to Mme. Pasteur, in one of those letters which resembled the loose pages of a laboratory notebook—

"Swine fever is not nearly so obscure to me now, and I am persuaded that with the help of time the scientific and practical problem will be solved.

"Three post-mortem examinations to-day. They take a long time, but that seems of no account to Thuillier, with his cool and patient eagerness."

Three days later : "I much regret not being able to tell you yet that I am starting back for Paris. It is quite impossible to abandon all these experiments which we have commenced; I should have to return here at least once or twice. The chief thing is that things are getting clearer with every experiment. You know that nowadays a medical knowledge of disease is nothing; it must be prevented beforehand. We are attempting this, and I think I can foresee success; but keep this for yourself and our children. I embrace you all most affectionately.

"P.S.—I have never felt better. Send me 1,000 fr. ; I have but 300 fr. left of the 1,600 fr. I brought. Pigs are expensive, and we are killing a great many."

At last on December 3 : "I am sending M. Dumas a note for to-morrow's meeting at the Academy. If I had time I would transcribe it for the laboratory and for René."

" Our researches "—thus ran the report to the Academy—
" may be summed up in the following propositions—

" I.   The swine fever, or rouget disease, is produced by a
special microbe, easy to cultivate outside the animal's body.   It
is so tiny that it often escapes the most attentive search.   It
resembles the microbe of chicken cholera more than any other;
its shape is also that of a figure 8, but finer and less visible
than that of the cholera.   It differs essentially from the latter
by its physiological properties; it kills rabbits and sheep, but
has no effect on hens.

" II.   If inoculated in a state of purity into pigs, in almost
inappreciable doses, it speedily brings the fever and death,
with all the characteristics usual in *spontaneous* cases.   It is
most deadly to the white, so-called improved, race, that which
is most sought after by pork-breeders.

" III.   Dr. Klein published in London (1878) an extensive
work on swine fever which he calls *Pneumo-enteritis of Swine*;
but that author is entirely mistaken as to the nature of the
parasite.   He has described as the microbe of the rouget a
bacillus with spores, more voluminous even than the bacteridium of splenic fever.   Dr. Klein's microbe is very different
from the true microbe of swine fever, and has, besides, no
relation to the etiology of that disease.

" IV.   After having satisfied ourselves by direct tests that
the malady does not recur, we have succeeded in inoculating in
in a benignant form, after which the animal has proved refractory to the mortal disease.

" V.   Though we consider that further control experiments
are necessary, we have already great confidence in this, that,
dating from next spring, vaccination by the virulent microbe of
swine fever, attenuated, will become the salvation of pigsties."

Pasteur ended thus his letter of December 3: " We shall
start to-morrow, Monday.   Adrien Loir and I shall sleep at
Lyons.   Thuillier will go straight to Paris, to take care of ten
little pigs which we have bought, and which he will take with
him.   In this way they will not be kept waiting at stations.
Pigs, young and old, are very sensitive to cold; they will be
wrapped up in straw.   They are very young and quite charming; one cannot help getting fond of them."

The next day Pasteur wrote to his son: " Everything has
gone off well, and we much hope, Thuillier and I, that preventive vaccination of this evil can be established in a practical

fashion. It would be a great boon in pork-breeding countries, where terrible ravages are made by the rouget (so called because the animals die covered with red or purple blotches, already developed during the fever which precedes death). In the United States, over a million swine died of this disease in 1879; it rages in England and in Germany. This year, it has desolated the Côtes-du-Nord, the Poitou, and the departments of the Rhone Valley. I sent to M. Dumas yesterday a *résumé* in a few lines of our results, to be read at to-day's meeting."

Pasteur, once more in Paris, returned eagerly to his studies on divers virus and on hydrophobia. If he was told that he over-worked himself, he replied : " It would seem to me that I was committing a theft if I were to let one day go by without doing some work." But he was again disturbed in the work he enjoyed by the contradictions of his opponents.

Koch's reply arrived soon after the Bolléne episode. The German scientist had modified his views to a certain extent; instead of denying the attenuation of virus as in 1881, he now proclaimed it as a discovery of the first order. But he did not beheve much, he said, in the practical results of the vaccination of charbon.

Pasteur put forward, in response, a report from the veterinary surgeon Boutet to the Chartres Veterinary and Agricultural School, made in the preceding October. The sheep vaccinated in Eure et Loir during the last year formed a total of 79,392. Instead of a mortality which had been more than nine per cent. on the average in the last ten years, the mortality had only been 518 sheep, much less than one per cent; 5,700 sheep had therefore been preserved by vaccination. Amongst cattle 4,562 animals had been vaccinated; out of a similar number 300 usually died every year. Since vaccination, only eleven cows had died.

" Such results appear to us convincing," wrote M. Boutet. " If our cultivators of the Beauce understand their own interest, splenic fever and malignant pustules will soon remain a mere memory, for charbon diseases never are spontaneous, and, by preventing the death of their cattle by vaccination, they will destroy all possibility of propagation of that terrible disease, which will in consequence entirely disappear."

Koch continued to smile at the discovery on the earthworms' action in the etiology of anthrax. " You are mistaken, Sir," replied Pasteur. " You are again preparing for yourself a

vexing change of opinion." And he concluded as follows :
" However violent your attacks, Sir, they will not hinder the
success of the method of attenuated virus. I am confidently
awaiting the consequences which it holds in reserve to help
humanity in its struggle against the diseases which assault it."

This debate was hardly concluded when new polemics arose
at the Académie de Médecine. A new treatment of typhoid
fever was under discussion.

In 1870, M. Glénard, a Lyons medical student, who had
enlisted, was, with many others, taken to Stettin as prisoner
of war. A German physician, Dr. Brand, moved with compassion by the sufferings of the vanquished French soldiers,
showed them great kindness and devotion. The French
student attached himself to him, helped him with his work,
and saw him treat typhoid fever with success by baths at 20° C.
Brand prided himself on this cold-bath treatment, which produced numerous cures. M. Glénard, on his return to Lyons,
remembering with confidence this method of which he had seen
the excellent results, persuaded the physician of the Croix
Rousse hospital, where he resided, to attempt the same treatment. This was done for ten years, and nearly all the Lyons
practitioners became convinced that Brand's method was
efficacious. M. Glénard came to Paris and read to the
Academy of Medicine a paper on the cold-bath treatment of
typhoid fever. The Academy appointed a commission, composed of civil and military physicians, and the discussion was
opened.

The oratorical display which had struck Pasteur when he
first came to the Académie de Médecine was much to the fore
on that occasion ; the merely curious hearers of that discussion
had an opportunity of enjoying medical eloquence, besides
acquiring information on the new treatment of typhoid fever.
There were some vehement denunciations of the microbe which
was suspected in typhoid fever. " You aim at the microbe and
you bring down the patient ! " exclaimed one of the orators,
who added, amidst great applause, that it was time " to offer
an impassable barrier to such adventurous boldness and thus
to preserve patients from the unforeseen dangers of that
therapeutic whirlwind ! "

Another orator took up a lighter tone : " I do not much
believe in that invasion of parasites which threatens us like
an eleventh plague of Egypt," said M. Peter. And attacking

the scientists who meddled with medicine, *chymiasters* as he called them, " They have come to this," he said, "that in typhoid fevers they only see *the* typhoid fever, in typhoid fever, fever only, and in fever, increased heat. They have thus reached that luminous idea that heat must be fought by cold. This organism is on fire, let us pour water over it; it is a fireman's doctrine."

Vulpian, whose grave mind was not unlike Pasteur's, intervened, and said that new attempts should not be discouraged by sneers. Without pronouncing on the merits of the cold-bath method, which he had not tried, he looked beyond this discussion, indicating the road which theoretically seemed to him to lead to a curative treatment. The first thing was to discover the agent which causes typhoid fever, and then, when that was known, attempt to destroy or paralyse it in the tissues of typhoid patients, or else to find drugs capable either of preventing the aggressions of that agent or of annihilating the effects of that aggression, "to produce, relatively to typhoid fever, the effect determined by salicylate of soda in acute rheumatism of the articulations."

Beyond the restricted audience, allowed a few seats in the Académie de Médecine, the general public itself was taking an interest in this prolonged debate. The very high death rate in the army due to typhoid fever was the cause of this eager attention. Whilst the German army, where Brand's method was employed, hardly lost five men out of a thousand, the French army lost more than ten per thousand.

Whilst military service was not compulsory, epidemics in barracks were looked upon with more or less compassionate attention. But the thought that typhoid fever had been more destructive within the last ten years than the most sanguinary battle now awakened all minds and hearts. Is then personal fear necessary to awaken human compassion?

Bouley, who was more given to propagating new doctrines than to lingering on such philosophical problems, thought it was time to introduce into the debate certain ideas on the great problems tackled by medicine since the discovery of what might be called a fourth kingdom in nature, that of microbia. In a statement read at the Académie de Médecine, he formulated in broad lines the rôle of the infinitesimally small and their activity in producing the phenomena of fermentations and diseases. He showed by the parallel works of Pasteur on the

one hand, and M. Chauveau on the other, that contagion is the
function of a living element. "It is especially," said Bouley,
"on the question of the prophylaxis of virulent diseases that
the microbian doctrine has given the most marvellous results.
To seize upon the most deadly virus, to submit them to a
methodical culture, to cause modifying agents to act upon them
in a measured proportion, and thus to succeed in attenuating
them in divers degrees, so as to utilize their strength, reduced
but still efficacious, in transmitting a benignant malady by
means of which immunity is acquired against the deadly
disease : what a beautiful dream ! ! And M. Pasteur has made
that dream into a reality ! ! ! . . "

The debate widened, typhoid fever became a mere incident.
The pathogenic action of the infinitesimally small entered into
the discussion ; traditional medicine faced microbian medicine.
M. Peter rushed once more to the front rank for the fight. He
declared that he did not apply the term *chymiaster* to Pasteur ;
he recognized that it was but "fair to proclaim that we owe
to M. Pasteur's researches the most useful practical applications in surgery and in obstetrics." But considering that
medicine might claim more independence, he repeated that
the discovery of the material elements of virulent diseases did
not throw so much light as had been said, either on pathological
anatomy, on the evolution, on the treatment or especially on
the prophylaxis of virulent diseases. "Those are but natural
history curiosities," he added, "interesting no doubt, but of
very little profit to medicine, and not worth either the time
given to them or the noise made about them. After so many
laborious researches, nothing will be changed in medicine,
there will only be a few more microbes."

A newspaper having repeated this last sentence, a professor
of the Faculty of Medicine, M. Cornil, simply recalled how,
at the time when the acarus of itch had been discovered, many
partisans of old doctrines had probably exclaimed, "What is
your acarus to me? Will it teach me more than I know
already?" "But," added M. Cornil, "the physician who had
understood the value of that discovery no longer inflicted
internal medication upon his patients to cure them of what
seemed an inveterate disease, but merely cured them by means
of a brush and a little ointment."

M. Peter, continuing his violent speech, quoted certain vaccination failures, and incompletely reported experiments, say-

ing, grandly : " M. Pasteur's excuse is that he is a chemist, who has tried, out of a wish to be useful, to reform medicine, to which he is a complete stranger.

" In the struggle I have undertaken the present discussion is but a skirmish ; but, to judge from the reinforcements which are coming to me, the *mêlée* may become general, and victory will remain, 1 hope, to the larger battalions, that is to say, to the 'old medicine.' "

Bouley, amazed that M. Peter should thus scout the notion of microbia introduced into pathology, valiantly fought this " skirmish " alone. He recalled the discussions à propos of tuberculosis, so obscure until a new and vivifying notion came to simplify the solution of the problem. " And you reject that solution ! You say, ' What does it matter to me? ' . . . What ! M. Koch, of Berlin—who with such discoveries as he has made might well abstain from envy—M. Koch points out to you the presence of bacteria in tubercles, and that seems to you of no importance? But that microbe gives you the explanation of those contagious properties of tuberculosis so well demonstrated by M. Villemin, for it is the instrument of virulence itself which is put under your eyes."

Bouley then went on to refute the arguments of M. Peter, epitomized the history of the discovery of the attenuation of virus, and all that this method of cultures possible in an extra-organic medium might suggest that was hopeful for a vaccine of cholera and of yellow fevér, which might be discovered one day and protect humanity against those terrible scourges. He concluded thus—" Let M. Peter do what I have done ; let him study M. Pasteur, and penetrate thoroughly into all that is admirable, through the absolute certainty of the results, in the long series of researches which have led him from the discovery of ferments to that of the nature of virus ; and then I can assure him that instead of decrying this great glory of France, of whom we must all be proud, he too will feel himself carried away by enthusiasm and will bow with admiration and respect before the chemist, who, though not a physician, illumines medicine and dispels, in the light of his experiments, a darkness which had hitherto remained impenetrable."

A year before this (Peter had not failed to report the fact) an experiment of anthrax vaccination had completely failed at the Turin Veterinary School. All the sheep, vaccinated and

non-vaccinated, had succumbed subsequently to the inoculation
of the blood of a sheep which had died of charbon.

This took place in March, 1882. As soon as Pasteur heard
of this extraordinary fiasco, which seemed the counterpart of
the Pouilly-le-Fort experiment, he wrote on April 16 to the
director of the Turin Veterinary School, asking on what day
the sheep had died the blood of which had been used for the
virulent inoculation.

The director answered simply that the sheep had died on the
morning of March 22, and that its blood had been inoculated
during the course of the following day. "There has been,"
said Pasteur, "a grave scientific mistake; the blood inoculated
was septic as well as full of charbon."

Though the director of the Turin Veterinary School affirmed
that the blood had been carefully examined and that it was in
no wise septic, Pasteur looked back on his 1877 experiments
on anthrax and septicæmia, and maintained before the Paris
Central Veterinary Society on June 8, 1882, that the Turin
School had done wrong in using the blood of an animal at least
twenty-four hours after its death, for the blood must have been
septic besides containing anthrax. The six professors of the
Turin School protested unanimously against such an interpretation. "We hold it marvellous," they wrote ironically, "that
your Illustrious Lordship should have recognized so surely,
from Paris, the disease which made such havoc amongst the
animals vaccinated and non-vaccinated and inoculated with
blood containing anthrax in our school on March 23, 1882.

"It does not seem to us possible that a scientist should
affirm the existence of septicæmia in an animal he has not even
seen. . . ."

The quarrel with the Turin School had now lasted a year.
On April 9, 1883, Pasteur appealed to the Academy of Sciences
to judge of the Turin incident and to put an end to this agitation, which threatened to cover truth with a veil. He read out
the letter he had just addressed to the Turin professors.

"Gentlemen, a dispute having arisen between you and
myself respecting the interpretation to be given to the absolute
failure of your control experiment of March 23, 1882, I have
the honour to inform you that, if you will accept the suggestion,
I will go to Turin any day you may choose; you shall inoculate
in my presence some virulent charbon into any number of
sheep you like. The exact moment of death in each case shall

be determined, and I will demonstrate to you that in every case the blood of the corpse containing only charbon at the first will also be septic on the next day. It will thus be established with absolute certainty that the assertion formulated by me on June 8, 1882, against which you have protested on two occasions, arises, not as you say, from an arbitrary opinion, but from an immovable scientific principle; and that I have legitimately affirmed from Paris the presence of septicæmia without it being in the least necessary that I should have seen the corpse of the sheep you utilized for your experiments.

"Minutes of the facts as they are produced shall be drawn up day by day, and signed by the professors of the Turin Veterinary School and by the other persons, physicians or veterinary surgeons, who may have been present at the experiments; these minutes will then be published both at the Academies of Turin and of Paris."

Pasteur contented himself with reading this letter to the Academy of Sciences. For months he had not attended the Academy of Medicine; he was tired of incessant and barren struggles; he often used to come away from the discussions worn out and excited. He would say to Messrs. Chamberland and Roux, who waited for him after the meetings, "How is it that certain doctors do not understand the range, the value, of our experiments? How is it that they do not foresee the great future of all these studies?"

The day after the Académie des Sciences meeting, judging that his letter to Turin sufficiently closed the incident, Pasteur started for Arbois. He wanted to set up a laboratory adjoining his house. Where the father had worked with his hands, the son would work at his great light-emitting studies.

On April 3 a letter from M. Peter had been read at the Academy of Medicine, declaring that he did not give up the struggle and that nothing would be lost by waiting.

At the following sitting, another physician, M. Fauvel, while declaring himself an admirer of Pasteur's work and full of respect for his person, thought it well not to accept blindly all the inductions into which Pasteur might find himself drawn, and to oppose those which were contradictory to acquired facts. After M. Fauvel, M. Peter violently attacked what he called "microbicidal drugs which may become homicidal," he said. When reading the account of this meeting, Pasteur had an impulse of anger. His resolutions not to return to the

Academy of Medicine gave way before the desire not to leave Bouley alone to lead the defensive campaign; he started for Paris.

As his family was then at Arbois, and the doors of his flat at the Ecole Normale closed, the simplest thing for Pasteur was to go to the Hôtel du Louvre, accompanied by a member of his family. The next morning he carefully prepared his speech, and, at three o'clock in the afternoon, he entered the Academy of Medicine. The President, M. Hardy, welcomed him in these words—"Allow me, before you begin to speak, to tell you that it is with great pleasure that we see you once again among us, and that the Academy hopes that, now that you have once more found your way to its precincts, you will not forget it again."

After isolating and rectifying the -points of discussion, Pasteur advised M. Peter to make a more searching inquiry into the subject of anthrax vaccination, and to trust to Time, the only sovereign judge. Should not the recollection of the violent hostility encountered at first by Jenner put people on their guard against hasty judgments? There was not one of the doctors present who could not remember what had been written at one time against vaccination!!!

He went on to oppose the false idea that each science should restrict itself within its own limitations. "What do I, a physician, says M. Peter, want with the minds of the chemist, the physicist and the physiologist?

"On hearing him speak with so much disdain of the chemists and physiologists who touch upon questions of disease, you might verily think that he is speaking in the name of a science whose principles are founded on a rock! Does he want proofs of the slow progress of therapeutics? It is now six months since, in this assembly of the greatest medical men, the question was discussed whether it is better to treat typhoid fever with cold lotions or with quinine, with alcohol or salicylic acid, or even not to treat it at all.

"And, when we are perhaps on the eve of solving the question of the etiology of that disease by a microbe, M. Peter commits the medical blasphemy of saying, 'What do your microbes matter to me? It will only be one microbe the more!'"

Amazed that sarcasm should be levelled against new studies which opened such wide horizons, he denounced the flippancy

with which a professor of the Faculty of Medicine allowed him·
self to speak of vaccinations by attenuated virus.

He ended by rejoicing once more that this great discovery
should have been a French one.

Pasteur went back to Arbois for a few days. On his return
to Paris, he was beginning some new experiments, when he
received a long letter from the Turin professors. Instead of
accepting his offer, they enumerated their experiments, asked
some questions in an offended and ironical manner, and concluded by praising an Italian national vaccine, which produced
absolute immunity in the future—when it did not kill.

"They cannot get out of this dilemma," said Pasteur;
"either they knew my 1877 notes, unravelling the contradictory statements of Davaine, Jaillard and Leplat, and Paul
Bert, or they did not know them. If they did not know them
on March 22, 1882, there is nothing more to say; they were
not guilty in acting as they did, but they should have owned it
freely. If they did know them, why ever did they inoculate
blood taken from a sheep twenty-four hours after its death?
They say that this blood was not septic; but how do they know?
They have done nothing to find out. They should have inoculated some guinea-pigs, by choice, and then tried some cultures
in a vacuum to compare them with cultures in contact with
air. Why will they not receive me? A meeting between
truth-seeking men would be the most natural thing in the
world ! "

Still hoping to persuade his adversaries to meet him at Turin
and be convinced, Pasteur wrote to them. "*Paris, May 9,*
1883. Gentlemen—Your letter of April 30 surprises me very
much. What is in question between you and me? That I
should go to Turin, if you will allow me, to demonstrate that
sheep, dead of charbon, as numerous as you like, will, for a
few hours after their death, be exclusively infected with
anthrax, and that the day after their death they will present
both anthrax and septic infection; and that therefore, when, on
March 23, 1882, wishing to inoculate blood infected with
anthrax only into sheep vaccinated and non-vaccinated, you
took blood from a carcase twenty-four hours after death, you
committed a grave scientific mistake.

"Instead of answering yes or no, instead of saying to me
'Come to Turin,' or 'Do not come,' you ask me, in a manu-

script letter of seventeen pages, to send you from Paris, in writing, preliminary explanations of all that I should have to demonstrate in Turin.

" Really, what is the good? Would not that lead to endless discussions? It is because of the uselessness of a written controversy that I have placed myself at your disposal.

" I have once more the honour of asking you to inform me whether you accept the proposal made to you on April 9, that I should go to Turin to place before your eyes the proofs of the facts I have just mentioned.

" P.S.—In order not to complicate the debate, I do not dwell upon the many erroneous quotations and statements contained in your letter "

M. Roux began to prepare an interesting curriculum of experiments to be carried out at Turin. But the Turin professors wrote a disagreeable letter, published a little pamphlet entitled *Of the Scientific Dogmatism of the Illustrious Professor Pasteur*, and things remained as they were.

All these discussions, renewed on so many divers points, were not altogether a waste of time; some of them bore fruitful results by causing most decisive proofs to be sought for. It has also made the path of Pasteur's followers wider and smoother that he himself should have borne the brunt of the first opposition.

In the meanwhile, testimonials of gratitude continued to pour in from the agricultors and veterinary surgeons who had seen the results of two years' practice of the vaccination against anthrax.

In the year 1882, 613,740 sheep and 83,946 oxen had been vaccinated. The Department of the Cantal which had before lost about 3,000,000 fr. every year, desired in June, 1883, on the occasion of an agricultural show, to give M. Pasteur a special acknowledgement of their gratitude. It consisted of a cup of silver-plated bronze, ornamented with a group of cattle. Behind the group—imitating in this the town of Aubenas, who had made a microscope figure as an attribute of honour—was represented, in small proportions, an instrument which found itself for the first time raised to such an exalted position, the little syringe used for inoculations.

Pasteur was much pressed to come himself and receive this offering from a land which would henceforth owe its fortune to him. He allowed himself to be persuaded, and arrived, accompanied as usual by his family.

The Mayor, surrounded by the municipal councillors, greeted him in these words : " Our town of Aurillac is very small, and you will not find here the brilliant population which inhabits great cities; but you will find minds capable of understanding the scientific and humanitarian mission which you have so generously undertaken. You will also find hearts capable of appreciating your benefits and of preserving the memory of them ; your name has been on all our lips for a long time."

Pasteur, visiting that local exhibition, did not resemble the official personages who listen wearily to the details given them by a staff of functionaries. He thought but of acquiring knowledge, going straight to this or that exhibitor and questioning him, not with perfunctory politeness, but with a real desire for practical information ; no detail seemed to him insignificant. " Nothing should be neglected," he said ; " and a remark from a rough labourer who does well what he has to do is infinitely precious."

After visiting the products and agricultural implements, Pasteur was met in the street by a peasant who stopped and waved his large hat, shouting, "Long live Pasteur ! " " You have saved my cattle," continued the man, coming up to shake hands with him.

Physicians in their turn desired to celebrate and to honour him who, though not a physician, had rendered such service to medicine. Thirty-two of them assembled to drink his health. The head physician of the Aurillac Hospital, Dr. Fleys, said in proposing the toast : " What the mechanism of the heavens owes to Newton, chemistry to Lavoisier, geology to Cuvier, general anatomy to Bichat, physiology to Claude Bernard, pathology and hygiene will owe to Pasteur. Unite with me, dear colleagues, and let us drink to the fame of the illustrious Pasteur, the precursor of the medicine of the future, a benefactor to humanity."

This glorious title was now associated with his name. In the first rank of his enthusiastic admirers came the scientists, who, from the point of view of pure science, admired the achievements, within those thirty-five years, of that great man whose perseverance equalled his penetration. Then came the manufacturers, the sericicultors, and the agricultors, who owed their fortune to him who had placed every process he discovered into the public domain. Finally, France could quote the words of the English physiologist, Huxley, in a public lecture at the London Royal Society : " Pasteur's discoveries alone would suffice to cover the war indemnity of five milliards paid by France to Germany in 1870."

To that capital was added the inestimable price of human lives saved. Since the antiseptic method had been adopted in surgical operations, the mortality had fallen from 50 per 100 to 5 per 100.

In the lying-in hospitals, more than decimated formerly (for the statistics had shown a death-rate of not only 100 but 200 per 1,000), the number of fatalities was now reduced to 3 per 1,000 and soon afterwards fell to 1 per 1,000. And, in consequence of the principles established by Pasteur, hygiene was growing, developing, and at last taking its proper place in the public view. So much progress accomplished had brought Pasteur a daily growing acknowledgment of gratitude, his country was more than proud of him. His powerful mind, allied with his very tender heart, had brought to French glory an aureole of charity.

The Government of the Republic remembered that England had voted two national rewards to Jenner, one in 1802 and one in 1807, the first of £10,000, and the second of £20,000. It was at the time of that deliberation that Pitt, the great orator, exclaimed, "Vote, gentlemen, your gratitude will never reach the amount of the service rendered."

The French Ministry proposed to augment the 12,000 fr. pension accorded to Pasteur in 1874 as a national recompense, and to make it 25,000 fr., to revert first to Pasteur's widow, and then to his children. A Commission was formed and Paul Bert again chosen to draw up the report.

On several occasions at the meetings of the commission one of its members, Benjamin Raspail, exalted the parasitic theory propounded in 1843 by his own father. His filial pleading went so far as to accuse Pasteur of plagiarism. Paul Bert, whilst recognizing the share attributed by F. V. Raspail to microscopic beings, recalled the fact that his attempt in favour of epidemic and contagious diseases had not been adopted by scientists. "No doubt," he said, " the parasitic origin of the itch was now definitely accepted, thanks in a great measure to the efforts of Raspail; but generalizations were considered as out of proportion to the fact they were supposed to rest on. It seemed excessive to conclude from the existence of the acarus of itch, visible to the naked eye or with the weakest magnifying glass, the presence of microscopic parasites in the humours of virulent diseases.   . Such hypotheses can be considered but as a sort of intuition."

"Hypotheses," said Pasteur, "come into our laboratories in armfuls; they fill our registers with projected experiments, they stimulate us to research—and that is all." One thing only counted for him : experimental verification.

Paul Bert, in his very complete report, quoted Huxley's words to the Royal Society and Pitt's words to the House of Commons. He stated that since the first Bill had been voted, a new series of discoveries, no less marvellous from a theoretical point of view and yet more important from a practical point of view, had come to strike the world of Science with astonishment and admiration." Recapitulating Pasteur's works, he said

"They may be classed in three series, constituting three great discoveries.

" The first one may be formulated thus : *Each fermentation is produced by the development of a special microbe.*

" The second one may be given this formula : *Each infectious disease* (those at least that M. Pasteur and his immediate followers have studied) *is produced by the development within the organism of a special microbe.*

" The third one may be expressed in this way : *The microbe of an infectious disease, cultivated under certain detrimental conditions, is attenuated in its pathogenic activity; from a virus it has become a vaccine.*

"As a practical consequence of the first discovery, M. Pasteur has given rules for the manufacture of beer and of vinegar, and shown how beer and wine may be preserved against secondary fermentations which would turn them sour, bitter or slimy, and which render difficult their transport and even their preservation on the spot.

"As a practical consequence of the second discovery, M. Pasteur has given rules to be followed to preserve cattle from splenic fever contamination, and silkworms from the diseases which decimated them. Surgeons, on the other hand, have succeeded, by means of the guidance it afforded, in effecting almost completely the disappearance of erysipelas and of the

purulent infections which formerly brought about the death of
so many patients after operations.

"As a practical consequence of the third discovery, M.
Pasteur has given rules for, and indeed has effected, the preservation of horses, oxen, and sheep from the anthrax disease
which every year kills in France about 20,000,000 francs'
worth. Swine will also be preserved from the rouget disease
which decimates them, and poultry from the cholera which
makes such terrible havoc among them. Everything leads us
to hope that rabies will also soon be conquered." When Paul
Bert was congratulated on his report, he said, "Admiration is
such a good, wholesome thing ! l "

The Bill was voted by the Chamber, and a fortnight later by
the Senate, unanimously. Pasteur heard the first news through
the newspapers, for he had just gone to the Jura. On July
14, he left Arbois for Dôle, where he had promised to be
present at a double ceremony.

On that national holiday, a statue of Peace was to be
inaugurated, and a memorial plate placed on the house where
Pasteur was born ; truly a harmonious association of ideas.
The prefect of the Jura evidently felt it when, while unveiling
the statue in the presence of Pasteur, he said : "This is
Peace, who has inspired Genius and the great services it has
rendered." The official procession, followed by popular acclamation, went on to the narrow Rue des Tanneurs. When
Pasteur, who had not seen his native place since his childhood, found himself before that tannery, in the low humble
rooms of which his father and mother had lived, he felt himself
the prey to a strong emotion.

The mayor quoted these words from the resolutions of the
Municipal Council : " M. Pasteur is a benefactor of Humanity,
one of the great men of France; he will remain for all Dôlois
and in particular those who, like him, have risen from the ranks
of the people, an object of respect as well as an example to
follow ; we consider that it is our duty to perpetuate his name
in our town."

The Director of Fine Arts, M. Kaempfen, representing the
Government at the ceremony, pronounced these simple words :
" In the name of the Government of the Republic, I salute the
inscription which commemorates the fact that in this little
house, in this little street, was born, on December 27, 1822,

he who was to become one of the greatest scientists of this century so great in science, and who has, by his admirable labours, increased the glory of France and deserved well of the whole of humanity."

The feelings in Pasteur's heart burst forth in these terms · "Gentlemen, I am profoundly moved by the honour done to me by the town of Dôle; but allow me, while expressing my gratitude, to protest against this excess of praise. By according to me a homage rendered usually but to the illustrious dead, you anticipate too much the judgment of posterity. Will it ratify your decision? and should not you, Mr. Mayor, have prudently warned the Municipal Council against such a hasty resolution?

" But after protesting, gentlemen, against the brilliant testimony of an admiration which is more than I deserve, let me tell you that I am touched, moved to the bottom of my soul. Your sympathy has joined on that memorial plate the two great things which have been the passion and the delight of my life : the love of Science and the cult of the home.

"Oh ! my father, my mother, dear departed ones, who lived so humbly in this little house, it is to you that I owe everything. Thy enthusiasm, my brave-hearted mother, thou hast instilled it into me. If I have always associated the greatness of Science with the greatness of France, it is because I was impregnated with the feelings that thou hadst inspired. And thou, dearest father, whose life was as hard as thy hard trade, thou hast shown to me what patience and protracted effort can accomplish. It is to thee that I owe perseverance in daily work. Not only hadst thou the qualities which go to make a useful life, but also admiration for great men and great things. To look upwards, learn to the utmost, to seek to rise ever higher, such was thy teaching. I can see thee now, after a hard day's work, reading in the evening some story of the battles in the glorious epoch of which thou wast a witness. Whilst teaching me to read, thy care was that I should learn the greatness of France.

" Be ye blessed, my dear parents, for what ye have been, and may the homage done to-day to your little house be yours !

"I thank you, gentlemen, for the opportunity of saying aloud what I have thought for sixty years. I thank you for this fête and for your welcome, and I thank the town of Dôle, which loses sight of none of her children, and which has kept such a remembrance of me."

"Nothing is more exquisite," wrote Bouley to Pasteur, "than those feelings of a noble heart, giving credit to the parents' influence for all the glory with which their son has covered their name. All your friends recognized you, and you appeared under quite a new light to those who may have misjudged your heart by knowing of you only the somewhat bitter words of some of your Academy speeches, when the love of truth has sometimes made you forgetful of gentleness."

It might have seemed that after so much homage, especially when offered in such a delicate way as on this last occasion, Pasteur had indeed reached a pinnacle of fame. His ambition however was not satisfied. Was it then boundless, in spite of the modesty which drew all hearts towards him? What more did he wish? Two great things : to complete his studies on hydrophobia and to establish the position of his collaborators—whose name he ever associated with his work—as his acknowledged successors.

A few cases of cholera had occurred at Damietta in the month of June. The English declared that it was but endemic cholera, and opposed the quarantines. They had with them the majority of the Alexandria Sanitary Council, and could easily prevent sanitary measures from being taken. If the English, voluntarily closing their eyes to the dangers of the epidemic, had wished to furnish a new proof of the importation of cholera, they could not have succeeded better. The cholera spread, and by July 14 it had reached Cairo. Between the 14th and 22nd there were five hundred deaths per day.

Alexandria was threatened. Pasteur, before leaving Paris for Arbois, submitted to the Consulting Committee of Public Hygiene the idea of a French Scientific Mission to Alexandria. "Since the last epidemic in 1865," he said, " science has made great progress on the subject of transmissible diseases. Every one of those diseases which has been subjected to a thorough study has been found by biologists to be produced by a microscopic being developing within the body of man or of animals, and causing therein ravages which are generally mortal. All the symptoms of the disease, all the causes of death depend directly upon the physiological properties of the microbe. . . . What is wanted at this moment to satisfy the preoccupations of science is to inquire into the primary cause of the scourge. Now the present state of knowledge demands that attention should be drawn to the possible existence within the blood, or within some organ, of a micro-organism whose nature and properties would account in all probability for all the peculiarities of cholera, both as to the morbid symptoms and the mode of its propagation. The proved existence of such a microbe would soon take precedence over the whole question of the measures to be taken to arrest the evil in its course, and might perhaps suggest new methods of treatment."

Not only did the Committee of Hygiene approve of Pasteur's project, but they asked him to choose some young men whose knowledge would be equalled by their devotion. Pasteur only had to look around him. When, on his return to the laboratory, he mentioned what had taken place at the Committee of Hygiene, M. Roux immediately offered to start. A professor at the Faculty of Medicine who had some hospital practice, M. Straus, and a professor at the Alfort Veterinary School, M. Nocard, both of whom had been authorised to work in the laboratory, asked permission to accompany M. Roux. Thuillier had the same desire, but asked for twenty-four hours to think over it.

The thought of his father and mother, who had made a great many sacrifices for his education, and whose only joy was to receive him at Amiens, where they lived, during his short holidays, made him hesitate. But the thought of duty overcame his regrets; he put his papers and notes in order and went to see his dear ones again. He told his father of his intention, but his mother did not know of it. At the time when the papers spoke of a French commission to study cholera, his elder sister, who loved him with an almost motherly tenderness, said to him suddenly, "You are not going to Egypt, Louis? swear that you are not!" "I am not going to swear anything," he answered, with absolute calm; adding that he might some time go to Russia to proceed to some vaccination of anthrax, as he had done at Buda-Pesth in 1881. When he left Amiens nothing in his farewells revealed his deep emotion; it was only from Marseilles that he wrote the truth.

Administrative difficulties retarded the departure of the Commission, which only reached Egypt on August 15. Dr. Koch had also come to study cholera. The head physician of the European hospital, Dr. Ardouin, placed his wards at the entire disposal of the French savants. In a certain number of cases, it was possible to proceed to post-mortem examinations immediately after death, before putrefaction had begun. It was a great thing from the point of view of the search after a pathogenic micro-organism as well as from the anatomo-pathological point of view.

The contents of the intestines and the characteristic stools of the cholera patients offered a great variety of micro-organisms. But which was really the cause of cholera? The most varied modes of culture were attempted in vain. The same negative results followed inoculations into divers animal species, cats, dogs, swine, monkeys, pigeons, rabbits, guinea-pigs, etc., made with the blood of cholerics or with the contents of their bowels. Experiments were made with twenty-four corpses. The epidemic ceased unexpectedly. Not to waste time, while waiting for a reappearance of the disease, the French Commission took up some researches on cattle plague. Suddenly a telegram from M. Roux informed Pasteur that Thuillier had succumbed to an attack of cholera.

"I have just heard the news of a great misfortune," wrote Pasteur to J. B. Dumas on September 19; "M. Thuillier died yesterday at Alexandria of cholera. I have telegraphed to the Mayor of Amiens asking him to break the news to the family.

"Science loses in Thuillier a courageous representative with a great future before him. I lose a much-loved and devoted pupil; my laboratory one of its principal supports.

"I can only console myself for this death by thinking of our beloved country and all he has done for it."

Thuillier was only twenty-six. How had this happened? Had he neglected any of the precautions which Pasteur had written down before the departure of the Commission, and which were so minute as to be thought exaggerated?

Pasteur remained silent all day, absolutely overcome. The head of the laboratory, M. Chamberland, divining his master's grief, came to Arbois. They exchanged their sorrowful thoughts, and Pasteur fell back into his sad broodings.

A few days later, a letter from M. Roux related the sad story "Alexandria, September 21. Sir and dear master—Having just heard that an Italian ship is going to start, I am writing a few lines without waiting for the French mail. The telegraph has told you of the terrible misfortune which has befallen us."

M. Roux then proceeded to relate in detail the symptoms presented by the unfortunate young man, who, after going to bed at ten o'clock, apparently in perfect health, had suddenly been taken ill about three o'clock in the morning of Saturday, September 15. At eight o'clock, all the horrible symptoms of the most violent form of cholera were apparent, and his friends gave him up for lost. They continued their desperate endeavours however, assisted by the whole staff of French and Italian doctors.

" By dint of all our strength, all our energy, we protracted the struggle until seven o'clock on Wednesday morning, the 19th. The asphyxia, which had then lasted twenty-four hours, was stronger than our efforts.

" Your own feelings will help you to imagine our grief.

" The French colony and the medical staff are thunder-struck. Splendid funeral honours have been rendered to our poor Thuillier.

" He was buried at four o'clock on Wednesday afternoon, with the finest and most imposing manifestation Alexandria had seen for a long time.

" One very precious and affecting homage was rendered by the German Commission with a noble simplicity which touched us all very much.

" M. Koch and his collaborators arrived when the news spread in the town. They gave utterance to beautiful and touching words to the memory of our dead friend. When the funeral took place, those gentlemen brought two wreaths which they themselves nailed on the coffin. 'They are simple,' said M. Koch, 'but they are of laurel, such as are given to the brave.'

" M. Koch held one corner of the pall. We embalmed our comrade's body ; he lies in a sealed zinc coffin. All formalities have been complied with, so that his remains may be brought back to France when the necessary time has expired. In Egypt the period of delay is a whole year.

" The French colony desires to erect a monument to the memory of Louis Thuillier.

" Dear master, how much more I should like to tell you ! The recital of the sad event which happened so quickly would take pages. This blow is altogether incomprehensible. It was more than a fortnight since we had seen a single case of cholera ; we were beginning to study cattle-plague.

" Of us all, Thuillier was the one who took most precautions ; he was irreproachably careful.

" We are writing by this post a few lines to his family, in the names of all of us.

" Such are the blows cholera can strike at the end of an epidemic ! Want of time forces me to close this letter. Pray believe in our respectful affection."

The whole of the French colony, who received great marks of sympathy from the Italians and other foreigners, wished to perpetuate the memory of Thuillier. Pasteur wrote, on October 16, to a French physician at Alexandria, who had informed him of this project :

" I am touched with the generous resolution of the French colony at Alexandria to erect a monument to the memory of Louis Thuillier. That valiant and beloved young man was deserving of every honour. I know, perhaps better than any one, the loss inflicted on science by his cruel death. I cannot console myself, and I am already dreading the sight of the dear fellow's empty place in my laboratory."

On his return to Paris, Pasteur read a paper to the Academy of Sciences, in his own name and in that of Thuillier, on the now well-ascertained mode of vaccination for swine-fever. He began by recalling Thuillier's worth ·

" Thuillier entered my laboratory after taking the first rank at the Physical Science Agrégation competition at the Ecole Normale. His was a deeply meditative, silent nature ; his whole person breathed a virile energy which struck all those who knew him. An indefatigable worker, he was ever ready for self-sacrifice."

A few days before, M. Straus had given to the Biology Society a summary statement of the studies of the Cholera Commission, concluding thus : " The documents collected during those two months are far from solving the etiological problem of cholera, but will perhaps not be useless for the orientation of future research."

The cholera bacillus was put in evidence, later on, by Dr. Koch, who had already suspected it during his researches in Egypt.

Glory, which had been seen in the battlefield at the beginning of the nineteenth century, now seemed to elect to dwell in the laboratory, that "temple of the future" as Pasteur called it. From every part of the world, letters reached Pasteur, appeals, requests for consultations. Many took him for a physician. "He does not cure individuals," answered Edmund About one day to a foreigner who was under that misapprehension; "he only tries to cure humanity." Some sceptical minds were predicting failure to his studies on hydrophobia. This problem was complicated by the fact that Pasteur was trying in vain to discover and isolate the specific microbe.

He was endeavouring to evade that difficulty; the idea pursued him that human medicine might avail itself of "the long period of incubation of hydrophobia, by attempting to establish, during that interval before the appearance of the first rabic symptoms, a refractory condition in the subjects bitten."

At the beginning of the year 1884, J. B. Dumas enjoyed following from a distance Pasteur's readings at the Académie des Sciences. His failing health and advancing age (he was more than eighty years old) had forced him to spend the winter in the South of France. On January 26, 1884, he wrote to Pasteur for the last time, à propos of a book [1] which was a short summary of Pasteur's discoveries and their concatenation :

"Dear colleague and friend,—I have read with a great and sincere emotion the picture of your scientific life drawn by a faithful and loving hand.

"Myself a witness and a sincere admirer of your happy efforts, your fruitful genius and your imperturbable method, I consider it a great service rendered to Science, that the accurate and complete whole should be put before the eyes of young people.

"It will make a wholesome impression on the public in general; to young scientists, it will be an initiation, and to those who, like me, have passed the age of labour it will bring happy memories of youthful enthusiasm.

"May Providence long spare you to France, and maintain in you that admirable equilibrium between the mind that observes, the genius that conceives, and the hand that executes with a perfection unknown until now."

This was a last proof of Dumas' affection for Pasteur. Although his life was now fast drawing to its close, his mental faculties were in no wise impaired, for we find him three weeks later, on February 20, using his influence as Permanent Secre-

[1] *La Vie d'un Savant*, by the author of the present work. [Trans.]

tary of the Academy to obtain the Lacaze prize for M. Cailletet, the inventor of the well-known apparatus for the liquefaction of gases.

J. B. Dumas died on April 11, 1884. Pasteur was then about to start for Edinburgh on the occasion of the tercentenary of the celebrated Scotch University. The "Institut de France," invited to take part in these celebrations, had selected representatives from each of the five Academies : the Académie Française was sending M. Caro ; the Academy of Sciences, Pasteur and de Lesseps ; the Academy of Moral Sciences, M. Gréard ; the Academy of Inscriptions and Letters, M. Perrot ; and the Academy of Fine Arts, M. Eugéne Guillaume. The Collége de France sent M. Guillaume Guizot, and the Academy of Medicine Dr. Henry Gueneau de Mussy.

Pasteur much wished to relinquish this official journey ; the idea that he would not be able to follow to the grave the incomparable teacher of his youth, the counsellor and confidant of his life, was infinitely painful to him.

He was however reconciled to it by one of his colleagues, M. Méziéres, who was going to Edinburgh on behalf of the Minister of Public Instruction, and who pointed out to him that the best way of honouring Dumas' memory lay in remembering Dumas' chief object in life—the interests of France. Pasteur went, hoping that he would have an opportunity of speaking of Dumas to the Edinburgh students.

In London, the French delegates had the pleasant surprise of finding that a private saloon had been reserved to take Pasteur and his friends to Edinburgh. This hospitality was offered to Pasteur by one of his numerous admirers, Mr. Younger, an Edinburgh brewer, as a token of gratitude for his discoveries in the manufacture of beer. He and his wife and children welcomed Pasteur with the warmest cordiality, when the train reached Edinburgh ; the principal inhabitants of the great Scotch city vied with each other in entertaining the French delegates, who were delighted with their reception.

The next morning, they, and the various representatives from all parts of the world, assembled in the Cathedral of St. Giles, where, with the exalted feeling which, in the Scotch people, mingles religious with political life, the Town Council had decided that a service should inaugurate the rejoicings. The Rev. Robert Flint, mounting that pulpit from which the impetuous John Knox, Calvin's friend and disciple, had breathed forth his violent fanaticism, preached to the immense assembly with a full consciousness of the importance of his discourse. He spoke of the relations between Science and Faith, of the absolute liberty of science in the realm of facts, of the thought of God considered as a stimulant to research, progress being but a Divine impulse.

In the afternoon, the students imparted life and merriment into the proceedings ; they had organized a dramatic performance, the members of the orchestra, even, being undergraduates.

The French delegates took great interest in the system of this University. Accustomed as they were to look upon the State as sole master and dispenser, they now saw an independent institution, owing its fortune to voluntary contributions, revealing in every point the power of private enterprise. Unlike what takes place in France, where administrative unity makes itself felt in the smallest village, the British Government effaces itself, and merely endeavours to inspire faith in political unity. Absolutely her own mistress, the University of Edinburgh is free to confer high honorary degrees on her distinguished visitors. However, these honorary diplomas are but of two kinds, viz. : Doctor of Divinity (D.D.) and Doctor of Laws (LL.D.). In 1884, seventeen degrees of D.D. and 122 degrees of LL.D. were reserved for the various delegates. "The only laws I know," smilingly said the learned Helmholtz, "are the laws of Physics."

The solemn proclamation of the University degrees took place on Thursday, April 17. The streets and monuments of the beautiful city were decorated with flags, and an air of rejoicing pervaded the whole atmosphere.

The ceremony began by a special prayer, alluding to the past, looking forward to the future, and asking for God's blessing on the delegates and their countries. The large assembly filled the immense hall where the Synod of the Presbyterian Church holds its meetings. The Chancellor and the Rector of the University were seated on a platform with a large number of professors ; those who were about to receive honorary degrees occupied seats in the centre of the hall ; about three thousand students found seats in various parts of the hall.

The Chancellor of the University of Edinburgh had arranged that the new graduates should be called in alphabetical order. As each of them heard his name, he rose and mounted the platform. The students took gréat pleasure in heartily cheer-

C C

ing those savants who had had most influence on their studies.
When Pasteur's name was pronounced, a great silence ensued ;
every one was trying to obtain a sight of him as he walked
towards the platform. His appearance was the signal for a
perfect outburst of applause ; five thousand men rose and cheered
him. It was indeed a splendid ovation.

In the evening, a banquet was set out in the hall, which was
hung with the blue and white colours of the University ; there
were a thousand guests, seated round twenty-eight tables, one
of which, the high table, was reserved for the speakers who were
to propose the toasts, which were to last four hours. Pasteur
was seated next to Virchow ; they talked together of the question
of rabies, and Virchow owned that, when he saw Pasteur in
1881 about to tackle this question, he much doubted the possibility of a solution. This friendly chat between two such men
proves the desirability of such gatherings ; intercourse between
the greatest scientists can but lead to general peace and fraternity between nations. After having read a telegram from
the Queen, congratulating the University and welcoming the
guests, a toast was drunk to the Queen and to the Royal Family,
and a few words spoken by the representative of the Emperor of
Brazil. Pasteur then rose to speak :

" My Lord Chancellor, Gentlemen, the city of Edinburgh is
now offering a sight of which she may be proud. All the great
scientific institutions, meeting here, appear as an immense Congress of hopes and congratulations. The honour and glory of
this international rendezvous deservedly belong to you, for it is
centuries since Scotland united her destinies with those of the
human mind. She was one of the first among the nations to
understand that intellect leads the world. And the world of
intellect, gladly answering your call, lays a well-merited homage
at your feet. When, yesterday, the eminent Professor Robert
Flint, addressing the Edinburgh University from the pulpit of
St. Giles, exclaimed, 'Remember the past and look to the
future,' all the delegates, seated like judges at a great tribunal,
evoked a vision of past centuries and joined in a unanimous wish
for a yet more glorious future.

" Amongst the illustrious delegates of all nations who bring
you an assurance of cordial good wishes, France has sent to
represent her those of her institutions which are most representative of the French spirit and the best part of French glory.
France is ready to applaud whenever a source of light appears in

the world; and when death strikes down a man of genius, France is ready to weep as for one of her own children. This noble spirit of solidarity was brought home to me when I heard some of you speak feelingly of the death of the illustrious chemist, J. B. Dumas, a celebrated member of all your Academies, and only a few years ago an eloquent panegyrist of your great Faraday. It was a bitter grief to me that I had to leave Paris before his funeral ceremony; but the hope of rendering here a last and solemn homage to that revered master helped me to conquer my affliction. Moreover, gentlemen, men may pass, but their works remain; we all are but passing guests of these great homes of intellect, which, like all the Universities who have come to greet you in this solemn day, are assured of immortality."

Pasteur, having thus rendered homage to J. B. Dumas, and having glorified his country by his presence, his speech and the great honours conferred on him, would have returned home at once; but the undergraduates begged to be allowed to entertain, the next day, some of those men whom they looked upon as examples and whom they might never see again.

Pasteur thanked the students for this invitation, which filled him with pride and pleasure, for he had always loved young people, he said, and continued, in his deep, stirring voice ·

"Ever since I can remember my life as a man, I do not think I have ever spoken for the first time with a student without saying to him, 'Work perseveringly; work can be made into a pleasure, and alone is profitable to man, to his city, to his country.' It is even more natural that I should thus speak to you. The common soul (if I may so speak) of an assembly of young men is wholly formed of the most generous feelings, being yet illumined with the divine spark which is in every man as he enters this world. You have just given a proof of this assurance, and I have felt moved to the heart in hearing you applaud, as you have just been doing, such men as de Lesseps, Helmholtz and Virchow. Your language has borrowed from ours the beautiful word *enthusiasm*, bequeathed to us by the Greeks: εν θεός, an inward God. It was almost with a divine feeling that you just now cheered those great men.

"One of those of our writers who have best made known to France and to Europe the philosophy of Robert Reid and Dugald Stewart said, addressing young men in the preface of one of his works:

"'Whatever career you may embrace, look up to an exalted goal; worship great men and great things.'

"Great things! You have indeed seen them. Will not this centenary remain one of Scotland's glorious memories? As to great men, in no country is their memory better honoured than in yours. But, if work should be the very life of your life, if the cult for great men and great things should be associated with your every thought, that is still not enough. Try to bring into everything you undertake the spirit of scientific method, founded on the immortal works of Galileo, Descartes and Newton.

"You especially, medical students of this celebrated University of Edinburgh—who, trained as you are by eminent masters, may aspire to the highest scientific ambition—be you inspired by the experimental method. To its principles, Scotland owes such men as Brewster, Thomson and Lister."

The speaker who had to respond on behalf of the students to the foreign delegates expressed himself thus, directly addressing Pasteur:

"Monsieur Pasteur, you have snatched from nature secrets too carefully, almost maliciously hidden. We greet in you a benefactor of humanity, all the more so because we know that you admit the existence of spiritual secrets, revealed to us by what you have just called the work of God in us.

"Representatives of France, we beg you to tell your great country that we are following with admiration the great reforms now being introduced into every branch of your education, reforms which we look upon as tokens of a beneficent rivalry and of a more and more cordial intercouse—for misunderstandings result from ignorance, a darkness lightened by the work of scientists."

The next morning, at ten o'clock, crowds gathered on the station platform with waving handkerchiefs. People were showing each other a great Edinburgh daily paper, in which Pasteur's speech to the undergraduates was reproduced and which also contained the following announcement in large print:

"In memory of M. Pasteur's visit to Edinburgh, Mr. Younger offers to the Edinburgh University a donation of £500."

Livingstone's daughter, Mrs. Bruce, on whom Pasteur had called the preceding day, came to the station a few moments before the departure of the train, bringing him a book entitled *The Life of Livingstone*.

The saloon carriage awaited Pasteur and his friends. They departed, delighted with the hospitality they had received, and much struck with the prominent place given to science and the welcome accorded to Pasteur. "This is indeed glory," said one of them. "Believe me," said Pasteur, " I only look upon it as a reason for continuing to go forward as long as my strength does not fail me."

CHAPTER XII

AMIDST the various researches undertaken in his laboratory, one study was placed by Pasteur above every other, one mystery constantly haunted his mind—that of hydrophobia. When he was received at the Académie Française, Renan, hoping to prove himself a prophet for once, said to him : " Humanity will owe to you deliverance from a horrible disease and also from a sad anomaly : I mean the distrust which we cannot help mingling with the caresses of the animal in whom we see most of nature's smiling benevolence."

The two first mad dogs brought into the laboratory were given to Pasteur, in 1880, by M. Bourrel, an old army veterinary surgeon who had long been trying to find a remedy for hydrophobia. He had invented a preventive measure which consisted in filing down the teeth of dogs, so that they should not bite into the skin ; in 1874, he had written that vivisection threw no light on that disease, the laws of which were " impenetrable to science until now." It now occurred to him that, perhaps, the investigators in the laboratory of the Ecole Normale might be more successful than he had been in his kennels in the Rue Fontaine-au-Roi.

One of the two dogs he sent was suffering from what is called *dumb madness* : his jaw hung, half opened and paralyzed, his tongue was covered with foam, and his eyes full of wistful anguish ; the other made ferocious darts at anything held out to him, with a rabid fury in his bloodshot eyes, and, in the hallucinations of his delirium, gave vent to haunting, despairing howls.

Much confusion prevailed at that time regarding this disease, its seat, its causes, and its remedy. Three things seemed positive : firstly, that the rabic virus was contained in the saliva of the mad animals ; secondly, that it was communicated through bites ; and thirdly, that the period of incubation might vary from a few days to several months. Clinical observation was reduced to complete impotence ; perhaps experiments might throw some light on the subject.

Bouley had affirmed in April, 1870, that the germ of the evil was localized in the saliva, and a new fact had seemed to support this theory. On December 10, 1880, Pasteur was advised by Professor Lannelongue that a five-year-old child, bitten on the face a month before, had just been admitted into the Hôpital Trousseau. The unfortunate little patient presented all the characteristics of hydrophobia : spasms, restlessness, shudders at the least breath of air, an ardent thirst, accompanied with an absolute impossibility of swallowing, convulsive movements, fits of furious rage—not one symptom was absent. The child died after twenty-four hours of horrible suffering—suffocated by the mucus which filled the mouth. Pasteur gathered some of that mucus four hours after the child's death, and mixed it with water ; he then inoculated this into some rabbits, which died in less than thirty-six hours, and whose saliva, injected into other rabbits, provoked an almost equally rapid death. Dr. Maurice Raynaud, who had already declared that hydrophobia could be transmitted to rabbits through the human saliva, and who had also caused the death of some rabbits with the saliva of that same child, thought himself justified in saying that those rabbits had died of hydrophobia.

Pasteur was slower in drawing conclusions. He had examined with a microscope the blood of those rabbits which had died in the laboratory, and had found in it a micro-organism ; he had cultivated this organism in veal broth, inoculated it into rabbits and dogs, and, its virulence having manifested itself in these animals, their blood had been found to contain that same microbe. "But," added Pasteur at the meeting of the Academy of Medicine (January 18, 1881), " I am absolutely ignorant of the connection there may be between this new disease and hydrophobia." It was indeed a singular thing that the deadly issue of this disease should occur so early, when the incubation period of hydrophobia is usually so long. Was there not some unknown microbe associated with the rabic saliva? This query was followed by experiments made with the saliva of children who had died of ordinary diseases, and even with that of healthy adults. Thuillier, following up and studying this saliva microbe and its special virulence with his usual

patience, soon applied to it with success the method of attenuation by the oxygen in air. "What did we want with a new
disease?" said a good many people, and yet it was making a
step forward to clear up this preliminary confusion. Pasteur,
in the course of a long and minute study of the saliva of mad
dogs—in which it was so generally admitted that the virulent
principle of rabies had its seat, that precautions against saliva
were the only ones taken at post-mortem examinations—discovered many other mistakes. If a healthy dog's saliva contains
many microbes, licked up by the dog in various kinds of dirt, what
must be the condition of the mouth of a rabid dog, springing upon
everything he meets, to tear it and bite it? The rabic virus is
therefore associated with many other micro-organisms, ready to
play their part and puzzle experimentalists; abscesses, morbid
complications of all sorts, may intervene before the development of the rabic virus. Hydrophobia might evidently be
developed by the inoculation of saliva, but it could not be confidently asserted that it would. Pasteur had made endless
efforts to inoculate rabies to rabbits solely through the saliva
of a mad dog; as soon as a case of hydrophobia occurred in
Bourrel's kennels, a telegram informed the laboratory, and a
few rabbits were immediately taken round in a cab.

One day, Pasteur having wished to collect a little saliva from
the jaws of a rabid dog, so as to obtain it directly, two of Bourrel's
assistants undertook to drag a mad bulldog, foaming at the
mouth, from its cage; they seized it by means of a lasso, and
stretched it on a table. These two men, thus associated with
Pasteur in the same danger, with the same calm heroism, held
the struggling, ferocious animal down with their powerful
hands, whilst the scientist drew, by means of a glass tube held
between his lips, a few drops of the deadly saliva.

But the same uncertainty followed the inoculation of the
saliva; the incubation was so slow that weeks and months
often elapsed whilst the result of an experiment was being
anxiously awaited. Evidently the saliva was not a sure agent
for experiments, and if more knowledge was to be obtained,
some other means had to be found of obtaining it.

Magendie and Renault had both tried experimenting with
rabic blood, but with no results, and Paul Bert had been
equally unsuccessful. Pasteur tried in his turn, but also in
vain. "We must try other experiments," he said, with his
usual indefatigable perseverance.

As the number of cases observed became larger, he felt a growing conviction that hydrophobia has its seat in the nervous system, and particularly in the medulla oblongata. "The propagation of the virus in a rabid dog's nervous system can almost be observed in its every stage," writes M. Roux, Pasteur's daily associate in these researches, which he afterwards made the subject of his thesis. "The anguish and fury due to the excitation of the grey cortex of the brain are followed by an alteration of the voice and a difficulty in deglutition. The medulla oblongata and the nerves starting from it are attacked in their turn; finally, the spinal cord itself becomes invaded and paralysis closes the scene."

As long as the virus has not reached the nervous centres, it may sojourn for weeks or months in some point of the body; this explains the slowness of certain incubations, and the fortunate escapes after some bites from rabid dogs. The *a priori* supposition that the virus attacks the nervous centres went very far back; it had served as a basis to a theory enunciated by Dɪ. Duboné (of Pau), who had, however, not supported it by any experiments. On the contrary, when M. Galtier, a professor at the Lyons Veterinary School, had attempted experiments in that direction, he had to inform the Academy of Medicine, in January, 1881, that he had only ascertained the existence of virus in rabid dogs in the lingual glands and in the buccopharyngeal mucous membrane. "More than ten times, and always unsuccessfully, have I inoculated the product obtained by pressure of the cerebral substances of the cerebellum or of the medulla oblongata of rabid dogs."

Pasteur was about to prove that it was possible to succeed by operating in a special manner, according to a rigorous technique, unknown in other laboratories. When the post-mortem examination of a mad dog had revealed no characteristic lesion, the brain was uncovered, and the surface of the medulla oblongata scalded with a glass stick, so as to destroy any external dust or dirt. Then, with a long tube, previously put through a flame, a particle of the substance was drawn and deposited in a glass just taken from a stove heated up to 200° C., and mixed with a little water or sterilized broth by means of a glass agitator, also previously put through a flame. The syringe used for inoculation on the rabbit or dog (lying ready on the operating board) had been purified in boiling water

Most of the animals who received this inoculation under the

skin succumbed to hydrophobia ; that virulent matter was therefore more successful than the saliva, which was a great result obtained.

" The seat of the rabic virus," wrote Pasteur, " is therefore not in the saliva only : the brain contains it in a degree of virulence at least equal to that of the saliva of rabid animals." But, to Pasteur's eyes, this was but a preliminary step on the long road which stretched before him ; it was necessary that all the inoculated animals should contract hydrophobia, and the period of incubation had to be shortened.

It was then that it occurred to Pasteur to inoculate the rabic virus directly on the surface of a dog's brain. He thought that, by placing the virus from the beginning in its true medium, hydrophobia would more surely supervene and the incubation might be shorter. The experiment was attempted : a dog under chloroform was fixed to the operating board, and a small, round portion of the cranium removed by means of a trephine (a surgical instrument somewhat similar to a fret-saw) ; the tough fibrous membrane called the dura-mater, being thus exposed, was then injected with a small quantity of the prepared virus, which lay in readiness in a Pravaz syringe. The wound was washed with carbolic and the skin stitched together, the whole thing lasting but a few minutes. The dog, on returning to consciousness, seemed quite the same as usual. But, after fourteen days, hydrophobia appeared : rabid fury, characteristic howls, the tearing up and devouring of his bed, delirious hallucination, and finally, paralysis and death.

A method was therefore found by which rabies was contracted surely and swiftly. Trephinings were again performed on chloroformed animals—Pasteur had a great horror of useless sufferings, and always insisted on anæsthesia. In every case, characteristic hydrophobia occurred after inoculation on the brain. The main lines of this complicated question were beginning to be traceable ; but other obstacles were in the way. Pasteur could not apply the method he had hitherto used, i.e. to isolate, and then to cultivate in an artificial medium, the microbe of hydrophobia, for he failed in detecting this microbe. Yet its existence admitted of no doubt ; perhaps it was beyond the limits of human sight. " Since this unknown being is living," thought Pasteur, " we must cultivate it ; failing an artificial medium, let us try the brain of living rabbits; it would indeed be an experimental feat!"

As soon as a trephined and inoculated rabbit died paralyzed, a little of his rabic medulla was inoculated to another; each inoculation succeeded another, and the time of incubation became shorter and shorter, until, after a hundred uninterrupted inoculations, it came to be reduced to seven days. But the virus, having reached this degree, the virulence of which was found to be greater than that of the virus of dogs made rabid by an accidental bite, now became fixed; Pasteur had mastered it. He could now predict the exact time when death should occur in each of the inoculated animals; his predictions were verified with surprising accuracy.

Pasteur was not yet satisfied with the immense progress marked by infallible inoculation and the shortened incubation; he now wished to decrease the degrees of virulence—when the attenuation of the virus was once conquered, it might be hoped that dogs could be made refractory to rabies. Pasteur abstracted a fragment of the medulla from a rabbit which had just died of rabies after an inoculation of the fixed virus; this fragment was suspended by a thread in a sterilized phial, the air in which was kept dry by some pieces of caustic potash lying at the bottom of the vessel and which was closed by a cotton-wool plug to prevent the entrance of atmospheric dusts. The temperature of the room where this desiccation took place was maintained at 23° C. As the medulla gradually became dry, its virulence decreased, until, at the end of fourteen days, it had become absolutely extinguished. This now inactive medulla was crushed and mixed with pure water, and injected under the skin of some dogs. The next day they were inoculated with medulla which had been desiccating for thirteen days, and so on, using increased virulence until the medulla was used of a rabbit dead the same day. These dogs might now be bitten by rabid dogs given them as companions for a few minutes, or submitted to the intracranial inoculations of the deadly virus: they resisted both.

Having at last obtained this refractory condition, Pasteur was anxious that his results should be verified by a Commission. The Minister of Public Instruction acceded to this desire, and a Commission was constituted in May, 1884, composed of Messrs. Béclard, Dean of the Faculty of Medicine, Paul Bert, Bouley, Villemin, Vulpian, and Tisserand, Director of the

Agriculture Office.　The Commission immediately set to work ;
a rabid dog having succumbed at Alfort on June 1, its carcase
was brought to the laboratory of the Ecole Normale, and a fragment of the medulla oblongata was mixed with some sterilized
broth.　Two dogs, declared by Pasteur to be refractory to
rabies, were trephined, and a few drops of the liquid injected
into their brains ; two other dogs and two rabbits received
inoculations at the same time, with the same liquid and in
precisely the same manner.

Bouley was taking notes for a report to be presented to the
Minister :

"M. Pasteur tells us that, considering the nature of the
rabic virus used, the rabbits and the two new dogs will develop
rabies within twelve or fifteen days, and that the two refractory
dogs will not develop it at all, however long they may be
detained under observation."

On May 29, Mme. Pasteur wrote to her children :

"The Commission on rabies met to-day and elected M.
Bouley as chairman.　Nothing is settled as to commencing
experiments.　Your father is absorbed in his thoughts, talks
little, sleeps little, rises at dawn, and, in one word, continues
the life I began with him this day thirty-five years ago."

On June 3, Bourrel sent word that he had a rabid dog in
the kennels of the Rue Fontaine-au-Roi ; a refractory dog
and a new dog were immediately submitted to numerous
bites ; the latter was violently bitten on the head in several
places.　The rabid dog, still living the next day and still able
to bite, was given two more dogs, one of which was refractory ;
this dog, and the refractory dog bitten on the 3rd, were
allowed to receive the first bites, the Commission having
thought that perhaps the saliva might then be more abundant
and more dangerous.

On June 6, the rabid dog having died, the Commission proceeded to inoculate the medulla of the animal into six more
dogs, by means of trephining.　Three of those dogs were
refractory, the three others were fresh from the kennels ; there
were also two rabbits.

On the 10th, Bourrel telegraphed the arrival of another
rabid dog, and the same operations were gone through.

"This rabid, furious dog," wrote Pasteur to his son-in-law,
"had spent the night lying on his master's bed ; his appearance
had been suspicious for a day or two.　On the morning of the

10th, his voice became rabietic, and his master, who had heard the bark of a rabid dog twenty years ago, was seized with terror, and brought the dog to M. Bourrel, who found that he was indeed in the biting stage of rabies. Fortunately a lingering fidelity had prevented him from attacking his master. .

"This morning the rabic condition is beginning to appear on one of the new dogs trephined on June 1, at the same time as two refractory dogs. Let us hope that the other new dog will also develop it and that the two refractory ones will resist."

At the same time that the Commission examined this dog which developed rabies within the exact time indicated by Pasteur, the two rabbits on whom inoculation had been performed at the same time were found to present the first symptoms of rabic paralysis. "This paralysis," noted Bouley, is revealed by great weakness of the limbs, particularly of the hind quarters; the least shock knocks them over and they experience great difficulty in getting up again." The second new dog on whom inoculation had been performed on June 1 was now also rabid; the refractory dogs were in perfect health.

During the whole of June, Pasteur found time to keep his daughter and son-in-law informed of the progress of events. "Keep my letters," he wrote, "they are almost like copies of the notes taken on the experiments."

Towards the end of the month, dozens of dogs were submitted to control-experiments which were continued until August. The dogs which Pasteur declared to be refractory underwent all the various tests made with rabic virus; bites, injections into the veins, trephining, everything was tried before Pasteur would decide to call them vaccinated. On June 17, Bourrel sent word that the new dog bitten on June 3 was becoming rabic; the members of the Commission went to the Rue Fontaine-au-Roi. The period of incubation had only lasted fourteen days, a fact attributed by Bouley to the bites having been chiefly about the head. The dog was destroying his kennel and biting his chain ferociously. More new dogs developed rabies the following days. Nineteen new dogs had been experimented upon : three died out of six bitten by a rabid dog, six out of eight after intravenous inoculation, and five out of five after subdural inoculation. Bouley thought that a few more cases might occur, the period of incubation after bites being so extremely irregular.

Bouley's report was sent to the Minister of Public Instruction at the beginning of August. "We submit to you to-day," he wrote, "this report on the first series of experiments that we have just witnessed, in order that M. Pasteur may refer to it in the paper which he proposes to read at the Copenhagen International Scientific Congress on these magnificent results, which devolve so much credit on French Science and which give it a fresh claim to the world's gratitude."

The Commission wished that a large kennel yard might be built, in order that the duration of immunity in protected dogs might be timed, and that other great problem solved, viz., whether it would be possible, through the inoculation of attenuated virus, to defy the virus from bites.

By the Minister's request, the Commission investigated the Meudon woods in search of a favourable site; an excellent place was found in the lower part of the Park, away from dwelling houses, easy to enclose and presumably in no one's way. But, when the inhabitants of Meudon heard of this project, they protested vehemently, evidently terrified at the thought of rabid dogs, however securely bound, in their peaceful neighbourhood.

Another piece of ground was then suggested to Pasteur, near St. Cloud, in the Park of Villeneuve l'Etang. Originally a State domain, this property had been put up for sale, but had found no buyer, not being suitable for parcelling out in small lots; the Bill was withdrawn which allowed of its sale and the greater part of the domain was devoted by the Ministry to Pasteur's and his assistants' experiments on the prophylaxis of contagious diseases.

Pasteur, his mind full of ideas, started for the International Medical Congress, which was now to take place at Copenhagen. Sixteen hundred members arranged to attend, and nearly all of them found on arriving that they were to be entertained in the houses of private individuals. The Danes carry hospitality to the most generous excess; several of them had been learning French for the last three years, the better to entertain the French delegates. Pasteur's son, then secretary of the French Legation at Copenhagen, had often spoken to his father with appreciative admiration of those Northerners, who hide deep enthusiasm under apparent calmness, almost coldness.

The opening meeting took place on August 10 in the large ball of the Palace of Industry; the King and Queen of Denmark and the King and Queen of Greece were present at that impressive gathering. The President, Professor Panum, welcomed the foreign members in the name of his country; he proclaimed the neutrality of Science, adding that the three official languages to be used during the Congress would be French, English, and German. His own speech was entirely in French, " the language which least divides us," he said, "and which we are accustomed to look upon as the most courteous in the world."

The former president of the London Congress, Sir James Paget, emphasized the scientific consequences of those triennial meetings, showing that, thanks to them, nations may calculate the march of progress.

Virchow, in the name of Germany, developed the same idea.

Pasteur, representing France, showed again as he had done at Milan in 1878, in London in 1881, at Geneva in 1882, and quite recently in Edinburgh, how much the scientist and the patriot were one in him.

" In the name of France," said he, " I thank M. le Président for his words of welcome . . . By our presence in this Congress, we affirm the neutrality of Science

Science is of no country. . . . But if Science has no country, the scientist must keep in mind all that may work towards the glory of his country. In every great scientist will be found a great patriot. The thought of adding to the greatness of his country sustains him in his long efforts, and throws him into the difficult but glorious scientific enterprises which bring about real and durable conquests. Humanity then profits by those labours coming from various directions.   "

At the end of the meeting Pasteur was presented to the King. The Queen of Denmark and the Queen of Greece, regardless of etiquette, walked towards him, " a signal proof," wrote a French contemporary, " of the esteem in which our illustrious countryman is held at the Danish Court."

Five general meetings were to give some of the scientists an opportunity of expounding their views on subjects of universal interest. Pasteur was asked to read the first paper; his audience consisted, besides the members of the Congress, of

many other men interested in scientific things, who had come
to hear him describe the steps by which he had made such
secure progress in the arduous question of hydrophobia. He
began by a declaration of war against the prejudice by which
so many people believe that rabies can occur spontaneously.
Whatever the pathological, physiological, or other conditions
may be under which a dog or another animal is placed, rabies
never appears if the animal has not been bitten or licked by
another rabid animal; this is so truly the case that hydrophobia
is unknown in certain countries. In order to preserve a whole
land from the disease, it is sufficient that a law should, as in
Australia, compel every imported dog to be in quarantine for
several months; he would then, if bitten by a mad dog before
his departure, have ample time to die before infecting other
animals. Norway and Lapland are equally free from rabies, a
few good prophylactic measures being sufficient to avert the
scourge.

It will be objected that there must have been a first rabid
dog originally. "That," said Pasteur, "is a problem which
cannot be solved in the present state of knowledge, for it par-
takes of the great and unknown mystery of the origin of life."

The audience followed with an impassioned curiosity the
history of the stages followed by Pasteur on the road to his
great discovery : the preliminary experiments, the demonstration of the fact that the rabic virus invades the nervous centres,
the culture of the virus within living animals, the attenuation of the rabic virus when passed from dogs to monkeys, and
simultaneously with this graduated attenuation, a converse
process by successive passages from rabbit to rabbit, the possibility of obtaining in this way all the degrees of virulence,
and finally the acquired certainty of having obtained a preventive vaccine against canine hydrophobia.

"Enthusiastic applause," wrote the reporter of the *Journal
des Débats*, "greeted the conclusion of the indefatigable
worker."

In the course of one of the excursions arranged for the
members of the Congress, Pasteur had the pleasure of seeing
his methods applied on a large scale, not as in Italy to the
progress of sericiculture, but to that of the manufacture of
beer. J. C. Jacobsen, a Danish citizen, whose name was
celebrated in the whole of Europe by his munificent donations
to science, had founded in 1847 the Carlsberg Brewery, now

one of the most important in the world; at least 200,000 hecto-litres were now produced every year by the Carlsberg Brewery and the Ny Carlsberg branch of it, which was under the direction of Jacobsen's son.

In 1879, Jacobsen, who was unknown to Pasteur, wrote to him, "I should be very much obliged if you would allow me to order from M. Paul Dubois, one of the great artists who do France so much credit, a marble bust of yourself, which I desire to place in the Carlsberg laboratory in token of the services rendered to chemistry, physiology, and beer-manu-facture, by your studies on fermentation, a foundation to all future progress in the brewer's trade." Paul Dubois' bust is a masterpiece: it is most characteristic of Pasteur—the deep thoughtful far-away look in his eyes, a somewhat stern expres-sion on his powerful features.

Actuated, like his father, by a feeling of gratitude, the younger Jacobsen had placed a bronze reproduction of this bust in a niche in the wall of the brewery, at the entrance of the Pasteur Street, leading to Ny Carlsberg.

This visit to the brewery was an object lesson to the members of the Congress, who were magnificently entertained by Jacobsen and his son; no better demonstration was ever made of the services which industry may receive from science. In the great laboratory, the physiologist Hansen had succeeded in finding differences in yeast; he had just separated from each other three kinds of yeast, each producing beer with a different flavour.

The French scientists were delighted with the practical sense and delicate feelings of the Danish people. Though they had gone through bitter trials in 1864, though France, England, and Russia had countenanced the unrighteous invasion, in the face of the old treaties which guaranteed to Denmark the possession of Schleswig, the diminished and impoverished nation had not given vent to barren recriminations or declama-tory protests. Proudly and silently sorrowing, the Danes had preserved their respect for the past, faith in justice and the cult of their great men. It is a strange thing that Shakespeare should have chosen that land of good sense and well-balanced reason for the surroundings of his mysterious hero, of all men the most haunted by the maddening enigma of destiny.

Elsinore is but a short distance from Copenhagen, and no

member of the Congress, especially among the English section, could have made up his mind to leave Denmark without visiting Hamlet's home.

A Transport Company organized the visit to Elsinore for a day when the Congress had arranged to have a complete holiday. Five steamers, gay with flags, were provided for the thousand medical men and their families, and accomplished the two hours' crossing to Elsinore on a lovely, clear day, with an absolutely calm sea. The scientific tourists landed at the foot of the old Kronborg Castle, ready for the lunch which was served out to them and which proved barely sufficient for their appetites; there was not quite enough bread for the Frenchmen, proverbially bread-eaters, and the water, running a little short, had to be supplemented with champagne.

Some of the visitors returned from a neighbouring wood, where they had been to see the stones of the supposed tomb of Hamlet, disappointed at having looked in vain for Ophelia's stream and for the willow tree which heard her sing her last song, her hands full of flowers. Evidently this place was but an imaginary scenery given by Shakespeare to the drama which stands like a point of interrogation before the mystery of human life; but his life-giving art has for ever made of Elsinore the place where Hamlet lived and suffered.

Pasteur, to whom the Danish character, in its strength and simplicity, proved singularly attractive, remained in Copenhagen for some time after the Congress was over. He had much pleasure in visiting the Thorwaldsen Museum. Copenhagen, after showering honours on the great artist during his lifetime, has continued to worship him after his death. Every statue, every plaster cast, is preserved in that Museum with extraordinary care. Thorwaldsen himself lies in the midst of his works—his simple stone grave, covered with graceful ivy, is in one of the courtyards of the Museum

Pasteur went on to Arbois from Copenhagen. The laboratory he had built there not being large enough to take in rabid dogs, he dictated from his study the experiments to be carried out in Paris; his carefully kept notebooks enabled him to know exactly how things were going on. His nephew, Adrien Loir, now a curator in the laboratory of Rue d'Ulm, had gladly given up his holidays and remained in Paris with the faithful Eugène Viala. This excellent assistant had come to Paris from Alais in 1871, at the request of Pasteur, who knew his family. Viala was then only twelve years old and could barely read and write. Pasteur sent him to an evening school and himself helped him with his studies; the boy was very intelligent and willing to learn. He became most useful to Pasteur, who, in 1885, was glad to let him undertake a great deal of the laboratory work, under the guidance of M. Roux; he was ultimately entrusted with all the trephining operations on dogs, rabbits, and guinea-pigs.

The letters written to him by Pasteur in 1884 show the exact point reached at that moment by the investigations on hydrophobia. Many people already thought those studies advanced enough to allow the method of treatment to be applied to man.

Pasteur wrote to Viala on September 19, " Tell M. Adrien (Loir) to send the following telegram : ' Surgeon Symonds, Oxford, England. Operation on man still impossible. No possibility at present of sending attenuated virus.' See MM. Bourrel and Béraud, procure a dog which has died of street-rabies, and use its medulla to inoculate a new monkey, two guinea-pigs and two rabbits. . I am afraid Nocard's dog cannot have been rabid ; even if you were sure that he was, you had better try those tests again.

" Since M. Bourrel says he has several mad dogs at present, you might take two couple of new dogs to his kennels ; when he has a good biting dog, he can have a pair of our dogs bitten, after which you will treat one of them so as to make him refractory (carefully taking note of the time elapsed between the bites and the beginning of the treatment). Mind you keep notes of every new experiment undertaken, and write to me every other day at least."

Pasteur pondered on the means of extinguishing hydrophobia or of merely diminishing its frequency. Could dogs be vaccinated ? There are 100,000 dogs in Paris, about 2,500,000 more in the provinces : vaccination necessitates several preventive inoculations ; innumerable kennels would have to be built for the purpose, to say nothing of the expense of keeping the dogs and of providing a trained staff capable of performing the difficult and dangerous operations. And, as M. Nocard truly remarked, where were rabbits to be found in sufficient number for the vaccine emulsions?

Optional vaccination did not seem more practicable ; it could only be worked on a very restricted scale and was therefore of very little use in a general way.

The main question was the possibility of preventing hydrophobia from occurring in a human being, previously bitten by a rabid dog.

The Emperor of Brazil, who took the greatest interest in the doings of the Ecole Normale laboratory, having written to Pasteur asking when the preventive treatment could be applied to man, Pasteur answered as follows—

" *September* 22.

" SIRE—Baron Itajuba, the Minister for Brazil, has handed me the letter which Your Majesty has done me the honour of writing on August 21. The Academy welcomed with unanimous sympathy your tribute to the memory of our illustrious colleague, M. Dumas; it will listen with similar pleasure to the words of regret which you desire me to express on the subject of M. Wurtz's premature death.

" Your Majesty is kind enough to mention my studies on hydrophobia; they are making good and uninterrupted progress. I consider, however, that it will take me nearly two years more to bring them to a happy issue. . . .

" What I want to do is to obtain prophylaxis of rabies *after* bites.

" Until now I have not dared to attempt anything on men, in spite of my own confidence in the result and the numerous opportunities afforded to me since my last reading at the Academy of Sciences. I fear too much that a failure might compromise the future, and I want first to accumulate successful cases on animals. Things in that direction are going very well indeed; I already have several examples of dogs made refractory after a rabietic bite. I take two dogs, cause them both to be bitten by a mad dog; I vaccinate the one and leave the other without any treatment : the latter dies and the first remains perfectly well.

" But even when I shall have multiplied examples of the prophylaxis of rabies in dogs, I think my hand will tremble when I go on to Mankind. It is here that the high and powerful initiative of the head of a State might intervene for the good of humanity. If I were a King, an Emperor, or even the President of a Republic, this is how I should exercise my right of pardoning criminals condemned to death. I should invite the counsel of a condemned man, on the eve of the day fixed for his execution, to choose between certain death and an experiment which would consist in several preventive inoculations of rabic virus, in order to make the subject's constitution refractory to rabies. If he survived this experiment—and I am convinced that he would—his life would be saved and his punishment commuted to a lifelong surveillance, as a guarantee towards that society which had condemned him.

" All condemned men would accept these conditions, death being their only terror.

" This brings me to the question of cholera, of which Your Majesty also has the kindness to speak to me. Neither Dr. Koch nor Drs. Straus and Roux have succeeded in giving cholera to animals, and therefore great uncertainty prevails regarding the bacillus to which Dr. Koch attributes the causation of cholera. It ought to be possible to try and communicate cholera to criminals condemned to death, by the injection of cultures of that bacillus. When the disease declared itself, a test could be made of the remedies which are counselled as apparently most efficacious.

" I attach so much importance to these measures, that, if Your Majesty shared my views, I should willingly come to Rio Janeiro, notwithstanding my age and the state of my health, in order to undertake such studies on the prophylaxis of hydrophobia and the contagion of cholera and its remedies.

" I am, with profound respect, Your Majesty's humble and obedient servant."

In other times, the right of pardon could be exercised in the form of a chance of life offered to a criminal lending himself to an experiment. Louis XVI, having admired a fire balloon rising above Versailles, thought of proposing to two condemned men that they should attempt to go up in one. But Pilâtre des Roziers, whose ambition it was to be the first aëronaut, was indignant at the thought that "vile criminals should be the first to rise up in the air." He won his cause, and in November, 1783, he organized an ascent at the Muette which lasted twenty minutes.

In England, in the eighteenth century, before Jenner's discovery, successful attempts had been made at the direct inoculation of small-pox. In some historical and medical *Researches on Vaccine*, published in 1803, Husson relates that the King of England, wishing to have the members of his family inoculated, began by having the method tried on six criminals condemned to death; they were all saved, and the Royal Family submitted to inoculation.

There is undoubtedly a beautiful aspect of that idea of utilizing the fate of a criminal for the cause of Humanity. But in our modern laws no such liberty is left to Justice, which has no power to invent new punishments, or to enter into a bargain with a condemned criminal.

Before his departure from Arbois, Pasteur encountered fresh and unforeseen obstacles. The successful opposition of the inhabitants of Meudon had inspired those of St. Cloud, Ville d'Avray, Vaucresson, Marnes, and Garches with the idea of resisting in their turn the installation of Pasteur's kennels at Villeneuve l'Etang. People spoke of public danger, of children exposed to meet ferocious rabid dogs wandering loose about the park, of popular Sundays spoilt, picnickers disturbed, etc., etc.

A former pupil of Pasteur's at the Strasburg Faculty, M. Christen, now a Town Councillor at Vaucresson, warned Pasteur of all this excitement, adding that he personally was ready to do his best to calm the terrors of his townspeople.

Pasteur answered, thanking him for his efforts. ". . I shall be back in Paris on October 24, and on the morning of the twenty-fifth and following days I shall be pleased to see any one desiring information on the subject. . . . But you may at once assure your frightened neighbours, Sir, that there will be no mad dogs at Villeneuve l'Etang, but only dogs made refractory to rabies. Not having enough room in my laboratory, I am actually obliged to quarter on various veterinary surgeons those dogs, which I should like to enclose in covered kennels, quite safely secured, you may be sure."

Pasteur, writing about this to his son, could not help saying, "Months of fine weather have been wasted! This will keep my plans back almost a year."

Little by little, in spite of the opposition which burst out now and again, calm was again re-established. French good sense and appreciation of great things got the better of the struggle; in January, 1885, Pasteur was able to go to Villeneuve l'Etang to superintend the arrangements. The old stables were turned into an immense kennel, paved with asphalte. A wide passage went from one end to the other, on each side of which accommodation for sixty dogs was arranged behind a double barrier of wire netting.

The subject of hydrophobia goes back to the remotest antiquity; one of Homer's warriors calls Hector a mad dog. The supposed allusions to it to be found in Hippocrates are of the vaguest, but Aristotle is quite explicit when speaking of canine rabies and of its transmission from one animal to the other through bites. He gives expression, however, to the singular opinion that man is not subject to it. More than three hundred years later we come to Celsus, who describes this disease, unknown or unnoticed until then. "The patient," said Celsus, "is tortured at the same time by thirst and by an invincible repulsion towards water." He counselled cauterization of the wound with a red-hot iron and also with various caustics and corrosives.

Pliny the Elder, a worthy precursor of village quacks, recommended the livers of mad dogs as a cure; it was not a successful one. Galen, who opposed this, had a no less singular recipe, a compound of cray-fish eyes. Later, the shrine of St. Hubert in Belgium was credited with miraculous cures; this superstition is still extant.

Sea bathing, unknown in France until the reign of Louis XIV, became a fashionable cure for hydrophobia, Dieppe sands being supposed to offer wonderful curing properties.

In 1780 a prize was offered for the best method of treating hydrophobia, and won by a pamphlet entitled *Dissertation sur la Rage*, written by a surgeon-major of the name of Le Roux.

This very sensible treatise concluded by recommending cauterization, now long forgotten, instead of the various quack remedies which had so long been in vogue, and the use of butter of antimony.

Le Roux did not allude in his paper to certain tenacious and cruel prejudices, which had caused several hydrophobic persons, or persons merely suspected of hydroprobia, to be killed like wild beasts, shot, poisoned, strangled, or suffocated.

It was supposed in some places that hydrophobia could be transmitted through the mere contact of the saliva or even by the breath of the victims; people who had been bitten were in terror of what might be done to them. A girl, bitten by a mad dog and taken to the Hôtel Dieu Hospital on May 8, 1780, begged that she might not be suffocated !

Those dreadful occurrences must have been only too frequent, for, in 1810, a philosopher asked the Government to enact a Bill in the following terms: "It is forbidden, under pain of death, to strangle, suffocate, bleed to death, or in any other way murder individuals suffering from rabies, hydrophobia, or any disease causing fits, convulsions, furious and dangerous madness; all necessary precautions against them being taken by families or public authorities."

In 1819, newspapers related the death of an unfortunate hydrophobe, smothered between two mattresses; it was said à propos of this murder that "it is the doctor's duty to repeat that this disease cannot be transmitted from man to man, and that there is therefore no danger in nursing hydrophobia patients." Though old and fantastic remedies were still in vogue in remote country places, cauterization was the most frequently employed; if the wounds were somewhat deep, it was recommended to use long, sharp and pointed needles, and to push them well in, even if the wound was on the face.

One of Pasteur's childish recollections (it happened in October, 1831) was the impression of terror produced throughout the Jura by the advent of a rabid wolf who went biting men and beasts on his way. Pasteur had seen an Arboisian of the name of Nicole being cauterized with a red-hot iron at the smithy near his father's house. The persons who had been bitten on the hands and head succumbed to hydrophobia, some of them amidst horrible sufferings; there were eight victims in the immediate neighbourhood. Nicole was saved. For years the whole region remained in dread of that mad wolf.

The long period of incubation encouraged people to hope that some preventive means might be found, instead of the painful operation of cauterization; some doctors attempted inoculating another poison, a viper's venom for instance, to neutralize the rabic virus—needless to say with fatal results. In 1852 a reward was promised by the Government to the finder of a remedy against hydrophobia; all the old quackeries came to light again, even Galen's remedy of cray-fish eyes!

Bouchardat, who had to report to the Academy on these remedies, considered them of no value whatever; his conclusion was that cauterization was the only prophylactic treatment of hydrophobia.

Such was also Bouley's opinion, eighteen years later, when he wrote that the object to keep in view was the quickest possible destruction of the tissues touched by rabietic saliva. Failing an iron heated to a light red heat, or the sprinkling of gunpowder over the wound and setting a match to it, he recommended caustics, such as nitric acid, sulphuric acid, hydrochloric acid, potassa fusa, butter of antimony, corrosive sublimate, and nitrate of silver.

Thus, after centuries had passed, and numberless remedies had been tried, no progress had been made, and nothing better had been found than cauterization, as indicated by Celsus in the first century.

As to the origin of rabies, it remained unknown and was erroneously attributed to divers causes. Spontaneity was still believed in. Bouley himself did not absolutely reject the idea of it, for he said in 1870 : " In the immense majority of cases, this disease proceeds from contagion ; out of 1,000 rabid dogs, 999 at least owe their condition to inoculation by a bite."

Pasteur was anxious to uproot this fallacy, as also another very serious error, vigorously opposed by Bouley, by M. Nocard, and by another veterinary surgeon in a *Manual on Rabies*, published in 1882, and still as tenacious as most prejudices, viz., that the word hydrophobia is synonymous with rabies. The rabid dog is *not* hydrophobe, he does *not* abhor water. The word is applicable to rabid human beings, but is false concerning rabid dogs.

Many people in the country, constantly seeing Pasteur's name associated with the word rabies, fancied that he was a consulting veterinary surgeon, and pestered him with letters full of questions. What was to be done to a dog whose manner seemed strange, though there was no evidence of a suspicious bite? Should he be shot? "No," answered Pasteur, "shut him up securely, and he will soon die if he is really mad." Some dog owners hesitated to destroy a dog manifestly bitten by a mad dog. "It is such a good dog!" "The law is absolute," answered Pasteur ; "every dog bitten by a mad dog must be destroyed at once." And it irritated him that village mayors should close their eyes to the non-observance of the law, and thus contribute to a recrudescence of rabies.

Pasteur wasted his precious time answering all those letters. On March 28, 1885, he wrote to his friend Jules Vercel

" Alas ! we shall not be able to go to Arbois for Easter ; I shall be busy for some time settling down, or rather settling my dogs down at Villeneuve l'Etang. I also have some new experiments on rabies on hand which will take some months.

I am demonstrating this year that dogs can be vaccinated, or
made refractory to rabies *after* they have been bitten by mad
dogs.

"I have not yet dared to treat human beings after bites from
rabid dogs; but the time is not far off, and I am much inclined
to begin by myself—inoculating myself with rabies, and then
arresting the consequences; for I am beginning to feel very
sure of my results."

Pasteur gave more details three days later, in a letter to his
son, then Secretary of the French Embassy at the Quirinal—

"The experiments before the Rabies Commission were
resumed on March 10; they are now being carried out, and
the Commission has already held six sittings; the seventh will
take place to-day.

"As I only submit to it results which I look upon as
acquired, this gives me a surplus of work to do; for those
control experiments are added to those I am now carrying out.
For I am continuing my researches, trying to discover new
principles, and hardening myself by habit and by increased
conviction in order to attempt preventive inoculations on man
after a bite.

"The Commission's experiments have led to no result so
far, for, as you know, weeks have to pass before any results
occur. But no untoward incident has occurred up to now; and
if all continues equally well, the Commission's second report
will be as favorable as that of last year, which left nothing to
be desired.

"I am equally satisfied with my new experiments in this
difficult study. Perhaps practical application on a large scale
may not be far off. . . ."

In May, everything at Villeneuve l'Etang was ready for the
reception of sixty dogs. Fifty of them, already made refractory to bites or rabic inoculation, were successively accommodated in the immense kennel, where each had his cell and his
experiment number. They had been made refractory by being
inoculated with fragments of medulla, which had hung for a
fortnight in a phial, and of which the virulence was extinguished, after which further inoculations had been made,
gradually increasing in virulence until the highest degree of it
had again been reached.

All those dogs, which were to be periodically taken back to
Paris for inoculations or bite tests, in order to see what was

the duration of the immunity conferred, were stray dogs picked up by the police. They were of various breeds, and showed every variety of character, some of them gentle and affectionate, others vicious and growling, some confiding, some shrinking, as if the recollection of chloroform and the laboratory was disagreeable to them. They showed some natural impatience of their enforced captivity, only interrupted by a short daily run. One of them, however, was promoted to the post of house-dog, and loosened every night; he excited much envy among his congeners. The dogs were very well cared for by a retired *gendarme*, an excellent man of the name of Pernin.

A lover of animals might have drawn an interesting contrast between the fate of those laboratory dogs, living and dying for the good of humanity, and that of the dogs buried in the neighbouring dogs' cemetery at Bagatelle, founded by Sir Richard Wallace, the great English philanthropist. Here lay toy dogs, lap dogs, drawing-room dogs, cherished and coddled during their useless lives, and luxuriously buried after their useless deaths, while the dead bodies of the others went to the knacker's yard.

Rabbit hutches and guinea-pig cages leaned against the dogs' palace. Pasteur, having seen to the comfort of his animals, now thought of himself; it was frequently necessary that he should come to spend two or three days at Villeneuve l'Etang. The official architect thought of repairing part of the little palace of Villeneuve, which was in a very bad state of decay. But Pasteur preferred to have some rooms near the stables put into repair, which had formerly been used for non-commissioned officers of the Cent Gardes; there was less to do to them, and the position was convenient. The roof, windows, and doors were renovated, and some cheap paper hung on the walls inside. " This is certainly not luxurious ! " exclaimed an astonished millionaire, who came to see Pasteur one day on his way to his own splendid villa at Marly.

On May 29 Pasteur wrote to his son—

" I thought I should have done with rabies by the end of April; I must postpone my hopes till the end of July. Yet I have not remained stationary; but, in these difficult studies, one is far from the goal as long as the last word, the last decisive proof is not acquired. What I aspire to is the possibility of treating a man after a bite with no fear of accidents.

" I have never had so many subjects of experiment on hand—

sixty dogs at Villeneuve l'Etang, forty at Rollin, ten at Frégis', fifteen at Bourrel's, and I deplore having no more kennels at my disposal.

"What do you say of the Rue Pasteur in the large city of Lille? The news has given me very great pleasure."

What Pasteur briefly called "Rollin" in this letter was the former *Lycée Rollin*, the old buildings of which had been transformed into outhouses for his laboratory. Large cages had been set up in the old courtyard, and the place was like a farm, with its population of hens, rabbits, and guinea-pigs.

Two series of experiments were being carried out on those 125 dogs. The first consisted in making dogs refractory to rabies by preventive inoculations; the second in preventing the onset of rabies in dogs bitten or subjected to inoculation.

CHAPTER XIII

PASTEUR had the power of concentrating his thoughts to such a degree that he often, when absorbed in one idea, became absolutely unconscious of what took place around him. At one of the meetings of the Académie Française, whilst the Dictionary was being discussed, he scribbled the following note on a stray sheet of paper

"I do not know how to hide my ideas from those who work with me; still, I wish I could have kept those I am going to express a little longer to myself. The experiments have already begun which will decide them.

"It concerns rabies, but the results might be general.

"I am inclined to think that the virus which is considered rabic may be accompanied by a substance which, by impregnating the nervous system, would make it unsuitable for the culture of the microbe. Thence vaccinal immunity. If that is so, the theory might be a general one : it would be a stupendous discovery.

"I have just met Chamberland in the Rue Gay-Lussac, and explained to him this view and my experiments. He was much struck, and asked my permission to make at once on anthrax the experiment I am about to make on rabies as soon as the dog and the culture rabbits are dead. Roux, the day before yesterday, was equally struck.

"*Académie Française, Thursday, January 29, 1885.*"

Could that vaccinal substance associated with the rabic virus be isolated? In the meanwhile a main fact was acquired, that of preventive inoculation, since Pasteur was sure of his series of dogs rendered refractory to rabies after a bite. Months were going by without bringing an answer to the question "Why ?" of the antirabic vaccination, as mysterious as the "Why ?" of Jennerian vaccination.

On Monday, July 6, Pasteur saw a little Alsatian boy, Joseph Meister, enter his laboratory, accompanied by his mother. He was only nine years old, and had been bitten two days before by a mad dog at Meissengott, near Schlestadt.

The child, going alone to school by a little by-road, had been attacked by a furious dog and thrown to the ground. Too small to defend himself, he had only thought of covering his face with his hands. A bricklayer, seeing the scene from a distance, arrived, and succeeded in beating the dog off with an iron bar; he picked up the boy, covered with blood and saliva. The dog went back to his master, Théodore Vone, a grocer at Meissengott, whom he bit on the arm. Vone seized a gun and shot the animal, whose stomach was found to be full of hay, straw, pieces of wood, etc. When little Meister's parents heard all these details they went, full of anxiety, to consult Dr. Weber, at Villé, that same evening. After cauterizing the wounds with carbolic, Dr. Weber advised Mme. Meister to start for Paris, where she could relate the facts to one who was not a physician, but who would be the best judge of what could be done in such a serious case. Théodore Vone, anxious on his own and on the child's account, decided to come also.

Pasteur reassured him; his clothes had wiped off the dog's saliva, and his shirt-sleeve was intact. He might safely go back to Alsace, and he promptly did so.

Pasteur's emotion was great at the sight of the fourteen wounds of the little boy, who suffered so much that he could hardly walk. What should he do for this child? could he risk the preventive treatment which had been constantly successful on his dogs? Pasteur was divided between his hopes and his scruples, painful in their acuteness. Before deciding on a course of action, he made arrangements for the comfort of this poor woman and her child, alone in Paris, and gave them an appointment for 5 o'clock, after the Institute meeting. He did not wish to attempt anything without having seen Vulpian and talked it over with him. Since the Rabies Commission had been constituted, Pasteur had formed a growing esteem for the great judgment of Vulpian, who, in his lectures on the general and comparative physiology of the nervous system, had already mentioned the profit to human clinics to be drawn from experimenting on animals.

His was a most prudent mind, always seeing all the aspects of a problem. The man was worthy of the scientist: he was absolutely straightforward, and of a discreet and active kindness. He was passionately fond of work, and had recourse to it when smitten by a deep sorrow.

Vulpian expressed the opinion that Pasteur's experiments on dogs were sufficiently conclusive to authorize him to foresee the same success in human pathology. Why not try this treatment? added the professor, usually so reserved. Was there any other efficacious treatment against hydrophobia? If at least the cauterizations had been made with a red-hot iron! but what was the good of carbolic acid twelve hours after the accident. If the almost certain danger which threatened the boy were weighed against the chances of snatching him from death, Pasteur would see that it was more than a right, that it was a duty to apply antirabic inoculation to little Meister.

This was also the opinion of Dr. Grancher, whom Pasteur consulted. M. Grancher worked at the laboratory; he and Dr. Straus might claim to be the two first French physicians who took up the study of bacteriology; these novel studies fascinated him, and he was drawn to Pasteur by the deepest admiration and by a strong affection, which Pasteur thoroughly reciprocated.

Vulpian and M. Grancher examined little Meister in the evening, and, seeing the number of bites, some of which, on one hand especially, were very deep, they decided on performing the first inoculation immediately; the substance chosen was fourteen days old and had quite lost its virulence : it was to be followed by further inoculations gradually increasing in strength.

It was a very slight operation, a mere injection into the side (by means of a Pravaz syringe) of a few drops of a liquid prepared with some fragments of medulla oblongata. The child, who cried very much before the operation, soon dried his tears when he found the slight prick was all that he had to undergo.

Pasteur had had a bedroom comfortably arranged for the mother and child in the old Rollin College, and the little boy was very happy amidst the various animals—chickens, rabbits, white mice, guinea-pigs, etc.; he begged and easily obtained of Pasteur the life of several of the youngest of them.

" All is going well," Pasteur wrote to his son-in-law on July 11 : " the child sleeps well, has a good appetite, and the inoculated matter is absorbed into the system from one day to another without leaving a trace. It is true that I have not yet come to the test inoculations, which will take place on Tuesday, Wednesday and Thursday. If the lad keeps well during the three following weeks, I think the experiment will be safe to succeed. I shall send the child and his mother back to Meissengott (near Schlestadt) in any case on August 1, giving these good people detailed instruction as to the observations they are to record for me. I shall make no statement before the end of the vacation."

But, as the inoculations were becoming more virulent, Pasteur became a prey to anxiety : " My dear children," wrote Mme. Pasteur, " your father has had another bad night ; he is dreading the last inoculations on the child. And yet there can be no drawing back now! The boy continues in perfect health."

Renewed hopes were expressed in the following letter from Pasteur—

" My dear René, I think great things are coming to pass. Joseph Meister has just left the laboratory. The three last inoculations have left some pink marks under the skin, gradually widening and not at all tender. There is some action, which is becoming more intense as we approach the final inoculation, which will take place on Thursday, July 16. The lad is very well this morning, and has slept well, though slightly restless ; he has a good appetite and no feverishness. He had a slight hysterical attack yesterday."

The letter ended with an affectionate invitation. " Perhaps one of the great medical facts of the century is going to take place ; you would regret not having seen it ! "

Pasteur was going through a succession of hopes, fears, anguish, and an ardent yearning to snatch little Meister from death ; he could no longer work. At nights, feverish visions came to him of this child whom he had seen playing in the garden, suffocating in the mad struggles of hydrophobia, like the dying child he had seen at the Hôpital Trousseau in 1880. Vainly his experimental genius assured him that the virus of that most terrible of diseases was about to be vanquished, that humanity was about to be delivered from this dread horror— his human tenderness was stronger than all, his accustomed ready sympathy for the sufferings and anxieties of others was for the nonce centred in " the dear lad."

The treatment lasted ten days ; Meister was inoculated

twelve times. The virulence of the medulla used was tested by trephinings on rabbits, and proved to be gradually stronger. Pasteur even inoculated on July 16, at 11 a.m., some medulla only one day old, bound to give hydrophobia to rabbits after only seven days' incubation; it was the surest test of the immunity and preservation due to the treatment.

Cured from his wounds, delighted with all he saw, gaily running about as if he had been in his own Alsatian farm, little Meister, whose blue eyes now showed neither fear nor shyness, merrily received the last inoculation; in the evening, after claiming a kiss from "Dear Monsieur Pasteur," as he called him, he went to bed and slept peacefully. Pasteur spent a terrible night of insomnia; in those slow dark hours of night when all vision is distorted, Pasteur, losing sight of the accumulation of experiments which guaranteed his success, imagined that the little boy would die.

The treatment being now completed, Pasteur left little Meister to the care of Dr. Grancher (the lad was not to return to Alsace until July 27) and consented to take a few days' rest. He spent them with his daughter in a quiet, almost deserted country place in Burgundy, but without however finding much restfulness in the beautiful peaceful scenery; he lived in constant expectation of Dr. Grancher's daily telegram or letter containing news of Joseph Meister.

By the time he went to the Jura, Pasteur's fears had almost disappeared. He wrote from Arbois to his son August 3, 1885: "Very good news last night of the bitten lad. I am looking forward with great hopes to the time when I can draw a conclusion. It will be thirty-one days to-morrow since he was bitten."

On August 20, six weeks before the new elections of Deputies, Léon Say, Pasteur's colleague at the Académie Française, wrote to him that many Beauce agricultors were anxious to put his name down on the list of candidates, as a recognition of the services rendered by science. A few months before, Jules Simon had thought Pasteur might be elected as a Life Senator, but Pasteur had refused to be convinced. He now replied to Léon Say

"Your proposal touches me very much and it would be agreeable to me to owe a Deputy's mandate to electors, several of whom have applied the results of my investigations. But

politics frighten me and I have already refused a candidature
in the Jura and a seat in the Senate in the course of this year.

"I might be tempted perhaps, if I no longer felt active
enough for my laboratory work. But I still feel equal to
further researches, and on my return to Paris, I shall be
organizing a 'service' against rabies which will absorb all my
energies. I now possess a very perfect method of prophylaxis
against that terrible disease, a method equally adapted to
human beings and to dogs, and by which your much afflicted
Department will be one of the first to benefit.

"Before my departure for Jura I dared to treat a poor
little nine-year-old lad whose mother brought him to me from
Alsace, where he had been attacked on the 4th ult., and
bitten on the thighs, legs, and hand in such a manner
that hydrophobia would have been inevitable. He remains
in perfect health."

Whilst many political speeches were being prepared, Pasteur
was thinking over a literary speech. He had been requested by
the Académie Française to welcome Joseph Bertrand, elected
in place of J. B. Dumas—the eulogium of a scientist, spoken
by one scientist, himself welcomed by another scientist. This
was an unusual programme for the Académie Française, perhaps
too unusual in the eyes of Pasteur, who did not think himself
worthy of speaking in the name of the Académie. Such was
his modesty; he forgot that amongst the savants who had been
members of the Académie, several, such as Fontenelle, Cuvier,
J. B. Dumas, etc., had published immortal pages, and that some
extracts from his own works would one day become classical.

The vacation gave him time to read over the writings of
his beloved teacher, and also to study the life and works of
Joseph Bertrand, already his colleague at the Académie des
Sciences.

Bertrand's election had been simple and easy, like everything
he had undertaken since his birth. It seemed as if a good fairy
had leant over his cradle and whispered to him, "Thou shalt
know many things, without having had to learn them." It is
a fact that he could read without having held a book in his
hands. He was ill and in bed whilst his brother Alexander
was being taught to read; he listened to the lessons and kept the
various combinations of letters in his mind. When he became
convalescent, his parents brought him a book of Natural History so that he might look at the pictures. He took the volume

and read from it fluently ; he was not five years old.   He learnt the elements of geometry very much in the same way.

Pasteur in his speech thus described Joseph Bertrand's childhood : " At ten years old you were already celebrated, and it was prophesied that you would pass at the head of the list into the Ecole Polytechnique and become a member of the Academy of Sciences?   No one doubted this, not even yourself.   You were indeed a child prodigy.   Sometimes it amused you to hide in a class of higher mathematics, and when the Professor propounded a difficult problem that no one could solve, one of the students would triumphantly lift you in his arms, stand you on a chair so that you might reach the board, and you would then give the required solution with a calm assurance, in the midst of applause from the professors and pupils."

Pasteur, whose every progress had been painfully acquired, admired the ease with which Bertrand had passed through the first stages of his career.   At an age when marbles and india-rubber balls are usually an important interest, Bertrand walked merrily to the *Jardin des Plantes* to attend a course of lectures by Gay-Lussac.   A few hours later, he might be seen at the Sorbonne, listening with interest to Saint Marc Girardin, the literary moralist.   The next day, he would go to a lecture on Comparative Legislation ; never was so young a child seen in such serious places.   He borrowed as many books from the Institute library as Biot himself ; he learnt whole passages by heart, merely by glancing at them.   He became a *doctor ès sciences* at sixteen, and a Member of the Institute at thirty-four.

Besides his personal works—such as those on Analytic Mechanics, which place him in the very first rank—his teaching had been brought to bear during forty years on all branches of mathematics.   Bertrand's life, apparently so happy, had been saddened by the irreparable loss, during the Commune, of a great many precious notes, letters, and manuscripts, which had been burnt with the house where he had left them.   Discouraged by this ruin of ten years' work, he had given way to a tendency to writing slight popular articles, of high literary merit, instead of continuing his deeper scientific work.   His eulogy of J. B. Dumas was not quite seriously enthusiastic enough to please Pasteur, who had a veritable cult for the memory of his old teacher, and who eagerly grasped this opportunity of speaking again of J. B. Dumas' influence on himself, of his admirable scientific discoveries, and of his political duties, undertaken in the hope of being useful to Science, but often proving a source of disappointment.

Pasteur enjoyed looking back on the beloved memory of J. B. Dumas, as he sat preparing his speech in his study at Arbois, looking out on the familiar landscape of his childhood, where the progress of practical science was evidenced by the occasional passing, through the distant pine woods, of the white smoke of the Switzerland express.

When in his laboratory in Paris, Pasteur hated to be disturbed whilst making experiments or writing out notes of his work. Any visitor was unwelcome ; one day that some one was attempting to force his way in, M. Roux was amused at seeing Pasteur—vexed at being disturbed and anxious not to pain the visitor—come out to say imploringly, " Oh ! not now, please ! I am too busy ! "

" When Chamberland and I," writes Dr. Roux, " were engaged in an interesting occupation, he mounted guard before us, and when, through the glazed doors, he saw people coming, he himself would go and meet them in order to send them away. He showed so artlessly that his sole thought was for the work, that no one ever could be offended."

But, at Arbois, where he only spent his holidays, he did not exercise so much severity ; any one could come in who liked. He received in the morning a constant stream of visitors, begging for advice, recommendations, interviews, etc.

"It is both comical and touching," wrote M. Girard, a local journalist, " to see the opinion the vineyard labourers have of him. These good people have heard M. Pasteur's name in connection with the diseases of wine, and they look upon him as a sort of wine doctor. If they notice a barrel of wine getting sour, they knock at the savant's door, bottle in hand ; this door is never closed to them. Peasants are not precise in their language ; they do not know how to begin their explanations or how to finish them. M. Pasteur, ever calm and serious, listens to the very end, takes the bottle and studies it at his leisure. A week later, the wine is ' cured.' "

He was consulted also on many other subjects—virus, silkworms, rabies, cholera, swine-fever, etc. ; many took him for a physician. Whilst telling them of their mistake, he yet did everything he could for them.

During this summer of 1885, he had the melancholy joy of seeing a bust erected in the village of Monay to the memory of a beloved friend of his, J. J. Perraud, a great and inspired sculptor, who had died in 1876. Perraud, whose magnificent statue of Despair is now at the Louvre, had had a sad life, and, on his lonely death-bed (he was a widower, with no children), Pasteur's tender sympathy had been an unspeakable comfort. Pasteur now took a leading part in the celebration of his friend's fame, and was glad to speak to the assembled villagers at Monay of the great and disinterested artist who had been born in their midst.

On his return to Paris, Pasteur found himself obliged to hasten the organization of a " service " for the preventive treatment of hydrophobia after a bite. The Mayors of Villers-Farlay, in the Jura, wrote to him that, on October 14, a shepherd had been cruelly bitten by a rabid dog.

Six little shepherd boys were watching over their sheep in a meadow; suddenly they saw a large dog passing along the road, with hanging, foaming jaws.

" A mad dog ! " they exclaimed. The dog, seeing the children, left the road and charged them ; they ran away shrieking, but the eldest of them, J. B. Jupille, fourteen years of age, bravely turned back in order to protect the flight of his comrades. Armed with his whip, he confronted the infuriated animal, who flew at him and seized his left hand. Jupille, wrestling with the dog, succeeded in kneeling on him, and forcing its jaws open in order to disengage his left hand ; in so doing, his right hand was seriously bitten in its turn ; finally, having been able to get hold of the animal by the neck, Jupille called to his little brother to pick up his whip, which had fallen during the struggle, and securely fastened the dog's jaws with the lash. He then took his wooden *sabot*, with which he battered the dog's head, after which, in order to be sure that it could do no further harm, he dragged the body down to a little stream in the meadow, and held the head under water for several minutes. Death being now certain, and all danger removed from his comrades, Jupille returned to Villers-Farlay.

Whilst the boy's wounds were being bandaged, the dog's carcase was fetched, and a necropsy took place the next day. The two veterinary surgeons who examined the body had not the slightest hesitation in declaring that the dog was rabid.

The Mayor of Villers-Farlay, who had been to see Pasteur during the summer, wrote to tell him that this lad would die

a victim of his own courage unless the new treatment intervened.   The answer came immediately : Pasteur declared that,
after five years' study, he had succeeded in making dogs refractory to rabies, even six or eight days after being bitten ; that
he had only once yet applied his method to a human being, but
that once with success, in the case of little Meister, and that,
if Jupille's family consented, the boy might be sent to him.
" I shall keep him near me in a room of my laboratory ; he will
be watched and need not go to bed ; he will merely receive a
daily prick, not more painful than a pin-prick."

The family, on hearing this letter, came to an immediate
decision ; but, between the day when he was bitten and Jupille's
arrival in Paris, six whole days had elapsed, whilst in Meister's
case there had only been two and a half !

Yet, however great were Pasteur's fears for the life of this
tall lad, who seemed quite surprised when congratulated on his
courageous conduct, they were not what they had been in the
first instance—he felt much greater confidence.

A few days later, on October 26, Pasteur in a statement at
the Academy of Sciences described the treatment followed for
Meister.   Three months and three days had passed, and the
child remained perfectly well.   Then he spoke of his new
attempt.   Vulpian rose

" The Academy will not be surprised," he said, " if, as a
member of the Medical and Surgical Section, I ask to be allowed
to express the feelings of admiration inspired in me by M.
Pasteur's statement.   I feel certain that those feelings will be
shared by the whole of the medical profession.

" Hydrophobia, that dread disease against which all therapeutic measures had hitherto failed, has at last found a remedy.
M. Pasteur, who has been preceded by no one in this path, has
been led by a series of investigations unceasingly carried on
for several years, to create a method of treatment, by means
of which the development of hydrophobia can *infallibly* be prevented in a patient recently bitten by a rabid dog.   I say
infallibly, because, after what I have seen in M. Pasteur's
laboratory, I do not doubt the constant success of this treatment when it is put into full practice a few days only after a
rabic bite.

" It is now necessary to see about organizing an installation
for the treatment of hydrophobia by M. Pasteur's method.
Every person bitten by a rabid dog must be given the oppor-

tunity of benefiting by this great discovery, which will seal the fame of our illustrious colleague and bring glory to our whole country."

Pasteur had ended his reading by a touching description of Jupille's action, leaving the Assembly under the impression of that boy of fourteen, sacrificing himself to save his companions. An Academician, Baron Larrey, whose authority was rendered all the greater by his calmness, dignity, and moderation, rose to speak. After acknowledging the importance of Pasteur's discovery, Larrey continued, " The sudden inspiration, agility and courage, with which the ferocious dog was muzzled, and thus made incapable of committing further injury to bystanders, . . . such an act of bravery deserves to be rewarded. I therefore have the honour of begging the Académie des Sciences to recommend to the Académie Française this young shepherd, who, by giving such a generous example of courage and devotion, has well deserved a Montyon prize."

Bouley, then chairman of the Academy, rose to speak in his turn—

" We are entitled to say that the date of the present meeting will remain for ever memorable in the history of medicine, and glorious for French science ; for it is that of one of the greatest steps ever accomplished in the medical order of things—a progress realized by the discovery of an efficacious means of preventive treatment for a disease, the incurable nature of which was a legacy handed down by one century to another. From this day, humanity is armed with a means of fighting the fatal disease of hydrophobia and of preventing its onset. It is to M. Pasteur that we owe this, and we could not feel too much admiration or too much gratitude for the efforts on his part which have led to such a magnificent result. . . ."

Five years previously, Bouley, in the annual combined public meeting of the five Academies, had proclaimed his enthusiasm for the discovery of the vaccination of anthrax. But on hearing him again on this October day, in 1885, his colleagues could not but be painfully struck by the change in him ; his voice was weak, his face thin and pale. He was dying of an affection of the heart, and quite aware of it, but he was sustained by a wonderful energy, and ready to forget his sufferings in his joy at the thought that the sum of human sorrows would be diminished by Pasteur's victory. He went to the Académie de Médecine the next day to enjoy the echo of the great sitting of the Académie des Sciences. He died on November 29.

The chairman of the Academy of Medicine, M. Jules Bergeron, applauded Pasteur's statement all the more that he too had publicly deplored (in 1862) the impotence of medical science in the presence of this cruel disease.

But while M. Bergeron shared the admiration felt by Vulpian and Dr. Grancher for the experiments which had transformed the rabic virus into its own vaccine, other medical men were divided into several categories : some were full of enthusiasm, others reserved their opinion, many were sceptical, and a few even positively hostile.

As soon as Pasteur's paper was published, people bitten by rabid dogs began to arrive from all sides to the laboratory. The " service " of hydrophobia became the chief business of the day. Every morning was spent by Eugène Viala in preparing the fragments of marrow used for inoculations : in a little room permanently kept at a temperature of 20° to 23° C., stood rows of sterilized flasks, their tubular openings closed by plugs of cotton-wool. Each flask contained a rabic marrow, hanging from the stopper by a thread and gradually drying up by the action of some fragments of caustic potash lying at the bottom of the flask. Viala cut those marrows into small pieces by means of scissors previously put through a flame, and placed them in small sterilized glasses; he then added a few drops of veal broth and pounded the mixture with a glass rod. The vaccinal liquid was now ready ; each glass was covered with a paper cover, and bore the date of the medulla used, the earliest of which was fourteen days old. For each patient under treatment from a certain date, there was a whole series of little glasses. Pasteur always attended these operations personally.

In the large hall of the laboratory, Pasteur's collaborators, Messrs. Chamberland and Roux, carried on investigations into contagious diseases under the master's directions ; the place was full of flasks, pipets, phials, containing culture broths. Etienne Wasserzug, another curator, hardly more than a boy, fresh from the Ecole Normale, where his bright intelligence and affectionate heart had made him very popular, translated (for he knew the English, German, Italian, Hungarian and Spanish languages, and was awaiting a favourable opportunity of learning Russian) the letters which arrived from all parts of the

world ; he also entertained foreign scientists. Pasteur had in
him a most valuable interpreter. Physicians came from all
parts of the world asking to be allowed to study the details of
the method. One morning, Dr. Grancher found Pasteur listening to a physician who was gravely and solemnly holding forth
his objections to microbian doctrines, and in particular to the
treatment of hydrophobia. Pasteur having heard this long
monologue, rose and said, "Sir, your language is not very
intelligible to me. I am not a physician and do not desire to
be one. Never speak to me of your dogma of morbid spontaneity. I am a chemist; I carry out experiments and I try
to understand what they teach me. What do you think,
doctor?" he added, turning to M. Grancher. The latter
smilingly answered that the hour for inoculations had struck.
They took place at eleven, in Pasteur's study ; he, standing by
the open door, called out the names of the patients. The date
and circumstances of the bites and the veterinary surgeon's
certificate were entered in a register, and the patients were
divided into series according to the degree of virulence which
was to be inoculated on each day of the period of treatment.

Pasteur took a personal interest in each of his patients, helping those who were poor and illiterate to find suitable lodgings
in the great capital. Children especially inspired him with a
loving solicitude. But his pity was mingled with terror, when,
on November 9, a little girl of ten was brought to him who had
been severely bitten on the head by a mountain dog, on October
3, thirty-seven days before ! ! The wound was still suppurating.
He said to himself, " This is a hopeless case : hydrophobia is
no doubt about to appear immediately ; it is much too late
for the preventive treatment to have the least chance of success.
Should I not, in the scientific interest of the method, refuse to
treat this child? If the issue is fatal, all those who have already
been treated will be frightened, and many bitten persons, discouraged from coming to the laboratory, may succumb to the
disease ! " These thoughts rapidly crossed Pasteur's mind.
But he found himself unable to resist his compassion for the
father and mother, begging him to try and save their child.

After the treatment was over, Louise Pelletier had returned
to school, when fits of breathlessness appeared, soon followed
by convulsive spasms; she could swallow nothing. Pasteur
hastened to her side when these symptoms began, and new
inoculations were attempted. On December 2, there was a

respite of a few hours, moments of calm which inspired Pasteur with the vain hope that she might yet be saved. This delusion was a short-lived one. After attending Bouley's funeral, his heart full of sorrow, Pasteur spent the day by little Louise's bedside, in her parents' rooms in the Rue Dauphine. He could not tear himself away ; she herself, full of affection for him, gasped out a desire that he should not go away, that he should stay with her ! She felt for his hand between two spasms. Pasteur shared the grief of the father and mother. When all hope had to be abandoned : " I did so wish I could have saved your little one ! " he said. And as he came down the staircase, he burst into tears.

He was obliged, a few days later, to preside at the reception of Joseph Bertrand at the Académie Française ; his sad feelings little in harmony with the occasion. He read in a mournful and troubled voice the speech he had prepared during his peaceful and happy holidays at Arbois. Henry Houssaye, reporting on this ceremony in the *Journal des Débats*, wrote, " M. Pasteur ended his speech amidst a torrent of applause, he received a veritable ovation. He seemed unaccountably moved. How can M. Pasteur, who has received every mark of admiration, every supreme honour, whose name is conse- crated by universal renown, still be touched by anything save the discoveries of his powerful genius ? " People did not realize that Pasteur's thoughts were far away from himself and from his brilliant discovery. He was thinking of Dumas, his master, of Bouley, his faithful friend and colleague, and of the child he had been unable to snatch from the jaws of death ; his mind was not with the living, but with the dead.

A telegram from New York having announced that four children, bitten by rabid dogs, were starting for Paris, many adversaries who had heard of Louise Pelletier's death were say- ing triumphantly that, if those children's parents had known of her fate, they would have spared them so long and useless a journey.

The four little Americans belonged to workmen's families and were sent to Paris by means of a public subscription opened in the columns of the *New York Herald* ; they were accompanied by a doctor and by the mother of the youngest of them, a boy only five years old. After the first inoculation, this little boy, astonished at the insignificant prick, could not help saying, " Is this all we have come such a long journey for ? " The children were received with enthusiasm on their return to New York, and were asked "many questions about the great man who had taken such care of them."

A letter dated from that time (January 14, 1886) shows that Pasteur yet found time for kindness, in the midst of his world-famed occupations.

"My dear Jupille, I have received your letters, and I am much pleased with the news you give me of your health. Mme. Pasteur thanks you for remembering her. She, and every one at the laboratory, join with me in wishing that you may keep well and improve as much as possible in reading, writing and arithmetic. Your writing is already much better than it was, but you should take some pains with your spelling. Where do you go to school? Who teaches you? Do you work at home as much as you might? You know that Joseph Meister, who was first to be vaccinated, often writes to me; well, I think he is improving more quickly than you are, though he is only ten years old. So, mind you take pains, do not waste your time with other boys, and listen to the advice of your teachers, and of your father and mother. Remember me to M. Perrot, the Mayor of Villers-Farlay. Perhaps, without him, you would have become ill, and to be ill of hydrophobia means inevitable death; therefore you owe him much gratitude. Good-bye. Keep well."

Pasteur's solicitude did not confine itself to his two first patients, Joseph Meister and the fearless Jupille, but was extended to all those who had come under his care; his kindness was like a living flame. The very little ones who then only saw in him a "kind gentleman" bending over them understood later in life, when recalling the sweet smile lighting up his serious face, that Science, thus understood, unites moral with intellectual grandeur.

Good, like evil, is infectious; Pasteur's science and devotion inspired an act of generosity which was to be followed by many others. He received a visit from one of his colleagues at the Académie Française, Edouard Hervé, who looked upon journalism as a great responsibility and as a school of mutual respect between adversaries. He was bringing to Pasteur, from the Comte de Laubespin, a generous philanthropist, a sum of 40,000 fr. destined to meet the expenses necessitated by the organization of the hydrophobia treatment. Pasteur, when

questioned by Hervé, answered that his intention was to found
a model establishment in Paris, supported by donations and
international subscriptions, without having recourse to the
State. But he added that he wanted to wait a little longer
until the success of the treatment was undoubted. Statistics
came to support it; Bouley, who had been entrusted with an
official inquiry on the subject under the Empire, had found
that the proportion of deaths after bites from rabid dogs had
been 40 per 100, 320 cases having been watched. The proportion often was greater still : whilst Joseph Meister was under
Pasteur's care, five persons were bitten by a rabid dog on the
Pantin Road, near Paris, and every one of them succumbed to
hydrophobia.

Pasteur, instead of referring to Bouley's statistics, preferred
to adopt those of M. Leblanc, a veterinary surgeon and a
member of the Academy of Medicine, who had for a long time
been head of the sanitary department of the *Préfecture de Police*.
These statistics only gave a proportion of deaths of 16 per 100,
and had been carefully and accurately kept.

On March 1, he was able to affirm, before the Academy,
that the new method had given proofs of its merit, for, out of
350 persons treated, only one death had taken place, that of the
little Pelletier. He concluded thus—

"It may be seen, by comparison with the most rigorous
statistics, that a very large number of persons have already been
saved from death.

" The prophylaxis of hydrophobia after a bite is established.

" It is advisable to create a vaccinal institute against
hydrophobia."

The Academy of Sciences appointed a Commission who
unanimously adopted the suggestion that an establishment for
the preventive treatment of hydrophobia after a bite should be
created in Paris, under the name of *Institut Pasteur*. A subscription was about to be opened in France and abroad. The
spending of the funds would be directed by a special Committee.

A great wave of enthusiasm and generosity swept from one
end of France to another and reached foreign countries. A
newspaper of Milan, the *Perseveranza*, which had opened a
subscription, collected 6,000 fr. in its first list. The *Journal
d'Alsace* headed a propaganda in favour of this work, " sprung
from Science and Charity." It reminded its readers that
Pasteur had occupied a professor's chair in the former brilliant

Faculty of Science of Strasburg, and that his first inoculation was made on an Alsatian boy, Joseph Meister.   The
newspaper intended to send the subscriptions to Pasteur
with these words : " Offerings from Alsace-Lorraine to the
Pasteur Institute."

The war of 1870 still darkened the memories of nations.
Amongst eager and numerous inventions of instruments of
death and destruction, humanity breathed when fresh news
came from the laboratory, where a continued struggle was
taking place against diseases.   The most mysterious, the most
cruel of all was going to be reduced to impotence.

Yet the method was about to meet with a few more cases like
Louise Pelletier's ; accidents would result, either from delay or
from exceptionally serious wounds.   Happy days were still in
store for those who sowed doubt and hatred.

During the early part of March, Pasteur received nineteen
Russians, coming from the province of Smolensk.   They had
been attacked by a rabid wolf and most of them had terrible
wounds : one of them, a priest, had been surprised by the
infuriated beast as he was going into church, his upper lip and
right cheek had been torn off, his face was one gaping wound.
Another, the youngest of them, had had the skin of his forehead
torn off by the wolf's teeth ; other bites were like knife cuts.
Five of these unhappy wretches were in such a condition that
they had to be carried to the Hôtel Dieu Hospital as soon as they
arrived.

The Russian doctor who had accompanied these mujiks
related how the wolf had wandered for two days and two
nights, tearing to pieces every one he met, and how he had
finally been struck down with an axe by one of those he had
bitten most severely.

Because of the gravity of the wounds, and in order to make
up for the time lost by the Russians before they started, Pasteur
decided on making two inoculations every day, one in the morning and one in the evening ; the patients at the Hôtel Dieu
could be inoculated upon at the hospital.

The fourteen others came every morning in their *touloupes*
and fur caps, with their wounds bandaged, and joined without a
word the motley groups awaiting treatment at the laboratory—
an English family, a Basque peasant, a Hungarian in his
national costume, etc., etc.

In the evening, the dumb and resigned band of mujiks came again to the laboratory door. They seemed led by Fate, heedless of the struggle between life and death of which they were the prize. "Pasteur" was the only French word they knew, and their set and melancholy faces brightened in his presence as with a ray of hope and gratitude.

Their condition was the more alarming that a whole fortnight had elapsed between their being bitten and the date of the first inoculations. Statistics were terrifying as to the results of wolf-bites, the average proportion of deaths being 82 per 100. General anxiety and excitement prevailed concerning the hapless Russians, and the news of the death of three of them produced an intense emotion.

Pasteur had unceasingly continued his visits to the Hôtel Dieu. He was overwhelmed with grief. His confidence in his method was in no wise shaken, the general results would not allow it. But questions of statistics were of little account in his eyes when he was the witness of a misfortune; his charity was not of that kind which is exhausted by collective generalities : each individual appealed to his heart. As he passed through the wards at the Hôtel Dieu, each patient in his bed inspired him with deep compassion. And that is why so many who only saw him pass, heard his voice, met his pitiful eyes resting on them, have preserved of him a memory such as the poor had of St. Vincent de Paul.

"The other Russians are keeping well so far," declared Pasteur at the Academy sitting of April 12, 1886. Whilst certain opponents in France continued to discuss the three deaths and apparently saw nought but those failures, the return of the sixteen survivors was greeted with an almost religious emotion. Other Russians had come before them and were saved, and the Tsar, knowing these things, desired his brother, the Grand Duke Vladimir, to bring to Pasteur an imperial gift, the Cross of the Order of St. Anne of Russia, in diamonds. He did more, he gave 100,000 fr. in aid of the proposed Pasteur Institute.

In April, 1886, the English Government, seeing the practical results of the method for the prophylaxis of hydrophobia, appointed a Commission to study and verify the facts. Sir James Paget was the president of it, and the other members were :—Dr. Lauder-Brunton, Mr. Fleming, Sir Joseph Lister, Dr. Quain, Sir Henry Roscoe, Professor Burdon Sanderson, and

Mr. Victor Horsley, secretary. The *résumé* of the programme was as follows—

Development of the rabic virus in the medulla oblongata of animals dying of rabies.

Transmission of this virus by subdural or subcutaneous inoculation.

Intensification of this virus by successive passages from rabbit to rabbit.

Possibility either of protectig healthy animals from ulterior bites from rabid animals,·or of preventing the onset of rabies in animals already bitten, by means of vaccinal inoculations.

Applications of this method to man and value of its results.

Burdon Sanderson and Horsley came to Paris, and two rabbits, inoculated on by Pasteur, were taken to England; a series of experiments was to be begun on them, and an inquiry was to take place afterwards concerning patients treated both in France and in England. Pasteur, who lost his temper at prejudices and ill-timed levity, approved and solicited inquiry and careful examination.

Long lists of subscribers appeared in the *Journal Officiel*— millionaires, poor workmen, students, women, etc. A great festival was organized at the Trocadéro in favour of the Pasteur Institute; the greatest artistes offered their services. Coquelin recited verses written for the occasion which excited loud applause from the immense audience. Gounod, who had conducted his *Ave Maria*, turned round after the closing bars, and, in an impulse of heartfelt enthusiasm, kissed both his hands to the savant.

In the evening at a banquet, Pasteur thanked his colleagues and the organizers of this incomparable performance. "Was it not," he said, "a touching sight, that of those immortal composers, those great charmers of fortunate humanity coming to the assistance of those who wish to study and to serve suffering humanity? And you too come, great artistes, great actors, like so many generals re-entering the ranks to give greater vigour to a common feeling. I cannot easily describe what I felt. Dare I confess that I was hearing most of you for the first time? I do not think I have spent more than ten evenings of my whole life at a theatre. But I can have no regrets now that you have given me, in a few hours' interval, as in an exquisite synthesis, the feelings that so many others scatter over several months, or rather several years."

A few days later, the subscription from Alsace-Lorraine brought in 43,000 fr.   Pasteur received it with grateful emotion, and was pleased and touched to find the name of little Joseph Meister among the list of private subscribers.   It was now eleven months since he had been bitten so cruelly by the dog, whose rabic condition had immediately been recognized by the German authorities.   Pasteur ever kept a corner of his heart for the boy who had caused him such anxiety.

Pasteur's name was now familiar to all those who were trying to benefit humanity ; his presence at charitable gatherings was considered as a happy omen, and he was asked to preside on many such occasions.   He was ever ready with his help and sympathy, speaking in public, answering letters from private individuals, giving wholesome advice to young people who came to him for it, and doing nothing by halves.   If he found the time, even during that period when the study of rabies was absorbing him, to undertake so many things and to achieve so many tasks, he owed it to Mme. Pasteur, who watched over his peace, keeping him safe from intrusions and interruptions. This retired, almost recluse life, enabled him to complete many works, a few of which would have sufficed to make several scientists celebrated.

Every morning, between ten and eleven o'clock, Pasteur walked down the Rue Claude-Bernard to the Rue Vauquelin, where a few temporary buildings had been erected to facilitate the treatment of hydrophobia, close to the rabbit hutches, hencoops, and dog kennels which occupied the yard of the old Collège Rollin.   The patients under treatment walked about cheerfully amidst these surroundings, looking like holiday makers in a Zoological Garden.   Children, whose tears were already dried at the second inoculation, ran about merrily. Pasteur, who loved the little ones, always kept sweets or new copper coins for them in his drawer.   One little girl amused herself by having holes bored in those coins, and hung them round her neck like a necklace ; she was wearing this ornament on the day of her departure, when she ran to kiss the great man as she would have kissed her grandfather.

Drs. Grancher, Roux, Chantemesse, and Charrin came by turns to perform the inoculations.   A surgery ward had been installed to treat the numerous wounds of the patients, and entrusted to the young and energetic Dr. Terrillon.

In August, 1886, while staying at Arbois, Pasteur spent much time over his notes and registers; he was sometimes tempted to read over certain articles of passionate criticism. " How difficult it is to obtain the triumph of truth ! " he would say. " Opposition is a useful stimulant, but bad faith is such a pitiable thing. How is it that they are not struck with the results as shown by statistics? From 1880 to 1885, sixty persons are stated to have died of hydrophobia in the Paris hospitals; well, since November 1, 1885, when the prophylactic method was started in my laboratory, only three deaths have occurred in those hospitals, two of which were cases which had not been treated. It is evident that very few people who had been bitten did not come to be treated. In France, out of that unknown but very restricted number, seventeen cases of death have been noted, whilst out of the 1,726 French and Algerians who came to the laboratory only ten died after the treatment."

But Pasteur was not yet satisfied with this proportion, already so low; he was trying to forestall the outburst of hydrophobia by a greater rapidity and intensity of the treatment. He read a paper on the subject to the Academy of Sciences on November 2, 1886. Admiral Jurien de la Gravière, who was in the chair, said to him, " All great discoveries have gone through a time of trial. May your health withstand the troubles and difficulties in your way."

Pasteur's health had indeed suffered from so much work and anxiety, and there were symptoms of some heart trouble. Drs. Villemin and Grancher persuaded him to interrupt his work and to think of spending a restful winter in the south of France. M. Raphael Bischoffsheim, a great lover of science, placed at Pasteur's disposal his beautiful villa at Bordighera, close to the French frontier, which he had on divers occasions lent to other distinguished guests, the Queen of Italy, Henri Sainte-Claire Deville, Gambetta, etc.

Pasteur consented to leave his work at the end of November, and started one evening from the Gare de Lyon with his wife, his daughter and her husband, and his two grandchildren; eighteen friends came to the station to see him off, including his pupils, M. Bischoffsheim, and some foreign physicians who were staying in Paris to study the prophylactic treatment of hydrophobia.

The bright dawn and the sunshine already appearing at

Avignon contrasted with the foggy November weather left behind in Paris and brought a feeling of comfort, almost of returning health ; a delegation of doctors met the train at Nice, bringing Pasteur their good wishes.

The travelling party drove from Vintimille to Bordighera under the deep blue sky reflected in a sea of a yet deeper blue, along a road bordered with cacti, palms and other tropical plants. The sight of the lovely gardens of the Villa Bischoffsheim gave Pasteur a delicious feeling of rest.

His health soon improved sufficiently for him to be able to take some short walks. But his thoughts constantly recurred to the laboratory. M. Duclaux was then thinking of starting a monthly periodical entitled *Annals of the Pasteur Institute*. Pasteur, writing to him on December 27, 1887, to express his approbation, suggested various experiments to be attempted. He attributed the action of the preventive inoculations to a vaccinal matter associated with the rabic microbe. Pasteur had thought at first that the first development of the pathogenic microbe caused the disappearance from the organism of an element necessary to the life of that microbe. It was, in other words, a theory of exhaustion. But since 1885, he adopted the other idea, supported indeed by biologists, that immunity was due to a substance left in the body by the culture of the microbe and which opposed the invasion—a theory of addition.

" I am happy to learn," wrote Villemin, his friend and his medical adviser, " that your health is improving ; continue to rest in that beautiful country, you have well deserved it, and rest is *absolutely* necessary to you. You have overtaxed yourself beyond all reason and you must make up for it. Repairs to the nervous system are worked chiefly by relaxation from the mental storms and moral anxieties which your *rabid* work has occasioned in you. Give the Bordighera sun a chance ! "

But Pasteur was not allowed the rest he so much needed ; on January 4, 1887, referring to a death which had occurred after treatment in the preceding December, M. Peter declared that the antirabic cure was useless ; at the following meeting he called it dangerous when applied in the "intensive " form. Dujardin-Beaumetz, Chauveau and Verneuil immediately intervened, declaring that the alleged fact was " devoid of any scientific character." A week later, MM. Grancher and Brouardel bore the brunt of the discussion. Grancher, Pasteur's representative on this occasion, disproved certain allegations, and added : " The medical men who have been chosen by M. Pasteur to assist him in his work have not hesitated to practise the antirabic inoculation on themselves, as a safeguard against an accidental inoculation of the virus which they are constantly handling.   What greater proof can they give of their bonâ fide convictions?"   He showed that the mortality amongst the cases treated remained below 1 per 100.   " M. Pasteur will soon publish foreign statistics from Samara, Moscow, St. Petersburg, Odessa, Warsaw and Vienna : they are all absolutely favourable."

As it was insinuated that the laboratory of the Ecole Normale kept its failures a secret, it was decided that the *Annals of the Pasteur Institute* would publish a monthly list and bulletin of patients under treatment.

Vulpian, at another meeting (it was almost the last time he was heard at the Académie de Médecine), said, à propos of what he called an inexcusable opposition, " This new benefit adds to the number of those which our illustrious Pasteur has already rendered to humanity. . . . Our works and our names will soon be buried under the rising tide of oblivion : the name and the works of M. Pasteur will continue to stand on heights too great to be reached by its sullen waves."   Pasteur was much disturbed by the noise of these discussions ; every post increased his feverishness, and he spoke every morning of returning to Paris to answer his opponents.

It was a pitiful thing to note on his worn countenance the visible signs of the necessity of the peace and rest offered by this beautiful land of serene sunshine ; and to hear at the same time a constant echo of those angry debates.   Anonymous letters were sent to him, insulting newspaper articles—all that envy and hatred can invent; the seamy side of human nature was being revealed to him.   " I did not know I had so many enemies," he said mournfully.   He was consoled to some extent by the ardent support of the greatest medical men in France.

Vulpian, in a statement to the Académie des Sciences, con· stituted himself Pasteur's champion.   Pasteur indeed was safe from attacks in that centre, but certain low slanderers who attended the public meetings of the Académie continued to accuse Pasteur of concealing the failures of his method.   Vulpian —who was furiously angry at such an insinuation against "a man like M. Pasteur, whose good faith, loyalty and scientific integrity should be an example to his adversaries as they are to his friends "—thought that it was in the interest both of science and of humanity to state once more the facts recently confirmed by new statistics; the public is so impressionable and so mobile in its opinions that one article is often enough to shake general confidence. He was therefore anxious to reassure all those who had been inoculated on and who might be induced by those discussions to wonder with anguish whether they really were saved. The Academy of Sciences decided that Vulpian's statement should be inserted *in extenso* in all the reports and a copy of it sent to every village in France. Vulpian wrote to Pasteur at the same time, "All your admirers hope that those interested attacks will merely excite your contempt. Fine weather is no doubt reigning at Bordighera : you must take advantage of it and become quite well. . . . The Academy of Medicine is almost entirely on your side; there are at the most but four or five exceptions."

Pasteur had a few calm days after these debates. Whilst planning out new investigations, he was much interested in the plans for his Institute which were now submitted to him. His thoughts were always away from Bordighera, which he seemed to look upon as a sort of exile. This impression was partly due to the situation of the town, so close to the frontier, and the haunt of so many homeless wanderers. He once met a sad-faced, still beautiful woman, in mourning robes, and recognized the Empress Eugénie.

Shortly afterwards, he received a visit from Prince Napoleon, who dragged his haughty *ennui* from town to town. He presented himself at the Villa Bischoffsheim under the name of Count Moncalieri, coming, he said, to greet his colleague of the Institute. Rabies formed the subject of their conversation. The next day, Pasteur called on the Prince, in his commonplace hotel rooms, a mere temporary resting place for the exiled Bonaparte, whose mysterious, uncompleted destiny was made more enigmatical by his startling resemblance to the great Emperor.

On February 23, the day after the carnival, early in the morning, a violent earthquake cast terror over that peaceful land where nature hides with flowers the spectre of death. At 6.20 a.m. a low and distant rumbling sound was heard, coming from the depths of the earth and resembling the noise of a train passing in an underground tunnel; houses began to rock and

ominous cracks were heard. This first shock lasted more than
a minute, during which the sense of solidity disappeared altogether, to be succeeded by a feeling of absolute, hopeless, impotence. No doubt, in every household, families gathered
together, with a sudden yearning not to be divided. Pasteur's
wife, children and grandchildren had barely had time to come
to him when another shock took place, more terrible than the
first; everything seemed about to be engulfed in an abyss.
Never had morning been more radiant; there was not a breath
of wind, the air was absolutely transparent.

An early departure was necessary : the broken ceilings were
dropping to pieces, shaken off by an incessant vibration of the
ground which continued after the second shock, and of which
Pasteur observed the effect on glass windows with much interest.
Pasteur and his family dove off to Vintimille in a carriage, along
a road lined with ruined houses, crowded with sick people in
quest of carriages and peasants coming down from their mountain dwellings, destroyed by the shock, leading donkeys loaded
with bedding, the women followed by little children hastily
wrapt in blankets and odd clothes. At Vintimille station,
terrified travellers were trying to leave France for Italy or
Italy for France, fancying that the danger would cease on the
other side of the frontier.

"We have resolved to go to Arbois," wrote Mme. Pasteur
to her son from Marseilles; "your father will be better able
there than anywhere else to recover from this shock to his
heart."

After a few weeks' stay at Arbois, Pasteur seemed quite
well again. He was received with respect and veneration on his
return to the Academies of Sciences and of Medicine. His best
and greatest colleagues had realized what the loss of him would
mean to France and to the world, and surrounded him with an
anxious solicitude.

At the beginning of July, Pasteur received the report presented to the House of Commons by the English Commission
after a fourteen months' study of the prophylactic method
against hydrophobia. The English scientists had verified every
one of the facts upon which the method was founded, but they
had not been satisfied with their experimental researches in Mr.
Horsley's laboratory, and had carried out a long and minute
inquiry in France. After noting on Pasteur's registers the
names of ninety persons treated, who had come from the same

neighbourhood, they had interviewed each one of them in their own homes. "It may therefore be considered as certain "— thus ran the report—"that M. Pasteur has discovered a prophylactic method against hydrophobia which may be compared with that of vaccination against small-pox. It would be difficult to overestimate the utility of this discovery, both from the point of view of its practical side and of its application to general pathology. We have here a new method of inoculation, or vaccination, as M. Pasteur sometimes calls it, and similar means might be employed to protect man and domestic animals against other virus as active as that of hydrophobia."

Pasteur laid this report on the desk of the Academy of Sciences on July 4. He spoke of its spirit of entire and unanimous confidence, and added—

"Thus fall to the ground the contradictions which have been published. I leave on one side the passionate attacks which were not justified by the least attempt at experiment, the slightest observation of facts in my laboratory, or even an exchange of words and ideas with the Director of the Hydrophobia Clinic, Professor Grancher, and his medical assistants.

"But, however deep is my satisfaction as a Frenchman, I cannot but feel a sense of deepest sadness at the thought that this high testimony from a commission of illustrious scientists was not known by him who, at the very beginning of the application of this method, supported me by his counsels and his authority, and who later on, when I was ill and absent, knew so well how to champion truth and justice; I mean our beloved colleague Vulpian."

Vulpian had succumbed to a few days' illness. His speech in favour of Pasteur was almost the farewell to the Academy of this great-hearted scientist.

The discussion threatened to revive. Other colleagues defended Pasteur at the Academy of Medicine on July 12. Professor Brouardel spoke, also M. Villemin, and then Charcot, who insisted on quoting word for word Vulpian's true and simple phrase : "The discovery of the preventive treatment of hydrophobia after a bite, entirely due to M. Pasteur's experimental genius, is one of the finest discoveries ever made, both from the scientific and the humanitarian point of view." And Charcot continued : "I am persuaded that I express in these words the opinion of all the medical men who have studied the question with an open mind, free from prejudice; the inventor of antirabic vaccination may, now more than ever, hold his head high and continue to accomplish his glorious task, heedless of the clamour of systematic contradiction or of the insidious murmurs of slander."

The Academy of Sciences begged Pasteur to become its Life Secretary in Vulpian's place. Pasteur did not reply at once to this offer, but went to see M. Berthelot : " This high position," he said, " would be more suitable to you than to me." M. Berthelot, much touched, refused unconditionally, and Pasteur accepted. He was elected on July 18. He said, in thanking his colleagues, "I would now spend what time remains before me, on the one hand in encouraging to research and in training for scientific studies,—the future of which seems to me most promising,—pupils worthy of French science ; and, on the other hand, in following attentively the work incited and encouraged by this Academy.

" Our only consolation, as we feel our own strength failing us, is to feel that we may help those who come after us to do more and to do better than ourselves, fixing their eyes as they can on the great horizons of which we only had a glimpse."

He did not long fulfil his new duties. On October 23, Sunday morning, after writing a letter in his room, he tried to speak to Mme. Pasteur and could not pronounce a word ; his tongue was paralyzed. He had promised to lunch with his daughter on that day, and, fearing that she might be alarmed, he drove to her house. After spending a few hours in an easy chair, he consented to remain at her house with Mme. Pasteur. In the evening his speech returned, and two days later, when he went back to the Ecole Normale, no one would have noticed any change in him. But, on the following Saturday morning, he had another almost similar attack, without any premonitory symptoms. His speech remained somewhat difficult, and his deep powerful voice completely lost its strength. In January, 1888, he was obliged to resign his secretaryship.

Ill-health had emaciated his features. A portrait of him by Carolus Duran represents him looking ill and weary, a sad look in his eyes. But goodness predominates in those worn features, revealing that lovable soul, full of pity for all human sufferings, and of which the painter has rendered the unspeakable thrill.

Pasteur's various portraits, compared with one another, show us different aspects of his physiognomy. A luminous profile, painted by Henner ten years before, brings out the powerful harmony of the forehead. In 1886, Bonnat painted, for the brewer Jacobsen, who wished to present it to Mme. Pasteur, a large portrait which may be called an official one. Pasteur is standing in rather an artificial attitude, which might be imperious, if his left hand was not resting on the shoulder of his granddaughter, a child of six, with clear pensive eyes. In that same year, Edelfeldt, the Finnish painter, begged to be allowed to come into the laboratory for a few sketches. Pasteur came and went, attending to his work and taking no notice of the painter. One day that Edelfeldt was watching him thus, deep in observation, his forehead lined with almost painful thoughts, he undertook to portray the savant in his meditative attitude. Pasteur is standing clad in a short brown coat, an experimental card in his left hand, in his right, a phial containing a fragment of rabic marrow, the expression in his eyes entirely concentrated on the scientific problem.

During the year 1888, Pasteur, after spending the morning with his patients, used to go and watch the buildings for the Pasteur Institute which were being erected in the Rue Dutot. 11,000 square yards of ground had been acquired in the midst of some market gardens. Instead of rows of hand-lights and young lettuces, a stone building, with a Louis XIII façade, was now being constructed. An interior gallery connected the main building with the large wings. The Pasteur Institute was to be at the same time a great dispensary for the treatment of hydrophobia, a centre of research on virulent and contagious diseases, and also a teaching centre. M. Duclaux's class of biological chemistry, held at the Sorbonne, was about to be transferred to the Pasteur Institute, where Dr. Roux would also give a course of lectures on technical microbia. The " service " of vaccinations against anthrax was entrusted to M. Chamberland. (The statistics of 1882-1887 gave a total of 1,600,000 sheep and nearly 200,000 oxen.) There would also be, under M. Metchnikoff's direction, some private laboratories, the monkish cells of the Pastorians.

At the end of October, the work was almost completed; Pasteur invited the President of the Republic to come and inaugurate the Institute. "I shall certainly not fail to do so," answered Carnot; "your Institute is a credit to France."

On November 14, politicians, colleagues, friends, collaborators, pupils assembled in the large library of the new Institute. Pasteur had the pleasure of seeing before him, in the first rank,

Duruy and Jules Simon; it was a great day for these former Ministers of Public Instruction. Like them, Pasteur had all his life been deeply interested in higher education. "If that teaching is but for a small number," he said, "it is with this small number, this élite that the prosperity, glory and supremacy of a nation rest."

Joseph Bertrand, chairman of the Institute Committee, knowing that by so doing he responded to Pasteur's dearest wishes, spoke of the past and recalled the memories of Biot, Senarmont, Claude Bernard, Balard, and J. B. Dumas.

Professor Grancher, Secretary of the Committee, alluded to the way in which not only Vulpian but Brouardel, Charcot, Verneuil, Chauveau and Villemin had recently honoured themselves by supporting the cause of progress and preparing its triumph. These memories of early friends, associated with that of recent champions, brought before the audience a vision of the procession of years. After speaking of the obstacles Pasteur had so often encountered amongst the medical world—

"You know," said M. Grancher, "that M. Pasteur is an innovator, and that his creative imagination, kept in check by rigorous observation of facts, has overturned many errors and built up in their place an entirely new science. His discoveries on ferments, on the generation of the infinitesimally small, on microbes, the cause of contagious diseases, and on the vaccination of those diseases, have been for biological chemistry, for the veterinary art and for medicine, not a regular progress, but a complete revolution. Now, revolutions, even those imposed by scientific demonstration, ever leave behind them vanquished ones who do not easily forgive. M. Pasteur has therefore many adversaries in the world, without counting those Athenian French who do not like to see one man always right or always fortunate. And, as if he had not enough adversaries, M. Pasteur makes himself new ones by the rigorous implacability of his dialectics and the absolute form he sometimes gives to his thought."

Going on to the most recently acquired results, M. Grancher stated that the mortality amongst persons treated after bites from rabid dogs remained under 1 per 100.

"If those figures are indeed eloquent," said M. Christophle, the treasurer, who spoke after M. Grancher, "other figures are touching. I would advise those who only see the dark side of humanity," he remarked, before entering upon the statement of accounts—"those who go about repeating that everything here below is for the worst, that there is no disinterestedness, no devotion in this world—to cast their eyes over the ' human documents ' of the Pasteur Institute. They would learn therein, beginning at the beginning, that Academies contain colleagues who are not offended, but proud and happy in the fame of another; that politicians and journalists often have a passion for what is good and true; that at no former epoch have great men been more beloved in France; that justice is already rendered to them during their lifetime, which is very much the best way of doing so; that we have cheered Victor Hugo's birthday, Chevreul's centenary, and the inauguration of the Pasteur Institute. When a Frenchman runs himself down, said one of M. Pasteur's colleagues, do not believe him; he is boasting! Reversing a celebrated and pessimistic phrase, it might be said that in this public subscription all the virtues flow into unselfishness like rivers into the sea."

M. Christophle went on to show how rich and poor had joined in this subscription and raised an amount of 2,586,680 fr. The French Chambers had voted 200,000 fr., to which had been added international gifts from the Tsar, the Emperor of Brazil, and the Sultan. The total expenses would probably reach 1,563,786 fr., leaving a little more than a million to form an endowment for the Pasteur Institute, a fund which was to be increased every year by the product of the sale of vaccines from the laboratory, which Pasteur and Messrs. Chamberland and Roux agreed to give up to the Institute.

"It is thus, Sir," concluded the treasurer, directly addressing Pasteur, "that public generosity, practical help from the Government, and your own disinterestedness have founded and consolidated the establishment which we are to-day inaugurating." And, persuaded that the solicitude of the public would never fail to support this great work, "This is for you, Sir, a rare and almost unhoped for happiness; let it console you for the passionate struggles, the terrible anxiety and the many emotions you have gone through."

Pasteur, overcome by his feelings, had to ask his son to read his speech. It began by a rapid summary of what France had done for education in all its degrees. "From village schools to laboratories, everything has been founded or renovated." After acknowledging the help given him in later years by the public authorities, he continued—

"And when the day came that, foreseeing the future which would be opened by the discovery of the attenuation of virus, I appealed to my country, so that we should be allowed, through the strength and impulse of private initiative, to build laboratories to be devoted, not only to the prophylactic treatment of hydrophobia,.but also to the study of virulent and contagious diseases—on that day again, France gave in handfuls. . . . It is now finished, this great building, of which it might be said that there is not a stone but what is the material sign of a generous thought.   All the virtues have subscribed to build this dwelling place for work.

"Alas! mine is the bitter grief that I enter it, a man 'vanquished by Time,' deprived of my masters, even of my companions in the struggle, Dumas, Bouley, Paul Bert, and lastly Vulpian, who, after having been with you, my dear Grancher, my counsellor at the very first, became the most energetic, the most convinced champion of this method.

"However, if I have the sorrow of thinking that they are no more, after having valiantly taken their part in discussions which I have never provoked but have had to endure; if they cannot hear me proclaim all that I owe to their counsels and support; if I feel their absence as deeply as on the morrow of their death, I have at least the consolation of believing that all that we struggled for together will not perish. The collaborators and pupils who are now here share our scientific faith. . . ."
He continued, as in a sort of testament : "Keep your early enthusiasm, dear collaborators, but let it ever be regulated by rigorous examinations and tests. Never advance anything which cannot be proved in a simple and decisive fashion.

"Worship the spirit of criticism. If reduced to itself, it is not an awakener of ideas or a stimulant to great things, but, without it, everything is fallible ; it always has the last word. What I am now asking you, and you will ask of your pupils later on, is what is most difficult to an inventor.

"It is indeed a hard task, when you believe you have found an important scientific fact and are feverishly anxious to publish it, to constrain yourself for days, weeks, years sometimes, to fight with yourself, to try and ruin your own experiments and only to proclaim your discovery after having exhausted all contrary hypotheses.

"But when, after so many efforts, you have at last arrived at a certainty, your joy is one of the greatest which can be felt by a human soul, and the thought that you will have contributed to the honour of your country renders that joy still deeper.

" If science has no country, the scientist should have one, and ascribe to it the influence which his works may have in this world. If I might be allowed, M. le Président, to conclude by a philosophical remark inspired by your presence in this Home of Work, I should say that two contrary laws seem to be wrestling with each other nowadays; the one, a law of blood and of death, ever imagining new means of destruction and forcing nations to be constantly ready for the battlefield—the other, a law of peace, work and health, ever evolving new means of delivering man from the scourges which beset him.

" The one seeks violent conquests, the other the relief of humanity. The latter places one human life above any victory; while the former would sacrifice hundreds and thousands of lives to the ambition of one. The law of which we are the instruments seeks, even in the midst of carnage, to cure the sanguinary ills of the law of war; the treatment inspired by our antiseptic methods may preserve thousands of soldiers. Which of those two laws will ultimately prevail, God alone knows. But we may assert that French Science will have tried, by obeying the law of Humanity, to extend the frontiers of Life."

CHAPTER XIV

In this Institute, which Pasteur entered ill and weary, he contemplated with joy those large laboratories, which would enable his pupils to work with ease and to attract around them investigators from all countries. He was happy to think that the material difficulties which had hampered him would be spared those who came after him. He believed in the realization of his wishes for peace, work, mutual help among men. Whatever the obstacles, he was persuaded that science would continue its civilizing progress and that its benefits would spread from domain to domain. Differing from those old men who are ever praising the past, he had an enthusiastic confidence in the future; he foresaw great developments of his studies, some of which were already apparent. His first researches on crystallography and molecular dissymmetry had served as a basis to stereo-chemistry. But, while he followed the studies on that subject of Le Bel and Van t'Hoff, he continued to regret that he had not been able to revert to the studies of his youth, enslaved as he had been by the inflexible logical sequence of his works. "Every time we have had the privilege of hearing Pasteur speak of his early researches," writes M. Chamberland, in an article in the *Revue Scientifique*, "we have seen the revival in him of a smouldering fire, and we have thought that his countenance showed a vague regret at having forsaken them. Who can now say what discoveries he might have made in that direction?" "One day," said Dr. Héricourt—who spent the summer near Villeneuve l'Etang, and who often came into the Park with his two sons—"he favoured me with an admirable, captivating discourse on this subject, the like of which I have never heard."

Pasteur, instead of feeling regret, might have looked back with calm pride on the progress he had made in other directions.

In what obscurity were fermentation and infection enveloped before his time, and with what light he had penetrated them! When he had discovered the all-powerful rôle of the infinitesimally small, he had actually mastered some of those living germs, causes of disease; he had transformed them from destructive to preservative agents. Not only had he renovated medicine and surgery, but hygiene, misunderstood and neglected until then, was benefiting by the experimental method. Light was being thrown on preventive measures.

M. Henri Monod, Director of Hygiene and Public Charities, one day quoted, à propos of sanitary measures, these words of the great English Minister, Disraeli—

"Public health is the foundation upon which rest the happiness of the people and the power of the State. Take the most beautiful kingdom, give it intelligent and laborious citizens, prosperous manufactures, productive agriculture; let arts flourish, let architects cover the land with temples and palaces; in order to defend all these riches, have first-rate weapons, fleets of torpedo boats—if the population remains stationary, if it decreases yearly in vigour and in stature, the nation must perish. And that is why I consider that the first duty of a statesman is the care of Public Health."

In 1889, when the International Congress of Hygiene met in Paris, M. Brouardel was able to say—

"If echoes from this meeting could reach them . . . our ancestors would learn that a revolution, the most formidable for thirty centuries, has shaken medical science to its very foundations, and that it is the work of a stranger to their corporation; and their sons do not cry Anathema, they admire him, bow to his laws. . . . We all proclaim ourselves disciples of Pasteur."

On the very day after those words were pronounced, Pasteur saw the realization of one of his most ardent wishes, the inauguration of the new Sorbonne. At the sight of the wonderful facilities for work offered by this palace, he remembered Claude Bernard's cellar, his own garret at the Ecole Normale, and felt a movement of patriotic pride.

In October, 1889, though his health remained shaken, he insisted on going to Alais, where a statue was being raised to J. B. Dumas. Many of his colleagues tried to dissuade him from this long and fatiguing journey, but he said: "I am alive, I shall go." At the foot of the statue, he spoke of his master, one of those men who are " the tutelary spirits of a nation."

The sericicultors, desiring to thank him for the five years he had spent in studying the silkworm disease, offered him an artistic souvenir : a silver heather twig laden with gold cocoons.

Pasteur did not fail to remind them that it was at the request of their fellow citizen that he had studied pébrine. He said, "In the expression of your gratitude, by which I am deeply touched, do not forget that the initiative was due to M. Dumas."

Thus his character revealed itself on every occasion. Every morning, with a step rendered heavy by age and ill-health, he went from his rooms to the Hydrophobia Clinic, arriving there long before the patients. He superintended the preparation of the vaccinal marrows; no detail escaped him. When the time came for inoculations, he was already informed of each patient's name, sometimes of his poor circumstances; he had a kind word for every one, often substantial help for the very poor. The children interested him most; whether severely bitten, or frightened at the inoculation, he dried their tears and consoled them. How many children have thus kept a memory of him! "When I see a child," he used to say, "he inspires me with two feelings : tenderness for what he is now, respect for what he may become hereafter."

Already in May, 1892, Denmark, Sweden, and Norway had formed various Committees of scientists and pupils of Pasteur to celebrate his seventieth birthday. In France, it was in November that the Medical and Surgical Section of the Academy of Sciences constituted a Subscription Committee to offer Pasteur an affectionate homage. Roty, the celebrated engraver, was desired to finish a medal he had already begun, representing Pasteur in profile, a skull cap on his broad forehead, the brow strongly prominent, the whole face full of energy and meditation. His shoulders are covered with the cape he usually wore in the morning in the passages of his Institute. Roty had not time to design a satisfactory reverse side; he surrounded with laurels and roses the following inscription : "To Pasteur, on his seventieth birthday. France and Humanity grateful."

On the morning of December 27, 1892, the great theatre of the Sorbonne was filled. The seats of honour held the French and foreign delegates from Scientific Societies, the members of the Institute, and the Professors of Faculties. In the amphitheatre were the deputations from the Ecoles Normale, Polytechnique, Centrale, of Pharmacy, Vétérinaires, and of Agriculture—deep masses of students. People pointed out to each other Pasteur's pupils, Messrs. Duclaux, Roux, Chamberland, Metchnikoff, in their places; M. Perdrix, a former Normalien, now an *Agrégé-préparateur*; M. Edouard Calmette, a former student of the Ecole Centrale, who had taken part in the studies on beer; and M. Denys Cochin, who, thirteen years before, had studied alcoholic fermentation in the laboratory of the Rue d'Ulm. The first gallery was full of those who had subscribed towards the presentation about to be made to Pasteur. In the second gallery, boys from *lycées* crowned the immense assembly with a youthful garland.

At half past 10 o'clock, whilst the band of the Republican Guard played a triumphal march, Pasteur entered, leaning on the arm of the President of the Republic. Carnot led him to a little table, whereon the addresses from the various delegates were to be laid. The Presidents of the Senate and of the Chamber, the Ministers and Ambassadors, took their seats on the platform. Behind the President of the Republic stood, in their uniform, the official delegates of the five Academies which form the Institut de France. The Academy of Medicine and the great Scientific Societies were represented by their presidents and life-secretaries.

M. Charles Dupuy, Minister of Public Instruction, rose to speak, and said, after retracing Pasteur's great works—

"Who can now say how much human life owes to you and how much more it will owe to you in the future! The day will come when another Lucretius will sing, in a new poem on Nature, the immortal Master whose genius engendered such benefits.

"He will not describe him as a solitary, unfeeling man, like the hero of the Latin poet; but he will show him mingling with the life of his time, with the joys and trials of his country, dividing his life between the stern enjoyment of scientific research and the sweet communion of family intercourse; going from the laboratory to his hearth, finding in his dear ones, particularly in the helpmeet who has understood him so well and loved him all the better for it, that comforting encouragement of every hour and each moment, without which

so many struggles might have exhausted his ardour, arrested
his perseverance, and enervated his genius. . . .

"May France keep you for many more years, and show you
to the world as the worthy object of her love, of her gratitude
and pride."

The President of the Academy of Sciences, M. d'Abbadie,
was chosen to present to Pasteur the commemorative medal of
this great day.

Joseph Bertrand said that the same science, wide, accurate,
and solid, had been a foundation to all Pasteur's works, each
of them shining "with such a dazzling light, that, in looking
at either, one is inclined to think that it eclipses all others."

After a few words from M. Daubrée, senior member of the
Mineralogical Section and formerly a colleague of Pasteur's at
the Strasburg Faculty, the great Lister, who represented the
Royal Societies of London and Edinburgh, brought to Pasteur
the homage of medicine and surgery. "You have," said he,
"raised the veil which for centuries had covered infectious
diseases; you have discovered and demonstrated their
microbian nature."

When Pasteur rose to embrace Lister, the sight of those
two men gave the impression of a brotherhood of science
labouring to diminish the sorrows of humanity.

After a speech from M. Bergeron, Life-Secretary of the
Academy of Medicine, and another from M. Sauton, President
of the Paris Municipal Council, the various delegates presented the addresses they had brought. Each of the large
cities of Europe had its representative. The national delegates were called in their turn. A student from the Alfort
Veterinary School brought a medal offered by the united
Veterinary Schools of France. Amongst other offerings,
Pasteur was given an album containing the signatures of the
inhabitants of Arbois, and another coming from Dôle, in which
were reproduced a facsimile of his birth-certificate and a photograph of the house in which he was born. The sight of his
father's signature at the end of the certificate moved him more
than anything else.

The Paris Faculty of Medicine was represented by its Dean,
Professor Brouardel. "More fortunate than Harvey and than
Jenner," he said, "you have been able to see the triumph of
your doctrines, and what a triumph ! . . "

The last word of homage was pronounced by M. Devise,

President of the Students' Association, who said to Pasteur, " You have been very great and very good ; you have given a beautiful example to students."

Pasteur's voice, made weaker than usual by his emotion, could not have been heard all over the large theatre; his thanks were read out by his son—

" Monsieur le Président de la République, your presence transforms an intimate fête into a great ceremony, and makes of the simple birthday of a savant a special date for French science.

" M. le Ministre, Gentlemen—In the midst of all this magnificence, my first thought takes me back to the melancholy memory of so many men of science who have known but trials. In the past, they had to struggle, against the prejudices which hampered their ideas. After those prejudices were vanquished, they encountered obstacles and difficulties of all kinds.

" Very few years ago, before the public authorities and the town councils had endowed science with splendid dwellings, a man whom I loved and admired, Claude Bernard, had, for a laboratory, a wretched cellar not far from here, low and damp. Perhaps it was there that he contracted the disease of which he died. When I heard what you were preparing for me here, the thought of him arose in my mind; I hail his great memory.

" Gentlemen, by an ingenious and delicate thought, you seem to make the whole of my life pass before my eyes. One of my Jura compatriots, the Mayor of Dôle, has brought me a photograph of the very humble home where my father and mother lived such a hard life. The presence of the students of the Ecole Normale brings back to me the glamour of my first scientific enthusiasms. The representatives of the Lille Faculty evoke memories of my first studies on crystallography and fermentation, which opened to me a new world. What hopes seized upon me when I realized that there must be laws behind so many obscure phenomena! You, my dear colleagues, have witnessed by what series of deductions it was given to me, a disciple of the experimental method, to reach physiological studies. If I have sometimes disturbed the calm of our Academies by somewhat violent discussions, it was because I was passionately defending truth.

" And you, delegates from foreign nations, who have come from so far to give to France a proof of sympathy, you bring me the deepest joy that can be felt by a man whose invincible belief is that Science and Peace will triumph over Ignorance and War, that nations will unite, not to destroy, but to build, and that the future will belong to those who will have done most for suffering humanity. I appeal to you, my dear Lister, and to you all, illustrious representatives of medicine and surgery.

"Young men, have confidence in those powerful and safe methods, of which we do not yet know all the secrets. And, whatever your career may be, do not let yourselves become tainted by a deprecating and barren scepticism, do not let yourselves be discouraged by the sadness of certain hours which pass over nations. Live in the serene peace of laboratories and libraries. Say to yourselves first : 'What have I done for my instruction?' and, as you gradually advance, 'What have I done for my country?' until the time comes when you may have the immense happiness of thinking that you have contributed in some way to the progress and to the good of humanity. But, whether our efforts are or not favoured by life, let us be able to say, when we come near the great goal, 'I have done what I could.'

"Gentlemen, I would express to you my deep emotion and hearty gratitude. In the same way as Roty, the great artist, has, on the back of this medal, hidden under roses.the heavy number of years which weigh on my life, you have, my dear colleagues, given to my old age the most delightful sight of all this living and loving youth."

The shouts "Vive Pasteur !" resounded throughout the building. The President of the Republic rose, went towards Pasteur to congratulate him, and embraced him with effusion.

Hearts went out to Pasteur even from distant countries. The Canadian Government, acting on the suggestion of the deputies of the province of Quebec, gave the name of Pasteur to a district on the borders of the state of Maine.

A few weeks after the fête, the Governor-General of Algeria, M. Cambon, wrote to Pasteur as follows—

" Sir—Desirous of showing to you the special gratitude which Algeria bears you for the immense services you have rendered to science and to humanity by your great and fruitful discoveries, I have decided that your name should be given to the village of Sériana, situated in the *arrondissement* of Batna, department of Constantine. I am happy that I have been able to render this slight homage to your illustrious person." " I feel a deep emotion," replied Pasteur, " in thinking that, thanks to you, my name will remain attached to that corner of the world. When a child of this village asks what was the origin of this denomination, I should like the schoolmaster to tell him simply that it is the name of a Frenchman who loved France very much, and who, by serving her, contributed to the good of humanity. My heart is thrilled at the thought that my name might one day awaken the first feelings of patriotism in a child's soul. I shall owe to you this great joy in my old age; I thank you more than I can say." The origin of Sériana is very ancient. M. Stéphane Gsell relates that this village was occupied long before the coming of the Romans, by a tribe which became Christian, as is seen by ruins of chapels and basilicas. It is situated on the slope of a mountain covered with oaks and cedars, and giving rise to springs of fresh water. A bust of Pasteur was soon after erected in this village, at the request of the inhabitants.

Enthusiasm for Pasteur was spreading everywhere. Women understood that science was entering their domain, since it served charity. They gave magnificent gifts; clauses in wills bore these words : " To Pasteur, to help in his humanitarian task." In November, 1893, Pasteur saw an unknown lady enter his study in the Rue Dutot, and heard her speak thus : " There must be some students who love science and who, having to earn their living, cannot give themselves up to disinterested work. I should like to place at your disposal four scholarships, for four young men chosen by you. Each scholarship would be of 3,000 fr.; 2,400 for the men themselves, and 600 fr. for the expenses they would incur in your laboratories. Their lives would be rendered easier. You could find amongst them, either an immediate collaborator for your Institute or a missionary whom you might send far away ; and if a medical career tempted them, they would be enabled by their momentary independence to prepare themselves all the better for their profession. I only ask one thing, which is that my name should not be mentioned."

Pasteur was infinitely touched by the scheme of this mysterious lady. The scholarship foundation was for one year only, but other years were about to follow and to resemble this one.

Many letters brought to Pasteur requested that he should study or order the study of such and such a disease. Some of these letters responded to preoccupations which had long been in the mind of Pasteur and his disciples. One day he received these lines :

"You have done all the good a man could do on earth. If you will, you can surely find a remedy for the horrible disease called diphtheria. Our children, to whom we teach your name as that of a great benefactor, will owe their lives to you.— A MOTHER."

Pasteur, in spite of his failing strength, had hopes that he would yet live to see the defeat of the foe so dreaded by mothers. In the laboratory of the Pasteur Institute, Dr. Roux and Dr. Yersin were obstinately pursuing the study of this disease. In their first paper on the subject, modestly entitled *A Contribution to the Study of Diphtheria*, they said : " Ever since Bretonneau, diphtheria has been looked upon as a specific and contagious disease ; its study has therefore been undertaken of late years with the help of the microbian methods which have already been the means of finding the cause of many other infectious diseases."

In spite of the convictions of Bretonneau, who had, in 1818, witnessed a violent epidemic of croup in the centre of France, his view was far from being generally adopted. Velpeau, then a young student, wrote to him in 1820 that all the members, save two, of the Faculty of Medicine were agreed in opposing or blaming his opinions. Another brilliant pupil of Bretonneau's, Dr. Trousseau, who never ceased to correspond with his old master, wrote to him in 1854 : " It remains to be proved that diphtheria always comes from a germ. I hardly doubt this with regard to small-pox ; to be consistent, I ought not to doubt it either with regard to diphtheria. I was thinking so this morning, as I was performing tracheotomy on a poor child twenty-eight months old ; opposite the bed, there was a picture of his five-year-old brother, painted on his death-bed. He had succumbed five years ago, to malignant angina."

Knowing Bretonneau's ideas on contagion, Trousseau wrote further down : " I shall have the beds and bedding burnt, the paper hangings also, for they have a velvety and attractive

surface ; I shall tell the mother to purify herself like a Hindoo
else what would you say to me ! ''

A German of the name of Klebs discovered the bacillus of
diphtheria in 1883, by studying the characteristic membranes;
it was afterwards isolated by Loeffler, another German.

Pure cultures of this bacillus, injected on the surface of the
excoriated fauces of rabbits, guinea-pigs, and pigeons, produce the diphtheritic membranes : Messrs. Roux and Yersin
demonstrated this fact and ascertained the method of its deadly
action.

Dr. Roux, in a lecture to the London Royal Society, in 1889,
said : '' Microbes are chiefly dangerous on account of the toxic
matters which they produce.'' He recalled that Pasteur had
been the first to investigate the action of the toxic products
elaborated by the microbe of chicken-cholera. By filtering
the culture, Pasteur had obtained a liquid which contained no
microbes. Hens inoculated with this liquid presented all the
symptoms of cholera. ''This experiment shows us,'' continued M. Roux, ''that the chemical products contained in
the culture are capable by themselves of provoking the
symptoms of the disease ; it is therefore very probable that the
same products are prepared within the body itself of a hen
attacked with cholera. It has been shown since then that
many pathogenic microbes manufactured these toxic products.
The microbes of typhoid fever, of cholera, of blue pus, of acute
experimental septicæmia, of diphtheria, are great poison-pro-
ducers. The cultures of the diphtheria bacillus particularly
are, after a certain time, so full of the toxin that, without
microbes, and in infinitesimal doses, they cause the death of
the animals with all the signs observed after inoculation with
the microbe itself. The picture of the disease is complete,
even presenting the ensuing paralysis if the injected dose is
too weak to bring about a rapid death. Death in infectious
diseases is therefore caused by intoxication.''

This bacillus, like that of tetanus, secretes a poison which
reaches the kidneys, attacks the nervous system, and acts on
the heart, the beats of which are accelerated or suddenly
arrested. Sheltered in the membrane like a foe in an ambush,
the microbe manufactures its deadly poison. Diphtheria, as
defined by M. Roux, is an intoxication caused by a very active
poison formed by the microbe within the restricted area
wherein it develops.

It was sufficient to examine a portion of diphtheritic membrane to distinguish the diphtheritic bacilli, tiny rods resembling short needles laid across each other. Other microbes were frequently associated with these bacilli, and it became necessary to study microbian associations in diphtheria. The Klebs-Loeffler bacillus, disseminated in broth, gave within a month or three weeks a richly toxic culture; the bottom of the vessel was covered with a thick deposit of microbes, and a film of younger bacilli floated on the surface. By filtering this broth and freeing it from microbes, Messrs. Roux and Yersin made a great discovery: they obtained pure toxin, capable of killing, in forty-eight hours, a guinea-pig inoculated with one-tenth of a cubic centimetre of it.

Now that the toxin was found, the remedy, the antitoxin, could be discovered. This was done by Behring, a German scientist, and by Kitasato, a Japanese physician. Drs. Richet and Héricourt had already opened the way in 1888, while studying another disease.

M. Roux inoculated a horse with diphtheritic toxin mitigated by the addition of iodine, in doses, very weak at first, but gradually stronger; the horse grew by degrees capable of resisting strong doses of pure toxin. It was then bled by means of a large trocar introduced into the jugular vein, the blood received in a bowl was allowed to coagulate, and the liquid part of it, the serum, was then collected; this serum was antitoxic, antidiphtheritic—in one word, the long-desired cure.

At the beginning of 1894, M. Roux had several horses rendered immune by the above process. He desired to prove the efficiency of the serum in the treatment of diphtheria, with the collaboration of MM. Martin and Chaillou, who had, both clinically and bacteriologically, studied more than 400 cases of diphtheria.

There are in Paris two hospitals where diphtheritic children are taken in. It was decided that the new treatment should be applied at the hospital of the *Enfants Malades*, whilst the old system should be continued at the Hôpital Trousseau.

From February 1, MM. Roux, Martin, and Chaillou paid a daily visit to the *Enfants Malades*; they treated all the little diphtheria patients by injection, in the side, of a dose of twenty cubic centimetres of serum, followed, twenty-four hours later, by another dose of twenty, or only of ten cubic centimetres.

Almost invariably, not only did the membranes cease to increase during the twenty-four hours following the first injection, but they began to come away within thirty-six or forty-eight hours, the third day at the latest; the livid, leaden paleness of the face disappeared; the child was saved.

From 1890 to 1893 there had been 3,971 cases of diphtheria, fatal in 2,029 cases, the average mortality being therefore 51 per 100. The serum treatment, applied to hundreds of children, brought it down to less than 24 per 100 in four months. At the Trousseau Hospital, where the serum was not employed, the mortality during the same period was 60 per 100.

In May, M. Roux gave a lecture on diphtheria at Lille, at the request of the Provident Society of the Friends of Science, which held its general meeting in that town. Pasteur, who was president of the Society, came to Lille to thank its inhabitants for the support they had afforded for forty years to the Society.

The master and his disciple were received in the Hall of the Industrial Society. Pasteur listened with an admiring emotion to his pupil, whose rigorous experimentation, together with the beauty of the object in view, filled him with enthusiasm. He who had said, "Exhaust every combination, until the mind can conceive no others possible," was delighted to hear the methodical exposition of the manner in which this great problem had been attacked and solved.

At the Hygiene and Demography Congress at Buda-Pesth, M. Roux, repeating and enlarging his lecture, made a communication on the serotherapy of diphtheria which created a great sensation in Europe.

In France, prefects asked the Minister of the Interior how local physicians might obtain this antidiphtheritic serum. The *Figaro* newspaper opened a subscription towards preserving children from croup; it soon reached more than a million francs. The Pasteur Institute was now able to build stables, buy a hundred horses, render them immune, and constitute a permanent organization for serotherapy. In three months, 50,000 doses of serum were about to be given away.

Pasteur, who was then at Arbois, followed every detail with passionate interest. Sitting under the old quinces in his little garden, he read the lists of subscribers, names of little children, offering charitable gifts as they entered this life, and names of sorrowing parents, giving in the names of dear lost ones.

When he started again for Paris, October 4, 1894, Pasteur was seized again with the melancholy feeling which had attended his first departure from his home, when he was sixteen years old. He saw the same grey sky, the same fine rain and misty horizon, as he looked for the last time upon the distant hills and wide plains he loved, perhaps conscious that it was so. But he remained silent, as was his wont when troubled by his thoughts, his sadness only revealing itself to those who lovingly watched every movement of his countenance.

On October 6, the Pasteur Institute was invaded by a crowd of medical men ; M. Martin gave a special lecture in compliance with the desire of many practitioners unaccustomed to laboratory work, who desired to understand the diagnosis of diphtheria and the mode in which the serum should be used. Pasteur, from his study window, was watching all this coming and going in his Institute. A twofold feeling was visible on his worn features : a sorrowing regret that his age now disarmed him for work, but also the satisfaction of feeling that his work was growing day by day, and that other investigators would, in a similar spirit, pursue the many researches which remained to be undertaken. About that time, M. Yersin, now a physician in the colonies, communicated to the *Annals of the Pasteur Institute* the discovery of the plague bacillus. He had been desired to go to China in order to study the nature of the scourge, its conditions of propagation, and the most efficient means of preventing it from attacking the French possessions. Pasteur had long recognized very great qualities in this pupil whose habits of silent labour were almost those of an ascete. M. Yersin started with a missionary's zeal. When he reached Hong-Kong, three hundred Chinese had already succumbed, and the hospitals of the colony were full ; he immediately recognized the symptoms of the bubonic plague, which had ravaged Europe on many occasions. He noticed that the epidemic raged principally in the slums occupied by Chinese of the poorer classes, and that in the infected quarters there were a great many rats which had died of the plague. Pasteur read with the greatest interest the following lines, so exactly in accordance with his own method of observation : " The peculiar aptitude to contract plague possessed by certain animals," wrote M. Yersin, " enabled me to undertake an experimental study of the disease under very favourable circumstances ; it was obvious that the first thing to do was to look for a microbe in the blood of the patients and in the bubonic pulp." When M. Yersin inoculated rats, mice, or guinea-pigs with this pulp, the animals died, and he found several bacilli in the ganglions, spleen, and blood. After some attempts at cultures and inoculations, he concluded thus : " The plague is a contagious and inoculable disease. It seems likely that rats constitute its principal vehicle, but I have also ascertained that flies can contract the disease and die of it, and may therefore become agents for its transmission."

At the very time when M. Yersin was discovering the specific bacillus of the plague in the bubonic pulp, Kitasato was making similar investigations. The foe now being recognized, hopes of vanquishing it might be entertained.

And whilst those good tidings were arriving, Pasteur was reading a new work by M. Metchnikoff, a Russian scientist, who had elected to come to France for the privilege of working by the side of Pasteur. M. Metchnikoff explained by the action of the white corpuscles of the blood, named " leucocytes," the immunity or resistance, either natural or acquired, of the organism against a defined disease. These corpuscles may be considered as soldiers entrusted with the defence of the organism against foreign invasions. If microbes penetrate into the tissues, the defenders gather all their forces together and a free fight ensues. The organism resists or succumbs according to the power or inferiority of the white blood-cells. If the invading microbe is surrounded, eaten up, and ingested by the victorious white corpuscles (also named *phagocytes*), the latter find in their victory itself fresh reserve forces against a renewed invasion.

On November 1, in the midst of all this laborious activity and daily progress, Pasteur was about to pay his daily visit to his grandchildren, when he was seized by a violent attack of uræmia. He was laid on his bed, and remained nearly unconscious for four hours ; the sweat of agony bathed his forehead and his whole body, and his eyes remained closed. The evening brought with it a ray of hope ; he was able to speak, and asked not to be left alone. Immediate danger seemed avoided, but great anxiety continued to be felt.

It was easy to organize a series of devoted nurses; all Pasteur's disciples were eager to watch by his bedside. Every evening, two persons took their seats in his room : one a member of the family, and one a "Pastorian." About one a.m. they were replaced by another Pastorian and another member of the family. From November 1 to December 25, the laboratory workers continued this watching, regulated by Dr. Roux as follows :—

Sunday night, Roux and Chantemesse ; Monday, Queyrat and Marmier ; Tuesday, Borrel and Martin ; Wednesday, Mesnil and Pottevin ; Thursday, Marchoux and Viala ; Friday, Calmette and Veillon ; Saturday, Renon and Morax. A few alterations were made in this order ; Dr. Marie claimed the privilege. M. Metchnikoff, full of anxiety, came and went continually from the laboratory to the master's room. After the day's work, each faithful watcher came in, bringing books or notes, to go on with the work begun, if the patient should be able to sleep. In the middle of the night, Mme. Pasteur would come in and send away with a sweet authority one of the two volunteer nurses. Pasteur's loving and faithful wife was straining every faculty of her valiant and tender soul to conjure the vision of death which seemed so near. In spite of all her courage, there were hours of weakness, at early dawn, when life was beginning to revive in the quiet neighbourhood, when she could not keep her tears from flowing silently. Would they succeed in saving him whose life was so precious, so useful to others? In the morning, Pasteur's two grandchildren came into the bedroom. The little girl of fourteen, fully realizing the prevailing anxiety, and rendered serious by the sorrow she struggled to hide, talked quietly with him. The little boy, only eight years old, climbed on to his grandfather's bed, kissing him affectionately and gazing on the loved face which always found enough strength to smile at him.

Dr. Chantemesse attended Pasteur with an incomparable devotion. Dr. Gille, who had often been sent for by Pasteur when staying at Villeneuve l'Etang, came to Paris from Garches to see him. Professor Guyon showed his colleague the most affectionate solicitude. Professor Dieulafoy was brought in one morning by M. Metchnikoff ; Professor Grancher, who was ill and away from Paris, hurried back to his master's side.

How often did they hang over him, anxiously following the respiratory rhythm due to the uræmic intoxication ! movements slow at first, then rapid, accelerated, gasping, slackening again, and arrested in a long pause of several seconds, during which all seemed suspended.

At the end of December, a marked improvement took place. On January 1, after seeing all his collaborators, down to the youngest laboratory attendant, Pasteur received the visit of one of his colleagues of the Académie Française. It was Alexandre Dumas, carrying a bunch of roses, and accompanied by one of his daughters. "I want to begin the year well," he said : "I am bringing you my good wishes." Pasteur and Alexandre Dumas, meeting at the Academy every Thursday for twelve years, felt much attraction towards each other. Pasteur, charmed from the first by this dazzling and witty intellect, had been surprised and touched by the delicate attentions of a heart which only opened to a chosen few. Dumas, who had observed many men, loved and admired Pasteur, a modest and kindly genius ; for this dramatic author hid a man thirsting for moral action, his realism was lined with mysticism, and he placed the desire to be useful above the hunger for fame. His blue eyes, usually keen and cold, easily detecting secret thoughts and looking on them with irony, were full of an expression of affectionate veneration when they rested on "our dear and great Pasteur," as he called him. Alexandre Dumas' visit gave Pasteur very great pleasure ; he compared it to a ray of sunshine.

As he could not go out, those who did not come to see him thought him worse than he really was. It was therefore with great surprise that people heard that he would be pleased to receive the old Normaliens, who were about to celebrate the centenary of their school, and who, after putting up a memorial plate on the small laboratory of the Rue d'Ulm, desired to visit the Pasteur Institute. They filed one after another into the drawing-room on the first floor. Pasteur, seated by the fire, seemed to revive the old times when he used to welcome young men into his home circle on Sunday evenings. He had an affectionate word or a smile for each of those who now passed before him, bowing low. Every one was struck with the keen expression of his eyes ; never had the strength of his intellect seemed more independent of the weakness of his body. Many believed in a speedy recovery and rejoiced. "Your health," said some one, "is not only national but universal property."

On that day, Dr. Roux had arranged on tables, in the large

laboratory, the little flasks which Pasteur had used in his experiments on so-called spontaneous generation, which had been religiously preserved; also rows of little tubes used for studies on wines; various preparations in various culture media; microbes and bacilli, so numerous that it was difficult to know which to see first. The bacteria of diphtheria and bubonic plague completed this museum.

Pasteur was carried into the laboratory about twelve o'clock, and Dr. Roux showed his master the plague bacillus through a microscope. Pasteur, looking at these things, souvenirs of his own work and results of his pupils' researches, thought of those disciples who were continuing his task in various parts of the world. In France, he had just sent Dr. Calmette to Lille, where he soon afterwards created a new and admirable Pasteur Institute. Dr. Yersin was continuing his investigations in China. A Normalien, M. Le Dantec, who had entered the Ecole at sixteen at the head of the list, and who had afterwards become a curator at the laboratory, was in Brazil, studying yellow fever, of which he very nearly died. Dr. Adrien Loir, after a protracted mission in Australia, was head of a Pasteur Institute at Tunis. Dr. Nicolle was setting up a laboratory of bacteriology at Constantinople. "There is still a great deal to do!" sighed Pasteur as he affectionately pressed Dr. Roux' hand.

He was more than ever full of a desire to allay human suffering, of a humanitarian sentiment which made of him a citizen of the world. But his love for France was in no wise diminished, and the permanence of his patriotic feelings was, soon after this, revealed by an incident. The Berlin Academy of Sciences was preparing a list of illustrious contemporary scientists to be submitted to the Kaiser with a view to conferring on them the badge of the Order of Merit. As Pasteur's protest and return of his diploma to the Bonn University had not been forgotten, the Berlin Academy, before placing his name on the list, desired to know whether he would accept this distinction at the hands of the German Emperor. Pasteur, while acknowledging with courteous thanks the honour done to him as a scientist, declared that he could not accept it.

For him, as for Victor Hugo, the question of Alsace-Lorraine was a question of humanity; the right of peoples to dispose of themselves was in question. And by a bitter irony of Fate, France, which had proclaimed this principle all over

Europe, saw Alsace torn away from her. And by whom? by
the very nation whom she had looked upon as the most ideal-
istic, with whom she had desired an alliance in a noble hope
of pacific civilization, a hope shared by Humboldt, the great
German scientist.

It was obvious to those who came near Pasteur that, in spite
of the regret caused in him by the decrease of his physical
strength, his moral energy remained unimpaired. He never
complained of the state of his health, and usually avoided speaking of himself. A little tent had been put up for him in the
new garden of the Pasteur Institute, under the young chest-
nuts, the flowers of which were now beginning to fall, and
he often spent his afternoons there. One or other of those
who had watched over him through the long winter nights frequently came to talk with him, and he would inquire, with all
his old interest, into every detail of the work going on.

His old friend Chappuis, now Honorary Rector of the Academy of Dijon, often came to sit with him under this tent.
Their friendship remained unchanged though it had lasted
more than fifty years. Their conversation now took a yet
more exalted turn than in the days of their youth and middle
age. The dignity of Chappius' life was almost austere, though
tempered by a smiling philosophy.

Pasteur, less preoccupied than Chappuis by philosophical
discussions, soared without an effort into the domain of spiritual things. Absolute faith in God and in Eternity, and a conviction that the power for good given to us in this world will
be continued beyond it, were feelings which pervaded his whole
life; the virtues of the Gospel had ever been present to him.
Full of respect for the form of religion which had been that
of his forefathers, he came to it simply and naturally for spiritual help in these last weeks of his life.

On June 13, he came, for the last time, down the steps of
the Pasteur Institute, and entered the carriage which was to
take him to Villeneuve l'Etang. Every one spoke to him of
this stay as if it were sure to bring him back to health. Did he
believe it? Did he try, in his tenderness for those around him,
to share their hopes? His face almost bore the same expression as when he used to go to Villeneuve l'Etang to continue his
studies. When the carriage passed through Saint Cloud, some
of the inhabitants, who had seen him pass in former years,

saluted him with a mixture of emotion and respectful interest.

At Villeneuve l'Etang, the old stables of the Cent Gardes had reverted to their former purpose and were used for the preparation of the diphtheria antitoxin. There were about one hundred horses there; old chargers, sold by the military authorities as unfit for further work; racehorses thus ending their days; a few, presents from their owners, such as Marshal Canrobert's old horse.

Pasteur spent those summer weeks in his room or under the trees on the lawns of the Park. A few horses had been put out to grass, the stables being quite full, and occasionally came near, looking over their hurdles towards him. Pasteur felt a deep thankfulness in watching the busy comings and goings of Dr. Roux and his curator, M. Martin, and of the veterinary surgeon, M. Prévôt, who was entrusted with the bleeding operations and the distribution of the flasks of serum. He thought of all that would survive him and felt that his weakened hand might now drop the torch which had set so many others alight. And, more than resigned, he sat peacefully under a beautiful group of pines and purple beeches, listening to the readings of Mme. Pasteur and of his daughter. They smiled on him with that valiant smile which women know how to keep through deepest anguish.

Biographies interested him as of yore. There was at that time a renewal of interest in memories of the First Empire; old letters, memoirs, war anecdotes were being published every day. Pasteur never tired of those great souvenirs. Many of those stories brought him back to the emotions of his youth, but he no longer looked with the same eyes on the glory of conquerors. The true guides of humanity now seemed to him to be those who gave devoted service, not those who ruled by might. After enjoying pages full of the thrill of battlefields, Pasteur admired the life of a great and good man, St. Vincent de Paul. He loved this son of poor peasants, proud to own his humble birth before a vainglorious society; this tutor of a future cardinal, who desired to become the chaplain of some unhappy convicts; this priest, who founded the work of the *Enfants Trouvés*, and who established lay and religious alliance over the vast domain of charity.

Pasteur himself exerted a great and charitable influence. The unknown lady who had put at his disposal four scholarships for young men without means came to him in August and offered him the funds for a Pasteur Hospital, the natural outcome, she said, of the Pastorian discoveries.

Pasteur's strength diminished day by day, he now could hardly walk. When he was seated in the Park, his grandchildren around him suggested young rose trees climbing around the trunk of a dying oak. The paralysis was increasing, and speech was becoming more and more difficult. The eyes alone remained bright and clear ; Pasteur was witnessing the ruin of what in him was perishable.

How willingly they would have given a moment of their lives to prolong his, those thousands of human beings whose existence had been saved by his methods : sick children, women in lying-in hospitals, patients operated upon in surgical wards, victims of rabid dogs saved from hydrophobia, and so many others protected against the infinitesimally small ! But, whilst visions of those living beings passed through the minds of his family, it seemed as if Pasteur already saw those dead ones who, like him, had preserved absolute faith in the Future Life.

The last week in September he was no longer strong enough to leave his bed, his weakness was extreme. On September 27, as he was offered a cup of milk : " I cannot," he murmured ; his eyes looked around him with an unspeakable expression of resignation, love and farewell. His head fell back on the pillows, and he slept; but, after this delusive rest, suddenly came the gaspings of agony. For twenty-four hours he remained motionless, his eyes closed, his body almost entirely paralyzed ; one of his hands rested in that of Mme. Pasteur, the other held a crucifix.

Thus, surrounded by his family and disciples, in this room of almost monastic simplicity, on Saturday, September 28, 1895, at 4.40 in the afternoon, very peacefully, he passed away.

THE END.

INDEX

H H

INDEX

H H 2

. :

284

Lightning Source UK Ltd.
Milton Keynes UK
UKOW05f1917170317
296920UK00023B/500/P